THE LIVING STREAM

Edna Longley

THE LIVING STREAM

LITERATURE & REVISIONISM IN IRELAND

BLOODAXE BOOKS

ISBN: 1 85224 216 7 hardback edition
1 85224 217 5 paperback edition

First published 1994 by
Bloodaxe Books Ltd,
P.O. Box 1SN,
Newcastle upon Tyne NE99 1SN.

Bloodaxe Books Ltd acknowledges
the financial assistance of Northern Arts.

CANTERBURY CHRIST CHURCH COLLEGE	
360429819	
Greenhead	17.07.98
820.99415LON	£9.95

Cover printing by J. Thomson Colour Printers Ltd, Glasgow.

Printed at Alden Press Limited,
Oxford and Northampton, Great Britain

In memoriam
FRANK KINAHAN

CONTENTS

'Make ten fanatics in a country and the mischief is irreparable. Having been created by idle thinking from the top layers of professors and propagandists, they work their way back through political channels to bully the top. They have been doing it here for twenty years until we now find ourselves caught in an enormous, ravelled, simple-minded web – which nobody knows how to disentangle – of Gaelic Revivalism, stark Isolationism, timid and therefore savage Puritanism, crazy Censorship...We do not need to look far for the revenge of Life. We find it in the people driven headlong from the loneliness of the land, driven from the barrenness of country life, driven even out of the country itself to a bombed world. Which is, surely, the ultimate commentary on this thing's disconnection with all practical history, all practical life.'

SEAN O'FAOLAIN, *The Bell* 3, 2 (November 1941)

Introduction: Revising 'Irish Literature'

I

It has grown harder to discuss Irish literature without being drawn into arguments about culture and politics. No doubt historical necess-ity is to blame. But although these essays have a political dimension, I see them as expanding rather than retracting a statement in my earlier book *Poetry in the Wars*. There I wrote: 'Poetry and politics, like church and state, should be separated.' By politics I meant predatory ideologies, fixed agendas and fixed expectations: the literary history of the 1930s is relevant to Northern Ireland since 1969. I did not claim that art was independent of politics, but that it could provide for political independence, for dissidence and reinvention. The radicalism of aesthetics is 'make it new'. Theodor Adorno, more commonly invoked as an anti-humanist, writes: 'In an age of repressive collectivism, the power of resistance to compact majorities resides in the lonely, exposed producer of art.'[1] Not every poem makes it new, and criticism legitimately finds significance in the overt politics or political unconscious of literary works. Yet poetry possesses the semantic means, the metaphorical audacity, to press beyond existing categories, to prepare the ground where, in Derek Mahon's words, 'a thought might grow'. Certainly literature has helped to erode the compact majorities that came to power in Ireland after 1921 and the censorships they brought with them. This book traces some Irish literary currents with regard to their cultural meaning in the context of Northern Ireland.

However, culture and context, never uncontroversial, bear unusually heavy political inscriptions where Ireland is concerned. In his book on Yeats, Louis MacNeice identifies the reading-difficulties:

> Most Irish people cannot see Ireland clearly because they are busy grind-ing axes. Many English people cannot see her clearly because she gives them a tear in the eye...[2]

Misty-eyed Americans add to the confusion. Complicity between Irish axes and foreign tears compounds it. As for seeing *Irish literature* steadily and seeing it whole, such an enterprise faces institutional, constitutional and theoretical obstacles. The latter surfaced when post-structuralism turned our quaking sod into a quaking text. And above (or beneath) all, the slow-motion Northern Irish civil war has exposed fault-lines half-buried for half a century.

Nevertheless, critics persist – and should persist – in trying to read how Irish literature reads Ireland. The essays collected here were written in the belief that literature, both as cultural artefact and cultural criticism, can help us to interpret Irish culture: its practices, signifying systems and the politicisation of both. (If culture is never 'unmediated', some mediations are more coercive than others.) My second belief is that any interpretive activity which involves literature should take into account its formal and aesthetic dimensions. 'Mechanisms of tradition', to use E.H. Gombrich's term, bear witness to context, while to exclude value-judgements is to exclude the cultural information offered by what works, what doesn't work and why. Conversely, the most explicit writings need not be the most revealing. The matter of Ireland sets traps for critic and artist alike, unless they look to manner as well.

In this preliminary essay I want to challenge some concepts which have shaped the profile of 'Irish literature'. Seamus Deane and others insist that perceptions of Ireland are unduly determined by stereotypical literary representations, especially by the afterglow of Matthew Arnold's broodings on the Celt. But it may also be the case that perceptions of Irish literature are unduly determined by assumptions – mainly Nationalist assumptions – about Ireland. If one reading produces too many peasants in the twilight, another may produce too many colonisers in the text. So whereas the *Field Day Anthology of Irish Writing* (1991) sets out to reclaim its contents from the invasive forces of Eng. Lit., I would argue that Irish canons have been equally rough-hewn by indigenous axes. And, since much Modernist thinking depends on literary events in Ireland at the turn of the century, to revise Irish literary history might lead to other revisions.

II *In a Minority*

My own critical approach owes something, though I hope not everything, to a particular background. Autobiographical angles on history seem as inescapable in Irish criticism as in Irish literature. So a few years ago, like the man who found out he had been speaking prose all his life, I realised that I might be a 'revisionist' literary critic. Revisionism is a shorthand and quasi-abusive term for historical studies held to be at odds with the founding ideology of the Irish Free State (Republic of Ireland since 1948). Whether malign historians have indeed caused subsidence under the Nationalist grand narrative, or whether its foundations have always quaked, I was brought up in one of the cracks that are now highly visible. Therefore, autobiography will colour the perspective in which I initially want to set current debates about literature and culture.

My father T.S. Broderick, Professor of Pure Mathematics at Trinity College Dublin (1944-62), was a Catholic teaching at a university whose history epitomises Irish sectarian differences. As James Lydon explains:

> From the very beginning Trinity was alienated from the vast majority of the catholic people of Ireland. Founded at a time when everywhere in Europe, and indeed overseas with colonial powers, religious conformity was being demanded as the norm in most states, the college from the start assumed openly a sectarian character. The English government was determined that converting the Irish to the reformed religion was a necessary part of the wider policy of teaching them civility, so that they could become full subjects of the king. Ireland must be ruled as England was and therefore the same penal laws which governed catholics in England must be applied also to Ireland. The Irish, and also the Old English, catholics must be converted, by force if necessary. But education would also have a vital role to play. Ironically, the protestant establishment believed every bit as strongly as did the catholic bishops in the nineteenth and twentieth centuries that education must be firmly based on, and generally informed by, orthodox religious beliefs.[3]

However, there were respites in the polarisation whereby Anglicans began by excluding Catholics (and Ulster dissenters) from Trinity, and Catholics finished by excluding themselves. At the end of the eighteenth century, with progress towards Catholic emancipation, Catholics could and did enter Trinity. They included Thomas Moore, the sons of Daniel O'Connell, and 'nearly all catholics of eminence in Ireland in the first half of the nineteenth century'.[4] Indeed, the cross-sectarian Young Ireland movement of the 1840s, according to its founder Thomas Davis, was 'made in the Historical Societies of Dublin, and belong[ed] to Trinity College Protestants and a few Roman Catholics in TCD'.[5] Perhaps political or literary advance in Ireland often belongs to some such cross-sectarian moment. But after 1850 the Irish Catholic Hierarchy, worried by secularising trends, insisted that Catholics must be educated by Catholic institutions. In Lydon's words: 'Keeping Irish catholicism pure meant a minimum of contact between catholics and protestants.'[6] This slowed, to its continuing crawl, the task which Samuel Ferguson defined in 1834 as being 'to make the people of Ireland better acquainted with one another'.[7]

Cardinal Paul Cullen, chief aborter of this incipient pluralism, had a twentieth-century counterpart in John Charles McQuaid, Archbishop of Dublin from 1940 to 1972. McQuaid's regime intensified and formalised the ban on Catholics attending TCD, and in a notorious

Lenten pastoral of 1961 he yet again forbade his flock 'under pain of mortal sin...to frequent that college'. Two decades earlier the Church's attitude had induced my father to leave the Church rather than Trinity. Since my mother, also a mathematician, came from a Scottish Presbyterian family, my sister and I, though baptised Catholics, were brought up within the Anglican compromise (the Church of Ireland). When, in 1986, I first read Hubert Butler's essays, they made sense of my sequestered childhood among the Southern Protestant minority.

During the 1940s and 1950s, despite his Protestant-Nationalist idealism, Butler challenged both the confessional nation-state and the minority's refusal of critical participation. His writings (discussed below in 'Defending Ireland's Soul') interpret the processes that made mid-century Southern Protestantism so inward-looking, self-protective, embalmed in genial euphemism, and wary of guilt by association with the North. When I was growing up, all Protestant social life, as well as education, revolved around Church of Ireland parishes. The *Ne Temere* decree (1907), enjoining the Catholic partner in a mixed marriage to bring up the children as Catholics (a decree my father disobeyed), aggravated fears that the Protestant community would dwindle still further if it did not keep itself to itself. *Ne Temere*, which influenced the Home Rule debate, caused religious apartheid to operate just as firmly in the Republic as in Northern Ireland. Hence Paul Durcan's satire 'What is a Protestant, Daddy?'

> Protestants were Martians
> Light-years more weird
> Than zoological creatures;
> But soon they would all go away
> For as a species they were dying out,
> Soon there would be no more Protestants...
> O Yea, O Lord,
> I was a proper little Irish Catholic boy
> Way back in the 1950s.

Durcan's own 'daddy' was a prominent judge, affiliated to the Fine Gael party.

Around 1958 I took part in a Church of Ireland youth club debate on the proposition: 'That the minority do not play their full part in the affairs of the Republic of Ireland.' Recently I found my paper for this debate – I was glad to see that it blamed both the minority and the Republic – inside an old copy of *The Bell* (June 1944) which someone must have put into my hands. The issue features an emblematic dispute between the editor, Sean O'Faolain, and W.B. Stanford. A polemic by Stanford, 'Protestantism Since the Treaty', faces a riposte from O'Faolain called 'Toryism in Trinity'. Stanford who died in 1984, was Professor of Greek at Trinity College, a well-known Homeric scholar, and a prominent Church of Ireland layman. His article, reprinted from a pamphlet, objects to 'symptoms of a pressure based on ecclesiastical policy',[8] including: difficulties about land-purchase, lack of Protestant access to public jobs and offices, the contention 'that to be a true Irishman one must be a Roman Catholic', and 'banning all literature which criticises the Roman Church and encouraging that which criticises any form of Protestantism'.[9] Although himself the shrewdest critic of retrogressive Nationalism, O'Faolain takes a tough line with this whining on the grounds that 'any Catholic knows more about grievances, ancient and modern, than all the Anglicans of Ireland and Great Britain put together'.[10] Perhaps his reaction marks some kind of boundary between a liberal *Catholic* Nationalist and a liberal *Protestant* Nationalist, such as Hubert Butler.

That even O'Faolain should 'resent' Stanford's raising of the religious question says much about its repression within Irish Nationalism:

> until I read these things I never think of myself, in relation to Ireland, as a Catholic at all, and I strongly resent being compelled to think of myself as a Catholic...when we should all feel quite content to think of ourselves as Irishmen...what [Professor Stanford] is...doing, in practice, is to foster something which is not *normal*, and which we *normally* and properly forget, to wit our religious differences [my italics][11]...

O'Faolain later employs the Nationalist trope of naming Protestant worthies (Parnell, Yeats, Douglas Hyde) in order to 'prove that where a man's political attitude was sound his religion has never been anyone's concern'.[12] But what if his or her political attitude were unsound? And what of O'Faolain's belief that religion and politics, religion and culture, had happily or 'normatively' gone their separate ways in Ireland of the 1940s? Although he gives Stanford credit for 'at least [showing] that Protestants are not all stone-dumb'[13] (a motif that recurs in recent commentary on Northern Ireland), the plaintive question 'What do Protestants want?' haunts his subtext.

When Hubert Butler tried to answer that question, he broke Southern Protestant silence in ways that pleased neither the Catholic church nor the Church of Ireland. For instance, he found Church of Ireland clergy guilty of 'appeasement' during a boycott on Protestants in Fethard-on-Sea, Co. Waterford in 1957 (an event which gave Ian Paisley his first political platform).[14] By writing as an Irishman and a Protestant, and pressing on the tension between these terms, he subverted the state-ideologies North and South. If we set Butler in the line of Anglo-Irish Nationalist literary intellectuals, it seems historically significant that he should take his stand on the Reformation, conscience, 'the right of private judgement'; that, like George Orwell, he should fuse individual voice and private judgement as prose style. Of course, the Unionist regime in the North has never exemplified Protestant conscience at its most acute. Nonetheless, Butler's oppositional forays in the Southern state, along with fellow-dissidents like Owen Sheehy-Skeffington,[15] exposed some of its contradictions and prefigured today's constitutional battle between moral authoritarianism and democratic liberties. In 1956 O'Faolain warned Butler against publishing an article on abortion because it would make him untouchable. In 1993 this is the stuff of Irish politics.

But the issue goes beyond particular libertarian questions to the structure of intellectual and public life in Ireland. Like O'Faolain, other mid-century writers and that small beacon *The Bell*, Butler stood for 'the art of free controversy'.[16] He saw critical argument on all fronts as frustrated by segregation between North and South ('Where there is disagreement, there should, at least, be the stimulus of conflict')[17] and by Protestant reluctance within the Republic to pursue 'a very real clash of philosophies'.[18] Despite much freer controversy since the 1950s, especially south of the Border, Ireland has not yet discarded these sectarian inhibitions – ironically, supposed to hold sectarianism at bay. Old habits of cohesion affect literary criticism too, producing alternations of hagiography and begrudgery. 'Critic' remains subliminally cognate with apostate or heretic, and different pulpits do not always engage one another.

It is at university that creative and critical encounters with the Other commonly occur. This has sometimes, but not always, been the case in twentieth-century Ireland. As we have seen, the history of Irish politics, culture and literature is bound up with the history of the universities. The National University of Ireland was founded in 1908 to link colleges established in the mid nineteenth century. Effectively the 'Catholic' university (Queen's College, Belfast now became a separate university), it supplied most of the Free State's establishment after Independence. The influence of its largest component, University College Dublin (UCD), was proportionate to Trinity's decline from ascendancy to marginalisation. Denis Donoghue, in an (inaccurate) account of Trinity which gave offence, exemplifies the long-term friction between Dublin's two universities:

> I resented the policy by which my colleagues and I were required to teach thousands of students, while our opposite numbers in Trinity dispensed sherry to their chosen few. When I protested to the President of UCD,

> he replied that Trinity was an irrelevance to Ireland and its development,
> it was merely an appendix to the country, the future was in the hands
> of the thousands of bright young men and women my colleagues and I
> would train. We would win...[19]

From one viewpoint, Trinity was a beleaguered liberal enclave;
from another, an élitist bastion of 'alien values'. A curious exception
to UCD rule was the warmth of Eamon de Valera towards Trinity
(though a later Fianna Fáil leader, Charles Haughey, never paid
an official visit to the college). My father played a part in this owing
to de Valera's interest in mathematics. As a Catholic mathematician
he was in a good position to build on his friendship with fellow-
mathematician Monsignor Patrick Browne of University College
Galway. This connection facilitated the foundation (in 1940) of the
Dublin Institute of Advanced Studies. De Valera used to ring up
my father about mathematical problems. But inter-university ani-
mosities continued. When, in 1967, the minister of education proposed
a merger between UCD and TCD, Donoghue's interlocutor (Michael
Tierney) wrote that this was an opportunity to 'clear the ground
completely of all the wrecks and relics of the Ascendancy'. Lydon
observes, however, that 'Tierney's was now very much a lone voice,
at least in public'.[20] Thus, although the merger never came off, the
episcopal ban was lifted in 1970. Catholic Dublin entered Trinity
and Trinity entered Catholic Dublin. A Trinity Catholic, Mary
Robinson, is now President of the Irish Republic.

This happy ending had one down side. The lifting of the ban,
at a time when the Northern Troubles were beginning, meant that
Ulster Protestants, hitherto a significant presence in TCD, lost
their sense of a traditional Dublin base. Again, with the founding
of a new university at Coleraine, students from Magee College in
Derry had ceased to spend two years at Trinity. Finally, the new
comprehensive entry-system for UK universities (UCCA) encouraged Northern sixth-formers to look across the Irish Sea. (More
recently, Ulster Catholics have joined this student 'brain-drain'.)
Such institutional shifts further weakened, both in the Republic
and Northern Ireland, any coherent understanding of Irish Protestant history. You might say, then, that an eccentric survivor from
pre-Partition Ireland died in 1970. Perhaps Trinity's sense of its
own traditions was also subject to revision. Gordon L. Herries
Davies, in an entertaining essay on the university's exploitation of
well-known alumni (Douglas Hyde Gallery, Samuel Beckett Centre
for Drama and Theatre Studies), notices an absent name:

> One of the greatest advocates of all time, [Edward Carson] represented
> his university in parliament from 1892 until 1918. He was the First Lord

of the Admiralty at a crucial stage of World War I...Yet for all that a
visitor to Trinity's campus will see, Carson might as well never have
existed. There is in his memory no bronze or stone, no canvas, and no
stained glass, and as for eponymy, I doubt whether the law school has
so much as a filing-cabinet named in his honour...[21]

Davies also observes that the 'single name of [Republican martyr]
Kevin Barry' was to prove of 'far more value to University College
Dublin than were the names of 454 imperial war dead to Trinity';
and that, possibly as a result, 'the names of those ninety or so Trinity
men and women who had died in [the Second World War]...were
never accorded any college memorial'.[22] War memorials, as I indicate
in 'The Rising, the Somme and Irish Memory', remain a political
and poetic issue. It's not surprising that Trinity should soft-pedal
its Unionist past. At the turn of the century there was warrant for
John Dillon's characterisation of the university as 'the centre and
fortress of all that was narrow and bitter and hostile to the national
life of Ireland'.[23] Trinity's literary Unionism, especially the opinions
of professor-poet Edward Dowden, the eminent Victorian critic,
tends to be a forgotten adversarial context for the Irish Literary
Revival. Because Southern Unionism no longer exists, analysts who
see Yeats as suffering from 'the pathology of literary unionism'[24]
overlook distinctions very alive to him in 1895 when he was fighting
on two fronts:

A very amusing proof of the unfounded nature of one of Professor
Dowden's charges against the Irish literary movement has just reached
me. At the very time Professor Dowden was sending to the Press an
introduction, saying that we indulged in indiscriminate praise of all things
Irish, and went about 'plastered with shamrocks and raving of Brian
Boru', a certain periodical was giving the hospitality of its pages to a
long anonymous letter making a directly contrary charge. The writer
of the letter accused some of the members of the Irish Literary Society
of discouraging 'worthy workers in the field', of endeavouring to substitute the pursuit of what he called 'high art' for the old, easy-going
days when every patriotic writer was as good as his neighbour, and even
of making allegations against the literary merits of the Young Ireland
Party.[25]

Yeats had already lost a struggle with a former Young Irelander,
Charles Gavan Duffy, over control of the New Irish Library. Here he
may be feeling the first chill of party pressures on the space opened
up by the literary movement.

   The *Field Day Anthology of Irish Writing* reprints a related controversy – one germane to its own genesis – which brings together
Trinity and Irish literary canons. In 1900 Stopford A. Brooke (great-

grandfather of the former Secretary of State for Northern Ireland) and T.W. Rolleston published *A Treasury of Irish Poetry in the English Tongue*. Brooke's introduction justifies the presence of TCD poets such as Dowden by proposing what Northern Irish politicians now term 'two traditions':

> This new movement took two lines, which ran parallel to one another, like two lines of railway. But now and again, as lines of railway meet and intersect at stations, these two mingled their motives, their subjects, and their manner. But, on the whole, they ran without touching; and one followed the English and the other the Irish tradition. The poets who kept the first line...have been so deeply influenced by Wordsworth, Keats, and in part by Shelley, that even when they write on Irish subjects the airs of England breathe and the waters of England ripple in their poetry...The other line on which Irish verse ran was backward to the recovery of the old Celtic stories and their modernising in poetry, and forward to the creation of a new form of the Celtic spirit...Amid the varied aims of these poets there is one element common to them all. It is their Nationalism.[26]

This tortuous rationale provoked a scornful response from D.P. Moran, editor of *The Leader*, champion of 'Irish Ireland' and the Irish language, and foe to mongrelism. In a sentence that sums up his philosophy of cultural separatism, he said: 'What is not real Irish you would as lief, in fact you would prefer, to have real English'.[27] Moran saw no distinction between Brooke's parallel lines and maintained that 'Men developed in Trinity College...can never [with the exception of Douglas Hyde, founder of the Gaelic League] reach the heart of Ireland...The haze of Trinity is around them, and the glamour of the Gael surrounds us.'[28] Rolleston now joined in by staking out a third – Irish Revival – position between Brooke and Moran. He accused the latter of

> going back I know not how many generations to the dismal conception of an Ireland divided into watertight compartments, with a separate religion in each, and no common thought, no national sentiment among them all. You cannot build a nation that way, nor a literature either.[29]

When I entered Trinity in 1958 it was largely a watertight compartment, despite a thin trickle of Irish Catholics including the poet Brendan Kennelly. The student-body, much smaller than it is today, mainly consisted of Southern and Northern Protestants, Catholics from England and further afield, other fairly upper-class English people who had not got into Oxbridge (a post-war constituency) and the sprinkle of overseas students which made Trinity then the most cosmopolitan, as well as the most mongrel, Irish university. Brian Fallon recently commented on Trinity's literary traditions:

> After independence, the National University of Ireland became the *alma mater* of most of the new writers and intelligentsia [he mentions Flann O'Brien and Denis Devlin]...The great exception was Samuel Beckett... In the Sixties, when Trinity seemed hardly to matter any longer as a 'literary' university, a vital new [poetic] generation emerged...[30]

I would argue for more continuity than Fallon, evidently a UCD graduate, allows. In 1950 the literary magazine *Icarus* was founded by Alec Reid – a friend of Beckett's, a wonderfully original lecturer in the English department – and others. *Icarus* was a going concern when Brendan Kennelly (1957) arrived in Trinity from Kerry, Michael Longley (1958) and Derek Mahon (1960) from Belfast. The two latter had attended the same state grammar-school (Royal Belfast Academical Institution) and benefited, like Northern Catholic literary contemporaries, from the Butler Education Act. *Icarus* reflected the unusual cultural make-up of this lost Trinity with its conduits to literary Dublin.

Autobiography leads me to stress the history of poetry at Trinity (*c.* 1957-64) because its omission from other literary histories seems representative of their rather lopsided construction. (Note: Eavan Boland came to Trinity after I had left.) In particular, misconceptions persist as to the contexts in which the sixties generation of Northern Irish poets began writing. And because the Trinity context has vanished, it needs all the more to be recalled. For example, John Wilson Foster refers a bit loosely to 'Philip Hobsbaum, the English critic and poet' as having 'galvanised the inert body of Ulster poetry into life from his post at Queen's University, Belfast'.[31] While Michael Longley (and I) attended the Hobsbaum 'Group' from autumn 1964, and first met Seamus Heaney there, Derek Mahon

> only went once and didn't like it. Too Leavisite and too contentious, intolerant. Philip was a good-hearted ruffian really, but I didn't understand his opinions. Much guff has been talked and published about the Group; in fact it had little influence, certainly not on me. I think the Belfast crowd (whom I saw during vacations) went along for something to do; but anyone who was any good went their own way.[32]

However, Mahon's vacation-impressions underestimate the catalytic importance of the Group for 'the Belfast crowd'. Hobsbaum was a talented talent-spotter, as his later career in Glasgow confirms. I remember him, back in Belfast for a brief visit, immediately noting the promise of the youthful Muldoon. He was also a generous promoter of his protégés, helping Michael Longley, as well as Seamus Heaney, to get published in London. (Through Hobsbaum I was commissioned to edit the poems of Edward Thomas.) More crucially, perhaps, he helped to create a recognisable and recognised focus for poetry in the North: a prototype for subsequent literary devolution in the British Isles. This distinctive focus has endured in various guises, despite historical shifts, and despite departures such as Heaney's (1972) and Muldoon's (1986). Hobsbaum himself left Belfast in 1966.

Nonetheless, most accounts of the Group over-stress a cosy fostering and ignore the aesthetic conflicts that pervaded its sessions: stimulating but tense debates in which not only poets, but critics like Arthur Terry, Michael Allen and Harry Chambers, joined. Over the years, Hobsbaum has written eclectically and enthusiastically about a range of twentieth-century poetry, including Yeats, Graves, Crane, Stevens and Lowell. In 1963 he appreciatively reviewed MacNeice's posthumous book of dark parables, *The Burning Perch*. My essay 'The Aesthetic and the Territorial' (in *Contemporary Irish Poetry*, edited by Elmer Andrews, 1992) gives the erroneous impression that Hobsbaum has never 'favoured' these poets at all. However, my remarks there do not constitute an overview of his career, but a recollection of the poetic models and values for which he generally argued at the Group when new writing was discussed. He did not, as a rule, endorse Romantic, symbolist, mythic, metaphysical and rhetorical tendencies, including those derived from the poets named above. Dylan Thomas was – and remains – anathema. Much of this echoed central emphases of the English Movement, and diverged from the aesthetic priorities established between Mahon and Longley in Dublin – where, for instance, Lowell represented a walk on the wild side and Larkin's dialogue with Yeats struck more chords than his relation to Kingsley Amis. Hence Mahon's inability to 'understand [Hobsbaum's] opinions'.

As Hobsbaum's own poetic practice suggests, his primary formal allegiances were to clearly-cut Movement patterns, though he was also an early advocate of Ted Hughes. (This has some bearing on the way in which Heaney, in *Death of a Naturalist*, manoeuvres between particular techniques of Larkin and Hughes.) Similarly, while stressing 'life', Hobsbaum was less at home with the psychic archetypes of *Life Studies* than with the novelistic dimension of Movement poetry: its disgruntled male personae, everyday narratives, and documentary nitty-gritty. His collection *In Retreat* (1966) includes dramatic monologues drawn from the lives of Cardinal Newman, Marx and Chopin, together with colloquial, satirical poems based on campus-life at Queen's. No doubt part of Hobsbaum's salutary purpose was to challenge the assumptions of all young writers invited to the Group. But certain assumptions were, perhaps, more relentlessly challenged than others. So there was indeed 'contention', some (but not all) of it fruitful, between the ideas about poetry that arrived in Belfast from London and Dublin.

As for Belfast itself: from the late 1950s Queen's University students (Seamus Heaney, Seamus Deane, Stewart Parker) had been publishing poetry and prose in the magazines *Gorgon* and *Interest*. (Deane had left Belfast by the time the Group was established.) It seems fair to say that this literary milieu was less well-developed than its Trinity-Dublin counterpart, whatever may have happened since, and that Hobsbaum's advent thus appeared more galvanic to the Queen's contingent. Heaney should be seen as generalising from his own experience and, ironically, from too Anglo-centric a viewpoint, when he says: 'all of us in this group [he includes Mahon] were harking to writers from the English cultural background' of 'the late fifties and sixties'.[33] That *Death of a Naturalist* (1966), *Night-Crossing* (1968) and *No Continuing City* (1969) are such different first collections proves the range of influences then at work. These early aesthetic differences have often been obscured or distorted by the political and theoretical batteries pounding away since 1970. If politics, as well as criticism, begins in aesthetics, close reading becomes all the more crucial.

Although distant constellations counted too – Baudelaire, Rimbaud, Frost, Stevens, Crane, Lowell, Wilbur, Penguin Modern European Poets – I suggest that three immediate literary environments, with their associated traditions, principally shaped Northern Irish poetry of the 1960s. Firstly, there was indeed the English/British dimension: perhaps not only the impact of Larkin or Hughes (or Dylan Thomas or Auden), and Hobsbaum's presence as bearer of recent developments, but a reading of the entire English lyrical tradition from new and contested ground. To assimilate Wordsworth in south Derry or Keith Douglas in Belfast is not the same as doing so in Hampshire or Yorkshire. Stopford Brooke, like other purists, underestimates the mutability of poetic airs and waters. Secondly, outside Queen's University, and perhaps despite Queen's University, there existed a few green shoots of the Ulster regionalism formulated and propagated by John Hewitt in the 1940s (see 'Progressive Bookmen' below). Hewitt himself was absent in Coventry (1957-72), but Sam Hanna Bell, John Boyd and the painter Colin Middleton encouraged young writers, as did Heaney's 'fosterer' Michael McLaverty. Although Heaney chiefly derives his own Ulster regional root from Patrick Kavanagh's Monaghan parish, from John Montague's transmutations

of Tyrone, and from Catholic-Gaelic sources, he implies a complementary debt to Hewitt when he recalls: 'In 1962...I had done
an extended essay on the history of literary magazines in Ulster,
as though I were already seeking a basis for faith in the possibility
of our cultural existence as northern, Irish and essentially ourselves.'[34]
If Heaney found that faith – with his poem 'A New Song' as its
ambiguous anthem – it would have been in Hewitt's evangelising
contributions to the magazines *Lagan* and *Rann*. And, thirdly, there
was Trinity College Dublin which placed in the foreground Anglo-
Irish literary traditions and their problematic continuance. Trinity
seems an apt nursery for Mahon's affinities with Yeats, Graves,
MacNeice and Beckett, and for his consequent dialectic between
formal order and anarchic alienation.

Yeats's formalism (not only metrical or stanzaic, but a matter of
linguistic and symbolic intensity) still pernes in the gyres of contemporary Northern Irish poetry. Perhaps because 'discontinuity'
is presumed, the evolution of Irish Revival poetic structures may
be under-appreciated. (This contrasts with the excessive attention
paid to 'big house' fiction: a more clearly weird species, comfortably
dying out.) If indigenous literary history is not respected in Ireland,
it will hardly be so in England. For example, Neil Corcoran refers
to Seamus Heaney's 'attempt to break through the crust of the "well-
made poem" which the first generation of Northern poets inherited
from their origins in the English Movement and the Belfast Group:
as Heaney observed at the time, he wanted " to take the English
lyric and make it eat stuff that it has never eaten before...and
make it still an English lyric" '.[35] If Corcoran's literary history
seems Heaney-centric, Heaney's once again seems Anglo-centric
in forgetting the Yeatsian stanzas that had ingested the turmoil of
the 1920s.

There is a distinction between Yeats's 'Sing whatever is well
made' – with all its attendant disorder and disturbance – and the
gentility-principle condemned by A. Alvarez. MacNeice sounded
the true note of Anglo-Irish impatience with England when he said:
'what distinguishes the "Movement" as a group from a poet like
Robert Graves is that the latter's neatness is always a means to an
end'.[36] (MacNeice exempted Larkin from this critique.) Northern
Irish formal concentration – still evident in its testing by the supposedly more freewheeling younger generation of poets – has origins
which are neither single nor simple. But they certainly include the
fact that the English lyric had already mutated under high pressure
in Anglo-Ireland. To stress this bit of Irish literary history is not

to wax sentimental over Ascendancy residues or make a sectarian point. It is to notice how the state-ideologies of the Republic and Northern Ireland have repressed cultural strands and cultural philosophies that lost out in the early twentieth-century power-struggles, but continue to declare themselves creatively. Pre-Partition Ireland has been a long time a-dying. It may yet help a new Ireland to be born.

III *Field Day and the Canon*

More attention should be paid to the fact that Yeats's pessimism after the Easter Rising included fears for literature and literary criticism:

> At the moment I feel that all the work of years has been overturned, all the bringing together of classes, all the freeing of Irish literature and criticism from politics.[37]

Here, writing to Lady Gregory, Yeats does not so much disown politics as fear polarisation, a squeeze on pluralism, and what might happen to the inside of his own head. He was not always to be so pessimistic, but these fears were realised in his lifetime (see 'Defending Ireland's Soul' below) and since 1969 the North has renewed their prophetic force.

The 1970s introduced a political strain into Northern Irish writing, especially its critical wing. By 1980 one group of writers (Seamus Deane, Brian Friel, Seamus Heaney, Tom Paulin), three of them also academics, had espoused an explicit and interventionist cultural politics behind the banner of the Field Day Theatre Company. Besides an annual touring play, the company has produced fifteen pamphlets – the majority by literary critics – and finally the key to all its mythologies: the *Field Day Anthology of Irish Writing* (1991). The anthology has received a bad press, particularly in the Republic, for an under-representation of women all the more striking in a compilation that suspects the aesthetic and favours the political. But this cock-up should not just be put down to general-purpose patriarchy. Its sources lie deep in Field Day's ideological direction since their first pamphlet-series. In an essay, 'Poetry and Politics in Northern Ireland'[38], and the pamphlet *From Cathleen to Anorexia* (reprinted here) I questioned the Field Day agenda. This was on two main grounds: firstly, that their chosen political model appeared to simplify the state of literary play, to ignore the cultural negotiations at work in poetry from the North, and to foreclose on the new politics they might symbolise; secondly, that a distinctively Northern Nationalist formation was claiming wider validity than it had earned, not only with respect to the North but to the whole island.

In overall design, if not in every sub-section, the *Field Day Anthology* confirms my earlier diagnosis. It would be churlish to deny the anthology's grand sweep, its valuable collation of out-of-print materials, the many contextual insights into the eighteenth and nineteenth centuries provided by W.J. McCormack, Seamus Deane and other editors. Nor am I either anxious or equipped to offer a critique from St Patrick onwards. What concerns me is how the twentieth century, above all the last twenty-three years, looms over the entire enterprise. In one sense this is inevitable, in another deliberate. Although Kevin Barry has praised 'the promiscuity of what is made available' [39] (showing that post-modernism is indeed in the eye of the beholder), the anthology is no do-it-yourself pick 'n' mix or harmless baggy monster, but a directive encyclopaedia, an interpretive centre packaged and signposted – especially for consumption abroad. Over half the first print-run was destined for the USA. The texts are ornately framed by introductions, headnotes, footnotes, categories. Seamus Deane, the General Editor, also edits or co-edits eleven sections – among them, the two sections of 'Political Writings and Speeches'. His insistent presence does much to freight the ship with Nationalist assumptions and priorities.

Before discussing the *Field Day Anthology* as a symptomatic yoking of 'Irish literature' to Nationalism, I should indicate the longer-term context. Field Day, responses to Field Day (and much that goes on outside this little orbit) continue a debate about culture and identity which has taken various forms, some of them literary, since the 1830s when Catholic emancipation began to alter Irish power-dynamics. The anthology rehearses earlier phases of that debate, not only in an analytical spirit but in furtherance of its own hegemonic ambitions. Three volumes, four thousand double-column pages and fifteen hundred years make a heavy gun-emplacement in the *kulturkampf* cheerfully heralded by 'Head' in Samuel Ferguson's 'Dialogue between the Head and Heart of an Irish Protestant' (1833):

> We must fight our battle now with a handful of types and a composing-stick, pages like this our field, and the reading public our arbiter of war. [40]

Today's textual battles are more often joined between Nationalists and 'revisionists' than between Catholic and Protestant Ireland as such. Northern Unionism, as a defender of the status quo, has only patchily developed the kind of self-validating discourse long practised

by Irish separatism; and with which, or in which, Southern Protestants have more readily engaged. John Wilson Foster is one of
the few literary critics who remedies what he terms 'the voicelessness
of Ulster unionist culture',[41] although historians are thicker on the
ground. Hence the tendency for revisionism and the Irish Literary
Revival to serve, in Nationalist intellectual quarters, as proxies or
scapegoats for Unionism. The genesis of the *Field Day Anthology*
invoked the Revival as anti-self. In his pamphlet *Heroic Styles: the
tradition of an idea* (1984) Deane floated 'a comprehensive [*sic*]
anthology' chiefly to counter the Celticism which Yeats absorbed
from Matthew Arnold, and expose the fact that

> the myth of Irishness, the notion of Irish unreality, the notions surround-
> ing Irish eloquence, are all political themes upon which the literature
> has battened to an extreme degree since the nineteenth century when
> the idea of national character was invented. The Irish national charac-
> ter...has been received as the verdict passed by history upon the Celtic
> personality. That stereotyping has caused a long colonial concussion.[42]

It is unclear that literature should bear all the blame for these
notions, even if these notions should bear all the blame. Yeats, in
touch with an indigenous cultural movement, one partly rooted in
Irish antiquarian studies, was by no means uncritical of Arnold's
ideas or of stereotypes prevailing in England. Also, nineteenth and
early twentieth-century literary images deserve to be treated with
some historical distance and caution. Deane responds to the Revival
in a curiously foreshortened way, as though it were breathing down
his neck. The stereotypes that pervade the contemporary political
arena have various sources and, as John Wilson Foster argues, may
equally essentialise Ulster Protestants by investing them with 'a
negative mystique'.[43] Better to be 'eloquent' than 'boot-faced', as
Declan Kiberd calls them in one Field Day pamphlet. When Kiberd
describes F.S.L. Lyons as documenting 'that curious blend of resolution and hysteria, of barbarous vulgarity and boot-faced sobriety,
which lies beneath the emotions of Ulster Protestantism', his para-
phrase tendentiously distorts Lyons's anthropology of the Twelfth
of July: 'Here was the visible contrast between the brilliant barbarity
of the setting, with its noise and glitter, and the sobriety of the
serried ranks of grim and serious and utterly respectable marchers,
each in his bowler hat and dark suit...the immobility and dynamism
of the Protestant culture, the mingling of resolution and hysteria.'[44]
    Aside from a glancing reference to 'the spiritual heroics of a
Yeats or a Pearse', Deane does not target Irish Ireland's contribution
to heroic rhetorics – D.P. Moran's 'glamour of the Gael' – and to

the essentialist 'mystique of Irishness' he so deplores. Indeed, *Heroic Styles* ends by reconceiving Moran's cultural separatism in sophisticated terms: 'Everything, including our politics and our literature, has to be re-written – i.e. re-read. That will enable new writing, new politics, unblemished by Irishness, but securely Irish.' [45] Deane's criticism frequently travels in a loop whereby he first seeks to disprove 'such a thing as an Irish national character or an Irish fate or an Irish destiny', but then reverts to Nationalist language: 'it is indeed true that *we* have in *this island, over a very long time*, produced a literature or a form of writing which is *unique* to *us*' [46] [my italics]. Deane's other loop, or contrary gyre, is to resist the 'promiscuous embrace of pluralism', even while scorning 'words like "tradition", "identity"...and their sticky swarm of relatives'.[47] 'Destiny' and 'promiscuity' seem to be the horns of binary dilemma: the former may make you (or Ireland) a character in somebody else's fiction; the latter may deprive you of any character at all.

This split, as in the case of Irish-Ireland thinking, fuels an intensive drive towards integration. For D.P. Moran, the Gael notoriously had to be 'the element that absorbs'. For Deane, re-reading will at least erase the Celtic 'blemish'. But 'the Celt' is ultimately code for Protestant as well as English versions of Ireland. John Wilson Foster diagnoses an Oedipal struggle complicated by sectarianism: 'The battle with Yeats is beginning to resemble The Everlasting Fight. He is the nationalist [some] Irish critics want and the higher-class Protestant they don't want.' [48] In certain lights, the Field Day writers seem dedicated to replacing the alleged cultural power of the Revival with their own myths and rhetorics. Thus the anthology gives remarkably little space to Yeats's prose-writings. The novelist Colm Tóibín has said:

> Each artist in the great Irish tradition has invented an Ireland. Each has done so in order to survive. Yeats's Protestant Ascendancy, Brian Friel's history lessons, Seamus Heaney's Catholic Derry childhood...In the Field Day enterprise itself, however, such manoeuvrings for the sake of art, such distortions, such single-mindedness have been stripped of their origin in artistic necessity and presented to us as a political manifesto, the political truth. A number of men have come to believe in their own dreams.[49]

However, in the anthology as we have it, counter-revivalism has merged or developed into counter-revisionism. Promiscuity now seems a greater threat than national-character-as-destiny. In an earlier Field Day publication Deane credited (discredited) Irish historians with a 'polemical ambition' to 'demolish the nationalist mythology that had been in place for over fifty years', and stated categorically: 'Field Day regards this new orthodoxy with disfavour'.[50] The anthology more elaborately challenges the extent to which 're-reading' Ireland has been the prerogative of historians. In one sense this is no bad thing as we move into a more inter-disciplinary age. Yet, Deane's General Introduction harbours its own polemical ambition while pretending to philosophical relativism. He outflanks both revivalists and revisionists by offering not so much literary history as a historicisation of writing. Writing demotes 'literature', ties it to the other texts of Irish history and turns Irish history into texts. This leads Deane to question not only the objectivity of certain historians, but objective history itself:

> Historians of limited philosophical resource still long to answer the question, 'What really happened then?' More modestly, this anthology asks the longer, less abrasive question: 'How, in the light of what is happening now, can we re-present what was, then and since, believed to have been the significance of what 'really' happened?'...It is part of the received wisdom that the Irish past has been (mis)interpreted by [Nationalist] historians who had a cause to plead and an axe to grind. It is equally the case that this anthology, like the works it presents to the reader, is at the mercy of the present moment and, also like them, derives its authority (such as it is) from that moment.[51]

By inviting readers on to purely textual ground, and loading the text, Deane tries to have his Nationalist history and eat it, to deconstruct and canonise in the same gesture. There are contradictions between his hostility towards revisionism, nostalgia for the old grand narrative, and tie-breaking proposal to make reader-reception 'our arbiter of war'. Without empirical checks, without argument over the *relative* persuasiveness of historical hypotheses, the authority of the present moment favours the sharpest axe over the sharpest eye. Perhaps some Nationalists now regard 'history' as a long-standing ally who has inexplicably defected. Hence their occasional exaltation of folk-memory (or some folks' memory) above 'scientific' history. Hence, too, this grasping at theoretical straws. In 'The Poverty of Theory' (1978) E.P. Thompson argues that Louis Althusser's attack on 'historicism', an attack which Deane echoes, is ultimately a form of idealism – 'the original heresy of metaphysics against knowledge'.[52] I also find Sabina Lovibond's ideas pertinent to Deane's sniper attacks on empiricism (he does not distinguish between empirical methods and empiricism as ideology) and to the whole *kulturkampf* opened up by Field Day. Lovibond argues that the 'doctrine of the autonomy of the *logos*' can dangerously detach language from being '*answerable* to reality', because: 'From one point of view...it encourages a vision of language as a medium of play and trickery rather than of communication...from another (related) point of view, it displays language as a battleground where speakers struggle for mastery'.[53]

In practice, the *Field Day Anthology* establishes its own master-version of history quite conventionally. It abounds in chronologies, periodisation and judgements as to 'what really happened'. Sections are headed: 'The Famine and Young Ireland', 'The Intellectual Revival 1830-1850', 'Poetry and Song 1800-1890'. Tom Dunne points out that Deane's 'introductions to the particular sections he edits – presumably written earlier' do not reflect 'the reservations of [his] General Introduction'.[54] Rather than liberating history into fiction, the anthology pegs literature to date, fact, event. Competition with historiography, obsession with politics, and the chimera of secure Irishness determine the leading emphases. For example, a hitherto unpublished story by Ronan Sheehan occupies fourteen pages of 'Irish Fiction 1965-1990' because it supposedly offers a 'brilliant metaphor of Anglo-Irish relationships'. Meanwhile John McGahern gets three pages. However, Declan Kiberd, charged with editing 'Contemporary Irish Poetry', found himself in difficulties since most contemporary Irish poets are not coming up with the right metaphors. They have, he laments, 'remarkably little to say' about politics 'in the past quarter century'.[55] This may simply mean that they don't say what Kiberd wants to hear. Many would agree that Paul Durcan is the Republic's most conspicuously 'political' poet. However, the *tendency* of his poetry can be termed 'revisionist'. Kiberd includes none of Durcan's political poems and, in a rare fit of aestheticism, he calls Durcan's style 'loose to the point of garrulity'.[56]

Irish history emerges as the author of Irish writing, rather than *vice versa*, whether *vice versa* signifies the aesthetic or the post-structuralist. Further, history itself is construed within a specific historical strand of Nationalist discourse – Republican as opposed to Home Rule. Thus Deane introduces the Irish grand narrative as an unvarying tale of conquest, from the Stone Age to the Northern Ireland Office:

> The island was conquered by pre-Christian invaders, Christian missionaries, the Normans, the pre-Reformation English, the Elizabethans, Cromwellians and by the Williamites. It was dominated by imperial England and it remains, to the present day, in thrall to many of the forces, economic and political, that affect the United Kingdom in its troubled post-imperial decline.[57]

By the same token, 'writing' turns out to be as selective a category as 'literature' ever was. Indeed, the anthology's originality, perhaps

its *raison d'être*, is that it highlights not lost literary gems but discursive texts: texts which themselves highlight politics, philosophy,
culture. As history of ideas (mainly ideas about Ireland), some
sections work very well. Yet, to admit this principle is to multiply
the difficulty of representing constituencies, women being the most
obvious case. 'Anthology' becomes an even more magnetic field,
medium as well as metaphor, for the selectivities of Irish politics.
Not every section takes a political line, but counter-revisionist polemic
zigzags through the entire fabric.

Early on, the presence of Spenser, other 'Early Planters', and
Cromwell signals anti-colonial intent. Nor does – say – Gladstone
turn up later to salvage some English self-respect. As we have seen,
Deane reads all Irish history up to and back from the present moment
as 'a long colonial concussion'. He has said: 'Field Day's analysis
of the situation derives from the conviction that it is, above all, a
colonial crisis.'[58] (True to his rejection of empiricism, the conviction
does not derive from the analysis.) That statement comes from Deane's
introduction to three Field Day pamphlets by Terry Eagleton, Fredric
Jameson and Edward Said. It must be admitted that all critics
involved in the Irish faction-fight tend to call upon the theoretical
support which suits their book – whether feminism, deconstruction,
or a more traditional Marxism. Field Day understandably favours
theorists who might help to insert Northern Ireland/Ireland into
the colonial/post-colonial frame (especially its simpler models). At
the same time, the theorists in question could have been productively
exposed to data about Ireland since the era of Yeats and Joyce. Strange
collusions are taking place: intellectual holiday romances in a post-
colonial never-never land. Joseph Lee's critique of how the Republic
has treated socio-economic ideas from abroad also applies to those
who throw theory at Ireland, hoping that bits of it will stick. Lee
asks: 'Did they conceive of imported ideas as raw materials, as
intermediate goods, or as finished products?'[59]

Jameson's pamphlet *Modernism and Imperialism* probes the 'underlying...Third World' features of Joyce's Dublin, without recourse
either to uneven civic development in the British Isles or to European
contexts. The latter might make Dublin pub-culture look less weird
to Jameson, on whose criterion it should not have outlived British
rule: 'the very fact of the pub itself, of public space in which you
meet and talk, is itself a happy survival of an older urban life, which
will have no equivalent in metropolitan literature...'[60] Social anthropology based on Duke University seems ill-equipped to understand
European cities and their art. Edward Said, although more friendly

towards Yeats's 'nativism' or essentialism than is Deane in *Heroic Styles*, fails to grasp the shifting sands of his position as a Protestant Nationalist. Thus he misreads Yeats's 'Fisherman' as, like Neruda's 'El pueblo', exemplifying 'an anonymous man of the people, who in his strength and loneliness is also a mute expression *of* the people'.[61] In fact, the poem marks extreme disaffection from 'my own race' in its contemporary 'reality'. Terry Eagleton, also author of the Field Day play *Saint Oscar* – axes, tears and cheap epigrams – takes an Anglo-centric tack when he warns Irish critics against prematurely pluralising identity or falling for the 'liberal humanist notion of culture [which] was constituted, among other things, to marginalise such peoples as the Irish'.[62] If Arnold flattered and colonised the Celt in one way, Eagleton may do so in another. He assumes (like Said) a homogeneous, unproblematic Irish people. Nor does he distinguish between cultural norms in Ireland and those obtaining somewhere called 'Britain' but evidently signifying southern England or Oxford. Liberal humanism may have been tried *on* Ireland, but has scarcely been tried *in* it, any more than have the politics of pluralism.

Irish liberals tensed between powerful opposites – witness Sean O'Faolain or Hubert Butler – inhabit a very different context to that of historical English liberalism (though this has been livened up by the Thatcherite threat). Hence, for instance, Butler's doubts about the seriousness of liberal English *literati* like Graham Greene and Stephen Spender: 'Their art and their reputation would not, I think, survive a real *kulturkampf* in which first principles were not only invoked but applied.'[63] Cultural differences should, more broadly, undermine 'liberal humanist' as a totalising reflex sneer. With regard to *Saint Oscar*, to Eagleton's co-option by Field Day, and to his theoretical entryism, the playwright Robin Glendinning protests:

> Apparently the Nobel prize-winning Wole Soyinka is much criticised in Nigeria these days for blaming the troubles of his country on his own countrymen and not on its colonial legacy. There does not seem to be much danger of Field Day falling into the trap of unsettling their Irish audience, or of providing their English audience with anything too complicated to understand...I did think that Field Day's *raison d'être* was that the language of Irish politics had petrified, and that the language of drama had, therefore, a vital and radical responsibility. If one of these petrified languages is Irish nationalism, surely a radical responsibility goes beyond finding novel ways of saying the same damned things? And surely inviting English left-wing intellectuals to use the petrified language in their own quarrel with their own establishment is also evading that responsibility?[64]

Similarly, Arnold's ideas also originated in English contexts, and were taken more seriously in England than in Ireland.

Although the term 'colonial' may fit some aspects of Irish experience, most historians would qualify or specify its uses, and dispute the one-size-fits-all zeal of most theorists. For instance, internal European colonialism might constitute an apter (if not necessarily happier) model than those elaborated by Fanon or Said. In the earlier period, the degree of parallelism between Irish and New World 'colonies' is the subject of continuing debate,[65] and the economic historian Liam Kennedy has challenged post-colonial (as opposed to secessionist) descriptions of the newly independent Free State. Kennedy's statistics place Ireland, then and now, very far indeed from any emergent Third World nation. He concludes: 'a much more fruitful comparative perspective – illuminating issues of industrialisation, urbanisation, demography, sectarian and ethnic tensions, and secessionist politics – may be derived from the experiences of Ireland's European neighbours'. (This is why Northern Irish people can now see themselves in the cracked looking-glass of Yugoslavia.) Kennedy surmises that 'ultra-nationalists' seek to update their traditional rhetoric 'through identification with genuine liberation struggles in the Third World'.[66] However, Robert Hughes enters a broader caveat:

> many 'radicals' seem to assume that, in looking at other cultures under the rubric of 'multiculturalism', one should gaze mainly at their versions of Marxism, 'liberation struggle', and so forth. But is this not just another Eurocentric caricature, to be asked to admire in other countries and cultures the ideological forms they have borrowed, recently, from the West?[67]

Thus home and abroad become mutually abstract.

Some intellectuals deny Ireland's European past because the Republic's European present, in a materialist EU, casts doubt on the victim-position to which Irish Nationalism has always appealed. The tenacious vision of a pure island Eden is recycled, thanks to Nationalist disinformation, in Edward Said's *Culture and Imperialism* (1993). Although Said's literary multiculturalism is generally more complex, the land of saints, scholars, missionaries and imperial civil servants seems to have gone float about – perhaps to the Caribbean: '*European* writing on Africa, India, parts of the Far East, Australia, and the Caribbean...I see as part of the general *European* effort to rule *distant* lands and peoples and, therefore, as related to Orientalist descriptions of the Islamic world, as well as to Europe's special ways of representing the Caribbean islands, *Ireland*, and the Far East'[68] [my italics]. Under various empires, theocracies and dynasties Europeans also had special ways of representing one another. Catholic Europe has been inclined to see the English, rather than the Irish, as 'a barbarian and degenerate race'.[69] Less innocently, David Lloyd's *Anomalous States: Irish Writing and the Post-Colonial Moment* (1993) cloaks familiar Marxist-Republican doctrines in theoretical euphemism. Lloyd refers to 'the negation of recalcitrant or inassimilable elements in Irish society' and desires to 'recover subterranean or marginalised practices which have been understood variously as aberrant, pre-modern and residual, or incoherent'.[70] This doubly mystifies the illegal organisation. For all his emphasis on 'heteroglossia', Lloyd's subversives, subalterns and hybridised street-ballads often turn out to sing the same old song when their 'occluded practices' come to light. Behind his piling of abstraction upon abstraction, his unmasking of the collusions between 'imperial ideology' and 'bourgeois National-ism', one glimpses once again a sinister purity.

It's true that some Ulster Protestant poets and critics have accepted (or unwittingly internalised) terminology associated with colonial-ism. John Hewitt's poem 'The Colony' (1950) allegorises Northern Ireland through the consciousness of a Roman settler aware that 'Already from other lands the legions ebb/and men no longer know the Roman peace'. John Wilson Foster takes the title of his collected essays, *Colonial Consequences* (1991), from a poem in which Hewitt complains that 'strangers from the mainland, eager men,/the latest jargon lively on the tongue,/here make their way among us'. However, the power-dynamics which these poems explore and exemplify – centring on land, religion, culture and the locus of authority – play out the tensions between province and capital(s), ethnically troubled region and seats of government (compare Transylvania), as much as between distant metropolis and colony. Foster's essay 'Culture and Colonisation' uses the North African analogy (Albert Memmi) to argue that the 'Ulster Protestant, feeling the perpetual threat of being taken over, already experiences in some sense, and exhibits the symptoms of, *the condition of being colonised*. His legendary intransigence is the anticipation of a calamity.'[71] But 'colonisation' may be too grand and romantic a term for the final sacrifice of Protestant Ascendancy – as 'decolonisation' for the attainment of Catholic Ascendancy. Equally, the 'injurious feeling of inferiority beside England'[72] with which Foster grew up can be duplicated by other cultural cringes within the UK 'multiple kingdom'. Thus Robert Crawford's *Devolving English Literature* (1992), with its Scottish perspectives on canonical matters, seems more relevant to Ireland than does Lloyd's application of the post-colonial pastry-cutter.

Comparative perspectives now abound: Frank Wright's *Northern Ireland : A Comparative Analysis* (1987) compares the North with 'frontier-societies' across the globe, detecting both similarity and difference in a range of political contexts. Wright's findings are complemented rather than contradicted by John Whyte's overview of the social-science literature in *Interpreting Northern Ireland* (1990). Whyte concludes that the 'internal-conflict approach' is close to becoming 'a dominant paradigm'.[73] Is it revisionist to suggest that there may be no dominant paradigm: that colonial readings might be spliced with approaches which show Ireland/Irish writing in other lights? Deane's exclusive focus on the colonial/Third World paradigm owes something to the persistent Nationalist belief in Irish exceptionalism (echoed by the title of Lloyd's book and by Jameson's reference to 'the uniqueness of the Irish situation').[74] It is not necessarily the case that 'The failure of...cultural versions to achieve hegemony in alliance with the political system is more remarkable in a European country than it would be in those parts of the world which have been subject to European domination.'[75]

One result of looking no further (or nearer) than 'colonialism' is to fudge the role of religion – sometimes supposed to wither away with the advent of true Republicanism. Deane consistently blames colonial false consciousness for 'sectarianism' and thus leaves the latter term unexamined too. For instance, writing on Joyce in the *Field Day Anthology*, he refers to 'the dual British-Roman catholic spiritual monarchy', and his General Introduction laments 'a society sectarianised by the Williamite confiscations and the Penal Laws'.[76] These encapsulations discount the historical politics of the Irish and European churches themselves. Ireland was not the only corner of Europe where the Reformation – and Counter-Reformation – had divisive consequences, and it was always unclear whether any eventual Irish state was to be for the Church or the Church for the state. Earlier, the goal of Irish Jacobites had been a Catholic monarch in London. When Brian Inglis maintained that the Penal Laws made it impossible for an Irish Protestant to criticise the status quo in the Republic, Hubert Butler argued:

> The Catholic Church prides itself on its universality so it must be judged by its universal and not by its local activities. Why not say the penal laws started not in Ireland in 1688 but rather in France three years earlier, when after the Revocation of the Edict of Nantes several hundred thousand Lost Sheep were bayoneted back into the Fold?[77]

Eleven hundred French Huguenots fought in King William's army.

Tom Paulin deserves credit for featuring religion in a section called 'Northern Protestant Oratory and Writing 1791-1985'. But Paulin, obsessed with the wilder shores of Presbyterianism, hears

Protestant orators – who include Ian Paisley and Paisley's nineteenth-century precursor Henry Cooke – as undifferentiated, marginal and doomed exotics from 'a solipsistic universe gnawed at its edges by anger and incoherence' (this would be essentialism and occlusion if done to Irish Catholics),[78] and thus removed from the intense theological-political dialectics that roared through the Irish nineteenth-century and beyond. In fact, the Hound of Heaven who fails to bark in this anthology, except courtesy of literature, is the Catholic Church. Where, for instance, is Archbishop John Charles McQuaid and *his* nineteenth-century precursor Cardinal Cullen? Balance, as well as information, requires a section with some such title as 'Catholic Apologetics from 1850 to the 1986 Divorce Referendum'.

If Protestantism looms larger theologically, Nationalism looms larger politically. Unionism, lumped in with Paulin's Presbyterian orators and thereby dehistoricised, consists of the Ulster Covenant, a patriotic speech from James Craig in 1940, and two speeches made in political defeat by Edward Carson (*not* a Northerner) and the late Harold McCusker. Neither nineteenth-century Ulster liberalism nor twentieth-century Ulster socialism gets a look-in. Deane's 'political' sections, and Luke Gibbons's cultural counterparts, overwhelmingly stress varieties of Nationalism (some varieties more than others). Thus 'Political Writings and Speeches 1900-1988' ends with a flourish of Charles Haughey, John Hume, Sean MacBride and Gerry Adams. The introduction to this section itself reads like a political speech, particularly its eulogy of ex-Taoiseach Charles Haughey:

> Charles Haughey, perhaps the most resourceful politician in Ireland, has repeatedly called Northern Ireland 'a failed entity' and seeks negotiation about its future on that basis. There is, in his policy, and in the attitudes of his party, Fianna Fáil, a recognition that a political crisis is not susceptible to genial gestures like those of [Garret] FitzGerald. It is a matter of interest and power, and most of the power is in the hands of the British. Haughey has still to show that he knows where the British see their interest to lie. But, in the interval, he skilfully combines de Valera's meticulously crafted republicanism with Seán Lemass's best possible blend of cosmopolitan modernity and ancestral loyalty for present-day Ireland. [79]

Here Deane nails his colours, his authority as General Editor, and 'Irish writing' to the Fianna Fáil mast – or, at least, to its Republican grain. Despite saluting Seán Lemass, he does not document Lemass's reforms of the late 1950s which, in steering the Republic away from economic protectionism, betokened the end of cultural protectionism too, and laid the fuse for controversies – abortion, divorce – now ablaze in the political foreground.

Church-state politics also bring feminism into the foreground, since control over women's minds and bodies is central to the argument. (Meanwhile, the Pope has intervened on the other side). In excluding women's politics and political women, of whatever stripe, in lauding Haughey but not Mary Robinson's libertarian crusades, in overlooking contemporary Irish feminism and its foremothers, in minimising the politics of the Catholic Church, the *Field Day Anthology* locates its own political heart north of the Border. It thus reflects the increasing tension between Northern Nationalism and revisionist processes – or social change – in the Republic (see 'From Cathleen to Anorexia'). A recent and symbolic case in point was Bernadette (Devlin) McAliskey's attack on blasé Southerners for 'laughing at grandmother's bare feet'. North-South differences within broadly Nationalist Ireland extend to the greater conservatism of the Catholic Church in the North. Radical nuns and priests are thinner on the ground there; the laity, though with some middle-class reservations, more obedient. There is an impulse from Armagh (seat of the all-Ireland Primate) to preserve the North as the last bastion of 'real' Irish Catholicism. In other words, Northern Catholics, for purposes of cultural defence and communal cohesion, still abide by the pact negotiated between Catholicism and Nationalism during the nineteenth century. That ambiguous bargain has not yet come unstuck, as it has in the Republic (hence Hierarchical hostility to the North's small band of integrated schools). The Northern Nationalist newspaper, the *Irish News* – originally founded by Catholic bishops as an anti-Parnellite organ – retains *pro fide et Patria* in its masthead. If, in west Belfast, Republicans sometimes clash with the Church, that too reproduces a nineteenth-century pattern. The Sinn Féin leader Gerry Adams took care to attend the funeral of the former Catholic Primate, Cardinal O'Fiaich. So it was always on the cards that, wittingly or unwittingly, whether impelled by conscious programme or programmed unconscious, Field Day would collide with progressive forces in the Republic. Colm Tóibín said in his review of the anthology:

> Unreconstructed Irish Nationalists have always had real difficulty with the 26 Counties. The 26 Counties are limbo, they believe, waiting for the day when our island will be united and the British will leave. This leaves out any idea that Southern Ireland has been forming its own habits and going its own way.[80]

Shocked, by the reaction from women, into recognising the Irish Republic, Field Day have embarked upon a damage-limitation exercise. To atone for their all-male directorate, and Deane's all-male editorial

team, they now plan a fourth volume edited by women writers,
critics and historians. Perhaps this afterthought might be called –
from Field Day's viewpoint – 'The Mad Women in the Annex'. Nor
should annexes be attached to fundamentally flawed structures. Such
a volume under such auspices, however powerful its own feminist
critique, would tie women to a totalising text whose patriarchal and
Nationalist compulsions are not easy to disentangle. A woman journal-
ist, who condemned the anthology from a feminist angle, asked how
Seamus Deane, 'one of my heroes', could do this. She might have
noted the blend of sectarianism, anti-Englishness and patronage of
women writers in Deane's attitude to George Eliot's 'evangelical,
female puritan spirit' in his *Celtic Revivals* (1985).[81] But the centripetal
imperatives of Catholicism/Nationalism encourage heroes and her-
oines to kiss and make up when it comes to the crunch. Conversely,
as a revisionist woman critic of Field Day, I may have given double
offence. Yet the anthology's sins of omission support the question-
marks which 'From Cathleen to Anorexia' attaches to the synchron-
isation of Nationalist and feminist objectives. When Terry Eagleton's
Field Day pamphlet compares Nationalism with feminism, and urges
both to resist premature deconstruction (see page 187 below), he
implicitly fears the latter's potential to deconstruct the former: partly
through its subversion of absolutes, partly through its reinstatement
of trans-cultural values. Sabina Lovibond makes feminism the test-
case when she argues that values assigned by cultures and groups
might be 'seen as answerable to a universal or quasi-universal standard
that would identify some discursive regimes, but not others, as
tolerable'.[82] In the Irish Republic feminist universals have proved
indispensable. The international women's movement liberated women
into politics, and into challenging legislation which enforced Catholic
teaching. Frances Gardiner's study, 'The Unfinished Revolution',
shows that – until the 1970s – women have been less politically
active there than in other Northern European countries. This is
because 'a budding feminist political consciousness' was subsumed
by Nationalist hegemony,[83] itself subsumed by Catholic hegemony.
Gardiner says:

> It has been noted that, following enfranchisement, women's political
> activity often seemed to recede, as if the effort of getting the vote had
> left suffragists temporarily exhausted. But, in many countries, within a
> matter of decades remobilisation occurred. This contrasted with the Irish
> experience, where women appeared to lose motivation to reinstate fem-
> inist concerns on the political agenda, or to participate in the shaping
> of the new state.[84]

Women were allowed no voice in drafting de Valera's 1937 Constitution, which upheld Catholic social teaching by recognising 'the
Family' as 'the natural primary and fundamental unit group of
Society' and by desiring women to concentrate on 'their duties in
the home'.

Like the 1937 Constitution, the *Field Day Anthology* tries to place
itself above argument. On the one hand, Deane's General Introduction
uses theoretical relativism to discredit 'revisionist' critiques: 'The
political animus informing...non-nationalist groups was concealed
as much as possible, and the most frequently worn disguise was,
in history, the pretence to "objectivity" and in literature the claim
to "autonomy".'[85] On the other hand, he throws theory to the winds
and advertises the anthology itself as transcending context, as not
merely an overview of texts but a unitary island-story:

> There *is* a story here, a meta-narrative, which is, we believe, hospitable
> to all the micro-narratives that, from time to time, have achieved promi
> nence as the official version of the true history, political and literary, of
> the island's past and present.[86]

At this stage I need not dwell on the ironies of 'hospitable'. However,
'meta-narrative' might be exposed to broader debates about canons and
history. I find Anne Rigney's *The Rhetoric of Historical Representation*
(1990) and Jan Gorak's *The Making of the Modern Canon* (1991)
relevant to the Irish interface between anthology and historiography.

Rigney examines three histories of the French Revolution written
at roughly the same distance from the event as Irish historians now
are from the upheavals of the 1920s. She shows that while historians
need to accept the theorists' point (i.e. that they are engaged in
representation as well as reproduction), their house-style is neither as
unphilosophical nor as unselfconscious as Deane makes out. Historical
narratives function within an 'intertextual antagonism', and historians
are constrained 'by the nature of their historiographical role and
the nature of the raw material with which they are dealing; the fact
that they are not free to produce whatever meaning they choose; the
fact that unlike fiction-writers they are not free to invent'.[87] (Rigney's
findings bear out E.P. Thompson's argument in 'The Poverty of
Theory'.) Thus J.H. Andrews, criticising Brian Friel's representation
of the nineteenth-century Ordnance Survey in his play *Translations*,
is bound by disciplines foreign to Friel (see page 155 below). Michael
Laffan, in 'Insular Attitudes: The Revisionists and their Critics',
points out that changes in Irish historiographical practices since
the 1960s were not simply dictated by new political exigencies (or
'political animus') but by the opening-up of crucial archives. Laffan

also insists that 'in looking critically at the past, in stressing complexity and ambivalence...Irish historians...have simply applied, in the Irish context, the same approaches and methods as are taken for granted by their counterparts in other countries'.[88] Nationalist history, resistant to the democracy of 'intertextual antagonism', desires to cast 'revisionism' in its own monolithic mould. But Laffan objects:

> Those historians who incur the wrath of radical or hyper-sensitive nationalists are a diverse collection of people: by nationality they are Irish, British and American; by political inclination they are conservative, liberal, radical and even (on rare occasions) Marxist...They disagree vehemently among themselves on numerous questions, and some of them would be inclined to repudiate the label 'revisionist', not merely because it is a label, but also because of the company they would be presumed to keep as members of any such group or faction.[89]

It is equally tendentious to identify a homogeneous literary faction who hide 'non-nationalist' politics behind doctrines of artistic autonomy. No Irish writer or critic can be so innocent as to divorce literature from context along the lines suggested by Tom Paulin's Anglocentric contention: 'We have been taught, many of us, to believe that art and politics are separated by the thickest and most enduring of partitions.'[90] The argument does not turn on *whether* to link literature and history, literature and politics, but on *how*.

Although Deane stresses 'the extent to which, in Irish conditions, canonical forms have not been established',[91] canons have been floating and floated for some time. How they relate to 'English' canons is another matter, to which I will return, and which I see as a more complex affair than 'repossessing some of the standard "English" names – Swift or Sterne, Burke or Wilde'.[92] In fact, the Irish canon has not always claimed these names. Yeats excluded the Anglo-Irish eighteenth century – to Dowden's protests – when he was canon-building in the 1890s.[93] So did Daniel Corkery when canon-building on behalf of Irish Ireland in *Synge and Anglo-Irish Literature* (1931). Indeed he went further and expunged Yeats together with much of the 'tribeless' Revival. The direction taken by the new state had already obliged Yeats to rethink his own Irish canon, to reinforce the Revival with the eighteenth century, and rebuild his Protestant literary 'ancestral stair' – 'Goldsmith and the Dean, Berkeley and Burke have travelled there' ('Blood and the Moon'). Deane has himself ridiculed Yeats's construction of the eighteenth century and accused him of 'literary unionism'.[94] Such shifts bear out Jan Gorak's conclusion that 'the canon' is neither single nor simple but the product of continual contestation:

> The history of canons...links them not with one permanently dominant ideology but with the ongoing and shifting construction of group goals. The group may consist of early Christian ecclesiastical authorities, fourteenth-century Florentine artists, eighteenth-century philologists, or late twentieth-century academicians. In each case, a special intensity of conviction about the cultural importance of their work encourages them to construct a canon.[95]

Gorak does not accept that 'proponents of cultural politics' behave any differently, despite harbouring a self-image whereby '*they* articulate, and therefore uncanonise, their principles to an unprecedented degree'.[96] This casts light on the internal contradictions of Deane's General Introduction. Field Day's 'group-goals' create a tension between canon-breaking (English literature) and canon-making (Irish literature). Nevertheless, Deane's meta-narrative remains a canonical venture.

Deane illustrates the unarticulated politics of *other* canon-makers by citing the case of Louis MacNeice:

> MacNeice for long has been an English thirties poet with an Irish background; today he is being recruited as an Ulster poet. His reputation to a large extent depends on his felt presence for a particular group or generation.[97]

As one of the 'recruiters' (what a drab term, and how Ferguson's military metaphor persists!) I began in the mid 1960s with an aesthetic question as to why such a good poet was relatively neglected in both Ireland *and* England. That question, a decade later, admittedly led me to issues of cultural politics, Irish Protestant history – forgotten or rewritten after Partition – and English ignorance of Ireland. But it also led to further questions about English-language poetic traditions in the twentieth century (see 'The Room Where MacNeice Wrote "Snow"'). Politics usurp aesthetics as much as aesthetics 'conceal' politics, since good stuff – not only by women – languishes uncanonised, ignored by academic fashions and national interests, dependent on purer kinds of enthusiasm (witness the initial rediscovery of Jean Rhys). Nor was MacNeice simply on tap to fulfil dubious needs implied by Deane's 'Ulster'. His felt presence has proved 'incorrigibly plural', to quote 'Snow', and can be verified by the old-fashioned tools of practical criticism and literary history. If reputation depended solely on politics, any expatriate Protestant hack would have filled the bill. Readings, though always incomplete, have not been arbitrarily imposed on MacNeice's poetry, just as Irish historians 'are not free to produce whatever meaning they choose'. Readers in the grip of conventional categories like 'English thirties poet' – a term which suggests partisan myopia in two countries – may have failed to switch on some of the lights in his text. Those which remain dark do not exist only in future reader-response.

Field Day's 'special intensity of conviction', to quote Gorak, derives from Northern Nationalism, or more strictly from Northern anti-Partitionism: the introverted, self-sustaining rhetoric of the Catholic community since the 1920s. And Field Day's group-goals centre on Derry as the locus of Jacobite restoration, the visionary city destined to redeem the shames of Belfast and Dublin. If the anthology is a shade triumphalist (and I find it so) this is triumphalism piled on top of trauma. The Unionist regime at Stormont neglected and gerrymandered Derry, with its incipient Catholic majority. Denial of city-council votes to non-ratepayers thus had the greatest political impact in Derry and made it the crucible of Civil Rights protest. Earlier in the 1960s, the city should have been selected (rather than Coleraine) as the site for the New University of Ulster. There was, indeed, Catholic-Protestant solidarity on that point, but not such as to withstand the fracturing pressures of the Troubles. Derry City Council now has a Nationalist majority and shares power, as most Unionist-dominated councils do not. The city has been revitalised and refurbished. At the same time, in a complex defensive manoeuvre that parallels the way in which Southern Protestantism shrank in upon itself, Derry Protestants have moved east across Lough Foyle, retreating towards the heartland. Thus Derry's self-image, boosted by Field Day and *vice versa*, belies a continuing sectarian split.

I read the *Field Day Anthology*, especially its binary inclinations, as a Derry meta-narrative. Eamonn McCann in *War and an Irish Town* (re-issued in 1993) records how St Columb's College nurtured a future (male) Catholic élite, including John Hume, Friel, Heaney and Deane. The school straddled tensions between rural and urban Derry, and class-differences within the city itself. Deane's background in the Bogside conditions his most interesting contribution to the anthology, and perhaps its epitome: 'Autobiography and Memoirs 1890-1988'. His selections here remain biased towards political record: the War of Independence, the Civil War, the Civil Rights movement (Bernadette Devlin, Eamonn McCann), Ulster Protestant 'fear and loathing of catholicism' – nothing in the other direction, 'piratical penetrations' from Britain.[98] Yet some of his choices suggest a fascination with the alienated outsider from both Irish communities: Hubert Butler, Noel Browne – a Southern politician who fell foul of the Catholic Hierarchy – and, surprisingly, Louis MacNeice. Indeed, Deane makes MacNeice the focus of powerful reflections on generic

alienation: 'MacNeice is one of those writers who helps us to understand the conflicts that exist within the North; he also helps us to
understand much other writing about the North because he creates
the self through that conflict rather than by an avoidance or over-
coming of it.' [99] Deane's empathy with MacNeice's 'expulsion and
emigration from [the] Edenic moment' [100] helps to interpret the
Palestinian as well as Jacobite element in Derry Nationalism – or,
more specifically, in the consciousness of Derry's inner émigrés, its
literary kings over the border. But when Deane transfers that doubly
split and dislocated communal psyche, perhaps his own autobiographical 'crisis' (a word he repeats obsessively), to the entire island,
the psycho-cultural meta-narrative collapses of its own extremity:
'[Ireland] is a place that takes precedence over all others and is, at
the same time, a nowhere, a utopia inverted and perverted.' [101]

Should Derry autobiographies take precedence over all others?
Neither Seamus Heaney's mellower rural Derry nor Brian Friel's
limbo-like Ballybeg are the whole story either. The curious a-histori-
cism of Friel's drama (for all its political concern with history) has
been little noted, although Colm Tóibín criticises Field Day writers
in general for propagating a time-warped 'world of haw lanterns,
wishing wells, station islands, hedge schools and cross-roads dancing'.[102]
Deane's news from nowhere again articulates a distinctively Northern
Nationalist perspective: destiny (the Republican ideal) betrayed by
promiscuity (the actual Republic which has messed things up).
Meanwhile, their own utopia has been infinitely deferred, their day
has not yet come. 'None of these autobiographies or memoirs,' says
Deane, 'can avoid the sense of a missing feature or energy', and he
diagnoses an 'incapacity to accept origin'.[103] But this is self-selection
speaking. It also perilously invests all identity in the 'national being'.
What Damian Smyth terms Deane's 'mourning of division…adulation
of coherence…passion for completeness' [104] underlies his efforts to
extricate himself from alien definitions: from Celticism, colonialism,
revivalism, revisionism, Free-statism, the Republic's modernising
self-images and – the bottom line – Unionism. But this spirited
resistance, which may mask deeper problems of personal and cultural
'origin', harbours its own hegemonic impulse. It is now the turn
of Irish Protestants to be silenced, misrepresented and stereotyped:
two contemporary Northern Protestant poets seem subtextually
willed off the stage of history by editorial notes which describe their
work as 'self-effacing' and written for 'posterities'.[105]

To give further credit where it is due, Luke Gibbons included my
earlier critique of Field Day (from *Poetry in the Wars*) in a section

of the anthology entitled 'Challenging the Canon: Revisionism and Cultural Criticism'. However, true revisionists here rub shoulders with Field Day pamphleteers – Field Day fends off challenge by self-anthologising to a remarkable extent – and carry ideological health-warnings. Perhaps Gibbons's intrusive anxiety to point out 'the underlying critical strategems in the revisionist approach to history'[106] indirectly admits that revisionism has spread beyond academe. Certain historians, particularly from Irish Protestant backgrounds, and even writers like Sean O'Faolain have come to be scapegoated as part of a wider struggle for hearts and minds. Again, despite complaining that revisionists have failed to set 'a new agenda ...for loyalist history'[107] too (untrue, and strangely dualistic from a Nationalist), Gibbons seems less interested in representing a range of Ulster Protestant opinion than in pursuing a quarrel within and about Nationalism. For instance, he omits the cultural politics of John Hewitt, yet celebrates Nationalist generosity and diversity: 'By denying the variegated pattern of nationalism, the fissures and tensions in a disparate set of responses to colonial domination, the revisionist enterprise gave back to the most conservative strands in nationalism the unity and cohesion they found so difficult to attain on their own terms.'[108] This is the anti-anti-racism argument, the don't-provoke-a-male-backlash argument. (In another section of the anthology Gibbons offers, as a variegated role-model, Aodh de Blacam – a Catholic convert who later fought for General Franco.) To legitimate the counter-revisionist backlash, revisionism must always figure as a concerted propagandist drive to 'establish myth, violence and catholicism as the co-ordinates of militant nationalism'.[109] Our endemic binary insists that, for Nationalism to be various, revisionism has to be monolithic. But revisionism, in its broader sense, may simply be a return of the repressed and therefore incorrigibly plural (which is why it worries Sinn Féin).

Backlash strikes more fiercely in contributions by Declan Kiberd and Seamus Deane to *Revising the Rising*, a publication that post-dates the *Field Day Anthology*. Kiberd's essay, 'The Elephant of Revolutionary Forgetfulness', castigates 'the designer-Stalinists who have so successfully impoverished the contemporary debate about the past', and even indicts Sean O'Casey for 'operating a kind of Section 31 [the Republic's act which bans Sinn Féin spokesmen from radio and television] ahead of its time...and never allow[ing a rebel] to make a full statement of the nationalist case'.[110] However, Stalinism and censorship may be in the eye of the beholder. Kiberd (who, after all, operates a kind of Section 31 against Paul Durcan) says menacingly of O'Casey: 'hardly the sort of portraiture expected in most countries of a people's playwright'.[111] The emerging tactic, also employed by Deane in 'Wherever Green is Read' – a direct assault on Roy Foster's 'popular' *Modern Ireland 1600-1972* – is simply to turn around, rather than empirically rebut, the charges which any spirit of doubt or compromise might bring against Nationalist absolutes. Thus Deane's version of liberalism and pluralism is idiosyncratic to say the least:

> The kindest view of liberalism in present-day Ireland would credit it with the wish to improve the existing political-economic system in such a manner that people would be as economically secure and as free as possible from all the demonic influences of 'ideologies', religious and political. Its buzz word is 'pluralism'; its idea of the best of all possible worlds is based on the hope of depoliticising the society to the point where it is essentially a consumerist organism...The full realisation of the individual self is regarded as an ambition that institutions exist to serve. Those that do not – religion, education, the 1937 Constitution, for example – are to be liberalised, gentrified or abolished...Pluralism has only one time – the present; everything else is, literally, anachronistic.[112]

Here Northern Nationalist alienation speaks loud and clear: alienation from the revisionist Republic, that is, where feminism could not function without the growth of liberalism and pluralism. Nor are rights of private judgement synonymous with privatisation. Deane's atavism has become more glaringly inconsistent with dismissing 'historians of little philosophical resource'. Once again, disagreement hinges not on *whether* we invoke the past(s) but on *how*. Deane's and Kiberd's tirades against 'media-led' pluralism display the hysteria of someone losing a political argument – or who has only just discovered that argument and politics exist. This betrays the extent to which Nationalism, like Unionism, has hitherto relied on undemocratic and unexamined loyalties. There is a telling vignette in John Waters's bestseller *Jiving at the Crossroads* (1991), a vivid but naive and unconsciously patriarchal narrative of Fianna Fáil's populist, clientalist grassroots culture. Sean Doherty, a TD for Roscommon, has just been made a minister:

> The faces flickered their way by, and yet were frozen in space, caught in the dancing torchlight. Most were faces we knew, local Fianna Fáil activists...There were people of different ages, shapes and sizes, though they were almost exclusively men...They were united as priests concelebrating a Mass of the Resurrection. They were the dogs whose day had finally arrived...[Doherty] was the chieftain among his people, and yet was one of them. This perhaps is what we mean when we speak of democracy.[113]

Actually, it isn't. And if the behaviour uncritically attributed to
Fianna Fáil in *Jiving at the Crossroads* were laid to the account of
Ulster Unionists, there would be an international outcry.

And what of 'literature'? The *Field Day Anthology* seems oddly
at a loss when it comes to Irish literary traditions in the twentieth
century. Apart from building in the obvious pillars (Joyce, an excellent
introduction to Beckett by J.C.C. Mays), volume three organises
political speeches and cultural criticism more confidently than what
we used to call primary texts – poems, drama and fiction. Nor does
literary criticism play much of a part, not even the manifestos published by individuals, groups and schools since the 1930s. Surely
these – like Yeats's missing mission-statements – are relevant to
our shifting canon. But Deane's problem was: How to divide the
century without dividing the country? British anthologies and literary
histories generally take a break, whether justifiable or not, at the
Second World War, but only Northern Ireland officially joined in
that skirmish. Deane's autobiographical section, despite its martial
emphases, includes memoirs of neither World War. The *Field Day
Anthology* may be the last work to observe the protocols of Irish
neutrality 1939-1945. To regionalise Irish writing, or to admit separate
literary developments North and South, was evidently unthinkable.
You don't have to be a Unionist to regret, with Damian Smyth,
'the absence of the border as an inscription on history':

> So great is the desire to totalise that even the rough stitching of the
> border, with its consequent realignment of imaginative forces and al-
> legiances in the two islands, is not addressed in terms of the writing it
> shaped in hidden and not so hidden ways...The poems of John Hewitt
> (1907-87), W.R. Rodgers (1909-69) and Louis MacNeice (1907-63), for
> example, are dumped into a mysterious category called 'Counter-Revival
> Poetry' with a motley assortment of southern poets...Hewitt's *The Colony*
> and MacNeice's *Autumn Journal* are attached to Kavanagh's *The Great
> Hunger* in terms of the revival of the 'long poem' – Hewitt's strenuous
> foundation myth and MacNeice's urbane international meditation are
> stripped of their relevance for contemporary northern verse and are
> reduced to considerations of mere length. In the process, of course, they
> are detached from the narrative of 'Ulster' 20th-century poetry. Over a
> thousand pages later...'Contemporary Irish Poetry' begins with Patrick
> McDonogh (1902-61) and Padraic Fallon (1905-74), who are conscript-
> ed as the forebears of Heaney, Longley, Mahon and Simmons...the
> consistencies of theme and style among the northern poets of the 60s
> are seen as unprecedented, tacked on to a disparate and less-contentious
> poetic narrative.[114]

Beside erasing the Border, the questionable term 'Counter-Revival'
merely gestures at the textual and political complexities of the post-

Revival period. Thus Terence Brown is given quite inadequate space to deal with the era of 'Provinciality and Censorship' in the Free State. The crucial bridge of the mid-century breaks down, until jagged planks reappear in the 1960s, because Northern Nationalist priorities marginalise the literary history of 'limbo' as well as the diverse literary and cultural traditions that have nourished contemporary Northern writing. The latter are either dispersed, as Smyth indicates, or – like Ulster Scots vernacular verse – absent. There might also be sound stylistic reasons for immediately preceding Heaney *et al* with Larkin and Hughes rather than with MacDonogh and Fallon. But only Northern *Protestant* poets are allowed anything 'in common with the semi-detached suburban muse of Philip Larkin and post-war England'.[115] The 'sense of a missing feature or energy' in volume three of the *Field Day Anthology* derives from arrested politics and from a refusal to give literature its pluralistic head. It is ironical that an anthology conceived by Northern Irish poets and critics should tell us so little either about the North or about poetry.

IV   *Nationalism and Poetic Canons*

I want to take a revisionist look at some of the critical vocabulary that surrounds Irish poetry. Then I will ask whether (and how) the term 'revisionism' can be applied to poetry itself. Nationalist literary history need not be deliberate; often it is unconscious or unexamined. Post-colonial readings have had their passage to Ireland eased by the relative absence of New Critical controls, while contextual checks, such as the valuable work of Terence Brown and W.J. McCormack, are a fairly recent development. Whereas Irish historiography has long been led by scholars bound up with Ireland's changing condition, homegrown literary criticism, though now increasing in influence, has been overwhelmed by the international fixation on Joyce and Yeats. This chronic deficit underlies the current stand-off between historians and theorists. But it also affects more conventional studies, in that scholars from elsewhere may founder in a swamp of untested assumptions. This is especially the case with twentieth-century Irish poetry. The flip side of theoretical chic is a disposition to read Ireland and its poetry flat, without dimensions or shades.

For example, Robert Garratt in *Modern Irish Poetry: Tradition and Continuity from Yeats to Heaney* (1986) succumbs to a vocabulary inflected with Nationalist premises. In the following collage Garratt, or his native guide, seems to be talking about something other than poetry: 'a conquered and dispossessed people who trace their lineage back beyond the Protestant Ascendancy...linguistic identity crisis ...[a] compulsion...to reconsider and redefine the Irishness of poetic expression is dominant...[Yeats's] deliberate isolation from the mainstream of twentieth-century Irish life...Irish subject matter disappears in some phases of Yeats's career, and at other times the Irish voice is only faintly audible...Joyce offered the next generation of poets a sense of continuity, and with it the means to widen the poetic tradition Yeats had narrowed...'.[116] Eliding 'subject matter', 'voice' and 'Irishness', Garratt confuses the evolution of independent (and Catholic) Ireland with how poems might relate to one another either on a historical or contemporary basis. To say that Joyce 'widened' the Yeatsian horizon is neither a literary-historical nor a literary-critical proposition. The confusion is intrinsic to Garratt's blurring of 'tradition' (the literary fabric) and 'continuity' (the social fabric). They are not disconnected, but should be distinguished. They converge here because Nationalist literary history requires both rupture and platonic unity: the 'continuity and discontinuity' so 'puzzling' to Seamus Deane.[117] Hugely totemic in its poetic mode, 'the tradition' carries male-Nationalist anxieties which have little to do with textual evidence for either rupture or unity.

Garratt's ideas about Irishness, the 'mainstream', and a tradition which, through Herculean effort, 'seems assured of some kind of continuity',[118] can be traced to Thomas Kinsella. In 'Poetic Forms and Social Malformations' I compare Kinsella's *New Oxford Book of Irish Verse* and Paul Muldoon's *Faber Book of Contemporary Irish Poetry*, both published in 1986. These anthologies reproduce a conflict between Nationalist and aesthetic priorities which goes back to the 1890s. Kinsella is fair to Yeats (though as guarantor of continuity), but other anthologists and commentators often slight his efforts on implicitly political grounds. Even when not interrogated as colonial, the Revival tends to be apologised for, got over as anomalous, caricatured as pastoral and unmodern – a reversal of the attacks it faced in 1900. Anthony Bradley introduces his anthology *Contemporary Irish Poetry* (1988 edition) with the assertion that its contents 'reflect (and in part constitute) the actual historical and social process of modern Ireland more accurately and intimately by far than Yeats's heroic myths and the mysticism of the Revival'.[119] This discounts actual literary-historical process, while posterity has yet to print its verdict on our contemporary poetic myths.

As we have seen, the influential mechanisms of tradition are sometimes transferred from Yeats to Joyce. (A study by Dillon

Johnston is called *Irish Poetry after Joyce*). Seamus Heaney, introducing the Yeats section of the *Field Day Anthology*, develops a broader contrast between these supposed literary opposites. Attempting to arbitrate in what Terence Brown has called 'Yeats, Joyce and the Irish Critical Debate',[120] Heaney says: 'while it is right that the questions continue to be pressed, it is imperative to recognise the immense contribution his work makes to our general intellectual and imaginative resource'.[121] Yet Heaney's own emphasis, though allied to the visionary individualism that he espouses in *Seeing Things* (1991), has once again the objective result of detaching Yeats from the mainstream:

> Yeats's singularity as a writer depended upon [a] uniquely elaborated command of the strategies of English verse; but it derived also from the off-centre view he deliberately maintained as a member of occult societies …Even an intelligence as strong and antagonistic as James Joyce's functioned within a set of cultural and intellectual forms that generally were shared and assented to. Homer and classical learning, Roman catholic liturgy and dogma, the medieval corpus of knowledge as represented by Dante and Aquinas…when Yeats called a character Red Hanrahan or Michael Robartes…he still could not endow the new-minted name with such canonical authority. There might well be a reservoir of doctrine and belief which sanctioned the imaginative archetype…but it had sunk underground…[122]

This is rather oddly argued: compare and contrast the eccentricity of Joyce and Yeats. Having failed to connect Yeats's underground streams with spilt Protestantism (and overlooked his claims on Greek and Irish myth), Heaney goes on to characterise 'an intelligence naturally solitary…self-born splendour…a vision of reality that possessed no surer basis than the ground of his own imagining'.[123] Since Heaney's norms are so tinged by spilt Catholicism ('canonical authority'), his silence about Yeats's cultural background (the word 'Protestant' occurs only with reference to the Senate speech on divorce) seems hardly more reassuring than Seamus Deane's direct obsession with the matter. In effect, both Deane and Heaney commit the historiographical heresy of reading Yeats's career backwards: from his late rhetoric of 'Anglo-Irish solitude'. Yeats did not set out to be solitary. But perhaps all this anxiety suggests where the most powerful influence lies. Indeed, Heaney's subtext may be the forbidden individualistic attractions of the Protestant imagination.

If the 'Contemporary Irish Poetry' section of the *Field Day Anthology*, at once politicised and chaotic, represents a nadir, few anthologies of Irish poetry nail any aesthetic colours to their metropolitan mastheads. Even Muldoon's revolt against political imperatives took cover in silence, exile and a cunning epigraph (see page 201 below). Michael Allen has called Peter Fallon's and Derek Mahon's *Penguin Book of Contemporary Irish Poetry* (1990) the product of 'sublimated regional fisticuffs' [124] with Muldoon-Faber's magnetic North. Following Kinsella, the *Penguin Book* denies any regional distinctiveness to Northern poetry, firmly locates 'centrality' in or around Dublin, and reinstates Nationalist literary history: 'as ever, poets from the North contribute to a national body of work which, in its turn, belongs to a global community'.[125] This professed 'map' of contemporary practice boasts that 'Irish poets...have always looked abroad' (unlike Shelley, one presumes) and stresses 'transatlantic neighbourhood' with the US – Ireland goes float about again – while dumping on MacNeice for having ventured across the Irish Sea: 'From the beginning MacNeice was associated with the English tradition.' [126]

The difference between Kinsella and Mahon-Fallon is that between Nationalist oldspeak ('a past heavy with loss')[127] and Nationalist newspeak, derived from the Republic's role in the EU – a language of export-markets, bulk-trading and product-recognition: 'The Irish publishing industry is now a busy and extensive one...If the present anthology can be said to have any polemical purpose, that purpose would be to correct imbalances created over the years by editors, publishers and critics, and to dispel the illusion that Irish poetry has been written exclusively by persons of Northern provenance'.[128] If this is, in fact, not merely a fit of temper but a form of literary counter-revisionism, the argument continues. Neil Corcoran, in his introduction to *The Chosen Ground: Essays on the Contemporary Poetry of Northern Ireland* (1992), defends the validity of the book's focus: 'the quality of the work produced in Northern Ireland since the mid-1960s constitutes one of the most remarkable facts in contemporary literary history'.[129] And a developing Southern revisionism, though without much to say about aesthetics, was heralded by Sebastian Barry's anthology *The Inherited Boundaries* (1986). For Barry, no 'unified poetic sensibility' exists, and the Northern poets 'are a fine part of the story of an island, but...no part of the story of the Republic' [130] – a story which Barry sees as only just beginning.

Reading through various anthologies and studies I began to personify 'Irish poetry' as a disturbed seeker after transcendental ego: now in 'two bodies', now in one, now an ancient staggering up from the psychiatrist's couch 'after more than a century of retrieval and self-analysis', now stepping forth as an 'energetic' contributor to the European Poetry Mountain, now a naked babe born 'nowhere' and offering 'a first if fragmentary map to a new country'. This collision between two (or three) rhetorics – Gaelic past, young or infant Europeans – points to unresolved tensions between North and South and within the Republic itself. Once again, it tells us something about Ireland, if little about poetry.

Dermot Bolger's introduction to his *Picador Book of Contemporary Irish Fiction* (1993) slides between two rhetorics in that he laments 'a seven-hundred-year occupation' by a 'foreign army', while celebrating 'a remarkably confident and yet challenging and dissenting young European literature'.[131] Not only the Northern writers whom Bolger anthologises inhabit this contradiction. Bolger is right to complain that colonial analyses, predicated on the North, have been applied to the whole island (though he blames external critics more than Northern Nationalists for this misreading). But, like Barry, who speaks of 'two poetries', he replaces the old unitary premise with a schizoid separatism. Neither the Southern state nor its literature can lay claim to a *tabula rasa*, since both are implicated in the Northern problem. Even Irish feminist thinking, innovatory in other quarters, sometimes recycles Nationalist vocabulary when the canonical chips are down. Ailbhe Smyth, editor of *Wildish Things: An Anthology of New Irish Women's Writing* (1989) fuses feminist theory with reflex resort to the post-colonial model: 'As Irish women, we are...doubly damned, doubly silenced.'[132] So much for Maria Edgeworth *et al.* And Smyth, like Bolger, announces a new spirit without giving it aesthetic as opposed to socio-political definition. Thus some up-to-date literary agendas from the Republic have yet to exorcise the gloomy ghost lurking in the version of Irish poetry that one dutiful American critic has absorbed: 'discrete strands of a hypothetically unified tradition, perhaps buried irrecoverably in prehistory and the Irish unconscious'.[133]

Let us tiptoe away and leave it there, but not before remembering that this essence which pre-empts its texts has a counterpart and antagonist in the attitudes behind Blake Morrison's and Andrew Motion's *Penguin Book of Contemporary British Poetry* (1982): an anthology which became notorious when Seamus Heaney objected to his inclusion on the grounds that 'My passport's green'. Deeper grounds for objection lie in the editors' ignorance of literary intercourse between 'these islands'. Thus they generalise about 'the spirit of post-modernism'[134] without reckoning that Heaney's appeal to English audiences might depend on his tap-root to Wordsworth, let alone his cuttings from Hughes or Larkin. Indeed, Heaney's poetry says something about the durability and redirection of traditions, rather than their collapse into trends. This is the phenomenon whereby, every now and then, metropolitan England discovers an Irish writer as a 'thing never known before', detached from literary contexts in both islands. In one contemporary frame, if Paul Muldoon is visited by the post-modernist spirit, it often materialises as a *critique* of Heaney's aesthetic. And in one historical frame, as I suggest in 'The Room Where MacNeice Wrote "Snow" ', 'certain contexts for Yeats went down the plughole of Irish separation from Britain'. Thus the 'symbolic and associative mode' which Morrison and Motion see Northern Irish poets as developing,[135] did not appear in a vacuum, any more than did Larkin's symbolist flights.

Northern Irish poetry should not – and cannot – be tidied up into one or other *Penguin Book*. The different environments show off different facets. At the same time, the dispersal of the poetry through these anthologies defuses its collective power, its distinctive narratives. Perhaps, too, a merged anthology would suggest that Paul Durcan and Tony Harrison breathe some of the same oxygen. Northern Irish poetry not only requires British Isles literary history: it questions national literary histories in the British Isles. The historian Hugh Kearney argues:

> the histories of what are normally regarded as four distinct 'nations' appear more intelligible if they are seen first within a general British Isles context and secondly if they are seen in terms of 'cultures', and 'sub-cultures'. Upon closer examination what seem to be 'national' units dissolve into a number of distinctive cultures with their own perceptions of the past, of social status...of religion...As with any historical approach, however, the problem is complicated by the inevitability of historical change. Cultures change and interact over time. Where nationally minded historians tend to stress a continuity over time between, say, the 'Scots' or the 'Irish' of different periods, a cultural approach involves the recognition that the perceptions of one period are radically different from those of another.[136]

This constitutes a more complex model than that proposed by Robert Crawford in *Devolving English Literature* (1992). While Crawford's Scottish appeal against 'a crude, unitary view of English Literature'[137] seems broadly unanswerable, it does not allow for the distortions produced by crude, unitary views of Irish literature. When Crawford takes the literary and linguistic politics of Seamus Heaney or Tom Paulin as speaking for ('barbarian') Ireland, he simplifies the aesthetic issues both within Ireland and between the islands.

Kearney coins the term 'Britannic melting pot'. North-east Ireland may be regarded as an incomplete melting pot within an incomplete melting pot. In one aspect, perhaps, Northern Irish poetry opens up the Britannic unconscious, exposing much that has been repressed by the Anglo-Celtic archipelago as a whole. In another, it melts down and re-forms poetic traditions that have flourished there historically. (The North's sense of tradition is not always negative.) And, since poetry has sometimes lent itself to the construction of national meanings, Northern Irish poetry may inscribe a double revisionism and a mutual deconstruction, as it negotiates what John Hewitt termed in 1945 'problems and cleavages for which we can find no counterpart elsewhere in the British archipelago'.[138] But this depends upon poetry revising itself. Problems and cleavages, which ultimately reside in cognition and language, have played a part in compelling poets not only to re-invent the *English* lyric, but to test lyrical structures, the lyric as construct, and the whole enterprise of poetry.

V *Poetry and Revisionism*

When national canons fade from view, the self-image of 'Ulster poetry' veers between John Hewitt's poles of 'rooted man' and 'airy internationalist':

> The Ulster writer must, if he is not to be satisfied in remaining 'one of the big fish in the little pond', seek and secure some recognition outside his native place. But the English language is the speech of millions. There is no limit to his potential audience. Yet I believe this had better not be achieved by his choosing materials and subjects outside or beyond those presented by his native environment. He must be a *rooted* man, must carry the native tang of his idiom like the native dust on his sleeve; otherwise he is an airy internationalist, thistledown, a twig in a stream.[139]

At one end of this spectrum or gyre, Hewitt's 'Once Alien Here' (1945) and Heaney's 'A New Song' (1972) set forth complementary – Protestant and Catholic – founding myths for a poetic tradition. Both poets use the word 'native' in adapting Nationalist literary ideology to a regionalist agenda. Hewitt portrays himself as 'lacking skill in either scale of song,/the graver English, lyric Irish tongue', and therefore seeking 'a native mode to tell/our stubborn wisdom individual'. 'A New Song' reinforces its nativism with Nature:

> But now our river tongues must rise
> From licking deep in native haunts
> To flood, with vowelling embrace,
> Demesnes staked out in consonants.

In each case, language and song are inseparable from territorial claim (Hewitt's 'let this rich earth so enhance the blood'). The poems also reproduce stereotypes: Hewitt's weighing of English and Irish specific gravities, Heaney's oblique gendering of 'river tongues' and 'demesnes'. In fact these politico-poetic manifestos internalise, from their different angles, similar images of literary self and other. As Hewitt associates the 'sullen Irish' with banished 'enchantments and...spells', so Heaney finds in Gaelic place-names 'a lost potent musk', twilight and 'Vanished music'. Evidently Celticism still serves rhetorical purposes. Its deconstructors might mark where the balance of lyrical power is deemed to lie, and how the Celtic note may be in tune with the Hidden Ireland. In 'A New Song' it is the Celtic-Gaelic element that proposes, however playfully, to absorb.

Twenty years on, these ideological configurations have been overtaken by poetic events (in the *oeuvres* of Heaney and Hewitt, too). Thus Paul Muldoon's *Madoc* (1990) is a satire, a *Dunciad*, whose miscegenations mock native modes. *Madoc* (of which more below) takes a poetic movement – Romanticism in its Pantisocratic apotheosis – on a nightmare trip to the village of 'Ulster' in Northern Pennsylvania, where all its founding myths are subjected to drastic shocks.

Yet, as fictive locus Ulster remains in view. The extent to which *Madoc* is an in-joke, with Southey and Coleridge representing Heaney and Muldoon in America, underlines the mutual awareness between poets – if transported – from a small place undergoing large upheavals. Their 'airy internationalist' alliances (such as that between Heaney, Derek Walcott and Joseph Brodsky) can seem less substantial. Tradition is more than the sum of individual talents, and it operates in the short term as well as the long. Writing these essays, I found that I was often tracing a textual web, and that the term 'intertextuality' applied to Northern Irish poetry in a special, living sense: not as a theoretical dead letter, but as a creative dynamic working upon mechanisms of tradition and cultural definitions alike.

Intertextual dialogues may be explicit variations on a theme: Heaney rewriting Hewitt from 'The Other Side', Muldoon taking oblique issue with Heaney's 'Punishment'; or they may unobtrusively tweak the threads of word or image: in this Muldoon's practice is paradigmatic. But poems can ignore one another yet be in touch. Because of the themes that go with the territory, and the territory that goes with the themes, they participate in a shifting system of aesthetic and cultural relations. Here lyric poetry, often damned as upholding the egotistical sublime, clearly subscribes to a dispersed collectivity, and observes disciplines akin to the historians' 'intertextual antagonism'. This is why we should take care not to collapse generational dialectics, as when Morrison and Motion (and latterly Stan Smith) press Heaney into the post-modernist mould or mould-lessness. What Smith terms 'destabilisation on the ground of language itself' [140] has various origins and takes various forms. All Northern Irish poetry is highly self-referential, but to different effects, and other dialogues depend on its dialogues about its own structures. Thus the formal order established by Heaney, Longley and Mahon has been challenged by the equally concentrated but more open-ended methods of Muldoon, Ciaran Carson and Medbh McGuckian. The elder poets have responded, but hardly surrendered, to the challenge. And, indeed, the diversity within each generation complicates a clearcut diagram. The (seeming) aesthetic paradox of Northern Irish poetry is that intense proximity has bred intense differentiation.

Is this 'the spirit of post-modernism'? Or, alternatively, to quote Carson's poem 'The Irish for No', 'What's all this to the Belfast business-man who drilled/ Thirteen holes in his head with a Black & Decker?' At one point in his essay 'Postmodern McGuckian' Thomas Docherty assigns her poetry to 'a literature of decolonisation'.[141] On the other hand, Alan Robinson depoliticises postmodern Muldoon when he reads 'The Frog' (discussed on page 168 below) as a rebuke to the 'over-ingenious hermeneutical probings of any critic who would see in poetry more than a game with language'.[142] Perhaps, rather than denying all meaning (an interpretation which has itself become a hermeneutical cliché), 'The Frog' parodies and questions specific ways in which poets might impose, or critics extract, contemporary significance. Neil Corcoran's fine essay on Ciaran Carson takes the point when he asks whether Carson's 'scepticism about how much can be made to cohere in any organisation of poetic language' may have 'affinities with postmodern theory' and yet be 'peculiarly appropriate to a poetry of the contemporary fate of Northern Ireland'.[143] Such a poetry might indeed find itself steering between the theoretical shoals of Marxism and post-modernism.

One context for Modernism itself should be kept in mind. In so far as it was shaped by a dialectic between Joyce and Yeats, it partook of Irish religio-cultural differences: differences still metaphysically and institutionally active in Northern Ireland. Hubert Butler's phrase about 'a very real clash of philosophies' (see page 14 above) has epistemological as well as ethical implications. As with Joyce, Catholic Ulster seems to have incubated its own deconstruction. Protestantism, less monolithic, has provided for literary dissent in a more heterogeneous fashion. All the spilt theology swirling around means that post-modernism need not be a remote theory, but grounded in Northern Irish culture as well as Irish literary history. Louis MacNeice's poetry revolves and transmits these issues in an earlier form. Thus some of the usual post-modernist markers may, in the case of Muldoon, Carson and McGuckian, combine aesthetic revisionism with local point. Like Joyce, they have formidable conceptual, social and literary constructions to assail, including the texts of their Northern precursors. This makes them, as Docherty remarks of McGuckian, 'keen readers of the dictionary'[144] and keen readers (or quoters) in general. Muldoon's '7, Middagh Street' and *Madoc* can be termed essays in criticism, and the critical stratum, always latent in poetry, stands out elsewhere.

For Ciaran Carson, it provides an opportunistic, anarchistic local strategy. Some of his poems unfold as critical dialogues with a pre-existing literary text – often poems, like Edward Thomas's 'Old Man' or Robert Frost's 'After Apple-Picking', that have already influenced Northern Irish poetry. Keats's Odes are the prime target in 'The Irish for No', but Frost and Heaney are also hit:

> They opened the door into the dark:
> *The murmurous haunt of flies on summer eves.* Empty jam-jars.
> Mish-mash. Hotch-potch. And now you rub your eyes and get acquainted
>   with the light.
> A dust of something reminiscent drowses over the garage smell of creo-
>   sote...

This mish-mash (grisly pun) seems more than collage for the sake of collage. As 'a game with language' it turns into a funeral game, to quote MacNeice: one that resembles the ironic echoes of nineteenth-century Romanticism in First World War poetry, or Charles Sorley and Edward Thomas re-writing Rupert Brooke. Carson's quotations, like his street-names and brand-names, belong to a semiotic kaleido-scope whereby bemused narrators revise literary history as history revises them. The 'dust of something reminiscent' drifting through the *oeuvres* of Carson, Muldoon and McGuckian is one of the ways in which Northern Irish poetry looks askance at inherited literary traditions, including its own. A recent predatory attention to great western texts – *Hamlet*, the *Odyssey*, the *Divine Comedy*, the *Meta-morphoses* – has stretched the intertextual web still further.

Medbh McGuckian's poetry offers itself as the antithesis, even the shadow-life, of Carson's: as an interior war of position rather than a problematic odyssey among Belfast's conflicting signs. Her imagination pivots on tensions between writing, sexuality, gender and motherhood. Clair Wills argues that 'McGuckian seems to wish to set up a new symbolic order, a "less official" faith which she can follow. In order to create this new symbolic order she takes on the role of both mother and priest.'[145] One re-ordering occurs at the

level of syntax. Carson and Muldoon put pressure on syntax though
not to breaking point. McGuckian keeps outward faith with traditional
periods, but inwardly suspends some of the usual contracts. She
writes – up to a point – a pseudo-syntax, its emphases displaced
by a subtler dialectic of images. Or, since her clothes, rooms, gardens,
flowers, weather and seasons (like Virginia Woolf's) give off only a
faint sensory aroma, she writes a symbolic meta-language with its
own emblematic grammar:

> Some patterns have
> A very long repeat, and this includes a rose
> Which has much in common with the rose
> In your drawing, where you somehow put the garden
> To rights. You call me aspen, tree of the woman's
> Tongue, but if my longer and longer sentences
> Prove me wholly female, I'd be persimmon,
> And good kindling, to us both.

('Aviary')

This typical dialogue between a female speaker-poet and a male artist-
lover refers to itself in terms of formal and syntactical difference
('pattern', 'sentences'). But the female challenges the sexual-aesthetic
line drawn by the male. She chooses the ambiguous 'persimmon'
(a hard wood whose fruit the dictionary terms 'very astringent until
softened by frost'), rather than the womanly, tremulously garrulous
aspen, as her symbol for poetry and sex. She thus retains a claim
on 'male' desire, the male rage for poetic order (putting 'the garden/
To rights'). The same 'rose' has figured in both their patterns. Yet
the persimmon's 'chambered pith' also promises new kinds of shape:
'good kindling' for poem-making and love-making.

McGuckian is celebrated for her teasing subversions, her dismantling of hierarchy and authority: 'A poem dreams of being written/
without the pronoun "I".' This is, perhaps, too self-unaware: irre-
ducible elements of lyric structure and authorial presence disguise
themselves more cunningly than theoretical readings of McGuckian
– and of Muldoon and Carson – realise. But, besides appealing to
post-modernist desire, McGuckian's seductive veils disquietingly
imply the repressive force of Ulster patriarchies. Her psychic wars
tend to have pyrrhic outcomes. Thus, partly through a subtextual
critical dialogue with her male peers, McGuckian may be absorbed
in the same kind of primary task as Woolf or Jean Rhys. Unlike
Woolf, but like Rhys, she lacks a discursive resort. Nevertheless, her
politics of the artistic process redistribute power behind the scenes.

If Paul Muldoon, too, postpones statement, this deferral dramatises
epistemological scruple rather than psychic irresolution or ever-

ramifying narratives. Indeed, the sense in which his poetry is a form of linguistic philosophy, an enquiry into its own first principles, into relations between 'the Way of Seeming and the Way of Truth', helped to release the talents of McGuckian and Carson. Elsewhere in this book, poems by Muldoon are discussed as specific acts of historical revisionism. These depend on a revisionism at the root. He has said of the poetic act itself: 'I want my own vision to be disturbed, I want never to be able to look at a hedgehog again or a...briefcase again – or at least the poem wants me never to be able to look at a hedgehog or a briefcase again – without seeing them in a different way.' [146] Muldoon's Frostian belief that 'all the fun's in how you see /say a thing' reaches a climax in *Madoc*, where the bracketed names of Western philosophers preside over much satirical negation of their attempts to establish cognitive (and thereby ethical, political and literary) order. Accordingly, those thinkers, who favour an unsteady-state universe go with the flow of the poem itself. (Heraclitus) marks the spot where the main narrative gets underway. However, this is preceded by a framing episode in which a fugitive who fails to break out of some constricting circumstance – perhaps Belfast, perhaps 'Ulster poetry' – ends up 'harnessed to a retinagraph'. Thereafter:

> all that follows
> flickers and flows
> from the back of his right eyeball.

Such constraint suggests that the cognitive riddles cannot simply be resolved by flux, but are tied in with social and ideological pressures. Like Carson's narrators (in *The Irish for No* and *Belfast Confetti*), trying to process a blizzard of data, Muldoon's retinagraph questions authorial control over the visions that present themselves.

These writing-difficulties merge into reading-difficulties and are, in part, a political metaphor. The 'web of textuality', like Stephen Dedalus's nets, in one sense represents entrapment. A poem's revision, its power to 'disturb', to change the perceptual angle, represents a blink of liberty. Thus poetic intertextuality differs from the local webs, and may unweave them. Whereas Paul Durcan's 'revisionism' works on discrepancies between the Republic's professed ideals and its actual conduct, rescues repressed histories, or imagines an alternative Ireland, Muldoon's deconstructive impulse functions in deeper strata where powerfully determining or determinist systems claim to constitute reality. Thus his poem 'Anseo' (see page 82 below) implies that a 'terrorist' is no psychopathic aberration, but produced by the codes, curriculum and pathology of a whole community.

Neither the origins nor the resonances of Muldoon's poetry can be confined to Ulster's theological and political absolutes. Indeed, *Madoc* is about going away and going solo – if also about luggage from home and home-thoughts already abroad. But I would dispute John Goodby's primary stress on the poem's linguistic games: 'Even the characteristically fine verbal discriminations, cited as proof of overall moral purpose by some critics, invite us to treat them as parodic pedantry: "he's couchant on a tavelin of vairs and minivers"'.[147] As one critic in question, I would suggest that Muldoon, for whom the pun is structural, rarely lacks a point or at least a target. This heraldic scene appears to satirise the relations between a poet ('Southey') and his camp-followers. If taken more literally, the 'vairs and minivers' (heraldic furs) advance a disturbing *leit-motif*. Throughout *Madoc* animals and humans contribute their fur, skin and bone to commodities or weapons: 'buffalo rug', 'elk-horn bow', 'skunk bonnet', 'tortoise-shell powder-flask', 'a tobacco-/pouch made from the scrotal sac//of a Conestoga'. The Pantisocrats have violated the Great Spirit which links the land, the animals and the Indians. However, the Indians, too, pursue tribal quarrels and interfere with Nature:

> The woodchuck has had occasion
> to turn into a moccasin.

Murder, rape, scalping and enslavement prevent a wholly ludic reading of *Madoc*. The poem conforms to MacNeice's precept that the poet must be 'both critic and entertainer (and his criticism will cut no ice unless he entertains)'.[148] At the same time, for Muldoon, all human ingenuity seems tainted with violence: poetry no less than tortoise-shell powder-flasks. *Madoc* is strongest when it hits the dark Jacobean groove of Muldoon's earlier long poem 'The More a Man Has the More a Man Wants',[149] and tracks to their literary lairs the chain-reactions of brutality and corruption that dominate his political vision. 'Overall moral purpose' may be out, along with idealist and humanist philosophers. But this, as in the case of William Golding's fables, need not exclude moral pattern. Textual nihilism – (Derrida) – is also sent up. 'What then?' sang Plato's ghost.

Clair Wills, in *Improprieties: Politics and Sexuality in Northern Irish Poetry* (1993), offers a political reading of *Madoc* which is at odds with John Goodby's response, and allows for the poem's Irish contexts. Despite the fact that Muldoon's 'recurrent narrative of decline from Utopian ideal to dangerous fiction suggests a cynical view of politics as a whole', Wills argues that his representation of both 'personal identities and political processes [as] constructed... bears a liberatory potential'.[150] This may be the case without a *caveat* ('cynical') that derives from her perception of Tom Paulin's poetry as a genuine, if flawed, form of radicalism. In Paulin's protests, as in his section of the *Field Day Anthology*, politics and culture coincide – a foreshortening that pre-empts analysis. In *Madoc* one thing alarmingly leads to another: not only image, word, rhyme, but idea, cultural practice, politics, literature. Wills's occasional emphasis on Muldoon's post-modernist 'heterogeneity' or the multi-vocal organisation of *Madoc* belies the logic that she generally discovers in his poems. Her central thesis – that Enlightenment and Romantic concepts contend in Northern Irish poetry – is often persuasive, but might be qualified by reference to some additional historical perspectives. Firstly, the congruence of these concepts with the Republican and Nationalist modes of Irish separatism cannot be divorced from religion, from the sectarian erosion of Enlightenment ideals. Secondly, the Catholic Church throughout Europe resisted such ideals on a broader front. Thus 'colonial (under)-development' is not solely to blame if the Enlightenment 'failed' in Ireland.[151] (Wills disregards its scientific dimension.) Nor does Muldoon's understanding of social constructions, any more than his challenge to cultural homogeneity, originate in an environment that cherishes 'the ideal of autonomy on which liberal definitions of privacy depend'.[152] He approaches the issue of self and society from the other end: from communities that idealise traditional and tribal cohesion. Further, Wills reads the politics of *Madoc* rather too conventionally when she refers to 'the irony of Southey's increasingly "Unionist" mentality [and] the refusal to... compromise with the indigenous population in Ireland, which led to the founding of the state of Northern Ireland, a state which, like Southeyopolis, was never viable'.[153] Muldoon's 'Southeyopolis' seems mainly a failed *literary* construction, with Seamus Heaney (and perhaps Field Day) especially implicated.

Coleridge and Southey were indeed inspired by the Enlightenment, French Republicanism, colonialism, Romantic utopianism – and the Muse: a heady ideological mix with various hangovers in Ireland. What interests Muldoon is the Muse's complicity in any brain-damage it might inflict, the fall from fantasy to brutality: 'A babble of blood out of the broken fount'. Early in *Madoc* the very tools of the literary trade became indistinguishable from arrows:

> Southey plucks a grey goose-quill from the sheaf;
> its nib is stiff with grume, de dum.

Thus, Muldoon's arrow-pointed phrases make discriminations that bear on their own ethical status. His refrain 'de dum' reduces poetry to an empty mechanism, automatic pilot, solipsistic indulgence, a mere reflex persistence that takes no account of grotesquely changed circumstances. Similarly, its transcendental ambitions collapse when 'Coleridge', under the sign of (Hobbes), cannot

> argue from this faded blue
> turtle's splay
> above the long-house door to a universal
> idea of 'blue' or 'turtle'...

All the nastiness and brutishness on display, including the Pantisocrats' vices and rivalries, imply an aesthetic-metaphysical revisionism in which few escape scalping. Like Václav Havel, Muldoon distrusts 'overly fixed (and therefore semantically empty) categories, empty ideological phrases and incantations that petrify thought in a hermetic structure of static concepts'.[154] In *Madoc* literary cliché becomes the stalking-horse for this wider petrifaction. The poem is not only designed to 'send a shiver' through the 'iridescent dome' of poetic, theoretical and critical constructs (including this essay). To read *Madoc* is to be exposed, however jokily, to Havel's desired politics of perpetual linguistic revolution.

The disintegrating Pantisocrats make a bad advertisement for poetic intertextuality. But, even as they self-destruct, *Madoc* itself continues the dialectic. Muldoon's chosen satirical ground confirms by default that dialogues about language, form and aesthetics reach out into culture, mentalities and politics. In his earlier poem, '7, Middagh Street', 'Salvador' (Dali) speaks for the surrealist 'integrity of our dream-visions', yet asks: 'Is it that to refer, however obliquely, //is to refer?' Muldoon has also volunteered Northern Irish poetry as a kind of cultural micro-chip: 'If you read [the Northern poets] you'll probably discover a lot more about this society... [than by] listening to every news bulletin for twenty years, or indeed reading every history of Ireland or every sociological text.'[155] Presumably this covers poetry's double function as encoder and decoder.

The dialectic between John Hewitt and Seamus Heaney encodes Ulster's territorial imperative in cultural as well as canonical terms. Heaney's 'The Other Side', in which a Catholic speaker remembers a Protestant farmer familiar to his childhood, answers Hewitt's 'The Hill Farm'. Here Hewitt – Protestant, urban, atheist – ponders his exclusion from the 'little ring of light' constituted by a Catholic family saying the rosary in the Glens of Antrim. Thus the farmer-patriarch in 'The Other Side' partly stands for Hewitt as perceived by Heaney. Although the poem suggests that different conceptual and linguistic orders divide Catholic and Protestant ('Your side of the house, I believe,/hardly rule by the book at all'), it also undermines the antithesis by exaggerating it into stereotype. Further, each figure is shadowed by the psychic 'other': 'a neighbour laid his shadow/on the stream'. This symbol suggests how the existential flow is made continuously problematic by the hidden sectarian narrative, with its mixture of exclusion-zones and secret sharing. The end of the poem, where stereotype vanishes, plays with the notion of a language that might heal the psycho-cultural splits, but implies that any talk about 'the price of grass-seed' will involve hard territorial bargaining. As 'The Other Side' both draws a line and steps across it, much Northern Irish poetry turns on boundaries, borders and barriers. In this context 'transgression', epitomised by Muldoon's criss-crossings, takes on its full heretical meaning.

The interwoven dialogues articulate differences within, as well as between, Protestant and Catholic Ulster. Poems vary in their readings and philosophies of history, their angles on gender, their concepts of self in society, their senses of place or Nature, their knowable or imagined communities, their critiques of religion and politics, their routes to secular transcendence, their trust in meta-narratives, their bearing towards Word and Image. One tension which might be brought into the critical and political foreground is that between traditionalism and modernity. Its pervasiveness, not only on the philosophical level addressed by Clair Wills, suggests how profoundly the nexus of religion and land has imprinted Ulster culture, and how *ancien régime* Europe lingers on. The strains do not simply show on a Catholic/Protestant, rural/urban basis. Rather, Northern Irish poetry interprets the way in which more contingent and fluid relations are breaching local, familial, clannish and theo-centric horizons. This is, perhaps, the deepest revisionism. Besides being, as he says, 'of the Troubles', Ciaran Carson's poems function as elegies and replacements for the communal narratives that a seanachie could once command. In my (1982) essay ' "A Barbarous Nook": The Writer and Belfast', I wonder whether Catholic imaginations have yet to take on the city. Carson's does so, but still with culture-shock. His litanies of city-names which have lost their referents (due to development as well as the Troubles) not only make a point about signifier and signified. They mark a break with older forms of cohesion which the Falls Road long maintained after its rite of passage from rural Ulster:

> The sleeve of Raglan Street has been unravelled; the helmet of
> Balaklava
> Is torn away from the mouth.
>
> ('Hamlet')

The 'Exiles Club', who meet in the 'Wollongong Bar' to reconstruct an obsolete map of a collapsing Belfast, are viewed with sympathy as well as irony. Carson's 'post-modernism' may really be a post-traditionalism; his return to poetry, like Edward Thomas's arrival there, triggered by memory and the dislocation of familiar landscapes. Not all the mnemonic confetti blow away. It is also relevant to his aesthetic that, being an exponent and interpreter of Irish traditional music, Carson views 'tradition' as always contemporary, always improvised in the present on a unique occasion, yet transmitted down long, multiple, intricate chains from the past. In a sense he revises, but does not wholly invalidate, some Yeatsian notions.

Kavanagh and MacNeice, placed first in the *Faber Book of Contemporary Irish Poetry*, started from world-pictures more distant in time than in space, both available to Ulster nativities in the early twentieth century. Kavanagh's 'A Christmas Childhood' draws a circle around a homogeneous medieval cosmos: 'And I had a prayer like a white rose pinned/On the Virgin Mary's blouse'. MacNeice's 'Carrickfergus' lays down a complementary model for the Ulster 'parish' poem: a site riven by the problems, cleavages, barriers and traffic of history: 'The Norman walled this town against the country'. It is the leap from 'Cassiopeia was over/Cassidy's hanging hill' to Belfast Lough 'Under the peacock aura of a drowning moon'. (The two parishes meet in Carson's 'Hamlet'.) The fabric of the lyric poem itself has been rent and remade by these alternatives.

Sociological texts may at last be catching up on poetry. John Whyte (in *Interpreting Northern Ireland*) ultimately traces a mosaic of parochial variables: 'Areas only a few miles from each other can differ enormously – in religious mix, in economic circumstances, in the level of violence, in political attitudes.' [156] And Frank Wright, relating Northern Ireland to other ethnic frontiers, shows how the 'internal conflict' is produced by the kind of fracturing 'force relationship' that metropolitans find incomprehensible.[157] Therefore the canonical issue reflects the deeper level at which Northern Irish poetry mediates between a frontier-society and two metropolises. Poetic intertextuality does not stop at unapproved roads or the Irish Sea. Even if its greatest intricacy is bound in with north-east Ireland, it also shows the frontier-zone to be culturally open-ended. Further, as a map of fractures and joinings, Northern Irish poetry contributes to the European argument about Nationalism.

Bosnia has thrown new light, and new dark, on the Ulster question. (There is a Bosnia Street in Belfast.) Years ago Hubert Butler was well aware of the uncomfortable parallels. For instance, he pointed out in 1956 that the 'Croats used to call themselves "the Ulster of Yugoslavia"' because they considered the Six Counties as progressive as themselves and in equal danger of being absorbed into the peasant economy of a more primitive people'.[158] However, Irish readers of South Slav history notice how the 'Catholics' and 'Protestants' keep changing places. Butler raised the Ulster connection to shock Catholic Ireland into realising how, under the quisling Ustashe regime in wartime Croatia, Orthodox Serbs had been bloodily converted to Catholicism. He risked (and achieved) unpopularity because:

> I felt that the honour of the small Protestant community in Southern Ireland would be compromised if those of us who had investigated the facts remained silent about what we had discovered. In many Roman Catholic pulpits the sufferings of the Catholics under Tito were being compared to the long martyrdom of Catholic Ireland under Protestant rule...If we agree that history should be falsified in Croatia in the interests of Catholic piety, how could we protest when our own history was similarly distorted?[159]

Neal Ascherson has argued for the necessity of Nationalism on the grounds that there comes an irreversible moment when 'a Catholic woman...finds that she has suddenly, helplessly turned into a Croat who must fear and mistrust the Muslim neighbours she has known all her life...There are now two communities, which can only fight or agree to separate for ever.'[160] But, as in Northern Ireland, the fear of such a moment does most to produce it. Ulster Unionism largely wrote its own nightmare scenario: 'not an inch', and you may lose everything. Nationalisms, powered by historical falsification and cultural distortion, by demonisation of the Other, are no more predestined or natural than regional co-existence. This would, ideally, recognise difference but maximise affiliation. Inter-culturalism (a tautology since no culture is pure) improves on the fragmentation latent in 'multi-culturalism'. Thus Anthony D. Smith's conclusion that 'All other visions, all other rationales, appear wan and shadowy by comparison' with Nationalism[161] might be tempered by Patrick Kavanagh's doubts in 'Nationalism and Literature': 'There have been many fine patriots but there must be some inherent defect in the whole business, seeing that men of little or no principle can readily weigh in with it and be accounted fine men.'[162] Irish sceptics, having survived such a heavy dose, should be heard.

   In Northern Ireland, too, inter-culturalism is threatened by the zero-sum game of 'fight or separate for ever'. Since the 1970s voluntary ethnic cleansing, the result of involuntary terrors, has consolidated Belfast's ghettoes, deepened Derry's binary split, and caused Protestant farmers to shrink away from the Fermanagh border. Mary Kaldor's redefinition of 'ethnic' is relevant:

> these [new] national identities have become ethnic, not in a genetic sense, but in the sense that people are born with these identities and cannot change them. You are Croat because your father was Croat not because you live in Croatia, are Catholic, or write with a Latin script. In this sense, the religious conflict in Northern Ireland, which shares many of the characteristics of the post-Communist conflicts, is also ethnic.[163]

Kaldor also suggests that 'an...approach which would address the nature of ethnic nationalism would have to include a bottom-up strategy. It would have to involve an extensive commitment to support all those groups and individuals who oppose ethnic nationalism and who are trying to preserve multi-ethnic communities.'[164]

Northern Irish poetry, itself the product of multi-ethnic cross-fertilisation, generally works from the bottom up. It draws on all the available literary traditions, cultural traditions, historical experiences – the world wars as much as 1690 or 1798 or 1916. Without evading political obstacles, it transgresses many supposed borders and breaks many imposed silences. And, in the variety of its concern with language, it exploits the full hybrid inheritance of Ulster English, whose vocabulary, structures and idioms have been influenced by Gaelic and Scots. It also places in the foreground the fact that we have a problem with language: with definition, representation, articulation, communication. The whole cognitive exercise shakes rigid concepts of identity built on the polarisations that occurred in the 1920s and the 1970s. Northern Irish poetry is revisionist (in more than one direction) because it exposes cultural phenomena and cultural permeations that political ideologies deny, as different scripts deny the common Serbo-Croat tongue.

The novelist Dzevad Karahasan (born into a Muslim family, educated by monks and married to a Serb) believes that western leaders fear 'the complexity of a truly united and multicultural Europe and...are therefore unable to understand Sarajevo...It is a war between a concept that embraces Bosnia's diversity and an ideology that backs excessive loyalty to one group.'[165] Even if Belfast was never the old Sarajevo, the same war is being fought here.

VI

Collecting these essays taught me something about revision. It confirmed, to quote Louis MacNeice's 'Variation on Heraclitus', that 'One cannot live in the same room twice'. Therefore, I have compromised between occasional updating and letting the record stand. Essays marked by a single date have been left as originally published, apart from minor corrections, deletions or additions. Two essays – 'Poetic Forms and Social Malformations' and 'The Room where MacNeice Wrote "Snow" ' – have been more extensively revised. 'Progressive Bookmen: Left-wing Politics and Ulster Protestant Writers' expands a short conference-paper written in 1987. The earliest piece, ' "A Barbarous Nook": The Writer and Belfast', remains largely a snapshot of how this kaleidoscopic relationship looked in 1982. Similarly, although the pamphlet 'From Cathleen to Anorexia' duplicates points made elsewhere, I have kept it more or less intact as a political statement.

The Living Stream is a quotation from Yeats's 'Easter 1916', a poem whose prophetic revisionism I discuss in the next essay:

> Hearts with one purpose alone
> Through summer and winter seem
> Enchanted to a stone
> To trouble the living stream.

This is no simple antithesis between obsession and flux. The stone actively 'troubles' the stream in the double sense of political turbulence and conceptual challenge. Years before reinventing Cathleen ni Houlihan as Medusa, Yeats had associated stone with opinion, abstraction and his own temptations thereto. In 1909 he described the lawyer John F. Taylor as probably thinking 'me effeminate. A stone is always stronger, more masculine than a living thing…his logic was but…the apologetics of a moment…instead of being, like living thought, an intricacy of leaf and twig'.[166] In the context of Irish Nationalism Yeats came to identify himself, the natural world and poetry with the female principle, and Maud Gonne (Cathleen), mechanism and opinion with the male. This may be partly why 'hens to moor-cocks call' and 'a mother names her child' in 'Easter 1916'. With regard to the Lane Gallery controversy Yeats said of Arthur Griffith's Sinn Féin: 'these men…expel from their own minds – by their minds' rigidity – the flowing and existing world'.[167] The symbolism of 'Easter 1916' turns this ultimately cognitive difference into a projection of the political and literary future. Tension between petrifaction and flux takes many forms in Irish literature after 1916. But it may be some kind of index that MacNeice's aesthetic should have been so profoundly shaped by a Heraclitean recoil, and that Kavanagh's should be haunted by the 'speechless muse' of Patrick Maguire, clay-suffocated amid the wheeling energies of the natural creation.

In 'Poetic Forms and Social Malformations' I argue that different cultural and political environments condition literature on each side of the border. Social change in the Republic, now a spate rather than a stream, seems to coincide with fluctuation and uncertainty as regards literary genres: the blurring of lines between poetry, prose and drama – sometimes an exhilarating transgression, sometimes an amorphous stew – collaboration or competition with newer media (film, rock), the emergence of urban-demotic modes to challenge artistic hierarchy, as if in a belated spirit of the 1930s. One might alliteratively stylise this challenge as Bolgerism *versus* Banvillism. John Banville's fiction, in *The Newton Letter* or *The Book of Evidence*, draws on the version of old high Modernism peculiar to Dublin. That is, it combines metafictional self-consciousness about the linguistic game and the deliquescent text, with an unshakable belief in itself as art, sentences polished to a bronze perfection. Banville has said in a celebration of Samuel Beckett: 'Beckett realises, as every true artist realises, that the raw material of life is that and no more…So much of modern fiction and drama – and, indeed, poetry – is mere journalism.' [168] The counter or complementary trend is, in fact, more adequately exemplified by Roddy Doyle than by Dermot Bolger. Most notably in *The Commitments*, Doyle's fiction exploits the phonetics, structures and codes of north Dublin working-class speech, and vibrates to the cultural transformations produced by Dublin's exponential growth since the 1960s. Although youth and rock have occasionally strayed into the 'Belfast novel', even Robert McLiam Wilson's iconoclastic *Ripley Bogle* (1989) manifests a very different sociology, not least in his use of an overweening alienated soliloquist as contrasted with Doyle's ensemble-playing.

A brief comparison between two collections of poetry might draw some threads together. These are Ciaran Carson's *Belfast Confetti* (1989) and Paul Durcan's *Daddy, Daddy* (1990). Their differences have to do with form, with cities and societies, with revision and revisionism, and with fathers. The literary father-fixation which I explore in 'When Did You Last See Your Father?' continues unabated, and its cross-border workings are part of the picture. Carson's book is dedicated to his father, and 'Ambition' and 'Bed-Time Story' draw on biographical details: the father's job as a postman, the sectarian injustices that went with the job, 'mistaken' internment:

> *God never shuts one door*, said my father, *but he opens up another*; and then,
> *I walked the iron catwalk naked in the freezing cold*: he's back into his
>   time
> As internee, the humiliation of the weekly bath. It was seven weeks before
> He was released: it was his younger brother they were after all the time.

The speech or eloquent silence of the father is an important motif in Northern Irish poetry. Here the father's talk comes over as pithy urban oral-history: a personal and communal saga caught in the process of translation into the fictions of his poet-son. Sometimes, like Muldoon, Carson doubts patriarchal 'nuts of wisdom': '*God never opens one door, but he shuts another*: my uncle was inside for seven years'. But 'Ambition' also follows in the footsteps of Seamus Heaney's 'Follower' and thus absorbs the father into a more positive scheme of values: a revision not a rejection of traditions. Although Carson opens up the generation-gap as a tension between roots and (upward) mobility, the structure of the poem and the generations hinges on another folk-saying: 'one step forward, two steps back'. 'Ambition' ends with father and son melting into one another:

> As I closed in on him, he coughed. I coughed. He stopped and turned,
> Made two steps back towards me, and I took one step forward.

'Hamlet' likens the literary and social effort 'to piece together the exploded fragments' to a father and son 'looking for' each other, and 'Bed-Time Story' elaborates the proximity of the father as proto-poet: not a rural reservoir of 'mellowed silence', as in Heaney, but a fecund fount of verbal and non-verbal languages: 'I step into the shoes again, and walk. I will deliver/Letters, cards, important gifts'. Yarn-spinning is the intertextuality that connects the oral and the written, culture and literature, country and city, tradition and this individual talent.

Carson's intricate yarns ramify from a particular historical patch of a patchworked city. Their post-modern appearance is tied in with an unresolved dualism between community and fracture. In contrast, Durcan's sequence 'Daddy, Daddy' plays the generational rite of passage discursively and purposefully across Irish history since the founding of the Free State:

> Outside on Pearse Street
> My mother weeps at the hospital gates.
> Such was your loyalty to the State,
> Your devotion and fidelity to the State,
> You took Mother on one holiday only in twenty-eight years –
> A pilgrimage by coach to the home of Mussolini
> And Clara Petachi near Lago di Como...

A judge and stalwart of the Catholic-bourgeois Fine Gael party, Durcan's father figures as an exaggerated epitome of the patriarchal roles assumed by state and Church: censor, fascist, landlord, sports-fanatic, (hypocritical) Irish-language fanatic, Abraham who would kill his deviant son, or destroy his mind, 'saint and murderer'. He speaks prescriptively in 'the tree-felling voice of a harsh judiciary', rather than in 'The Mayo Accent', Durcan's version of pacific mellowed silence: 'Peatsmoke of silence unfurls over turf fires of language'. This symbolises and idealises an originary speech which the state or Nation has forgotten, but poetry, women and the father's better self remember. Durcan's future-oriented (epochal) vision undermines patriarchal foundations by imagining, more confidently and tangibly than McGuckian, a new symbolic order. The fact that he can even conceive such a matriarchal utopia, wish-fulfilment or no, throws into relief Carson's projection of a masculine milieu where women chiefly figure as mute victims or muted custodians of a fraying fabric. In Carson's poem 'Patchwork' 'my granny' is 'buried/Beneath the patchwork quilt./*It took me twenty years to make that quilt* – I'm speaking for her, now'. Thus women may, at least, be associated with the disturbance of patrilinear patterns in the poetry's own fabric. Decisive valediction as well as elegy, Durcan's 'Daddy, Daddy' gets further with the rite of passage on which it embarks. In 'Cot' the father becomes the son, and in 'The One-Armed Crucifixion' an exhausting generation game, perhaps a parable of the revisionist struggle, can only end in the son's favour:

> How many thousands of hours on the shore at Galway,
> In the drizzle off the back of the sea,
> On the sodden sands,
> Did we spend hurling together, father and son?
> Pucking the sliothar, one to the other,
> Hour in, hour out, year in, year out.
> How many thousands of times, old man,
> Did you strike a high ball for your young son
> To crouch, to dart, to leap,
> To pluck the ball one-handed out of the climbing air?

*   *   *

This essay has been concerned with the relation of literature to the academy and to the body politic. In Ireland (although the temptation to court American academe exists) the former relation has not utterly usurped the latter: the revision of literary idioms – whatever these might be – does not take place in a vacuum. By the same token, Irish literature presents an inter-disciplinary challenge to which vulgar 'theory' can be insensitive. Peter Washington in *Fraud* (1989) and David Bromwich in *Politics by Other Means* (1992) criticise the political pretensions of literary theory: a retreat of the radical Left masquerading as advance. Bromwich remarks sardonically: 'If I say in a lecture, "The figuration of Prospero's last speech in *The*

Tempest betrays a slippage from subversion to containment which the occlusive presence of Caliban tends to undermine," I may, in some fantastic dialogue of the mind, be singing the equivalent of a Sandinista Wedding March...' [169] Washington writes:

> We are exhorted either to take up the radical cause, or to defend the academy from its dangers. But taking sides is surely only one part of politics, unavoidable though it may sometimes be? There is a preliminary move – namely, knowing why we should take one side rather than the other...it is precisely *because* knowledge is largely conditioned by interests, and because our existence is irretrievably political, i.e., subject to conflicting demands and powers, that the cultivation of detachment, rational enquiry and scepticism (in the general sense) are absolutely essential...[170]

This seems relevant to some of the intersections between theory and Ireland. The attack on 'liberal humanism' appeals to counter-revisionist intellectuals in the Republic because it reinstates the old polarities and closes up the doubly 'critical' space where different positions might at least be required to argue their case. Counter-revisionists, swimming against the current of etymology, try to stigmatise 'pluralism' as itself a tyrannical dogma rather than a demanding intellectual and socio-political objective. Here neo-Republicans and religious reactionaries, the 'real' Ireland and the 'true' Church, are at one. In *Postmodernism, Reason and Religion* (1992) Ernest Gellner observes: 'The [post-modernist] relativist endorses the absolutism of others, and so his relativism entails an absolutism which also contradicts it.' [171] But, as Ireland indicates, this self-deceiving manoeuvre can take place inside one country and one head. 'Fantastic dialogues of the mind' are, in fact, rather less remote from actual politics than is the case elsewhere. The harmless radical chic of California reads differently in Northern Ireland.

I began by noting how the enterprise of stabilising or even establishing the Irish 'text' can be frustrated by internal splits and by distances and diaspora that influence literary criticism as well as politics. Today cultural materialists from England and post-colonialists from America beat upon our shores in succession to the Celticism and shamrockery of yore (not that these tides have entirely ebbed). Other theoretical models, too, have sponsored some dubious readings, whether inside-out or outside-in. E.P. Thompson's argument with Althusser seems relevant to the Irish situation – not least, because Thompson understands the theological as well as epistemological issues that divide historiography and theory. He writes:

> internationalism...ought not to consist in lying prostrate before the ('Western Marxist') theorists of our choice, or in seeking to imitate their modes of discourse. The reasons why this kind of imitation can never

> produce more than a sickly native growth are complex...The 'adoption'
> of other traditions – that is, adoption which has not been fully worked
> through, interrogated and translated into the terms of our own traditions
> – can very often mean no more than the evacuation of the real places
> of conflict within our own intellectual culture...[172]

This strikes home, even if eliciting 'the terms of our own traditions'
is one of those 'places of conflict'. The perceptual, yet simultaneously
practical, difficulties long associated with Irish history, culture and
literature may have a special bearing on wider debates about the
application of literary theory to specific texts and contexts. Northern
Irish poetry is again paradigmatic in being compelled to reflect on
the perspectives from which it comes. It also broaches religious
differences that have left their metaphysical mark on current academic
schisms.

Perhaps Irish Studies, as we now call them, have inherited two
broad modes of enquiry. One, derived from the Enlightenment, is
the empirical quest for data: an inter-disciplinary burden not only
borne by historians. But this approach can never be wholly detached
from another tradition: the discursive tradition of 'talking about
Ireland' which grew up with nineteenth-century Nationalism and
is, indeed, politics by other means. At the moment Irish literary
studies (including this book) are uneasily caught between the two.

The Rising, the Somme and Irish Memory

We know their dream; enough
To know they dreamed and are dead...
    W.B. Yeats, 'Easter 1916'

Say only this, 'They are dead.'
    Charles Sorley

Commemorations are as selective as sympathies. They honour *our* dead, not your dead. Charles Haughey cannot visit Béal na Bláth to honour Michael Collins, let alone wear a poppy. And even when the same person or event is being commemorated, splits occur. Witness Christianity or the rival claimants to Wolfe Tone's bones at Bodenstown. We might observe, too, that 'processions' to Bodenstown follow a Catholic model, despite the secularist beneath the sod, and that Protestant Ulster desired a Union Jack to hang forever over Carson's tomb in St Anne's Cathedral, Belfast. Perhaps all public commemoration seeks authenticity by appeal to the religious instinct. In Ireland, however, the cross-overs between religious and political behaviour are peculiarly pervasive, subtle and unconscious. This essay borrows its title and some ideas from *The Great War and Modern Memory*, Paul Fussell's classic study of World War I in relation to English writing and English mentalities. Parts of Fussell's analysis also apply to Ireland. But the issue of the Somme and Ulster Protestant memory opens up further theological, as well as historical, contexts. Equally, Easter Week, in consummating the alliance between Nationalism and Catholicism, had special designs on Catholic memory. Thus, when the Rising and the Somme came to be processed by state ideologies, the manner of their commemoration was shaped by sectarian idioms. I suggest that Irish Catholics and Ulster Protestants not only tend to remember different things, but to remember them in different ways. The mnemonic structures differ: the categories, tropes, rituals. Religion, still the major psycho-cultural force in Ireland, has powerfully influenced the forms of Irish memory.

Commemoration is a means whereby communities renew their own *religio*: literally, what ties them together, the rope around the individual sticks. Seamus Heaney, whose poetry sometimes exemplifies and always understands *religio* in this sense, has evoked its operation at the Bloody Sunday funerals in Derry:

> The common funeral
> Unrolled its swaddling band,
> Lapping, tightening

> Till we were braced and bound
> Like brothers in a ring.
>
> ('Casualty')

Since all Northern Irish funerals remember other funerals, commemoration is a factor in funerals, as funeral in commemorations. Heaney's poem 'Casualty' itself commemorates a renegade who 'broke/Our tribe's complicity' by disobeying an IRA order. Thus the word 'swaddling' may hint at a regressive or restrictive element in tribal cohesion. Similarly, 'bound' hovers between bond and bind, between solidarity and suffocation. Nonetheless (or all the more), Heaney's image captures Northern Irish tribal *religio* as it might also be found, though differently manifested, on a similar Protestant occasion. Perhaps Catholic Ireland was especially shocked by the Enniskillen bombing on Remembrance Day 1987 because a commemorative rite had been violated and the broken taboo, the *nefas*, was understood at a deep cultural level. Did even the murders at the church in Darkley cause as much revulsion?

But commemoration, communal *religio*, does not merely remember. It reinvents and reconstitutes according to present needs. For instance, 1641, the supposed Protestant race-memory of massacre at Catholic hands, took on a new lease of life during the Home Rule crisis. And the Wolfe Tone cult did not really get off the ground until the centenary of his death in 1898 (a good many Irish 'traditions' were invented in the 1890s), or even later. Tom Dunne maintains that 'Tone's reputation was created long after his death [principally] by Pearse's claim that Tone was the founder of Irish Nationalism – a claim that became part of official nationalist orthodoxy after 1916, and has been a central cliché of official and popular political culture since 1922'.[1] Hence the musical group 'the Wolfe Tones' rather than, say, 'the Henry Joy McCrackens'. As for 1916 itself, the 1966 commemoration actually revived a waning piety. And 1966 fed into 1969. Although the Republic's fiftieth anniversary celebrations turned off the incipiently post-Nationalist generation of Fintan O'Toole – 'If Pearse is Christ, give us Barabbas'[2] – they roused the atavisms of the North, Protestant as well as Catholic. Tricolours in west Belfast fanned the flames of Paisleyism.

Here again Seamus Heaney's response seems relevant – the response of a younger, innocent, pre-Troubles Heaney. In 'Feeling into Words', a lecture given in 1974, Heaney explained how he came to write 'Requiem for the Croppies':

> [The poem] was written in 1966 when most poets in Ireland were straining to celebrate the anniversary of the 1916 Rising. That rising was the

harvest of seeds sown in 1798, when revolutionary republican ideals
and national feeling coalesced in the doctrines of Irish republicanism
and in the rebellion of 1798 itself – unsuccessful and savagely put down...
The oblique implication was that the seeds of violent resistance sowed
in the Year of Liberty had flowered in what Yeats called 'the right rose
tree' of 1916.[3]

Some of the assumptions here derive from the cliché noted by Tom
Dunne. Heaney assumes that you can commemorate one historical
event in terms of another; that there was organic continuity (seeds),
as well as absolute identity, between 1798 and 1916; that 'most poets
in Ireland' were keenly sharpening their nibs; that Yeats unambigu-
ously welcomed the 'right Rose Tree'. In fact 'Requiem for the
Croppies' concentrates on the Wexford rather than the Antrim mode
of 1798, thereby omitting the Northern Presbyterian contribution,
which would have upset seamless and timeless unities: 'The *priest*
lay behind ditches with the tramp./A *people*, hardly marching...'
(my italics). Marianne Elliott has pointed out that Presbyterian
United Irishmen were not all that tolerant of priests, and that secular
Republicans expected popish superstition to wither away.[4]

But if Heaney commemorates the Easter Rising by (partially)
commemorating 1798, Pearse prepared the way by making the
Rising itself a commemoration. He invoked not only Tone, but all
previous resistance to British rule, all 'the dead generations'. W.I.
Thompson, in *The Imagination of an Insurrection* (1967), sees Pearse
as embarked upon a *Liebestod*: perhaps loving the dead led him to
love death, to regard death as the finest tribute to the dead: 'the
fools, the fools, the fools! – they have left us our Fenian dead'. Pearse,
assisted by General Maxwell, passed on a legacy that now includes
the hunger strikes and the funeral-culture of west Belfast.

But the Rising paid tribute to the past as well as to the dead.
Was it a back-formation? A pastiche? Why did the Dublin people
stare? It is not just that cultural Nationalism, whether Yeats's or
Douglas Hyde's, had invested heavily in 'the ancient ways'. Some of
the leading takers for Irish Nationalism have always absorbed it at
a social, geographical or historical remove. They set out from locations
in the diaspora; from the perspectives of English Romanticism or
leftism; from the class-guilt of the Anglo-Irish; from the political
guilt of an Ulster Protestant. Such adherents sometimes confuse
ancient ways with contemporary actualities. My favourite recent
example was Ken Livingstone, MP, rebuking the Republic's government for its minimalist commemoration of 1916. But several participants in the Rising also represented earlier strata, or *kitsch* versions,

of national feeling: Tom Clarke factoring in American Fenianism through the Irish Republican Brotherhood; James Connolly, whose *Labour in Irish History* (1910) reads more like a work of émigré romance than of Marxist materialism; Constance Markievicz, whose big-house amateur theatricals may have personified that romance for Connolly. (Sean O'Faolain remembers her giving lectures which were 'an extraordinary medley of Marx, Republicanism and Gaeldom'.[5]) And did back-formations continue, yielding diminishing returns? Was all the self-absorbed isolationism of the Free State really necessary? Is it not appalling to think of Bobby Sands – an authentic 'Republican rebel' – memorising Leon Uris's *Trinity* to entertain prisoners in Long Kesh? Today, commemorations and funerals multiply upon one another in geometric regression.

Pearse is said to have been abstracted in the Post Office: perhaps because his imagination did not inhabit the present and its responsibilities, but concentrated on keeping faith with the past and impressing the future. Never has an insurrection been so deliberately memorable as well as commemorative, so conscious of its audience: 'They shall be spoken of among their people' (Pearse, 'The Mother'). Yeats, with a mixture of guilt, horror and envy, understood this poetic and dramatic attention-seeking:

> 'But where can we draw water,'
> Said Pearse to Connolly,
> 'When all the wells are parched away?
> O plain as plain can be
> There's nothing but our own red blood
> Can make a right Rose Tree.'
>   ('The Rose Tree')

Rather like stage-directors, Pearse and Connolly are represented as planning to pool, and thereby maximise, the historical symbolism available to them: the French republican liberty tree, Dark Rosaleen, the blood of patriots and Catholic martyrs.

It has often been noted that Pearse's appetite for martyrdom marks the point of elision between his Nationalism and his Catholicism. He saw Douglas Hyde as John the Baptist and looked for a messiah:

> I do not know if the Messiah has yet come, and I am not sure that there will be any visible and personal Messiah in this redemption. The people itself will perhaps be its own Messiah, the people labouring, scourged, crowned with thorns, agonising and dying, to rise again immortal and impassible...[6]

The above passage is quoted by W.I. Thompson in his persuasive psychoanalysis of Pearse as 'eliminating his humanity in his remorseless fixation of the will upon martyrdom'.[7] (The nineteenth-century poet Mickiewicz bestowed the same self-image on Catholic Poland.) But Thompson also records the extent to which Pearse's writings *rehearsed* the role and rhetoric that brought him death, not as 'the cost but [as] the reward of sacrifice'.[8] Pearse can be seen as a narcissist performing before the mirror of history. The poet's consciously 'noble house of my thought' prepares its own reception. The rebel-leader arranges not only his martyrdom but his martyrology. The son anticipates the mother/Mary mourning her lost paragon:

> Dear Mary, that didst see thy first-born Son
> Go forth to die amid the scorn of men...
> ('A Mother Speaks')

Pearse organising his Pietà resembles a suicide who thinks he will be able to watch everyone being sorry watching him.

Everyone, that is, whose cultural programming can receive his signals and their continuing transmission. I suspect that even very sympathetic non-Catholics found the symbolism and psychology of the hunger strikes hard to take. It is not only because individuals lack stamina that loyalist hunger strikes have always fizzled out: the gesture also lacks cultural support. Protestantism – and even Anglican-ism is low-church in Ireland – eschews iconography, martyrology, mariolatry, saints, Christ on the Cross. In Protestant theology, Pearse's self-identification with Christ appears more obviously blasphemous. Orange insignia stick to the Old Testament, not only out of savage affinities, but because of the ban on representing the New. As a result, the Protestant equivalent of martyrology is a biblical narrative of persecution (paranoia rather than masochism). Anthony D. Buckley, after analysing the Old Testament 'texts' behind the 'emblems' worn by members of the Black Preceptory, concludes:

> It would indeed be difficult for a unionist who encountered these stories in detail and in depth in the context of the Black Institution not to recognise a similarity between the situation of the Ulster Protestant and that of the heroes of the various stories. Like the people of Israel in the land of Canaan, Ulster Protestants have been given, and now occupy, an alien land. The foreigners whose land they occupy are, like the Canaanites, the Midianites, the Philistines and all the others, adherents of an alien religion. Like Jacob, they steadfastly avoid marrying the daughters of their enemies. Like the heroes of the stories, they lay great stress on loyalty, whether to their religion or to the crown.[9]

Buckley's article is called 'God's Chosen People'. This religious archetype contrasts with that of the Irish people as Christ.

It also involves a contrast between the verbal and the visual, text and image. Even visual signs themselves are not all read in the same way. Black Preceptory emblems – listed by Buckley as including 'gardeners' tools; a dove with olive branch; Noah's Ark; a seven-stepped ladder; a skull and cross-bones; a burning bush; Moses; Aaron's Rod; two crossed trumpets; a square and compasses...'[10] – do not yield up their meaning in an encompassing visual experience. They require exegesis, translation – not only for outsiders. And where historical 'stories' rather than their metaphorical surrogates or religious archetypes, are in the foreground, this verbal/visual priority may also hold good. Seamus Heaney, in a lecture called 'The Sense of the Past', reflected on the power of 'those images and objects which signify common loyalties and are recognised as emblems of a symbolic past which also claims to be the historical past'.[11] While admitting the dangers that can stem from 'idealising images of the political past', Heaney still feels the cultural tug of pictured scenes like a mass-rock or Wolfe Tone's profile presiding over 'the local AOH hall' and reinforced by 'an illustration in an old *Wolfe Tone Annual*'. He says: 'this image of a noble nature sto-ically enduring had a deeply formative effect on my notion of the United Irishmen, the 1798 rebellion and the whole tradition of Irish nationalism...[this] dream of the past...enhanced the learning process even when that process involved the demystification and dismantling of the original image'.[12] Here Heaney again seems to be receiving Tone via Pearse and Catholic iconography. Thus he may make an unwarranted cross-cultural leap when he refers to 'emblematic scenes such as the mass-rock or Tone in the dock or King William on his charger or Edward Carson signing the Covenant at Belfast City Hall'.[13] Are the latter scenes 'emblematic' in quite the same way? Do they evoke the same kind of response?

Belinda Loftus, in *Mirrors: William III and Mother Ireland* (1990), provides a fascinating history of how these figures have been rep-resented. But in one sense of her title they are not 'mirrors': King Billy originates in history, Mother Ireland in myth, even if both function mythically in history. Heaney makes the same error when he writes that 'the sovereignty' of 'an indigenous territorial numen, a tutelar of the whole island...call her Mother Ireland... has been temporarily usurped or infringed by a new male cult whose founding fathers were Cromwell, William of Orange and Edward Carson'.[14] Aside from the tactic which assigns all 'female' vulnerability to Nationalism and all 'masculine' aggression to Unionism, Heaney assumes that Unionist politics are totalised in King Billy as Nationalist

politics in Mother Ireland. When Loftus asked two Republican
women what Mother Ireland meant to them, they replied 'Everything'.[15]
Loftus considers Mother Ireland, despite the problems she raises
for feminism, better 'suited to handling the complexities of Irish
politics today [than] the simple, clear-cut symbolism of male figures
like William III whose fine-art development came to a full stop at
the end of the eighteenth century'.[16] It is also true that loyalist
imagery has not diversified much since 1968; whereas, despite their
late start in the mural-stakes, Republican areas have been adorned
with phoenixes, Celtic crosses, Cúchulainn, freedom-fighters, and
Bobby Sands as a lark in barbed wire, besides Mother Irelands
beckoning to battle and a few daughter-Irelands in battle-dress. One
mural consists of a masked and bereted IRA man, a flame, and
EASTER 1916. However, the Somme, if not King Billy, may be
represented in a visionary manner: an apocalyptic mural depicting the
battlefield centres on an idealised soldier linked to the heavens by
rays of light. (Incidentally, art students help to produce all this 'popular'
art.)

Yet in finding the Orange visuals comparatively static or limited,
we may once again not be comparing like with like. Protestant arches
and marches function emblematically in the strict sense, *not* 'symbolically'. An emblem is 'a silent parable', a morality, not a mystery
like a symbol. As in sixteenth-century emblem-books, the historical
narratives on walls and banners are framed by words. And the few
images without words also implicitly urge: Rem 1690, No Surrender,
This We Will Maintain, Lest We Forget. This Protestant memory-
bank links emblem with selective chronicle. In addition to the larger
chronicle from the Boyne to the Somme, banners carry, like *lares*
and *penates*, the ancestral details of every local lodge. That extraordinary spectacle, the Twelfth of July, must be strangely unconscious
of itself as such. Otherwise it would not feature endless uncharismatic
portraits of temperance-campaigning clergy. As Ulster's Solemn
League and Covenant associated the 'threatened calamity' of Home
Rule with earlier 'days of stress and trial', so Orange insignia work
as reminders which are also warnings. They are not icons, but
exempla or history-lessons: a heritage-pack as survival-kit. Republican
iconography, on the other hand, merges memory into aspiration.
It has yet to enter history as such. *Tiocfaidh ár lá* ('Our day will
come') underwrites a visionary symbolism that cannot or need not
be spelled out. Not Rem Easter 1916, but the rebel and the eternal
flame. Similarly, Protestants march, rather than process or 'mass'.
They express their territoriality in a martial rhetoric of music and

movement which matches King Billy's prancing charger and pointing sword. In contrast, Republican ritual appears to commune with itself: *Sinn Féin*. Protestants read this self-communion, this silent rather than vocal bigotry, this indifference to their own insistent rhetorical display, this refusal to notice or argue with Unionism, as exclusive and threatening. But iconography too is a rhetoric, albeit one that tries to place itself beyond argument. Similarly, Catholics misread Protestant rhetoric as wholly anti-Catholic, rather than also as inner-directed mnemonic. Thus the two forms of commemorative *religio*, of cultural defence or maintenance, bypass one another.

Ulster Protestants perceive their security as resting on a contract with the British crown. The Anglo-Irish Agreement might have caused less of a *frisson* if it had been less textual (just as civil rights sit-ins might have got a bit further than marches). Gordon Lucy in *The Ulster Covenant: A Pictorial History* waxes lyrical about the *language* of the Covenant as subsuming a historical community:

> The Ulster people, seeing a common danger, shared a common bond, an unbreakable determination, which found expression in one document, their Solemn League and Covenant. In its simple but eloquent phrases Ulster men and women found the expression of their deepest convictions, their deepest loyalties and their most fervent hopes for their future and that of their children.[17]

Despite 'pictorial' in the book's title, Lucy's commentary does not emphasise the visual. Later he calls the Covenant 'masterly [in] construction; concise in its wording; comprehensive in its scope', and refers to its author as 'modern Ulster's Thomas Jefferson'.[18] He also points to the Covenant's origins in the 'religious history of Scotland in the sixteenth and seventeenth centuries'.[19] The Bible and Presbyterian fundamentalism underlie a document that begins: 'Being convinced in our consciences', just as Catholic hyperdulia and transcendentalism underlie a proclamation that believes: 'Ireland, through us, summons her children to her flag'. The Covenant, like Pearse's profile, hung in living-rooms.

Paul Fussell calls one of his chapters 'Oh What a Literary War'. Nineteenth-century Romanticism, in various conjunctions with Nationalism, had a pervasive effect on twentieth-century wars. But Fussell singles out the chivalric language associated with 'Christian self-abnegation ("sacrifice"), as well as with more violent actions of aggression and defence'. He lists the literary tutors of 'this "raised", essentially feudal language' as 'the boys' books of George Alfred Henty; the male-romances of Rider Haggard; the poems of Robert Bridges; and especially the Arthurian poems of Tennyson and the pseudo-medieval romances of William Morris'.[20] No doubt some members of the Ulster Volunteer Force (and of the National Volunteers too) had been exposed to this tutoring, as to the more immediate wartime propaganda-effort and the Victorian culture of empire. However, indigenous religious and political traditions put further pressure behind 'a just war' and clichés like 'staunch', 'heritage', 'liberty' and 'loyal'; while Kipling, in his anti-Home Rule poem 'Ulster 1912', had given 'sacrifice' a special gloss: 'What need of further lies?/We are the sacrifice'. Philip Orr, in his illuminating *The Road to the Somme* (1987), quotes the following verse from the *Newtownards Chronicle* (12 September 1914):

> A hundred years ago your fathers fought
> As you must fight for liberty today.
> Beside that heritage all else was naught,
> And shall you prove yourselves less staunch than they?
> The hour has struck, and Britain asks your vow
> Of loyal and ungrudging service – now!

Perhaps 'staunch' has stayed current only in Ulster (where there seem to be no staunch Catholics or devout Protestants). Ulster/Irish Catholic recruitment-figures remain in dispute (and their deaths doubly uncommemorated North and South) because Unionist leaders inflated their own followers' eagerness to join up. As Orr says, 'it was in the Ulster Unionists' interests to portray Ulstermen as rallying to the Empire's defence in throngs whilst the mutinous Catholic population sat unmoved and unpatriotic at home'.[21] (Men from Catholic west Belfast usually joined the 16th (Irish) Division as opposed to the 36th (Ulster) Division.) Ulster Protestant participation in the war, later mainly of internal significance, was meant to be remembered in the context of Home Rule. Orr quotes a poem by F.S. Boas which exemplifies a 'sense of anticipated contract':

> The sword half drawn on her own behalf
> In Ulster's Red Right Hand
> Will leap from the scabbard and flash like fire
> For the common Motherland.
>
> And wherever the fight is hottest,
> And the sorest task is set,
> ULSTER WILL STRIKE FOR ENGLAND
> AND ENGLAND WILL NOT FORGET.[22]

As for after the war, Keith Jeffery quotes Sir James Craig speaking on 11 November 1922: 'those who have passed away have left behind a great message...to stand firm, and to give away none of Ulster's soil'.[23] Recently Ian Paisley and James Molyneaux revived the

outer-directed mnemonic role of Ulster's embattled past – the
reminder to Britain – when they personified staunchness during
the Gulf War debate at Westminster. Meanwhile the television
cameras showed the body-language of John Hume and Seamus
Mallon as more slumped than staunch. If not exactly 'mutinous',
they appeared to exclude themselves from somebody else's communal
religio. At any rate, seventy-five years ago the Somme, 1 July 1916,
complicated the politics produced by the Rising on 24 April: two
sacrificial shrines – the people crucified, a chosen people massacred
– demanded their incompatible due.

Demythologising retrospects on World War I developed more
slowly in Northern Ireland, where Edward Carson hymned 'the
glory and the honour [the dead] have won for the Imperial Province',[24]
though 'heroes' returned to find themselves unemployed, and Wilfred
Owen and the rest could be read there too. Among the unpublished
juvenilia of John Hewitt, already a socialist in the mid-1920s, are
attacks on the war's futility. Despite an early admiration for Connolly
in particular, Hewitt was also revising the Rising (see page 114
below). Orr observes that by 1936 'homage to the men who had
died [at the Somme] was mingled with a preparedness to criticise
the military strategy of the leaders and, indeed, the attitude of the
ordinary soldiers'.[25] In 1966 a veteran wrote an article for the *Belfast
Telegraph* which said: 'we were locked in chains for execution'.[26]

Pearse's mind-set is often compared to Rupert Brooke's: the
association of self-sacrifice with a 'cleansing' or 'cleanness' next to
godliness; the parallels between Brooke's public-school athletic
idealism and Pearse's 'devout Catholic' version of *Boys' Own*; the
vision of noble death as a 'royal gift' or 'rarer gifts than gold'. Pearse's
poetry shares with Brooke's patriotic sonnets an inversion – some
might say perversion – of normative values. Words and images,
more usually mustered for poetic celebrations of life, are turned to
the service of death. Brooke calls war 'peace'; danger 'safety'; death
'rich'. Like Pearse, he presents renunciation – of all things earthly,
bodily, sensory, human – as fulfilment:

> These laid the world away; poured out the red
> Sweet wine of youth; gave up the years to be
> Of work and joy...
>
> ('The Dead')

> These had seen movement, and heard music; known
> Slumber and waking; loved; gone proudly friended...
>
> ('The Dead', II)

Pearse's 'Renunciation' is quicker to mortify the flesh. He lingers
less on life in imaginatively taking leave:

> I heard thy music,
> O melody of melody,
> And I closed my ears
> For fear I should falter.

The poem's sequence of sensory self-deprivations resembles the
masochistic penances undertaken by Stephen Dedalus. Charles Sorley's
sonnet, 'When you see millions of the mouthless dead', written
before the Somme, attacks the doctrines of sacrificial inversion and
sentimental remembrance:

> When you see millions of the mouthless dead
> Across your dreams in pale battalions go,
> Say not soft things as other men have said,
> That you'll remember. For you need not so.
> Give them not praise. For, deaf, how should they know
> It is not curses heaped on each gashed head?
> Nor tears. Their blind eyes see not your tears flow.
> Nor honour. It is easy to be dead.
> Say only this, 'They are dead'...

Sorley's ironic reversals of Brooke's inversions initiate the role of
literary criticism in anti-war poetry. His sonnet also pre-empts the
'soft things' written in remembrance-poems and said at official
Remembrance Day ceremonies – ceremonies that ease further deaths.
One might compare 'blind eyes' with Pearse's 'I blinded my eyes'
in 'Renunciation'.

The literary construction of the Rising, of course, drew heavily
on native sources for its 'raised' language and its iconography: the
tropes of Jacobite Gaelic poems; Catholic devotional literature; the
ballads of Young Ireland. But Yeats had also acted as a catalytic
converter of English and European Romantic idioms. His pseudo-
Celticism (with help from Samuel Ferguson's Ulster Protestant
aggrandisement of mythic heroes) was his answer to Morris and to
Tennyson's Arthur. Also, Yeats imported the *fin-de-siècle* into Ireland:
febrile, apocalyptic, prostrated before 'forgotten beauty' symbolised
by iconic females. The *fin-de-siècle* was profoundly Catholic in
sensibility: only some instinct of 'No Surrender' held Yeats back
from the Rome-ward path of Lionel Johnson or Maud Gonne. The
poetry of Joseph Mary Plunkett (ill, as were so many of Yeats's
'tragic generation') was influenced by the English Catholic mystic,
Francis Thompson, and it exemplifies the Catholic-Gaelic – rather
than Protestant-Celtic – mode of the *fin-de-siècle*. (Hence the contra-

diction on which the Gaelic League eventually impaled Douglas Hyde.) His poem for Joan of Arc (does the French Catholic-Nationalist poet Péguy lurk in the background?) begins: 'She walks the azure meadows where the stars/Shed glowing petals on her moon-white feet' and concludes with divinely sanctioned war:

> The battle-ranks of Heaven are marching past
> Squadron by squadron, battalion, and brigade,
> Both horse and foot – Soundless their swift parade,
> Silent till she appears – then quick they cast
> Upon the wind the banner of the Maid
> And heaven rocks with Gabriel's trumpet-blast.

Such apocalypse may parallel, rather than imitate, James Clarence Mangan's vision of Dark Rosaleen with 'holy delicate white hands' who inspires the earth to 'rock beneath our tread'. Either way, the devotional structure – to which Yeats's poetry ceased to approximate soon after 1900 – seems a cultural constant. Thomas MacDonagh, of whom W.I. Thompson says 'his self-image was the tortured soul, his self-myth...a Byronism converted to a Christian cause' [27], wrote a poem to Mangan's grand Byronian soul: 'Poor splendid Poet of the burning eyes'. The poem shares the doctrine of Pearse's 'Fool' – that a mad dream may be truest wisdom – and it ends:

> thy single love
> Was, in high trust, to hymn thy Gaelic land
> And passionate proud woes of Róisín Dubh.

Where is the Republic's tradition of anti-war poetry (until Paul Durcan), for all its stress on virtuous neutrality? (The fate of Sean O'Casey's anti-war play *The Silver Tassie* is significant in this connection.) There are obvious historical and political reasons why the Rising could not be equated with the Great War's 'futility'. Nonetheless, the Civil War, if not the Anglo-Irish War, cast the dream into question. The Civil War made it more difficult to believe Irish versions of 'The old Lie: Dulce et Decorum est/Pro patria mori'. And, of course, the brutalities of the European war came home to Ireland in the shape of returning service-men and the Black-and-Tans. In 'Nineteen Hundred and Nineteen', Yeats makes a Black-and-Tan atrocity the focus for his 'lamentation over lost peace and lost hope'. The poem is also a belated World War I poem, and a critique of Orange/British and Green violence. It dates from 1912 the destruction of faith in principle and progress:

> We, who seven years ago
> Talked of honour and of truth,
> Shriek with pleasure if we show
> The weasel's twist, the weasel's tooth.

'Meditations in Time of Civil War' echoes that quatrain, now seeming
to date disillusionment from 1916:

> We had fed the heart on fantasies,
> The heart's grown brutal from the fare;
> More substance in our enmities
> Than in our love...

The Civil War has not yet fully emerged from a traumatised silence.
Many participants, like veterans of the Great War, simply refused
to say anything about it (there are numerous family testimonies to
this). As Wilfred Owen asked: 'Why speak they not of comrades
that went under?' Owen, while his own poetry kept on speaking,
knew that silences do not only mark the place where enormity seems
beyond words: they mark the place where cultures are thrown into
extreme psychic confusion. The end of 'Meditations in Time of
Civil War' bitterly echoes the utopian apocalypses of the *fin-de-siècle*
as it dramatises the 'senseless tumult' that created the trauma:

> The rage-driven, rage-tormented, and rage-hungry troop,
> Trooper belabouring trooper, biting at arm or at face,
> Plunges towards nothing, arms and fingers spreading wide
> For the embrace of nothing; and I, my wits astray
> Because of all that senseless tumult, all but cried
> For vengeance on the murderers of Jacques Molay.

Perhaps not until Brendan Kennelly (*Cromwell; The Book of Judas*)
and Paul Durcan (*Daddy, Daddy*) did poetry in the Republic really
begin to confront the psychic fall-out of political 'fantasies'. But Eoin
MacNeill, before the Rising he tried to stop, had already psycho-
analysed it as 'impelled by a sense of feebleness or despondency or
fatalism or by an instinct of satisfying their own emotions or escaping
from a difficult and complex and trying situation'.[28]

For the last twenty-three years Northern Irish poetry, like Northern
Irish society, has found itself back in that 'difficult and complex and
trying situation' – a return of the repressed, which can be resolved
neither by paramilitary sublimation nor by the politics of commemoration. When poetry engages with the vocabularies, emblems and icons
that condition this fresh outbreak of war, it has evidently absorbed the
precedents of Yeats, Owen, Rosenberg and others: literary models
bound in with historical origins. For instance, Tom Paulin has
satirised the ugly, neo-imperial 'old lies' which Unionism still parades,
and Michael Longley has redirected the Great War protest-elegy in
circumstances where futile deaths raise even more difficult issues.
His poem 'The War Poets' obliquely links Northern Irish poets
with the dead 'soldier-poets' for whom the armistice never comes:

> It was rushes of air that took the breath away
> As though curtains were drawn suddenly aside
> And darkness streamed into the dormitory
> Where everybody talked about the war ending
> And always it would be the last week of the war.

Paul Muldoon's 'Aisling' revises the Rising by asking whether Cathleen ni Houlihan, inspirer of hunger-strikes, should be renamed 'Anorexia' (see 'From Cathleen to Anorexia' p.173 below). Another poem, 'Anseo', probes the psychology, rather than the ideology, of Northern Nationalism. A delinquent schoolboy is trained by his 'Master' to fetch from the hedge 'A stick with which he would be beaten'. This parable of cultural sado-masochism, of a self-scourged people, ends with the victim becoming authoritarian in his turn: 'fighting for Ireland' as a leader of 'volunteers'. 'Volunteers' ironises a construction, a conscription, which includes the boy's commemorative name: Joseph Mary Plunkett Ward. To single out this particular 1916 leader is to highlight the role of poetry (and religion) in imagining insurrection. The stick also figures as a Yeatsian 'salley-rod' and 'hazel-wand': once the emblem of mysterious art, now 'whittled down to a whiplash'. Further, in quoting Auden's 'In Memory of W.B. Yeats' – 'Joe Ward' is said to be 'Making things happen' – Muldoon gives a new nuance to the old debate about poetry and action. He implies, not the impotence of the former, but the insignificance of the latter. Thus Northern Irish poetry, in so far as it can be called meditations in time of civil war, addresses the literary and political complexity it has inherited, by working very close to the grain of language and image. The local pathologies demand from poets the precision of a bomb-disposal team: delicate dismantling which is also a matter of life and death.

Perhaps it all started with Yeats revising Thomas Davis. Yeats's early aesthetic challenge to Davis's language ('worn down to mere abstraction by perpetual mechanical use')[29] reaches a literary-political culmination in 'Easter 1916'. It was Davis who mass-produced the Nationalist rhetorical strategy of commemoration:

> On Fontenoy, on Fontenoy, like eagles in the sun
> With bloody plumes the Irish stand – the field is fought and won!
>
> For often, in O'Connor's van
> To triumph dash'd each Connaught clan...

Yet in adapting the devices of nineteenth-century English patriotic verse, Davis may have been more akin to emblem-minded Orangemen than to the deep symbolic penetration of Mangan. Yeats terms the songs and ballads a 'rhymed lesson book'.[30] Davis invoked a vigorous past to promote action in the present, not so that the dead generations might be venerated for their own sake. The nostalgic mantras of Thomas Moore, themselves in tune with some Gaelic poetic structures, influenced the Catholic-Nationalist reception of Davis's exhortations. Thus Davis may have been partly misread by Pearse's commemorative Rising.

Yeats's 1916 poems are not straightforward commemorations, but reflections on commemoration: on symbol, word and memory. They exploit and achieve ballad-memorability, yet frustrate the notion that remembering the Rising will be a simple matter. In the very form of his poem, Yeats criticises Pearse's iconography as Sorley criticises Brooke's 'raised' language. Refrains particularly carry, or intensify, poetic memorability. They drive home Davis's history-lessons, and perhaps the idea that Irish history merely repeats itself. If 'Easter 1916' were an orthodox Young Ireland ballad, it would not have an ambiguity as its main refrain: 'A terrible beauty is born'. What should have been the refrain – commemoration of the dead leaders – is postponed until the last moment and thereby qualified. Also, at the end of the third stanza Yeats denies us the expected refrain. Instead we come up against 'The stone's in the midst of all'. Stone, for Yeats, signifies monistic fixity, 'opinion', 'Hearts with one purpose alone'.[29] He contrasts the stone with another image, 'the living stream', which signifies the flux of life and history. By imitating this flux, the movement of 'Easter 1916' subverts the stony predetermined repetitions of the Davisite ballad:

> The horse that comes from the road,
> The rider, the birds that range
> From cloud to tumbling cloud,
> Minute by minute they change...

The paradox here is that the rebels, who have changed everything, themselves remain unchanging – not only through their deaths and transfiguration. Yeats's rhythms, shuttling the same word into different slots, undermine this fixity: 'Minute by minute they change...Changes minute by minute...Minute by minute they *live*' (my italics). The pulse of the lines breaks out of the mausoleum imposed by Pearse's belief that 'life springs from death'. Yeats's 1916 poems admit that symbolic action – the rose tree, 'MacDonagh's bony thumb' – has proved more potent than 'politic words'. Pearse's bad poetry has made something happen. Yet in 'Easter 1916' the fluidity of Yeats's own medium, its metaphoric and metamorphic powers, suggests that the Nationalist icon may stand still, while 'the living stream' moves on. (The same, of course, applies to the frozen historical emblems of

Ulster Unionism.) It might also be said that words *argue* with symbol by proving themselves more flexible.

'Easter 1916' at once *makes* the Davisite tradition, and *breaks* it. The power of Yeats's whole literary enterprise cracks the 'mechanical' mould. Today, Yeats's 'living stream' might represent the last seventy-five years and Southern revisionism, while his 'stone' might represent either Northern Republicanism or neo-Pearsean efforts to 'Reclaim the Spirit of 1916'. 'Easter 1916' is, in fact, the first work of revisionist poetry, revisionist history, revisionist literary criticism. But the poem involves a double revisionism, a revisionist double-take, successive 'changes' in perspective. The speaker acknowledges that he has been a sceptic of the kind that the historian (and priest) Brendan Bradshaw now deplores. On meeting Nationalist idealists, he 'thought before I had done/Of a mocking tale or a gibe'. But the Rising has forced him to see tragedy, 'terrible beauty', where formerly he saw comedy, and to see men and women he had criticised as 'transformed utterly'. But the second pair of stanzas has second thoughts about that trans-formation. After meditating on stream and stone, the poem proceeds to revisionist questions which still hang in the air: 'Was it needless death after all?' 'And what if excess of love/Bewildered them till they died?' 'Excess of love' was Pearse's own phrase and 'bewilder', with its hint of the irrational or neurotic, echoes Eoin MacNeill's doubts. Yet this does not detract from the tragic dignity with which the names 'MacDonagh and MacBride/And Connolly and Pearse' are ultimately invested. 'Easter 1916', in so finely balancing tribute and question ('what if' is both), might be a model for revisionism without devaluation. Tread softly because you tread on my myths.

Reclaiming the *spirit* of 1916 indeed appears to be a religious project. Brendan Bradshaw depicts himself as crying in the wilderness against 'a sceptical empiricism [which] resulted in sterile reductionism'. Meanwhile he depicts his opponents as a monolithic group, a con-spiracy, of historians, called 'the revisionists', who have extracted the heroism, tragedy and 'play of national consciousness' from Irish history. Bradshaw's own studies, on the other hand, have led him to reinstate 'the popular perception of Irish history as a struggle for the liberation of "faith and fatherland" from the oppression of the Prot-estant English'.[31] (He appears to be fighting the Reformation as much as revisionism.) If Bradshaw seeks to make Nationalist doctrines absolute and sacrosanct again, others have endorsed the redemptive function of 1916 – an endorsement which logically implies that redemp-tive politics did not work first time round. In Dermot Bolger's sym-posium *16 on 16*, Anthony Cronin says we are 'a craven people;

but...craven before our own gods', and Francis Stuart calls the 1916 leaders 'people of one's race whose memory redeems at least some of the shame that race has brought on itself since'.[32] Elsewhere Robert Ballagh, one of the reclaimers, contrasts 'the vision and self-sacrifice of the men and women who participated in the rising' with 'the poverty of spirit [and] narrow-minded, self-seeking attitudes' in contemporary Ireland. For Ballagh, the spirit of 1916 denotes a kind of shock-therapy, which could transform the Republic's 'catalepsy', 'stupor', and 'miasma of mediocrity'.[33] It seems dangerous, even fascistic, to dream of a golden moment in the past which might dissolve the ills of the present. (How ironical that Ballagh's article should take its title from Robert Graves's demythologising memoir of the Great War.) To desire Pearse's Second Coming is to shirk the tough problems of contemporary politics. It is to escape – into commemoration – 'from a difficult and complex and trying situation'.

A baying, witch-hunting, heretic-hunting note sometimes enters these anti-revisionist calls. Among the targets are: 'academics', 'status-seekers' with 'expensive residences', 'media pundits', 'scribblers and chatterers', 'bourgeois shoneens', 'West Britons', 'foreign dross' and 'the serried ranks of the Southern establishment'. It is no apostasy to treat Pearse and Co. as historical figures rather than as saints; to set the Rising in its early twentieth-century contexts; to demystify its transcendental permanence. Equally, Ulster Protestants will need to accept that texts and covenants can become slippery in the living stream of history. It is no good shouting 'Lundy' at the Anglo-Irish Agreement while the people perish and 'conscience' withers. The spirits of 1912 and 1916 froze all kinds of energy, diversity and possibility. The snail's progress of 'talks' exemplifies their mutually paralysing effect in the North. Thank – not God, but women and men – that living streams have begun to flow in the Republic; that what Sean O'Faolain foresaw as 'the revenge of Life'[34] is now taking place. Those who mourn a lost spirit are really mourning their own emotional investment. But emotion does not become devalued when its object recedes or changes in aspect. At the moment, Eastern Europe causes socialists pain which is partly excessive, partly a growing-pain. Sanctified histories are Ireland's equivalent of Marxist-Leninism, all the more insidious because their roots go deeper. Eastern Europe itself now has to confront sanctified histories placed in the deep freeze by Communism. But we may be in a luckier position since we have been so long exposed to the consequences of letting our demons loose. The deconsecration of Irish memory is overdue – and underway.

[1991]

'A Barbarous Nook': The Writer and Belfast

> *He who could sing of martial deeds,*
> *Where Valor struggles, falls, and bleeds,*
> *Fond of the saint that whispers peace,*
> *Bids the war-tempest's horrors cease –*
> *Calls the high-wing'd Urania down,*
> *With civic wreaths BELFAST to crown.*
> SAM LYONS

My topic, 'The Writer and Belfast', makes me feel as inadequate as Belfast itself made the writer Sam Lyons feel in 1822. Introducing 'Belfast: A Poem, Descriptive and Tributary', Lyons was 'aware that the subject which [the author] has undertaken is very extensive, and one in which it is impossible for him to meet the wishes of all; nay, in fact it might admit of a continuation to much larger bounds than he has at present prescribed'.[1] However, at the risk of crass generalisation, I decided to opt for a broad canvas. As with politics, so with literature: if you pull out one thread of the Belfast tangle, others tug in opposition. My main purpose is to survey the vision of Belfast presented in some twentieth-century fiction and poetry, including work by St John Ervine, Michael McLaverty, Sam Hanna Bell, Brian Moore, Louis MacNeice, John Hewitt, Seamus Heaney and Derek Mahon. I shall also briefly mention several other writers in order to fill out the Joycean issue of whether the 'conscience' of the city has been imaginatively created. Again, I shall occasionally look at this 'writer and city' question from the alternative viewpoint: not 'Belfast in Literature' but 'Literature in Belfast'.

As regards 'Literature in Belfast', Belfast's image, through most of its history, has combined Philistia with its other possible aspects as 'Bigots-borough' (James Douglas's coinage)[2] or Cokestown-across-the-water. (In fact, the North of Ireland has never been a 'black country' in the sense of producing iron, steel, coal or widespread smog.) The narrator of George Birmingham's *The Red Hand of Ulster*, himself a 'peer...with a taste for literature',[3] offers a conventional analysis: 'Belfast – perhaps because of the religious atmosphere of the city, perhaps because of the interest taken by its inhabitants in money-making – has not given to the world many eminent poets, philosophers or scholars'.[4] This may not have been quite accurate in 1912: it's less accurate now. But E.M. Forster's obituary of Forrest Reid in 1947 saw him as exceptional: 'He was the most important person in Belfast, and...I have sometimes smiled to think how little that great city, engaged in its own ponderous purposes, dreamed of him or indeed of anything.'[5] Derek Mahon in 1964 still considered the city impervious to dreams. He published in the magazine *Icarus* (from Trinity College Dublin), the first version of his poem 'In Belfast' (re-titled 'The Spring Vacation'). The last stanza, since wholly revised, then ironically prescribed:

> Poetry and fluent drivel, know your place –
> Take shape in some more glib environment
> Away from shipyard gantry, bolt and rivet.
> Elsewhere assess existence, ask to what end
> It tends, wherefore and why. In Belfast live it.[6]

There was of course Belfast's fabled Athenian age, of the late eighteenth and early nineteenth century, vividly reflected in *The Drennan Letters*. However the picture painted by Mrs Martha McTier, William Drennan's lively sister, is not always rosy. She refers in 1807 to 'the talk and puffing of that taste for the fine arts which was said to have arisen here'.[7] Yet Mrs McTier's own critical powers seem a mark of some civilisation. For instance, of Mrs Siddons's second visit to Belfast (in 1805) she remarks: '[Mrs Siddons] is grown very large, which is not inconsistent with the sublime, though it detracts from the beautiful' .[8] But, in the words of Denis Ireland's essay, 'Smoke Clouds in the Lagan Valley': 'The little Georgian town on the Lagan' was to be 'smothered by Victorianism and the Manchester School'.[9] The population of Belfast multiplied faster than that of any comparable Victorian city, from 53,000 in 1830 to over 250,000 in 1891. Its area grew from two and a half square miles in the 1830s to twenty-three square miles by the end of the century. Commercial and scientific materialism, together with the puritanical evangelism let loose by the 'Year of Grace' (1859), drove literature underground. Poetry was published pseudonymously or posthumously. Already Thackeray in 1842 had found the bookshop full of 'portraits of reverend gentlemen', whereas the 'poor neglected Dramatic Muse of Ulster hid herself'.[10] Samuel Ferguson had transferred his linguistic and antiquarian researches to Dublin, becoming one of those 'invisible exports', self-exiled writers, much lamented by John Hewitt and John Boyd in articles during the 1940s and early 50s. The export list includes AE, Joseph Campbell, St John Ervine, George Birmingham, Louis MacNeice, W.R. Rodgers, Flann O'Brien, Benedict Kiely, Brian Moore, Seamus Heaney and Derek Mahon. Rodgers complained in 1941 of being 'schooled in a backwater of literature out of sight of the running stream of contemporary verse'.[11] John Hewitt, a stayer, sums up the problem in 'The Bitter Gourd': 'The Ulster ideology...offered the writer no inspiration. The Ulster public offered him no livelihood.'[12] While advocating rootedness and regionalism, Hewitt has to admit: 'It is only in recent years that minds of even a moderate sensitivity have been able to endure and remain.'[13] So while both Ulster and Belfast have produced numerous writers, Belfast, their natural metropolis, has often in the past sped them through the double swing-doors to Dublin or London and beyond.

Of course Belfast's inhospitality to writers may have operated in a vicious circle to reinforce the unfavourable aspects of its literary image. John Milton unwittingly set a trend by calling the place 'a barbarous nook', sight unseen, in reaction to the royalist loyalties of its presbyters.[14] I collected some adjectives which convey the force of that mutual rejection: Michael McLaverty's recurrent 'desolate', MacNeice's 'hard', 'cold', 'melancholy', 'lurid' (in his poem 'Belfast'), Hewitt's 'harsh', Mahon's 'desperate'. John Montague packs into the first stanza of The Rough Field 'iron bleakness', 'narrow huckster streets', 'stern', 'dour, despoiled', 'shabby' and 'grimy'.[15] And of course Brian Moore's fusillade of 'run-down', 'provincial', 'grey', 'black, 'ugly', 'dull', 'dead'. Sometimes, especially in recent thrillers, all this acquires an exotic tinge, as of 'down these mean streets a man must go'. But the blackest picture of all appears in a novel by M.F. Caulfield, actually called The Black City. The first paragraphs explain:

> It is the Black City because of what is between Protestant and Catholic, between mongrel Briton and mongrel Irishman, that is, narrow hatred and bigotry. It is not much of a place as cities go, a nineteenth-century industrial profusion of shipyard gantries, linen-mills, factory chimneys, flaking pubs, oily river basins and mile after mile of narrow, mean streets... It is an awfully wet place. The wettest place on earth...The rain...persists all day almost every day. It clogs the streets, mixes with the dust to create a fine, gluey mud that adheres to everything.[16]

The Black City is a serious, if melodramatic and impressionistic, study of sectarian violence. But that opening, and the adjectives quoted earlier, suggest the high degree of pathetic fallacy that obtains in writing about Belfast. ('The inevitable rain', for instance, often accompanies the frustrations of Brian Moore's characters.)[17] Forrest Reid's beloved quotation 'Tout paysage est un état d'âme' overstates the case, though should be kept in mind.[18]

Yet it does not always rain in the literature of Belfast, or in Belfast itself. A company filming Gerald Seymour's grim thriller Harry's Game (1975) had their symbolism upset by a fortnight of mediterranean weather. The alleviating gleam of sunlight, literal and meta-phorical, breaks through. Louis MacNeice's *Zoo* contains a chapter of 'Personal Digression' (originally entitled 'Recantation') which starts with a change of weather, and continues as a revision of stereotype:

> The weekend was all sunshine. I could not remember Belfast like this, and the continuous sunshine delighted but outraged me. My conception of Belfast, built up since early childhood, demanded that it should always be grey, wet, repellent and its inhabitants dour, rude, and callous...my family's house lay under the Black Mountain – not black, but a luminous grey-blue. There was no speck of wetness on the streets. The macabre elements seemed to have vanished – no El Greco faces under shawls... It was very possible that Ulstermen were bigots, sadists, witch-doctors, morons. I had seen their Twelfths of July. But I had always dramatised them into the Enemy. They were not really grandiose monsters. If they were lost, they were lost with a small 'l'.[19]

In fact MacNeice's angriest version of Belfast was yet to come – in section XVI of *Autumn Journal*. But that passage typifies a number of recantations, qualifications, tensions, paradoxes, in the physical and metaphysical perception of other writers too: one of the most succinct is John Hewitt's '*betraying, violent city/ irremediably home*'.[20] Even Caulfield lightens the gloom: 'But it is not all a horror. The city is well set in natural beauty – better than the setting for London, Paris, Rome, Florence, Milan, Turin, Amsterdam, The Hague, Brussels, Manchester, Liverpool, Cambridge, Oxford or Dublin.'[21] This incongruity between city and setting recurs as the most comprehensive paradox, as a symbol of the unintegrated, unfinished state of Belfast. The visiting E.M. Forster felt the city to be 'haunted by a ghost, by some exile from the realms of the ideal who has slipped into her commonsense, much as the sea and the dispossessed fields, avenging nature, have re-emerged as dampness and as weeds in her streets'.[22] At the end of Mary Beckett's short story 'A Belfast Woman' the protagonist is told: 'Belfast has the most beautiful sunsets in the world...It's because of all the smoke and dirt and dust and pollution.'[23] The hills around Belfast fed the religious vision of C.S. Lewis, and possibly his fantasy-land Narnia. In *Surprised by Joy* he celebrates Belfast seen over the Lough as 'one of those great contrasts which have bitten deeply into my mind – Niflheim and Asgard, Britain and Logres...air and ether, the low world and the high'.[24] Within such cosmic suggestiveness the geography, history and society of Belfast afford plenty of subsidiary myths and conflicts: Cave Hill, the Titanic, and of course the sectarian division, reduced to its bones by the British Army's 'tribal map' which the undercover agent in *Harry's Game* must memorise. The

fact that the literature, too, is largely a 'tribal map', doubly subjective
and relativistic: that there are Catholic and Protestant experiences
of Belfast, again suggests that Belfast as a literary, let alone a political,
concept is still evolving. (One Belfast writer, a little maliciously,
speaks of Joyce *'embalming'* Dublin.)[25] Some novels by Forrest Reid
and Janet McNeill come as not only a relief but a surprise, when
the city fails to be a protagonist, there chiefly as a backcloth for
personal relationships. Few unifying emblems emerge from the
fiction: the backward look to 1798, Moore's anarchic, apocalyptic Blitz
in *The Emperor of Ice-Cream*, some equally levelling dole queues,[26]
the non-sectarian homosexual pub in Maurice Leitch's *The Liberty
Lad*[27] – a novel in which Belfast gets a much-needed fling as an
outpost of the swinging sixties. Belfast thus confronts the writer
with a spiritual, political and social complexity that is capable of
testing the imagination to its limits. In the finished version of 'In
Belfast' Mahon alters his earlier view of poetry's irrelevance to
Belfast or *vice versa*. Presenting the city as not a melodramatic but
a tragic scenario, he equates 'knowledge' of it with an advance in
human and artistic responsibility, and rhymes 'city' with 'pity':

> One part of my mind must learn to know its place.
> The things that happen in the kitchen-houses
> And echoing back-streets of this desperate city
> Should engage more than my casual interest,
> Exact more interest than my casual pity.[28]

Whether Mahon defines Belfast in terms of artistic responsibility
or artistic responsibility in terms of Belfast, the assumption of such
responsibility has been chiefly, and properly, the prerogative of
Protestant writers. Most of my quotations have, in fact, characterised
the city in terms of its founding Protestantism. Catholic writers, on
the other hand, or people in fiction by Catholic writers, tend to
regard Belfast as less their fault than their fate. By the mid nineteenth century the proportion of Catholics in Belfast had risen from
5 to 35 per cent. Their arrival from rural Ulster turned Belfast into
an immigrant city, dominated by ethnic/sectarian tensions similar
to those that shaped Boston or Glasgow. The fiction of Michael
McLaverty, although set 100 years later, has the extraordinary
quality of seeming to repeat this cultural migration. It archetypally
re-enacts the loss of the fields and the shock of the streets. Thus
McLaverty also captures Ireland's violation by the Industrial Revolution: Belfast remains the only Irish city with an industrial *history*.
John Wilson Foster emphasises what is left behind, the motif of
'the blighted land' in McLaverty.[29] But perhaps the blighting city

is often his real subject. It insists on being the central reality of
Call My Brother Back (1939) and *Lost Fields* (1942). The main
consciousness in each novel undergoes an adjustment to Belfast.
McLaverty's most inclusively 'desolate' symbol for the city is the
cage, the prison – a symbolism Mahon emphasises in Brian Moore's
fiction;[30] although to McLaverty Belfast traps the wild bird, to Moore
it chains the free spirit. In *Call My Brother Back* the grounds of
Colm MacNeill's Belfast school lie between a 'dark jail wall' and the
overlooking 'top windows of terrace houses'.[31] Colm makes distant
contact with an actual prisoner whose waving handkerchief flutters
'like a captured gull against the grey stone of the jail'.[32] The first
paragraphs of *Lost Fields* introduce us to the claustrophobic domestic
interior of the Griffin household, where 'A lark's cage hung close
to the window'.[33] When the Griffin grandmother is coaxed there
from the country, so that she can help out with her pension during
bad times, she often reacts to her room in the small house as to a
cell: 'Lying awake she would think of…the sleepy hum of the wind
in the hedges, and the absence of chiming clocks to measure out for
her the inexorable drag of the night hours.'[34] That old Mrs Griffin
is not an idealised figure but irritable and irritating, reinforces the
impression of bewilderment between two worlds. The Catholic edge
of the city supplies a half-tantalising, half-consoling glimpse of the
countryside. It epitomises an incomplete rite of passage not just from
the country but towards economic, cultural and political integration.

But the 'lost fields', with a big or a small 'l', may also of course be
the city itself. Hugh Griffin works in the ironically named 'brickfields',
and the whole environment thickens the sense of purgatory, torture,
a sentence to hard labour. The river has 'black sluggish pools that
stank',[35] or becomes 'a clayey flood'[36] that once carries 'a bloated
bed-tick':[37] an image of the Depression to rival Orwell's young
woman 'poking a stick up a foul drain-pipe'.[38] Hugh is physically
engulfed by 'the dust coarsening his throat and lying in the sweaty
wrinkles of his brow'.[39] Similarly, his father Johnny who pushes a
handcart can be 'splashed to the neck with gutters and my feet in
a slobber the whole day'.[40] Hugh gets married, and stays behind
when the other Griffins leave Belfast. Foster comments: 'Hugh
represents the end of innocence as he cynically prepares to breast
his way through the rigours of city life that broke his father…in
losing intimacy with nature he has irrevocably lost part of himself.'[41]
Still, the return to the country has disadvantages: McLaverty does not
romanticise small townland life – and the 'quare changes'[42] Hugh
makes in the Belfast house show energetic realism as much as cyni-

cism. (Perhaps the city has developed in him supposedly *Protestant* qualities.) At the end of the novel his wife Eileen smiles at him and looks 'up the waste ground to where little girls were gathering in a ring to play some kind of a game':[43] a colonising of the waste ground by play, by custom – the process that begets street lore to replace country lore.

Young Colm MacNeill goes further than this. One of the embryonic poets who curiously abound in Ulster fiction (including the heroine of Janet McNeill's *The Maiden Dinosaur*), he begins to *imagine* the city. Belfast is first a postcard from his brother Alec: 'twelve little photographs...folded together like a melodeon...Try as he could Colm failed to bring them to life'.[44] With images more familiar, words must now be assimilated: 'Oxford Street, Victoria Street, Cromac Street...and he thought of the island names – Lagavristeevore, Killaney, Crocnacreeva – words full of music.'[45] Since *Call My Brother Back* evokes the 1920 Troubles, it is the city's violence rather than poverty that Colm's and McLaverty's imagination ultimately confront. Before Alec is murdered, sucked into the political vortex of Belfast as Hugh and Johnny into the economic vortex, Colm has already reflected: 'It was a strange city...to be living two lives, whereas on Rathlin Catholics and Protestants mixed and talked and danced together'[46] – another emblem there. At the end of the novel Colm's mind 'swirls' with partly integrated, partly contradictory impressions: 'rabbits wild and free on the hills around Belfast...a rusty tin in the fork of a thorn bush...a rickle of bones falling dead in York Street'.[47] What Colm's stream of consciousness fails to resolve, McLaverty's naturalism does not resolve either. His method veers between the epic and the episodic in that neither crises – deaths, departures – nor more positive Belfast experiences, generate much emotional or moral analysis on the part of the novel and its characters. Joseph Tomelty praises *Call My Brother Back* for representing the 'awful fatalism' of the Falls Road.[48] Similarly, in *Lost Fields* the grandmother's Good Friday attendance at Tenebrae, a tribal as well as devotional rite, merges into the purgatorial ordeal of Belfast itself: 'the voices of the choir filling the bleak air with black desolation... a coldness crawled over her and she thought of death, of clay, and of corruption'.[49] McLaverty's equivalent fatalism, almost medieval at times, and his pre-psychological approach, may have their simplicities and limitations. But he establishes an open-ended empathy which captures the psychic disturbance of a community in relation to the city. Mary Beckett's short stories, especially those collected in *A Belfast Woman* (1980), give the women of Catholic Belfast more voice in the narrative at a later stage of their history. Anne Devlin's first-person story 'Naming the Names' (reprinted in *The Way-Paver*, 1986) focuses on the mixed familial, sexual and political emotions of a young woman from the Falls Road, whose life has been changed by the Troubles. Her mantra of street-names – 'Osman, Serbia, Sultan, Raglan, Bosnia, Belgrade, Romania, Sebastopol' – like the lilt of Colm's island-names, represents a lost childhood stability.

Here I would like to make a brief comparison between McLaverty and a poet he 'fostered',[50] Seamus Heaney: another empathetic imagination finely attuned to the psychic signals of Catholic Ulster, and a comer to Belfast from the country. Heaney's most 'Belfast' collection of poems is *Wintering Out* (1972) poised, like *Call My Brother Back*, between countryside and city in time of trouble. Indeed, the very title expresses ordeal or endurance in a term derived from bygone rural labouring conditions. The sequence, 'A Northern Hoard', constitutes the emotional centre of the book. It contains such specifically urban images as 'the streetlamp's glow', 'the burnt-out gable', and 'the din/Of gunshot, siren and clucking gas/Out there beyond each curtained terrace'. The metaphorical 'my smeared doorstep' condenses McLaverty's special horror of blood on streets. 'A Northern Hoard' probes the poet's relation to the city's suffering, to 'the needy'. But a striking aspect of this relation is the paralysis of faculties, the effort required to overcome deafness, dumbness, numbness: 'What do I say if they wheel out their dead?' Similarly Heaney's article about Belfast, 'Christmas, 1971', speaks of 'the weary twisted emotions that are rolled like a ball of hooks and sinkers in the heart'.[51] The first poem 'Roots' hints at what may be primarily an imaginative choice: 'We petrify or uproot now': paralysis is thus assimilated to the stone of the city, whereas the poet's 'dream' goes on to interpret the Troubles more adequately in terms of a 'wounded' mandrake, literally a rural root, to which he commits himself. The poem preceding 'Roots' significantly looks back to Belfast as a 'Linen Town' in 1786 before 'They hanged young McCracken' (the Presbyterian United Irishman). The vision is of a decisively vanished ideal: 'one of the *last* afternoons/Of reasonable light' (presumably a pun on the Enlightenment), 'a *last* turn/In the tang of possibility' (my italics). There may also be a subtextual farewell to the literary rapprochements of the 1960s. 'A Northern Hoard' thus poses the problem of Belfast or Belfast as the problem: 'Where the fault is opening'. Heaney's pun here combines earthquake-centre with accusation – *whose* 'fault'? However, the bulk of *Wintering Out* actually follows the faultline deep into Heaney's Derry country-

side, the rural hinterland, the rural battlefield. It is an emphasis
comparable to his impatience in 'Whatever You Say Say Nothing'
with the urban languages of newspapers and neighbours, as against
the mythic language he opts for in Part I of *North*. Thus in one
sense Heaney reverts to the rural end of McLaverty's straddle, as he
'politicises' the Mossbawn terrain.[52] But if this perspective disregards
Belfast's specifically urban concentration of Ulster's and Ireland's
divisions – and poets have no duty to be comprehensive – Heaney
finds a good deal more than Colm MacNeill's 'music' in his poems
based on local names.

I should mention that Padraic Fiacc's streetwise sensibility affords
a raw and nervous reflection of the Catholic ghettos. And, in a
reversal of Heaney's trajectory, Paul Muldoon's collections *Why
Brownlee Left* (1980) and *Quoof* (1983) move towards the city as
imaginative epicentre. 'Immram', the blackly comic narrative poem
at the end of *Why Brownlee Left*, casts Ulster's atavisms into the
metropolitan idioms of Byron and Raymond Chandler. By relocating
an Irish voyage-tale in the Californian cityscape (or thriller-scape)
Muldoon highlights motifs of vendetta, corruption, violence against
women. There is, accordingly, some ambiguity as to whether 'the
city' closes down or opens up horizons. 'Immram' leaves its harrassed
protagonist on the verge of merging 'happily' into the 'steady stream'
of an urban crowd. However, this 'flow in one direction' may point
beyond Belfast to wider confluences. 'Gathering Mushrooms', the first
poem in *Quoof*, evokes a violated Belfast which has lost a sanctum
of tradition, beauty, femininity – now incidental to a drug-trip:

> The pair of us
> tripping through Barnett's fair demesne
> like girls in long dresses
> after a hail-storm.
> We might have been thinking of the fire-bomb
> that sent Malone House sky-high
> and its priceless collection of linen
> sky-high.

The final stanza's images of 'bare cement', 'concrete wall' and 'soiled
grey blanket', images which derive from the dirty protest and hunger-
strikes, brutally renew the old notion of Belfast itself as a concrete
prison. Thus the course of the poem seems to echo Yeats's lament:
'Many ingenious lovely things are gone'. Among the bleak urban
impressions in 'The More a Man Has the More a Man Wants',
the last poem in *Quoof*, is a group of skinhead glue-sniffers who 'have
formed a quorum/round a burnt-out heavy-duty tyre' (a less

glamorous drug-scene) near 'the once-sweet stream' of Stranmillis. Here Muldoon ironically translates the Gaelic name of a district in south Belfast, while 'quorum' tilts at the barrenness of the political environment too. However, Muldoon's poetry ascribes no unpolluted pastoral innocence to rural Ulster. In 'The More a Man Has' a trail of blood circles between Belfast, Co. Armagh and the USA – where the American dream affords little liberty either.

Before proceeding to the 'Protestant' novel of Belfast I would like to consider an approach and a genre which are licensed to cross boundaries. The approach is comedy or humour, the genre reminiscence, and they cross each other's boundaries as well. Even if overwhelming questions remain unanswered, if Forster's exiled ghost has not returned from the realms of the ideal, or Wolfe Tone to Cave Hill, life goes on and pushes towards expression. Comedy and reminiscence could, I suppose, be described as 'modes of reassurance' in that they emphasise shared or interchangeable experience in the city. And practised by Protestant writers, they carry a non-political implication of identity and roots. Mahon's 'In Belfast' may criticise such modes as 'yield[ing] instead to the humorous formulae,/The spurious mystery in the knowing nod', or perhaps they come under his heading of the 'tide of sunlight between shower and shower'. In any case they have burgeoned in recent years, perhaps because the Troubles have made such reassurance more necessary. As regards reminiscence, interest in local history has always been strong, exemplified by Cathal O'Byrne's enthusiastic researches in *As I Roved Out* (1946).[53] The development of publishing firms in Belfast, Blackstaff, Friars Bush and Appletree, has encouraged photographic record: *The Narrow Streets*[54] is a book on Belfast's lanes and entries whose title is not pejorative. But it also seems as if the Troubles since 1969 have unlocked individual memories, compelled a number of older writers to express their Belfast past. John Hewitt's autobiographical sonnet sequence, *Kites in Spring: A Belfast Boyhood* (1980) is a case in point.

As my next essay shows, Hewitt's social vision complicates the polarity between country and city that Raymond Williams criticises in post-industrial English literature. For Hewitt, and for Northern Ireland, it is only true up to a point that:

> the common image of the country is now an image of the past, and the common image of the city an image of the future...The pull of the idea of the country is towards old ways, human ways, natural ways. The pull of the idea of the city is towards progress, modernisation, development. In what is then...a present experienced as tension, we use the contrast of country and city to ratify an unresolved division and conflict of impulses...[55]

Belfast's proximity to rural Ulster, the persistence of 'old ways' after their transplantation to the city, the double sense in which 'we were too slow to make them citizens' (Hewitt, 'The Colony'), the ambiguity attached to 'progress' in Ulster – all directly exposed Hewitt to conflicting impulses. Due to his sojourns in the Glens of Antrim, he generally characterises the city as Protestant and the country as Catholic. Seamus Heaney's tropes have a similar tendency; and, as if to realise the fears of Hewitt's 'colonist', he sometimes opposes superior strengths of nature/nativeness to a built environment: 'each planted bawn'. At the same time, Hewitt's Ulster countryside is socially imprinted. It registers sectarian fences, the unequal allocation of good land, hard labour on all sides, and it reflects the ancestral pull of Armagh orchards ('some meander of my country blood'). Admittedly 'Conacre' (1943) summons 'perspectives of the Golden Age', salutes Nature as 'the world my pulses take for true', and looks forward to Belfast's ruin: 'Should these high chimneys tumble down,/the gantries sag and fall...' But Hewitt's troubled movement between city and country enacts his 'lonely rage' for an integrated society: a quest saved from pastoral or mere (William Morris) utopianism by his driving civic sense. The only poet to be made a freeman of Belfast (in March 1983), a bitter-sweet compensation for many political defeats, Hewitt interprets Protestant responsibility as a form of creative civics. For the Silver Jubilee of the Belfast Museum and Art Gallery (1954) he wrote verses which play on the ironies of the city's motto 'Pro tanto quid retribuamus'. Having rehearsed Belfast's fall from Northern Athens to a conurbation 'consumed by progress of that sort/the men who kept the ledgers reckoned with', Hewitt goes on to praise as role-models the Victorian naturalists, anthropologists, topographers, collectors and antiquarians who stand behind the museums's foundation, and William Gray who fought reluctant councillors to 'make life the richer for this hill-rimmed city'.

Kites in Spring is itself a kind of museum and gallery in that it incorporates personal memories, public events and figures, local history, popular culture and a 'mesh of kin' stretching back to the countryside. The first sonnet begins: 'This is the story of a happy boy'. Hewitt keeps his promise despite *unhappy* personal and period details – family deaths, the Ulster Volunteers, sectarian riots and the murder of Catholics, the First World War. The idiom of *Kites in Spring* appropriately combines Hewitt's habitual slightly archaic formality with a youthful simplicity. These qualities are evident in a sonnet entitled 'The Irish Dimension', which puts that portentous phrase in its childish place. He remembers meeting a Catholic boy whose

> magazines were full
> Of faces, places, named, unknown to me.
> Benburb, Wolfe Tone, Cuchullain, Fontenoy.
> I still am grateful, Willie Morrissey.[56]

Kites in Spring and Hewitt's related Belfast poems may insinuate what 'The Colony' or 'Once Alien Here' assert: 'this is our country also, nowhere else'.

Belfast also belongs to John Campbell, and John Campbell to Belfast, in the very different idiom of vernacular verse. In *Saturday Night in York Street* Campbell's nostalgic, non-sectarian local pride illustrates relativity of perception, as the street name acquires a contrasting resonance to the last words of *Call My Brother Back*: ' "Buck Alec", Rinty Monaghan,/James Galway, Gerry Fitt,/All are first-class York Street men/With talent, strength and grit.'[57] In another poem Campbell himself allows the possibility that others may just see 'a dirty street'. Of course the working-class voice of Belfast has entered literature through McLaverty, Sam Thompson, Joseph Tomelty and others. Tomelty's *The Apprentice*[58] is a novel of the working-class, and more unusually of work, at a slightly more skilled level than McLaverty's people. But *Saturday Night in York Street*, which includes a poem about the abilities of an old-time docker, might represent the liberation of the Belfast working class from the aesthetic patronage once extended to them in Herbert Moore Pim's collection of character sketches, *Unknown Immortals in the Northern City of Success* (1917). For instance, 'That which is called Johnston' salutes a fish-and-chip seller with fey facetiousness: 'Who is this that cometh forth in the darkness to the streets of Arthur and Chichester? Who is this that spreadeth tubers from the earth, and fish stolen from the sea...upon the pages of salvation?'[59] (The latter allude to the *War Cry*.) There is no need to dwell on the literary and social sins of Mr Pim. But the excesses of his style may be related to a feeling that the Belfast working class is particularly hard to make picturesque. Much later Robert Harbinson marred pioneering memoirs such as *No Surrender*[60] with some defensive stylistic inflation. He also provided for the Faber reader a self-conscious glossary that includes 'King Billy = William III', and 'Jinny = Effeminate Person'. Sam McAughtry, confident of his local audience, and indeed his radio audience, addresses it in confidently local terms. His union of reminiscence with humorous invention, in compilations like *Play it again, Sam* and *Sam McAughtry's Belfast*,[61] depends on the button-

holing conversational manner as of someone met in a pub or a bookie's
(frequent settings). For example: 'The working classes are in the
grip of very severe changes. Take funerals. There's no great distance
walked nowadays. Two or three yards for the sake of appearances,
then pull in to the side and everybody into the motors.' [62] At its
best, McAughtry's humour has the succinct, deflationary, ironic
qualities that are genuinely characteristic of Belfast speech. And
his anecdotes value the realism, sharpness and shrewdness of those
who live by their wits and their wit in the city. John Morrow's more
elaborately wrought, demythologising comedy draws on a similar
idiom and value-system. His book of short stories, *Northern Myths*, [63]
contains an apt image for his own and McAughtry's significance.
Writing about the ecstatic reception that visiting artists receive
from 'entertainment-starved fans in our embattled city', Morrow
diagnoses ' "the-campfire-in-the-clearing" syndrome – the warmth
in front heightened by the coldness of the dark forest at your back'. [64]
However there comes a point where some of the 'humorous formulae'
break down. Morrow may reach it in his novel, *The Confessions of
Proinsias O'Toole*, [65] a brave but not wholly successful effort to view
the Troubles through the eyes of a talented con-man, on the make
from all sides. Another instance is Martin Lynch's play, *The Interrogation of Ambrose Fogarty*. [66] Lynch's first play, *Dockers*, has a strong
element of humorous-reminiscence-as-drama: celebrating the now
disappearing culture of the 'Sailortown' territory he shares with
Campbell and McAughtry. But when Lynch's west Belfast following
came to see themselves on the stage in *Ambrose Fogarty*, they seemed
confused between laughing at the comic Willie Lagan, based on a
local character, and fiercely egging on Ambrose to defy the RUC
detectives. Lynch, too, may as yet be artistically confused between
a mode of reassurance or acceptance, and a mode of rejection or
protest: a gap he seeks to bridge by means of his socialist politics.
Socialism does seem to be a factor common to writers who have
attempted the neutral evocation of Belfast working-class life.

I will now turn to Protestant novelists whose critique of Belfast is
neither socialist nor comic but predominantly moral. I will also
suggest that the morality of Birmingham, Ervine, and Bell amounts
in each case to the readjustment of a morality which the city itself
has developed, or which has developed the city. The Protestant
writer's responsibility for Belfast began with its rise and ends with
its fall: a Marlovian rather than a medieval pattern. It's perhaps
hard now to recall Belfast as Pim's 'City of Success' – that was well
over fifty years ago. We can catch the primal flush of industrial

and commercial pride in Sam Lyons's poem. (In 1822 the population of Belfast was 40,000.) Having lavished praise on the 'beautiful demesnes' of prosperous citizens, Lyons asks:

> How shall I style thee, famed BELFAST?
> (On whom let none aspersions cast)
> Wilt thou be styled Imperial Rome?
> Where wealth and splendor had their home...?[67]

Perhaps Belfast and what Lyons calls 'the beautifying Mirror of decent Poetic Composition'[68] were never so far apart. However, Samuel Ferguson, in 'The Forging of the Anchor' (1832) which 'became one of the best-known pieces of verse in the nineteenth-century',[69] sees one of Belfast's growing industries in equally lofty, indeed epic and heroic terms: 'the ruddy lurid row/Of smiths that stand, an ardent band, like men before the foe'. Shipbuilding alone provides a microcosm both of relativistic perceptions and of rise and fall. Aside from treatments of the sectarian question in the yard, notably Sam Thompson's play *Over the Bridge* (1960), one might contrast 'The Forging of the Anchor' – a hymn to technological capitalism – with Stewart Parker's radio-play *The Iceberg*,[70] a dialogue for the ghosts of two workers killed during construction of the Titanic. Derek Mahon's poem 'A Refusal to Mourn' is not only an elegy for his boiler-maker grandfather but a requiem for the Titanic and for Belfast as a shipbuilding city:

> And his boilers lie like tombs
> In the mud of the sea bed
> Till the next ice age comes...[71]

Perhaps the Greek myth should have been remembered by those who named the ship – still an uneasy portent for Protestant Belfast.

George Birmingham (really the Rev James Hannay) preserves the tone of pride, while also mocking it. His autobiography *Pleasant Places* begins: 'I was born in Belfast and brought up to believe that, like St Paul, I am a citizen of no mean city'.[72] In *The Red Hand of Ulster* Birmingham respects as well as caricatures the Belfast business-man Cahoon: 'His contempt, not only for our fellow-countrymen in Leinster, Munster and Connaught, but for all the other inhabitants of the British Isles was absolute. He had a way of pronouncing final judgment on all the problems of life which fascinated me. "That's all well enough in its way", he would say; "but it won't do in Belfast. We're businessmen." ' [73] This is related to the more fully-fledged irony of the first version of 'In Belfast', where Mahon affirms: 'The incontestable priorities of life/Are best expounded by a man in a hat/In a Belfast pub, in a voice you could cut with a knife'. In fact *The Red Hand of Ulster* is a utopian – in Irish terms – satire, which shows the practical, independent spirit of Protestant Belfast and Ulster accepting Home Rule, which it fails to recognise as such.

St John Ervine, closer to the commercial life of Belfast than the clergyman Hannay, son of a clergyman father, treats it at once more seriously and more ambivalently. The similarity between Ervine and Arnold Bennett goes deeper than the conventional association of Ervine's technique with the Bennett-Galsworthy-Wells tendency. Not only do Ervine's shopkeeping scenes aspire to Bennett's meticulous detail; his literary 'industry' seems, like Bennett's, itself a product of the environment it depicts. Ervine's admiration for the energies of commercial and industrial life is directly displayed in *Some Impressions of My Elders*, when he visits Bennett's fictional milieu, and utters some very Bennett-like sentiments: 'I saw the whole of "the Five Towns"...and realised how strangely moving such a scene can be because of its suggestion of human presences. It was not without beauty, in spite of the gloom of an industrial area, but it impressed me most by its air of effort and power and achievement. I became conscious...of great labours, of confused strivings out of which some human need is satisfied, and I came away, as I always come away from such sights, immensely impressed by human organisation and very satisfied with great machines.'[74] (The anti-mechanistic philosophies of MacNeice and Mahon may be the result of an equal and opposite reaction.) Ervine also shares Bennett's emotional inhibition, perhaps with an added Calvinist pad-lock. *Mrs Martin's Man* (1914)[75] is ripe in incestuous potential. One sister first loves the other's husband, then has a special feeling for her nephew, as the long-lost father has for his daughter. The novel may, indeed, be an allegory of divided Ireland, including a prophecy of Partition when the family splits. But on the emotional level, all that the courageous Mrs Martin can manage, when confronted by the mystery of human motive, is the idiomatic but inadequate 'It's quare'. And when really baffled: 'It's quaren quare'. Despite its solid qualities, one comes away from *Mrs Martin's Man* feeling that not all life's problems can be solved by opening a shop in Belfast. Ervine himself seems partly to come round to this view in *The Wayward Man* (1927).[76] His hero, Robert Dunwoody, shuttles between the security of shops and the romance of ships. This exploits Belfast's maritime aspect as a port, rather than yard or dock: the Lough's recurrent role as the threshold of escape or exile. Robert's mother, another Belfast Protestant incarnation of the Irish matriarch, is less sympathetic than Mrs Martin, and rules her children's lives with the firmness of Bennett's miserly fathers. Robert marries an even less sympathetic wife, the grasping Brenda, who prefers to make money rather than have babies. This presumably validates the older Mrs Dunwoody, whose worldly ambition is for the sake of the family, not an end in itself. The final situation corresponds to that of Bennett's *Anna of the Five Towns*. Robert makes pregnant the clinging Sadie, whose father his wife has helped to ruin, just as Anna loves the ineffectual son of her father's victim. Both novelists leave the issues unresolved: they rebuke the work ethic without really replacing it; and Ervine's approach is not only 'pre-Joycean', as John Wilson Foster says,[77] but also pre-Lawrentian.

If Ervine's morality amounts to a compassionate worldliness, Sam Hanna Bell's is based on an ideal version of Presbyterian principles. These principles are tested on their original rural ground in Bell's first and richest novel, *December Bride* (1951). They are partly manifest in the behaviour of the patriarch Andrew Echlin, who sacrifices his own life to save others from drowning. Echlin has fundamentalist objections to an organ being installed in the church; but he rejects Orangeism because on the Twelfth of July:

> Not once did he hear a simple man like himself speak from a platform or a longcar. The final revulsion came when he saw a mill-owner whom he knew by repute stand up...It was for this man that women blinded themselves working embroidery at ha'pence a dozen. He saw him lift up his hands as if he bore aloft, visible, like sacred relics, the shrivelled and relinquished liberties that he and his kind had fought and bled for.[78]

December Bride is set at the turn of the century; and Bell's two Belfast novels are also historical. *The Hollow Ball* (1961) goes back to the Depression, *A Man Flourishing* (1973) to 1798 and the Act of Union. Indeed, the fact that Birmingham, McLaverty, Bell and Moore have all written historically suggests a search for what went wrong in the evolution of the city, or for the missed moment: 1798, 1921, 1941? In *December Bride* a visit to Belfast precipitates disaster in the heroine's life. But *A Man Flourishing* really gets down to fundamentals in portraying Belfast's very origins as perverted, and in identifying the career of its protagonist with that of the city itself. James Gault, a Presbyterian from County Down, leaves his theological studies in Glasgow to join the United Irishmen. After the suppression of the Rising he hides out in the Belfast underworld while 'Flies fed...on the spiked heads withering high on the Market House'.[79] Gault emerges from hiding and gradually succeeds as a

businessman. The more he 'flourishes' with the city, the more his
political and religious beliefs become eroded, 'shrivelled and relinquished liberties'. Bell has a Trollopian finger on the fine gradations
whereby morality crumbles before worldly temptation, as the spirit
of '98 crumbled before the Union, prosperity, and change. *The Hollow
Ball* inscribes a similar moral pattern of decline and fall. David
Minnis, like James Gault, disappoints a religious and 'obdurate'
mother in order to win fame and fortune at professional football.
By a series of selfish self-deceptions Minnis simultaneously lets
down his girl and his best friend, also a Protestant. The friend's
contrasting devotion to others finds expression first in socialism,
then in Republicanism[80] a latterday spirit of '98. Bell's critique is
often deep enough, in both these novels, to move from details of
corrupt individual behaviour, to Belfast's general worldliness, to
the betrayals at its source. He thus cuts deeper than Birmingham
in his '98 novel *The Northern Iron* (1909). Birmingham gives a vivid
and sympathetic picture of the compound in Belfast of Presbyterian
'iron' with French Republican doctrines. But the end of the novel
is weakened by Birmingham's desire not to think *too* badly of the
Irish episcopalian and aristocratic architects of the Union.[81] Indeed,
the construction of Birmingham's novels and of his sentences chimes
with the tolerant, rounded liberalism of his attitudes: Anglican as
opposed to Bell's spikier ethic and prose. (Birmingham, by the way,
began as a Nationalist and supporter of the Gaelic League, but ended
up in England disillusioned with politics.)

The last part of this essay will be concerned with the poetry of
Derek Mahon via that of Louis MacNeice. But I want to get back
to poetry by noting the reflexive strand in Brian Moore's fiction: a
strand which reintroduces the issue of 'Literature in Belfast'. Moore
has been so well and thoroughly discussed by others that drastic
summary seems permissible. There is a consensus among Moore's
critics, including Derek Mahon, about the parallel with Joyce. Mahon
says: 'Joyce's obsession with paralysis and death in *Dubliners* has its
counterpart in Moore's concern with the immutability of his Belfast
society, and with the effect of this stagnancy on its inhabitants.'[82]
This Joycean parallel implies, first: the Belfast Catholic bourgeoisie
may now be regarded as a 'problem' in themselves. A measure of
gradual Catholic advance beyond McLaverty's fringes is that Gavin
Burke in *The Emperor of Ice-Cream* can be said to rebel against the
Catholic work ethic. By joining the ARP and the war effort, Gavin
rejects matriculation, university. a professional career blessed by
the church, a 'Holy Catholic Virgin',[83] 'Pillion-riding girls with

Hons. English degrees and an eye for a man with a future'.[84]
Secondly, such symbiosis guarantees that the experiences of Judith
Hearne and of Diarmuid Devine in *The Feast of Lupercal* speak for
the condition of the whole city. Judith literally batters against a
rigid, uncaring religion that might as well, or as ill, be Protestant.
Diarmuid, finding inclusion as oppressive as Judith's exclusion,
becomes trapped in a small-minded community-network that has
its Protestant equivalent: a climate of gossip and espionage stretching
from peeping-Tom schoolboy to the President of St Michan's.
Thirdly and centrally, as with Joyce, the necessary liberation of the
artist from a spiritual grave constitutes both an implicit and an explicit
theme. The moral of Moore's fiction is thus the most comprehensive
of all, and returns us to Belfast as Philistia. In *The Emperor of Ice-
Cream* Moore says goodbye to all that by effectively conducting his
own blitz on the city, in terms both of the actual Blitz and the anarchic
consciousness of Gavin Burke. With non-sectarian impartiality,
Gavin and his left-wing Protestant friend Freddy Hargreaves together entreat the friendly bombs to fall on Belfast: ' "blow up St
Michan's"..."Blow up City Hall". "And Queen's University." "And
Harland and Wolff's." "Blow up the Orange Hall".'[85] Gavin's
interest in poetry, probably a portrait of the author as a young man,
is not Moore's first glance at this art in relation to Belfast. *Judith
Hearne* contains that dreadful advertisement for Queen's poetry of
the 1950s, Bernard Rice. Fat and lazy, Bernard is 'writing a great
poem. A *great* poem and it may take years to finish. And in the
meantime, I'm forced to live here and let Mama support me. Which
is as it should be'.[86] Bernard's torpor certainly makes him the centre
of the literary paralysis.

   To move now from fiction to fact. Paralysis also figures in the
first sentences of Seamus Heaney's memoir of Philip Hobsbaum's
Belfast writers' 'Group': ' "If a coathanger knocked in a wardrobe/
That was a great event" – Derek Mahon's evocation of the unfulfilled
expectancy of an old man living in Belfast could be extended to
the young men around Queen's in the late fifties and early sixties.'[87]
Heaney goes on to suggest how the Group helped to change things
(see Introduction, p.18). And it might also be said that by the
mid-sixties a provincial city – whether of Ireland or the UK – was
no longer felt to be quite so unpromising a creative nursery. Writers
were not now obliged to choose between the metropolis and the
country cottage. Heaney also emphasises a lull in Belfast literary
activity since Hewitt's departure to England (1957) and the final
issue in 1953 of *Rann*, Roy McFadden's poetry magazine. In fact

magazines do supply a rough graph of Belfast's cultural confidence. *Uladh* (1904-5), despite the involvement of Joseph Campbell, displays little real confidence, being a slavish clone of the literary movement in Dublin. *Uladh* is defined by its extravagantly Celtic cover (designed by Campbell's brother), and the extragavantly Gaelicised names of several contributors.[88] It had close links with the Ulster Literary Theatre, whose productions David Kennedy sums up as 'dim giants from the Irish sagas [declaiming] in blank verse to blanker halls'.[89] The very name *Lagan* announces a more limited and local ambition. In 1943 John Boyd began to edit this Belfast equivalent of *Penguin New Writing* very much in the spirit of wartime realism to which *The Emperor of Ice-Cream* harks back, although Moore's portrayal of Belfast's forties intelligentsia as joss-stick-burning Protestant homosexuals seems mostly wide of the mark. Boyd's contributors include McLaverty, Bell, Tomelty, Rodgers and Hewitt. He is very cautious about announcing any kind of Ulster 'renaissance'.[90] *Rann* similarly, and I am afraid accurately, says: 'At present we have poets but not a poetry'.[91] However, it builds up the sense of a regional tradition through John Hewitt's regular feature, 'Ancestral Voices', reprints of poems by older Ulster poets.[92] Ulster's current leading literary magazine *The Honest Ulsterman* (founded in 1968 by James Simmons) exhibits neither *Uladh*'s self-consciousness, nor the apologetic attitudes of *Lagan* or *Rann* . Indeed, its occasionally abrasive confidence, particularly evident in reviews, has attracted resentment from literary Dublin. One of the editors of the Dublin periodical *Cyphers* refers, like an aristocrat snubbing an upstart, to the *Ulsterman* and *Ulsterman* publications 'blow[ing] their own trumpet raucously'.[93] This sourness, by the way, contrasts with Sean O'Faolain's warm generosity in *The Bell* both to Belfast and to Ulster writing.[94] In any case *The Honest Ulsterman* lays the Twilight ghost of *Uladh*.

Perhaps the fact that 'poetry arrived in that city', to quote Heaney, had been prophetically inscribed. Belfast is notorious for street-names associated with religion and empire. For instance, its 'Holy Land' includes Jerusalem, Damascus, and Palestine Streets; its military and imperial roll-call runs from Cromwell to Lucknow to Sebastopol to Kitchener. But what optimistic and extravagant alderman christened two obscure streets near (Protestant) Sandy Row with the names of Thalia and Euterpe? However, Bentham and Utility lurk watchfully nearby, and the chosen Muses – of flute-playing and comedy – may make a precise local point.

Of course no city, whatever the condition of its literary culture, may presume to call the Muses home. Joyce lived in Paris and wrote about Dublin. Conversely, Forrest Reid could live happily in Belfast yet 'cried for Elysium'.[95] It is finally the treatment of Belfast by two exiles that I want to consider: MacNeice and Mahon. One of the ways in which *The Emperor of Ice-Cream* brings together fiction and poetry is through Gavin's obsession with the thirties poets. He asks himself: 'How could you tell Owen [his brother] that the real future of your generation had been foreseen by a group of modern poets whom Owen had never read, would never read?'[96] And he quotes (elsewhere too) MacNeice's 'Eclogue for Christmas': 'We shall go down like paleolithic man/Before some new Ice Age or Gengiz Khan.'[97] Freddy Hargreaves, perhaps not an entirely convincing representative of the thirties spirit in forties Belfast, reads *Letters from Iceland* at the ARP post.[98] It is interesting that MacNeice, for whom Belfast was the first city, should have been in the vanguard of absorbing the city into English poetry generally. Whereas Auden's city tends to be more abstract and generalised, close to civilisation itself, MacNeice's city is a matter of flesh rather than bones, of particular images and people and the socio-economic relations between the two. Mahon's essay, 'MacNeice in England and Ireland', suggests that as early twentieth-century Dublin notoriously might be reconstructed from *Ulysses*, so MacNeice together with Graham Greene preserves 'the pre-war urban England of rainy tramlines, Corner Houses, Bisto Kids and Guinness Is Good For You'.[99] In *Modern Poetry* MacNeice equates Birmingham – city not novelist – with artistic responsibility, as Mahon equates Belfast. Birmingham made MacNeice realise that Eliot's ' "short square fingers stuffing pipes" were not brute romantic objects...but were living fingers attached to concrete people – were even, in a sense, *my* fingers'.[100] In fact MacNeice's 'Belfast' poem focuses the difference between 'MacNeice in England and Ireland', between his perceptions of Birmingham and Belfast. One quatrain, which seems imported from 'Birmingham', sticks out like a sore thumb, or a less sore thumb: 'glaring/Metal patents, parchment lampshades, harsh/Attempts at buyable beauty'. Such shoddy capitalism in part belongs to a different universe from the other stanzas: with their 'carrion' or 'stained water', the 'murderous' hammers and men, the 'cowled and haunted faces', the gantries 'Like crucifixes'. In these images Belfast's industry provides the correlatives for some infinitely worse affliction. MacNeice's 'Belfast' establishes a pattern (sometimes a stereotype) in gendering Belfast as dominated by 'the male kind', while representing its victims as female: 'A shawled factory-woman as if shipwrecked there'. (His 'Dublin' figures that city as female – déclassée Anglo-Irish – with 'her seedy elegance...her gentle veils of rain'.) It may be that MacNeice's 'Recantation' had this poem in mind as a 'lurid' *Black City* melodrama. His critique in the sixteenth section of *Autumn Journal* constitutes a deeper if savage analysis: 'A city built upon mud;/A culture built upon profit;/Free speech nipped in the bud,/The minority always guilty'. But this brilliant précis of Belfast's own historical guilt takes its place in the poet's larger indictment of 'Ireland, my Ireland', where the whole country functions as a correlative for what is rotten in the state of Europe.

The difference between MacNeice's Belfast and Mahon's Belfast is that Mahon lived all his early life in the city, which thus entered and shaped his 'soul landscape' (as nearby Carrickfergus shaped MacNeice's). MacNeice in 'Belfast' does convict of indifference 'us who walk in the street so buoyantly and glib'. But Mahon's poem *begins*: 'Walking among *my own* this windy morning' (my italics). It should be said that Mahon's childhood Belfast was, specifically, north Belfast, Belfast Lough, and the post-war suburb Glengormley. His imagery evokes a precariously domesticated locale: raw estates threatened by sea-wind; houseproud, pathetic washing-lines; fear that the repressed might return, even though 'Clothes pegs litter the window-ledge/And the long ships lie in clover' ('Glengormley'). If MacNeice's poems about Birmingham, imply the need for some expansion of the spirit, Mahon's 'In Belfast' envisages more drastic change. The poem profoundly concentrates the 'problem' of Belfast because it draws together all that sense of the city as hell or purgatory, political and psychological repression: 'the unwieldy images of the squinting heart'. The incongruity between city and setting is definitively crystallised in religious language: 'We could *all* be saved by keeping an eye on the hill/At the top of every street, for there it is, /Eternally, if irrelevantly, visible.' Further, that 'We' again admits the poet's implication and complicity in the evil ('This thing of darkness I/Acknowledge mine'). Mahon's use of the word 'saved' indicates that once more a Protestant writer is turning Protestant orthodoxy, Protestant conscience, against itself, to conceive a very different kind of salvation to that offered by evangelism.

Night-Crossing does, however, contain some life-affirming glimpses of the Belfast working class. 'Grandfather' and 'My Wicked Uncle' complement the ancestors of Seamus Heaney's poems. They are the poetic apotheosis of the McAughtry or Morrow worlds, and also complement each other as styles of Belfast wit. The grandfather, 'Wounded but humorous', is 'cute as they come', 'shrewd', 'Nothing escapes him; he escapes us all'. The uncle's 'Wicked-avuncular fantasy' defines other qualities of Mahon's own humour, which itself may be seen as the apotheosis of Belfast's ironic tendency. I need hardly comment on the extent to which Mahon, like MacNeice, revels in urban demotic usage, in what MacNeice calls the city's 'spontaneous colouring of speech'.[101] But the city in *Night-Crossing* expands from Belfast into wider orbits. For instance, in 'An Unborn Child', the womb becomes the awaiting city of the world: 'I must compose myself in the nerve-centre/Of this metropolis, and not fidget'. Mahon's triple pun on 'compose' fuses organic creation, equilibrium and creativity in relation to the world as city. As with the microcosm, so with the macrocosm. 'Death of a Film-Star', Mahon's Marilyn Monroe poem,[102] symbolises neurotic destructiveness and self-destruction as 'Stars...scattering ash/Down the cold back-streets of the Zodiac'. The 'back-streets' of Belfast echoing far indeed. There is much walking of the streets in early Mahon, in a way that confirms his city as a 'nerve-centre'. Clearly Mahon's experience of Belfast has coalesced with his experience of other more cosmopolitan cities: in *Night-Crossing* as a whole his sensibility remarkably conflates the 'desperate city' with the Baudelairean city, with 'windworried terraces/Of nineteenth-century Paris'. In this respect Mahon surpasses Moore, perhaps only as poetry surpasses prose, in that Moore *contrasts* rather than *connects* alienation at home and abroad. Mahon's first city is also his last city. Moore's Belfast dwindles, in *The Doctor's Wife*, to a mixture of crude Troubles headlines and a cartoon rendering of provincialism.[103] Mahon when absent still 'remembers not to forget'.[104]

Again, besides artistic stature, it may be a matter of whether you consider Belfast your fault or your fate. I have used the word 'tragic' in connection with Mahon's vision of Belfast. The simplest definition of tragedy is that it confronts the worst possibilities about human beings and their world. I think that Mahon's poetry does this in relation to Belfast, in reaction to Belfast, and thus creates a 'conscience' for the city in an ultimate sense beyond either moral or political analysis. He skirts a Jacobean borderline between tragedy and satire, where his 'germinal irony'[105] imagines 'the twilight of cities', the eradication of 'human society'.[106] This anarchism, more strategic than Moore's in *The Emperor of Ice-Cream*, returns to Belfast, just as do those contrasting evocations of an 'ideal society' or 'a sunken city/Sea-changed at last':[107] redemption after the fall. However, in 'Rage for Order' Belfast and the writer once again figure at a distance from each other:

> Somewhere beyond
> The scorched gable end
> And the burnt-out
> Buses there is a poet indulging his
> Wretched rage for order…

Yet such deprecation is not to be taken literally. Mahon does hold up the imagination at its most stretched to Belfast at its most extreme: 'a world of/Sirens, bin-lids/And bricked-up windows'.[108] The first poem of *The Snow Party*, 'Afterlives', more explicitly redeems this blind and deaf world. Mahon as before identifies Belfast with responsibility, with 'growing up'. By a subtle system of assonance he also gives the name itself the most beautiful resonance I know, and makes the hills less 'irrelevantly visible'. Thus while 'home' rhymes with 'bomb', a trail of sound integrates the hills with the city:

> But the hills are still the same
> Grey-blue above Belfast.
> Perhaps if I'd stayed behind
> And lived it bomb by bomb
> I might have grown up at last
> And learnt what is meant by home. [109]

[1982-3]

Progressive Bookmen
Left-wing Politics and Ulster Protestant Writers

I

Left-wing Ulster Protestants have a distinctive tale to tell. In 1921 they inherited a messy palette of Red, Orange and Green, and faced a Unionist regime which was quite as anxious about socialism as about Nationalism. Then Northern Ireland entered the Slump and the 1930s:

> Thousands of men whom nobody will employ
> Standing at the corners, coughing.
> (Louis MacNeice, *Autumn Journal*)

After the Second World War, the Left, though split, won an astonishing 126,000 votes in the 1945 Stormont election. But support collapsed four years later when the Irish Republic had been declared and, as a result, Westminster consolidated Unionism with the Ireland Act. In the early 1960s, polarisation having eased once more, the Northern Ireland Labour Party began to make modest advances. This provoked a strong Unionist counter-attack. When the Troubles began, class-politics were sucked into the tribal maw which had always threatened their survival. In his novel *The Hollow Ball* (1961) Sam Hanna Bell, one of the writers whose reminiscences helped me with this essay, satirises a political meeting in 1930s Belfast:

> The man behind the table struck a push-bell and stood up.
> 'Comrades and friends, this meeting is called by the Unemployed Workers' Organisation and other progressive bodies to consider the problem of Ulster men and women – '
> 'Irish men and women,' said a voice from the front...
> The chairman paused and allowed his glance to linger thoughtfully over the audience so that they should be quite clear as to who was wasting whose time. 'Comrade,' he said, 'this problem is above any petty partisanship.'
> 'That's what I mean,' said the voice, unabashed, 'so call us something we can all accept – Irish.'
> The audience watched the man behind the table discarding the rest of his introductory remarks. 'I call therefore on Brother McKelvey to give us the trade union view.'
> 'On what?' prompted Brother McKelvey without leaving his chair. Reluctantly the chairman straightened up again: '– the trade union point of view on workers being forced across the water to seek employment.' With his backside poised over his chair he added, 'And I hope the meeting's time won't be wasted by comrades dragging in issues dead as Brian Boru.'[1]

Similarly, John Hewitt's short story 'Insurrection' (1930) shows a communist, an anarchist and a trade unionist failing to make common cause with the Republican movement.[2]

I want to outline a view of relations between Northern Irish writing and left-wing politics from the late 1920s until 1960, the year in which the performance of Sam Thompson's play *Over the Bridge*, an exposé of sectarianism in the shipyards, consummated such relations. Among those who sweated it out in the dark ages before the world media arrived were John Hewitt (1907-87), my principal subject, Sam Hanna Bell (1909-90) and the playwright and autobiographer John Boyd (*b.* 1912). I also want to develop a contrast between Hewitt's politics and those of his expatriate contemporary, Louis MacNeice. Different environments influenced their approach to the issues that obsessed their literary generation. While Hewitt shared W.R. Rodgers's feelings about being 'schooled in a backwater of literature out of sight of the running stream of contemporary verse',[3] MacNeice's poetry abounds in images and self-images of water on the move – 'river turning tidal' – images that represent the flux of consciousness and of history. Domicile in England placed MacNeice close to certain historical currents: *Autumn Journal* (1939) capitalises on that proximity. On the other hand, although his poetry suffered from aesthetic time-lags, Hewitt was closer than MacNeice to direct political involvement. Neither joined the Communist Party, but the passionately committed Hewitt wavered on the brink, and would never have said with MacNeice: 'My sympathies are Left. On paper and in the soul. But not in my heart or my guts.'[4]

Even if sponsored by Samuel Hynes's fine book, the term 'Auden Generation' should be laid to rest. Its Anglo-centric and metropolitan assumptions contradict the pluralistic tumult sketched by Valentine Cunningham in *British Writers of the Thirties*:

> Orthodoxies impose unities. And perhaps the most important cautionary note to sound about the '30s is one against the too ready professions and appearances of unity. If we think of the '30s as a seamless political whole we are grossly distorting them. Even on the Left there was great disunity. The United Front was a seamed patchwork of revolutionaries, old Liberals, young liberals, pacifists, Trotskyites, Stalinists, members of the Communist, the Labour, and the Independent Labour Parties, as well as members of no party at all. To call all the Front's sympathisers Red would be exaggerating mightily…And within the literary United Front, if that's how we may think of the sphere commanded by the Left Book Club and other associations for thinking and creative Leftist people, the same mixed shades and ragged divisions obtained…And politics exacerbated the usual proneness to such differences of opinion and divisive dealings within the cultural world.[5]

Yet, although MacNeice is prominent (Hugh MacDiarmid and Lewis Grassic Gibbon much less so), *British Writers of the Thirties* might as well be called *English Writers of the Thirties*. The dust-jacket photographs are of Auden, Isherwood and Spender, the perspectives English. MacNeice's cultural-political chemistry eludes Cunningham, who notes his interest in 'the divided self' and discusses 'The Hebrides' as an instance of travelogue (to 'Seedy Margins'), without recognising that Ireland might have disposed him both to self-division and to island-fancying.[6] But on the other island neither Hewitt nor MacNeice figures in Michael Smith's anthology *Irish Poetry: The Thirties Generation* (1971). And does 'thirties generation' have the same resonances in the context of the Free State? Seemingly the literary 1930s and the political 1930s look different according to the point on the archipelago from which they are surveyed now or were experienced then. Specifically, Belfast complicates the perspectives as it once upset the manifestoes. Hewitt's still mostly unpublished autobiography *A North Light* contains a chapter about the 1930s: 'My Generation'. This memoir both belongs to and deviates from Cunningham's scenario. Indeed, its subtext might be a struggle (within Hewitt himself too) between local particularism and metropolitan party-lines. In 1942 Hewitt wrote a defiant uncollected poem 'On Reading Auden and Others' (the others possibly include Mac-Neice), which begins: 'These men have spoken for a generation/But not for me...'

II

'Dead as Brian Boru' – an epitaph that the plot of *The Hollow Ball* shows to be premature – parallels a strand in John Hewitt's political formation and vocabulary:

> Then, by the mid-1920s, with the new ministries in gear and the non-entities trooping to the Westminster back benches, it seemed evident that the Unionists were a right-wing offshoot of the British Tory Party, who at home fought every election on the border, and that the Nationalists, the representatives of the Catholic minority, were merely obsolete clansmen with old slogans, moving in an irrelevant dream, utterly without the smallest fig-leaf of a social policy. So my concern went to the Labour Party – I was branch delegate at one annual conference – the party of Sam Kyle and Billy McMullen, who had a policy about 'the ownership of the means of production, distribution and exchange'.[7]

Here Hewitt was building on shaky foundations. Kyle and McMullen had been elected to Stormont in 1925 'after a campaign in which

the anti-partitionist positions of prominent members of the Labour
Party had been repressed rather than discarded'.[8] This, like the
Republican comrade in *The Hollow Ball*, raises the ghost of James
Connolly and his still-contested legacy to the Irish Left. In 1912
Connolly had clashed with William Walker, anti Home Ruler and
leading light of the Independent Labour Party, on the grounds that
Walker's professed internationalism was really a disguised colonialism.
During its prosperous years bourgeois Unionism used a rhetoric of
'progress' to fend off domination by the economically more backward
South (compare the tensions between the Northern League and
Rome). So when Ulster Protestant socialists invoke 'progress' – as
do Hewitt's adjectives 'obsolete', 'old', 'irrelevant' – they might be
complicit in unexamined Unionism or a sense of superior civilisation.

In 1942 Hewitt called Northern Nationalists 'sectarians, a Redmondite rump stupefying in snugs and clubs'.[9] Similarly, his poem
'An Irishman in Coventry' (1958) is based on a clash between
progressivist utopianism and the 'whiskey-tinctured' behaviour of
Irish brickies. (Hewitt's Methodist background explains his attitude
to alcohol.) The poem sets up a rather schematic opposition between
Coventry's 'eager', 'tolerant', welfarist spirit – 'image of the state
hope argued for' – and the dystopian, atavistic fatalism of 'my creed-
haunted, God-forsaken race'. In fact, the brickies were rebuilding
Coventry, and Irish immigrant votes, not necessarily motivated by
Marx, helped to keep the local Labour Party in business. For all
Hewitt's identification with 'my race', 'An Irishman in Coventry'
appears blind to its own political unconscious. It also points to contradictions in his view of the relation between ideology (always
understood as conscious manifesto) and practical politics. And,
just as Ulster Unionism historically attached itself to the Tories, so
Hewitt tends to idealise Labour England as the locus of political
thought and action. Despite some homesickness, Hewitt's years in
Coventry (1957-1972), where he became friendly with E.P. Thompson
and other Left intellectuals, brought him closest to an earthly paradise.

However, Connolly's own contradictions anticipated his advent
in the General Post Office. Witness his theoretical evasion of the
religious question (relegated to a personal matter), instinct for Irish
Catholic cohesion, rejection of 'foreign' i.e. English values, and
romance with the Gael as opposed to the 'hybrid Irishman'.[10] Connolly
offers *Labour in Irish History* (1910) as a contribution to 'the literature of the Gaelic revival' and locates his proto-socialist utopia in
'the Gaelic principle of common ownership'.[11] Sean O'Faolain was
later to hold him chiefly responsible for propagating 'the grand

delusion' of the 'Gaelic mystique':[12] a susceptibility fanned by his upbringing outside Ireland. Altogether, it is not surprising that Connolly had limited sympathy with the skilled Protestant working-class in Belfast. This class (now reduced in numbers and influence) has, indeed, proved unsympathetically prone to put Unionism before trade unionism when exhorted to do so. In *Over the Bridge* violent bigotry defeats the language of brotherhood. Yet traditional Connolly-ite concepts may over-stress the degree to which Protestant workers have been manipulated or duped, and over-mythologise strategic cross-sectarian solidarity during essentially economic campaigns like the Outdoor Relief strike of 1932. Peadar O'Donnell notes: 'it is often in the name of his fierce Orange beliefs that [an Orangemen] enters a progressive fight'.[13] Henry Patterson argues that more 'serious analysis of Protestant politics...might have prevented the easy identification of intransigent class opposition to bourgeois Unionism with a nationalist or republican position'.[14] (In today's recession working-class loyalists may criticise middle-class Unionist indifference to their needs, but see the Fair Employment Agency as a device for transferring jobs to Catholics.)

What of John Hewitt's attitude to Connolly? In 'No Rootless Colonist' he recalls his youthful 'vague sense of a romantic Irish nationalism, with Oisin and Connolly, Maeve and Maud Gonne, bright in the sky'; but also insists: 'our politics looked beyond to the world. Sacco and Vanzetti were, for us, far more significant than any of the celebrated "felons of our land".'[15] Once again Hewitt questionably severs Ireland's myths and mists from the real or great world. In fact his *juvenilia*, verse written in the late 1920s, establish no clear hierarchy of political values. He did indeed write a poem about the controversial death-sentences passed on the American anarchists Sacco and Vanzetti (1927). But he also wrote two elegies for Connolly and 'Song for Mayday' (1928), which ends:

> ...in my dreams I see a host of hero martyrs
> who are dead:
> John Brown, James Connolly, and Christ, for you
> I wear my ribbon red.

'Easter Tuesday' and 'To the Memory of James Connolly' also equate Connolly with Christ. However, in Hewitt's early notebooks salutes to the dead of 1916 mingle with laments for First World War victims and veterans, attacks on Ulster Unionists and English Tories, and scorn for Ramsay MacDonald's betrayal of the British Labour Party. His radicalism seems at once ardent and promiscuous.

What does begin to emerge is a Northern dissidence. 'Dublin: Easter 1928' notices 'the barefoot children in the street', and ends: 'The only change wrought by new law – the pillarboxes now are green'. In 1929 Hewitt wrote 'Two sonnets on the Free State Censorship Bill' which call up Swift

> to say the bitter thing
> Or pen the words that hiss and stab and sting
> And flay the foul flesh of the Pope's brigade.

Certainly this puts the issue more bluntly than do Yeats's resorts to Swift's 'sibylline frenzy blind'. A year later in ''98' Hewitt doubts his credentials, as a non-Dubliner, to write about 'MacDonagh, Plunkett, Pearse', whereas: 'I know well where William Orr,/ McCracken, Dixon, talked before/those brief bright weeks of '98/bore them away to brutal fate.'

This is an early sign of the Ulster Protestant writer's tendency to use 1798 rather than 1916 as a radical benchmark – and one which may define difference from, rather than solidarity with, the Southern state. (Tom Paulin's excoriations of the Republic are a recent case in point.[16]) Sam Hanna Bell, who described his younger self as 'a radical with a faint Nationalist colouration' and 'a nostalgic hankering for 1798', found the Presbyterian radicals attractive partly as an alternative to most versions of Nationalism then on offer.[17] His novel *A Man Flourishing* (briefly discussed in the previous essay) measures the moral decline of a former '98 Volunteer by the fact that he becomes a capitalist and strike-breaker, rather than by any culpable indifference to the rest of the island. Bell at one time helped to edit *Labour Progress*. Similarly, Hewitt's favourite United Irishman was James Hope, the weaver of Templepatrick, whom he salutes along with William Thompson as 'the brave old pre-Marx Marxists of Ireland'.[18] He also revered Mary Ann McCracken. These emphases contrast with those of an older writer, the Protestant Republican Denis Ireland (1894-1974). Whereas Hewitt and Bell dwell on the Northern and proto-socialist '98, Ireland wrote a book on Wolfe Tone called *Patriot Adventurer* (1936) and turned out courageous but repetitious polemics with titles like *Six Counties in Search of a Nation* (1947). He carried consistency so far as to abstain from a *Bell* symposium nominating 'The Best Books on Ulster', because 'the books that have enlightened me about Ulster have always been books about Ireland as a whole'.[19] No socialist (as well as no regionalist) Ireland rejected 'Connolly the economic thinker', while declaring: 'Connolly the patriot will live for ever'.[20] Thus Connolly's choice of 1798 (let alone a conjectural Gaelic collective) as the cornerstone for an all-Ireland socialist edifice, does not understand the potential fissures within the tradition he claims.

One obvious fissure is religion: presumably Hewitt was an atheist by 1930 when he castigated the Pope's resolve to 'pray for Russia', doubting his moral authority to 'point/a jewelled finger at the Slav's disgrace'. Like later references to Catholicism in Hewitt's poetry – 'the lifted hand between the mind and truth'[21] – this shows how hard it is for an Ulster Protestant radical to tread the line between atheism or secularism and anti-Catholicism. Any 'superstition' destined to wither away is bound to have a popish aura. (This was true in 1798 – and 1789.) However, the campaigns of 'the Pope's brigade' were then alienating socialists and writers throughout Ireland. This is why MacNeice's 'Eclogue from Iceland' (1936) celebrates Connolly in a roll-call of 'Soldiers of fortune, renegade artists, rebels and sharpers' who have kept the faith but lost the battle: 'There was Connolly/Vilified now by the gangs of Catholic Action'. Catholic Action was an umbrella for para-religious groups, flourishing in the 1920s and 1930s, and part of Rome's wider anti-Communist front, whose propaganda helped to ensure that Catholic doctrine would prevail in the institutions of the Free State.

A North Light spells out Hewitt's distaste for the Republican-socialist axis. Looking back from the early 1960s, he tells how he met fellow radicals in a Belfast pub, the Brown Horse, in 1937, and agreed to become literary editor of a new journal, the *Irish Democrat*. (He had long been contributing poems to leftist periodicals such as the *Irishman* and *Worker's Voice*.) His inaugural manifesto urged: 'Proletarian writers of Ireland Unite! We must mobilise against War and fascism.'[21] Yet the unity of the *Democrat* itself fell apart after it began to be edited from London. Hewitt says:

> By means I have never been able to understand, *The Democrat* became the monthly organ of the Connolly club, a Communist-inspired Irish Association in London, and continues to this day. It seems to me now an altogether deplorable production, its pages well padded with the words of sentimental Irish songs…Wildly wrong in its interpretation of Irish affairs, foolishly supporting the reactionary I.R.A., lacking in frankness, blatantly opportunist, it has nothing to do with what we intended.

But he adds, movingly:

> Yet when, on the fringes of an open-air meeting in an English city, a young man with a thick brogue invites me to buy a copy, I always experience a momentary thrill of emotion for those far away days of the Left Book Club, The Popular Front, Aid for Spain, the snug in the Brown Horse, and take my copy and, turning its pages, rage at the betrayal of our dream.

The poetic corollary to all this can be traced in Hewitt's and Mac-
Neice's similar reactions to *Goodbye, Twilight* (1936), an anthology
edited by Leslie Daiken. Daiken's introduction attacks 'the capitalist
Free State', 'Ireland's unregenerate manhood', 'the *betrayal of the
national aspirations by the Treaty of 1921* ' (his italics), Joyce's
'thorough-going isolationism' and Yeats's 'Twilight renaissance'.[22]
One of Hewitt's two reviews, while hankering after 'a real sharp and
singing contribution...from the workers and peasants', runs into a
conflict between Marxism and aesthetics:

> We recognise that no art can...be entirely independent of its economic
> background...But we will not submit to the crying down of Browning,
> say, as a middle-class tourist, or the crying up of 36 of these 40 poets
> as poets...this book is...final. Rockbottom.[23]

His review in the *Irish Democrat* queries the anthology's unitary
subtitle – *Songs of the Struggle in Ireland*. Because of 'Too much
weight on the Southern contributions', 'the Irish Struggle becomes
the Free State or Republican Struggle'; whereas: 'The Irish struggle
has many variations and is being fought out in Derry and Strabane,
in Sandy Row and Short Strand.'[24] Hewitt's keenest thrusts conflate
stylistics and politics: 'The old counters are proffered again and
again...Ireland's Dead, The People, The Name of Tone...Dark
Rosaleen'. He remarks that the 'majority of these poets, if they
write from experience, must have spent the greater part of their
lives at republican conventions'.[25] Thus, despite his hostility to
Yeats's politics, Hewitt accepts Yeats as the public voice to beat,
rather than to be dispatched into the twilight zone: 'If anyone can
make poetry of the stuff of politics he can...Stand on his shoulders,
and there get your wider vision.'[26]
      MacNeice discusses *Goodbye, Twilight* in the chapter of *The
Poetry of W.B. Yeats* (1941) which compares Yeats to contemporaries
and successors, both Irish and English. From his own double vantage-
point, and perhaps staking his own double claim, MacNeice too
finds literary cliché and political contradiction:

> proletarian poetry will have to become a great deal less bourgeois; at the
> moment it relies upon clichés, and is trying to fight the bourgeois with his
> own discarded weapons...Some of the poems...are marked by a deliberate
> irreverence towards the Celtic renaissance...such poems, being conditioned
> by Irish dislikes, are still specifically Irish. Other poems...are the conven-
> tional utterance of the international working class ...Many, however, are
> still blatantly nationalistic and some are even devoutly Roman Catholic.[27]

Goodbye, Twilight irritates MacNeice and Hewitt into taking particularly fierce issue with the Marxist axiom that propaganda and liter-

ature are indistinguishable. Perhaps Irish factors, including the
influence of Yeats, made it unlikely that either could ever endorse a
wholly materialist account of poetry. Here and elsewhere MacNeice
argues that poetry is conditioned, but not determined, by its socio-
economic context: 'The Marxist historian is…employing bad logic
if, having proved that poetry in any period is *conditioned* by the
social and economic background, he goes on to assume that either
the *cause* or the function or the end of poetry can be assessed in
sociological or economic terms.'[28] Today, *Goodbye, Twilight* seems
'dead as Brian Boru'.

III

Hewitt's nostalgia over the *Irish Democrat* proves that it can be
difficult to draw clear boundaries between the pan-Irish, British,
and Northern Irish 1930s. Nevertheless, by the end of the 1920s a
left-wing literary conscience was struggling to be born in the Ulster
environment that MacNeice characterises in *Autumn Journal* XVI
as 'A culture built upon profit;/Free speech nipped in the bud'. The
mystical point of origin, the Helicon of protest, is usually identified
as David (Davy) McLean's Progressive Bookshop, which opened
in 1928. In 1929 Hewitt wrote a touchingly naive 'Sonnet for the
Progressive Bookshop, 17 Union Street, Belfast':

> This is the Mermaid Tavern of Belfast.
> The young men come to talk, argue and show
> brave lyrics to their friends. They seek to know
> how long the dark conspiracy will last
> that holds men chained to wheels embedded fast
> in old Tradition's bog.

Sam Hanna Bell recalled the Unionist ethos at the time as 'so
cloying that almost anything came as a relief'.[29] John Boyd writes
that 'we despised Belfast for its political and religious obscurantism',
and that John Hewitt 'was the centre of a small circle of left-wingers
who thought the intellectual life of the city stagnant and who, by
political action and thought, were trying to stir things up'.[30] Boyd
was a working-class scholarship boy from Ballymacarett with trade
union activists in his family. Hewitt had absorbed socialism from
his father, a Methodist schoolteacher who admired James Larkin
and Keir Hardie, and introduced his son to the English radical
tradition (see page 147). If Yeats owed his soul to William Morris,
Hewitt owed to Morris the soul of his politics.

In his *juvenila*, some of which can be found in Frank Ormsby's excellent edition of the *Collected Poems* (1992), Hewitt speaks as a revolutionary, rebel, Jacobin, anarchist, man with a secret mission, 'The Agitator in the Dock'. He discovered barricades before the 1930s had got underway, and set out to champion the poor and unemployed. These verses scourge complacent Unionists/Tories, such as the Duke of Abercorn opening the Stormont parliament in 1927, or the residents of 'Malone Park' (re-titled 'Aristocratic Area'): 'There is one thing I mean to do:/When spring runs down this leafy length:/I'll gather in this avenue/The slum folk in their ragged strength'. Even if he never kept this promise, Hewitt was not all talk. During the 1930s, despite the energy that he put into his work at the Municipal Museum and Art Gallery (now the Ulster Museum and Art Gallery), he became an activist – indeed, hyper-activist: public speaker, committee-founder, manifesto-addict. By the end of the decade he was lamenting that politics 'devour the time/that I could better spend at rime': a couplet that makes it own point. For instance, Hewitt and his wife Roberta assisted the National Council for Civil Liberties with their investigation into the B-Specials. He says in *A North Light*: 'Although we had no sort of sympathy with the gunmen, some of us considered that there were provisions in [the Special Powers Act] which diverged a long way from sound democratic practice, as, for instance, the authority to dispense with inquests in any given area.' During the investigation he became 'acquainted with the nature of state authority and its techniques of the opened letter and the tapped telephone'.[31]

Another cause was the Belfast Peace League, which the Hewitts helped to found, and of which Roberta became secretary. Hewitt's manifesto for the League includes a 1930s waiting-for-the-end scenario: 'Air raid on London and Home Counties. Whitehall in ruins...Gas fog stretches from Victoria to Piccadilly.'[32] At the same time, he understood the 'paradox' of 'working for international peace [while] in my native city, Catholics were burnt out of the York Street area'.[33] Hence *The Bloody Brae* (1936), his dramatised apology for planter blood-guilt. Besides doing his bit for civil rights and following global issues, he attended to the nitty-gritty of political action – watching out for anti-Catholic discrimination in the Gallery, befriending the manual workers there. He also had to defend art: against a curator who pandered to Unionist aldermen; and against a notorious Lord Mayor, Sir Crawford McCullagh, who ordered him to remove 'disgusting' prints of Van Gogh and Monet from the walls of Belfast Castle.

If Hewitt might have shared such problems with aesthetes in Dublin, he shared others with comrades in Britain. Today when the British Left has virtually cut its Ulster links, with the Labour Party nominating the Nationalist SDLP (whose 'L' has been a dead letter since the departure of Paddy Devlin and Gerry Fitt) as its 'sister party', we forget the interpenetration that once existed. The Progressive Bookshop mustered 350 members for the Left Book Club: names reputed to be on RUC lists. The common interests of Lagan and Clyde generated much political traffic. When Hewitt met and liked James Maxton, leader of Red Clyde, at an Independent Labour Party Summer School in Welwyn Garden City (1933), he had already heard Maxton speak several times at the Ulster Hall. Yet, crossing the water, Hewitt was apt to be disillusioned by more theoretical and literary socialists such as those who frequented a summer school run by John Middleton Murry. MacNeice, longer acclimatised, writes sardonically about 'militant socialist' neighbours ('The word Proletariat hung in festoons from the ceiling'), preferring his Birmingham students because, 'coming from the proletariat themselves, they were conscious of the weaknesses of the Prolet-Cult'.[34] Similarly, Hewitt preferred 'the warmth and affection of fellowship and neighbourliness with the I.L.P. at Welwyn' to Murry's 'steaming fish tank of supercharged egos'.[35]

The dream betrayed is a 1930s narrative to which Hewitt's disappointments bring a Northern Irish accent. For MacNeice, resistant to 'slogans' and totalising claims, the poets' 'great flirtation...with the Third International'[36] had always harboured a suspect Romanticism. His poem 'To a Communist' (1933), possibly addressed to Anthony Blunt, warns:

> Your thoughts make shape like snow; in one night only
> The gawky earth grows breasts,
> Snow's unity engrosses
> Particular pettiness of stones and grasses.
> But before you proclaim the millennium, my dear,
> Consult the barometer –
> This poise is perfect but maintained
> For one day only.

But if MacNeice's eye for 'Particular pettiness' now makes him look more politically intelligent than many of his contemporaries, it does not make him look conservative. He could be ironical about Blunt's switch of creeds from aestheticism to Marxism, yet respond to John Cornford as 'the first inspiring communist I had met'.[37] Years later Cornford's lover, Margot Heinemann, returned the

compliment, when she argued that 'though [MacNeice] is usually
presented in surveys of the period as a "sceptical liberal" in contra-
distinction to the more radical and Marxist Auden, Spender and Day
Lewis...his work of the later thirties is if anything more "political"
than theirs'.[38] In the later 1930s Hewitt was still radical, Marxist
and activist, as international politics penetrated Belfast in the shape
of Basque and Jewish refugees, and the imperatives of Republican
Spain. He wrote finely in *Irish Jewry*: 'the Jew, who made German
science distinguished, German music significant, German painting
discussed, and German literature admired, is in exile, his books
burnt, his apparatus smashed, his fiddle shattered in a thousand
fragments'.[39]

    Hewitt's anti-fascism was more clear-sighted than his devotion
to the Soviet Union – a dream that endured into the post-war
period. MacNeice resembled George Orwell in being undeceived
by 'the Soviet myth' and in criticising its totalitarian and millenarian
effects on English intellectuals. In *The Strings are False* he attacks
the Marxist who 'finds it such fun practising strategy – i.e. hypocrisy,
lying, graft, political pimping, tergiversation, allegedly necessary
murder – that he forgets the end in the means...Siberia fills with
ghosts'.[40] It can be no coincidence that he proceeds to an ironic
précis of Anthony Blunt's political and artistic opinions. Judging
by his ingenuous rebuke to the Pope, Hewitt began a romance with
Russia in his early twenties. He also wrote 'A Chant for the Workers
of the World on the 13th Anniversary of the Revolution', which
has the regrettable chorus: 'Shoulder to shoulder, woman and man,/
Another heave for the five-year plan'. In 1937 he praised the social-
realist Soviet contributions to a touring exhibition of children's
art, while condemning Finnish works as 'escape into romance,
adventure, or the supernatural'. (The Winter War fills with ghosts).
'What troll,' Hewitt asks, 'is so grotesque and interesting as a blast
furnace?' He tolerates 'not particularly good' drawings (of the 'Red
Army...children helping at socially necessary tasks...collective farms'),
because 'one can't help feeling behind them the growing up of a
new kind of man'.[41] He should have trusted the political acuteness
of his aesthetic sense. Hewitt was later to charge his friend John
Luke, the Ulster painter, with too much emphasis on technique
and a disappointing 'lack of any comment, direct or indirect, on
social relationships'.[42] One might compare MacNeice's argument
with Blunt over Diego Rivera (see page 234).

    Hewitt had already met (in 1936) George Orwell whom he calls
in *A North Light* 'the first man of the Left in my acquaintance

who could have fairly been called Anti-Soviet'. He continues with an apologia for himself and others: 'while, from time to time, we learned things about the Russian régime which disturbed us, in so much it seemed on the right side, that we felt public criticism was letting the side down, playing into the capitalists' hands'. He then says that reports from Spain, about the behaviour of the Communists to the Anarchists, later made him and Roberta 'more objective'. Yet on 11 April 1945, in a letter to Patrick Maybin, he condoned Soviet treatment of the Poles on the grounds that they were rooting out wartime corruption: 'And so the Reds have had to clean up and so the Poles have yelled murder.' More forgiveably, he complained that, when Belfast was celebrating the European armistice, 'somebody deliberately kept the supply of Red Flags short – at most they flew on a few public buildings'.

IV

If some dreams failed, the dynamics of the 1930s produced the Welfare State. This dragged Stormont in its wake: both towards reform and towards new kinds of abuse. The literary energies of the decade also had consequences for Northern Ireland, influencing poetics and cultural ideology. If, as my next essay argues, the utopianism of Hewitt and MacNeice can ultimately be seen as a displaced form of Protestant Nationalism, it also stems from the intersection between the British 1930s and the flawed political entities in Ireland. This intersection, which cuts two ways and may have implications for culture and poetry in the other island too, was itself subject to change during the years 1939-1945.

The Second World War, spent by MacNeice (mainly) in London and by Hewitt in Belfast, redefined their concepts of the relation between poetry and society. In blitzed London, in 'the bandaging dark which bound/This town together' ('Aftermath'), MacNeice found true community for the first (and last) time: a classless warmth that temporarily healed his deepest wounds. Before the war *Autumn Journal* had raised – if only to dash – the Irish literary intellectual's perennial hope of doing 'local work which is not at the world's mercy'. During the war MacNeice praised Orwell's meditation on Englishness, *The Lion and the Unicorn*, for its 'insistence on *local* factors' as opposed to 'the dogma of the pedants and the jargon of arm-chair reformists'; and in 1952 he criticised thirties 'social consciousness' for promoting a 'narrow and inhuman conception of society – a "society" in which neither personal relationships (or at

any rate the sense of family) nor regional loyalties nor religious
ties should count'.[43] Perhaps in the 1930s the social thrust of his
poetry had been really about reconceiving, in more collective terms,
the local ties which centralised urban England was allowing to
lapse – Raymond Williams's 'knowable community'. (This concern
has been put to new tests in contemporary Northern Irish poetry.)
MacNeice differs from Patrick Kavanagh as a democratiser of the
Yeatsian sublime because he stresses 'community', rather than 'parish'
– perceiving words themselves as a community-product. Despite
its particularist virtues, the parish constitutes a nuclear model for
poetry and society: one that assumes homogeneity and pre-modern
forms of contract. 'Community', with its 1930s nuance, is MacNeice's
humanising of 'communism'. He agreed with the Marxist poet-
critic Christopher Caudwell that 'the instinctive ego of art is the
common man into which we retire to establish communion with
our fellows'[44] – the socialism of the poem, perhaps.

   John Hewitt's war work was indeed local work. He tried, not
very enthusiastically, to join up, but being in a reserved occupation
found himself (like MacNeice in the BBC) aiding civil defence
and the cultural wing of the war effort. Confinement to Northern
Ireland incubated the philosophy of 'regionalism' which was to
keep Hewitt – and others – going for fifteen years and beyond.
Yet Hewitt's writings had always contained a potentially regionalist
substratum. It first came to the surface when, in the mid-1930s,
he gathered into one notebook all his verse featuring Ulster people,
places, placenames and dialect. He called the sequence 'The Red
Hand: a poemosaic' and gave it the epigraph: 'How can I write of
Ulster? Every word/I ever wrote has Ulster back of it.' Patriotic
emotion had been crystallised by an experience that Hewitt recounts
in his poem 'The Return' (1935). A professional visit to Bristol,
during which he was stirred by English local heritage, 'a microcosm
of England', had sensitised him to Ulster's own distinctiveness.
'The Return' links this revelation with a holiday spent on Rathlin
Island at a time of international and local violence: Mussolini's
invasion of Abyssinia, sectarian riots in Belfast. Here Hewitt records
the kind of epiphany which Irish Protestant poets more often attach
to a western island than to one off the north coast: 'islands are well-
heads of the world's salvation'. Like MacNeice's 'Western Landscape'
(1945), the poem briefly grasps transcendence in 'the lair of light'
but moves back into history:

       Not once a social conscience troubled us.
       Leaning on rocks, or perched precarious

on the stone walls between bare field and field,
we let the free heart flutter...

But in the city of our dreadful night
men fought with men because of a threadbare flag...

Hewitt's knowledge of Ulster became deeper, more locally particular, as a result not only of renting a cottage in the Glens of Antrim, but of lecturing to troops stationed all over Northern Ireland. When Hitler attacked the Soviet Union, he was even conscripted to interpret the new ally: 'And so the Marxian Dialectic was wafted from Ballymoney to Newry'.[45] John Wilson Foster has argued that Hewitt's later position was 'at best a radicalism stiffened by tradition and nostalgia into conservatism' and that his 'thirties socialism... rings truer'.[46] Hewitt's socialism did not end with the thirties, although his Marxism weakened. I would suggest that in the 1940s he and others converted rather than diverted political aims and energies into cultural channels which might accelerate a progressive flow. Peadar O'Donnell said in 1942: 'It is not really very important whether Belfast writers speak from the Stormont camp or from the Customs House Steps: a Balzac would perhaps be more destructive than a Zola. What is vitally important is that Belfast writers should write. But they need more than a magazine. They need a full size literary movement.'[47]

They were, at least, to get a magazine – *Lagan*, founded in 1943 by John Boyd, Sam Hanna Bell and Bob Davidson. *Lagan*, which lasted for three years, always disclaimed other than modest beginnings. But its impulse if not its achievement was Balzacian, complementing Sean O'Faolain's ambition as founding editor of *The Bell* (in 1940) to 'blueprint the society' rather than theorise about Irishness.[48] A prominent mode, as in *The Bell*, and in 1930s Britain, was the social-realist short story. John Boyd's editorials, while pleading against '"reportage" that tries too obviously to align us with a political group', keep social ends in view: 'the struggle for a way of writing is part of the struggle for a way of life'.[49] Besides impeding other traffic between North and South, the war made Dublin more distant as a literary capital. Meanwhile literati in the Forces, such as Rayner Heppenstall and the Australian poet John Manifold, enlivened Belfast. But neither *Lagan* nor Hewitt's regionalism – the magazine's ideological engine – involved a declaration of literary separatism. *Lagan* was modelled on, not oppositional to, *The Bell*. One of the few Dublin-based organs to take an empirical interest in Ulster life, *The Bell* published Hewitt, MacNeice, Sam Hanna Bell, Thomas

Carnduff (the shipyards poet and playwright) and other Northern writers alongside O'Faolain and Hubert Butler. It sponsored debates about Protestantism and about the North. Peadar O'Donnell, Donegal man and socialist (also a somewhat erratic Republican), was an important bridge. O'Donnell, who later became editor, understood the North better than O'Faolain, generous but sometimes inaccurate. Hewitt pays tribute to his friend O'Donnell in a poem which originally appeared in *The Bell* (July 1942): 'Calling on Peadar O'Donnell at Dungloe'.

Yet O'Faolain did stimulate Hewitt's regionalism on a partly oppositional basis – just as England had triggered his sense of Ulster. He was annoyed by O'Faolain's response to the North, and to the Museum and Art Gallery, in his book *An Irish Journey* (1940). In *A North Light* Hewitt criticises O'Faolain's interesting assumption that exhibits such as 'Viking ornaments, the inauguration chair of the O'Neill's...a skeleton of the extinct Irish elk' must somehow be 'foreign' to 'the Six Counties'. He remarks, for instance:

> Mr O'Faolain could hardly be expected to know that in the entrance hall of almost every big house in the North the antlers of a great Irish deer dug out of an adjacent bog will hang opposite the half-length portrait of King William from the Kneller factory: by the first totem the family is making its assertion of Irishry, by the second of its membership of the Protestant Ascendancy.

But, on the other hand, O'Faolain's strictures provoked Hewitt into examining the deficiencies of cultural policy and cultural self-understanding in the North: 'I was compelled to meditate more deeply and analytically on what the purpose and scope of our museum and art gallery should be, in the context of a split nation and divided allegiance.' One of his first moves in the museum after the war was to 'add a meagre halfcase illustrating the Social Life of the Handloom Weaver [and including] the tattered remnants of one old weaver's book of verse'. The 'rhyming weavers', poets of the pre-industrial rural working class who wrote in the Ulster Scots vernacular, were to remain a touchstone for Hewitt. That he began his important work on them at this period suggests how socialism and regionalism were fusing in his imagination.

Hewitt's radical pantheon was augmented rather than deposed by new influences like Lewis Mumford, who warned of 'apoplexy at the centre and paralysis at the extremities', or the geographer Estyn Evans who showed that 'Ulster, even the Irish-Ulster, has its legacy of difference and individuality since the horned cairns were built'.[50] However, writing to Patrick Maybin in 1945, he was unsure whether the Northern Ireland Labour Party had the capacity 'to be the instrument for effecting my regionalist conception'. Thus Hewitt set about effecting it himself, with all the energy he had formerly brought to socialist activism. In *A North Light* he has the grace to quote the satire on his zeal in F.L. Green's Belfast novel *Odd Man Out*:

> There was hardly a platform which [Griffin] could prevent himself from taking, and from which he theorised in a robust, crisp fashion. There was scarcely a stranger to the city who, coming to the North for information regarding its history, literature, drama, painting, politics, commerce, hopes, was not swiftly and adroitly contacted by Griffin and as swiftly loaded with facts. And, similarly, when a new artist or novelist, poet, politician, playwright, appeared from amongst the population, Griffin was there to study him from some vantage point and thereafter applaud him or dismiss him in a few theorising remarks.[51]

'Freehold', Hewitt's verse-manifesto for regionalism (written in 1944-46), presses several vocabularies into its utopian prospectus:

> Mine is historic Ulster, battlefield
> of Gael and Planter, certified and sealed
> by blood, and what is stronger than the blood,
> by images and folkways understood
> but dimly by the wits, yet valid still
> in word and gesture, name of house or hill...
> But there is much to do before our pride
> can move with mercy in its equal stride;
> wet fields to drain, bare hills to plant with trees,
> and power to gather from the plunging seas
> and sprawling rivers, sagging walls to shore,
> lost acres to resume, and skills restore,
> and towns to trim to decency – and more,
> bright halls for art and music, rambling parks
> not fenced or gravelled by some board of works,
> and simple trades to nurture, till again
> potter and miller are familiar men...

The trace-elements here include Estyn Evans, the Protestant work-ethic, the rationales of planter and commissar, progressivist machine-socialism, nostalgic craft-socialism, post-war reconstruction, Thomas Davis and Young Ireland, even blood and soil. But for all its contradictions, for all its primary focus on cultural definitions that might serve the Ulster Protestant, Hewitt's new way of thinking about the North rephrases the political impasse which had blocked socialist advance: 'Wales and Scotland are, after all, well-defined geographical and national entities...Where then does Ulster stand? After all, we have a frontier. What then of Donegal?'[52] The cultural-

political vista that opens up at the end of 'Regionalism: The Last
Chance' (1947) is being revisited and revised forty years on:

> Ulster, considered as a region and not as the symbol of any particular
> creed, can, I believe, command the loyalty of every one of its inhabitants.
> For regional identity does not preclude, rather it requires, membership of
> a larger association. And, whether that association be, as I hope, of a
> federated British Isles, or a federal Ireland, out of that loyalty to our own
> place, rooted in honest history, in familiar folkways and knowledge, phrased
> in our own dialect, there should emerge a culture and an attitude individual
> and distinctive, a fine contribution to the European inheritance and no mere
> echo of the thought and imagination of another people and another land.[53]

But in 1953 Hewitt missed an important chance to implement his
vision when Unionist intrigue denied him the directorship of the
museum. This was largely due to his 'communist' opinions. In the
same year he published 'The Colony', which translates his cultural
meditations into his most sophisticated poetic model of Ulster politics.
The poem permits itself one utopian simile: 'as goat and ox may
graze in the same field/and each gain something from proximity'.

Regionalism, the quest for 'a native mode', certainly improved on
textbook socialism as a stimulus to Hewitt's poetry. But he had never
been *only* a man of the Left – hence, perhaps, John Wilson Foster's
remark about conservatism – always evincing the holistic ambition
of Belfast's Victorian polymaths. Hewitt refers to 'my thought' as to
something more organic and moral than theoretical. His copiousness
and didacticism smack of the nineteenth century as well as the 1930s.
To the detriment of art, he generally had something to say. As Foster
shows,[54] another ancestral prompter must be Methodism. Vivian
Mercier has analysed the evangelical origins of the Irish Literary
Revival, and a similar missionary spirit links the Hewitt who urged
proletarian writers to mobilise, with the Hewitt who tried to enthuse
Ulster Young Farmers about their poetic heritage in a journal otherwise devoted to flax policy. Behind both incarnations lurks Alexander
Irvine, the Antrim-born preacher, social-reformer and writer. Irvine,
in Hewitt's words, 'had exposed the outrages of the chain-gangs in
the Southern States [and]...stood shoulder to shoulder with Jack
London'[55] – an unusually attractive 'Scotch Irish' exemplar. Hewitt
in the early 1930s was inspired first by a sermon of Irvine's, then
by a controversial speech at the Labour Hall celebrating 'the agitator
Christ, and the communism of the early disciples'.[56] Then there
was a private occasion when Irvine told him that in Ulster 'Someone
was needed to say the unpopular things, to maintain the imperilled
values'. Hewitt turned this episode into a short story called 'The
Laying on of Hands'.[57]

From the mid 1940s a small number of cultural missionaries were at work in various savage quarters – for instance, Sam Hanna Bell and John Boyd in the BBC. Although Hewitt later abandoned regionalism as a coherent theory, it served or caught its time. My Introduction indicates some artistic and intellectual continuities, including Seamus Heaney's attention to the regionalist era. When Hewitt reviewed Heaney's *Death of a Naturalist* in 1966, he employed the value-terms of his regionalist aesthetic: 'actual...grounded...concrete...firm...spare', and related Heaney to Ulster writers like Michael McLaverty and Peadar O'Donnell who 'inhabit the same region of our national feeling'.[58] Hewitt has been castigated for (in 'The Bitter Gourd') nominating Protestant New England as a regional role-model. Yet, he possibly guided Heaney towards Robert Frost.

At this point MacNeice may seem to have fallen out of the frame. Indeed, his flat *Autumn Sequel* (1954) contrasts with the evangelical conviction of 'Freehold'. Both these long poems celebrate friends and creative spirits, but the former fails to locate any larger 'knowable community'. What Hewitt criticised as MacNeice's lack of 'roots' may finally show in his inability to reanimate the unifying communitarian impulse of *Autumn Journal* or his wartime poetry. Yet MacNeice's legacy to his Northern Irish successors had not become wholly aesthetic in that the Kafka-esque world of his last dark parables reflects the politics of the BBC in London and Belfast. MacNeice took a hand in the three-year fight to get Sam Thompson's *Over the Bridge* on to the stage: a juncture where culture and politics effectively reunited and won a famous victory over the Unionist establishment which had attempted to suppress the play. Thompson, the working-class socialist who shattered Unionist censorship in a way from which it never quite recovered, was encouraged (to write for the BBC) by Sam Hanna Bell. He was also guided by Bell's friend the literary lawyer and socialist, Martin McBirney, later assassinated by the IRA. John Hewitt had taught Thompson in a WEA Class. It was MacNeice who had recruited Bell for the BBC. MacNeice consistently used his own clout in the London Features Department to fortify Bell and Boyd in their constructive subversion of the Unionist grip on BBC Northern Ireland. Douglas Carson has said of these two producers: 'together they democratised local radio'.[59] *Over the Bridge*, which could not have existed without this left-wing literary milieu, without the Progressive Bookshop and all that, was used by Unionists opposed to Lord Brookeborough (whom the scandal weakened) in their campaign to replace him with Terence O'Neill. And we know what that led to.

Douglas Carson, in a lecture partly based on conversations with Sam Hanna Bell, has shown how MacNeice's support for *Over the Bridge* preceded the review in which he greeted it as a revival of the thirties spirit: 'a play *about* something. Social consciousness seems to have become, among the younger generation, a dirty phrase [so] it is very refreshing to encounter a work such as this which reaffirms the eternal commonplaces of the misery – and the dignity – of man'.[60] *Over the Bridge*, originally scheduled for production at the Belfast Group Theatre in 1957, was dropped when a member of the theatre's board of management set the alarm bells ringing at Stormont. The same man was Head of Programmes at BBC Northern Ireland. In Carson's words:

> The result was the famous battle which lasted three years. Most of the Group company resigned. Thompson sued the management. They settled out of court, but controversy raged in the press and at Stormont.
>
> Behind the scenes Sam Hanna Bell was working for Thompson. Mac-Neice was less inhibited and took Thompson's side openly.
>
> The BBC was not well pleased...[61]

Unlike MacNeice, Hewitt lived to rethink his politics and cultural politics in the context of Northern Ireland after October 1968. 'The Coasters', written in 1969 and published in *An Ulster Reckoning* (1971), has unique authority to tell the Unionist middle class 'I told you so':

> Now the fever is high and raging;
> who would have guessed it, coasting along?
> The ignorant-sick thresh about in delirium
> and tear at the scabs with dirty fingernails.
> The cloud of infection hangs over the city,
> a quick change of wind and it
> might spill over the leafy suburbs.
> You coasted too long.

This eerily echoes Hewitt's 'Malone Park' of forty years before. Here, too, a characteristic trope of the 1930s – metaphors of physical and psychic illness – finds a belated occasion. Hewitt's coasters have also ignored his early warning of Protestant crisis in 'The Colony'. 'Sure that Caesar's word/is Caesar's bond', most 'colonists' do not see the need to 'convince/my people and this people we are changed/from the raw levies which usurped the land...' In 1986 Hewitt published *Freehold and Other Poems*. This collection reprinted (for the first time in book-form) both 'The Bloody Brae', product of the pessimistically political 1930s, and the title-poem, product of the optimistically cultural 1940s. In his preface to *An Ulster Reckoning* Hewitt ruefully recalls 'an apparent softening of the hard lines and a growing tolerance between the two historic communities'. *Freehold* also juxtaposes two poems which sugggest how cultural visions must accept the reality and challenge of political forces. 'Ulster Names', written in 1950, proclaims the regionalist spirit: 'I take my stand by the Ulster names,/each clean hard name like a weathered stone'. Its dark twin, 'Postscript, 1984' lists:

> Banbridge, Ballykelly, Darkley, Crossmaglen,
> summoning pity, anger and despair,
> by grief of kin, by hate of murderous men
> till the whole tarnished map is stained and torn,
> not to be read as pastoral again.

Two complementary poems by Hewitt and MacNeice can be interpreted as epitaphs or elegies for their own literary-political endeavours, and for the utopianism of a generation. Hewitt's 'A Local Poet' (1975), which again revises and darkens an earlier text, measures the distance between ambition and achievement:

> He followed their lilting stanzas
> through a thousand columns or more,
> and scratched for the splintered couplets
> in the cracks on the cottage floor,
> for his Rhyming Weavers fell silent
> when they flocked through the factory door.

Besides regretting the failure of literature to unite weavers, factory-workers and the 'mannerly' middle-class poet, the poem – perhaps Hewitt's best – registers the obduracy of the political 'problems and cleavages' [62] that had been his starting-point:

> He'd imagined a highway of heroes
> and stepped aside on the grass
> to let Cuchullain's chariot through,
> and the Starry Ploughmen pass;
> but he met the Travelling Gunman
> instead of the Galloglass.

MacNeice's 'Epitaph for Liberal Poets' (1942) foresees the obsolescence of free thought, the death of the individual and the poet, the triumph of 'Those who shall supersede us and cannot need us – /The tight-lipped technocratic Conquisitadores'. Yet MacNeice did not cease to question and resist the Conquistadores any more than Hewitt ever relinquished his local burdens.

[1986/1993]

'Defending Ireland's Soul'
Protestant Writers and Irish Nationalism after Independence

I

Irish Nationalism, considered as ideology rather than practice, or faith rather than works, involves an intricate series of misunderstandings between Catholic Ireland, Anglican Ireland, and Presbyterian Ireland. This is because 'Republican' doctrines, mainly formulated by Northern Presbyterians, were modified by liberal Anglicans and Catholics in Dublin, according to the rather different spirit of nineteenth-century Nationalism, and then came to serve the needs of Catholic hegemony. Misunderstandings are reproduced in what I regard as misreadings by some contemporary Irish writers and critics. Of course, at the present historical juncture no critic or writer can be detached from continuing processes. The critique of the past is the critique of the present. Yet a deconstructionist 'thirst for accusation' may lead us in circles. Thus W.J. McCormack might find a 'repressed ideology of sectarianism'[1] in more places than *Purgatory* (first published in *On the Boiler*, 1938) and Yeats's other versions of Irish Protestant history. Republicanism or Nationalism itself, as articulated by Protestants like Wolfe Tone and Thomas Davis, had to repress sectarianism in order to include its authors. This has enabled Catholic Nationalism to deny its own sectarian constituents by invoking 'the Common Name of Irishman'. But perhaps we should approach all repression with analysis rather than accusation.

In his lecture 'Varieties of Irishness'[2] Roy Foster observed that Yeats's 'over-compensation as a marginalised Irish Protestant often led him into rigid and declamatory attitudes'. He then told an anecdote about a Dubliner who, after a similar remark on Foster's part, had protested: 'You can't talk about Yeats like that! *He was as Irish as I am.*' In this essay I want to review some different strategies and rhetorics whereby Yeats, and a few of his Protestant literary successors, negotiate their marginalisation at the hands of Irishness as a Nationalist construct. During the fallout after Partition and after Yeats the following writers found themselves implicated in the question of Protestantism and Nationalism: Hubert Butler (1900-1991), Louis MacNeice (1907-1963) and John Hewitt (1907-1987). I will occasionally bring into view the fallout after 1969.

MacNeice occupies a point of intersection or transition between Anglo-Irish and Northern Protestant consciousness. He was, perhaps, partially rescued from each by the other, as well as by England. In his autobiography *The Strings are False* (mostly written

in 1940) a memory from Sherborne, his English prep school, epitomises divided allegiance:

> On the Twelfth of July Powys came into my dormitory and said: 'What
> is all this they do in your country today? Isn't it all mumbo-jumbo?'
> Remembering my father and Home Rule and the bony elbows of Miss
> Craig and the black file of mill-girls and the wickedness of Carson and
> the dull dank days between sodden haycocks and foghorns, I said Yes
> it was. And I felt uplifted. To be speaking man to man to Powys and
> giving the lie to the Red Hand of Ulster was power, was freedom, meant
> I was nearly grown up. King William is dead and his white horse with
> him, and Miss Craig will never put her knuckles in my ears again. But
> Powys went out of the dormitory and Mr Cameron came in, his under-
> lip jutting and his eyes enraged. 'What were you saying to Mr Powys?'
> Oh this division of allegiance! That the Twelfth of July was mumbo-
> jumbo was true, and my father thought so too, but the moment Mr
> Cameron appeared I felt rather guilty and cheap. Because I had been
> showing off to Powys and because Mr Cameron being after all Irish I
> felt I had betrayed him.[3]

MacNeice's situation as 'an Irishman of Southern blood and Northern
upbringing, whose father was a Protestant bishop and also a fervent
Home Ruler',[4] also points to longstanding strains between Northern
and Southern Protestants, not only with respect to Home Rule.
This friction derived from Ulster's virtual monopoly of Presbyterianism. The established church throughout the island conspired to
defeat the radical Presbyterians in 1798, and to secure the Act of
Union and its own privileges. During the nineteenth century, with
nonconformist disabilities removed and Catholic solidarity advanced,
Northern Protestants drew closer together. In 1834 the 'Old Light'
Presbyterian minister Henry Cooke 'proclaimed the banns of marriage
between the Presbyterians and the traditionally conservative Anglicans
...a move of great significance for the future of Irish politics'.[5] Yet
today's split between Official and Democratic (Paisleyite) Unionists
reflects the original faultlines. And the differing class-balance of
Southern Protestants, whether Unionist or Nationalist, has often
set them rather snobbishly apart from the industrialised bourgeoisie
and working class of the North East.

Thus, for example, Tom Paulin overlooks Yeats's share in these
inter-Protestant prejudices when he regards his dislike of the Northern Irish as instancing 'the paradoxical, even lop-sided nature of
Yeats's nationalism'.[6] (As we shall see, there is a lot of paradoxical,
lopsided literary Nationalism about.) In 1938 MacNeice, on more
empirical grounds than Yeats's, favourably contrasted the (remaining)
Southern landed gentry with the cultural cringe of their Northern
Unionist counterparts:

I still think, however, that the Ulster gentry are an inferior species.
They lack the traditions and easy individuality of the southern Anglo-
Irish landowners; comparatively new to their class, they have to keep
proving that they are at home in it. A few may try to ape the *bonhomie*
of the South, but most of them set out to be more English than the
English. All the boys go to English public schools...[7]

It should be said that the Southern gentry, too, usually sent their
sons to be educated in England. Again, in 'Portrait of a Minority'
(1954) Hubert Butler, speaking as a member of this class, regretted
that it had abdicated from its natural leadership of Irish Protestantism:

I do not like solid blocks of opinion but, in fact, there is nothing very
reassuring about our Southern Protestant incapacity for congealing into
aggressive or defensive blocks. It merely means that the Ulster Protestant,
a more fanatical and bitter champion of the Reformation, assumes the
leadership of Irish Protestant opinion. And that leadership really belongs
by tradition to the Protestants of the South, the people of Swift and
Berkeley, Lord Edward Fitzgerald, Smith O'Brien, Parnell, men who
often jeopardised their careers and even sacrificed their lives in the
cause of an Ireland, free and united. So now our amiable inertia, our
refusal to express grievances or cherish hopes about Ireland, are really
delaying our ultimate unity and the reconciliation of our two diverging
communities.[8]

That the eminently reasonable Butler should echo Yeatsian pedigrees
leads me to question some readings of Yeats's own relation to 'Protestant Ascendancy' in W.J. McCormack's *Ascendancy and Tradition*
and Seamus Deane's *Celtic Revivals*. I put the term in quotation-
marks because the historical geographer Kevin Whelan recently
objected[9] to its being used in social and cultural contexts, whereas
it strictly signified constitutional and political discrimination in
favour of Anglicans after 1690. The Unionist regime at Stormont
developed a latter-day brand of 'Ascendancy' which explains the
term's currency in Irish literary-critical debates. Yeats himself in
his 'Commentary on A Parnellite at Parnell's Funeral' associates
Ascendancy with an eighteenth-century Protestant 'sense of responsibility' which gave way to the nineteenth-century 'Garrison, a political
party of Protestant and Catholic landowners, merchants and officials'.[10]
McCormack uses the Commentary effectively to show that *Purgatory*
broods on this decline, and also that the daughter of the great
house who marries a 'groom' has implicitly transgressed sectarian
boundaries as well as those of class: 'Evidence of the play's genesis,
in the manuscript scenario and in earlier utterances of Yeats's,
specifies its assumption of the Protestant/Catholic antagonism as
tribal if not racial, as the operational field of taboo and totem.'[11]

But McCormack does not discuss the mid-1930s context which links 'Parnell's Funeral', the Commentary, *Purgatory* and Yeats's sense that two tribal forces were still fighting 'in our blood' to generate the Irish nation.[12] The Commentary begins with the Battle of the Boyne and ends with the Parnellite window of opportunity. Even Parnell's fall meant that many 'Unionists and Nationalists' stopped living behind a 'party wall': 'we began to value truth...free discussion appeared among us for the first time'.[13] However, 'Parnell's Funeral' suggests, in the wake of Yeats's disillusionment over divorce, censorship and other matters, that Parnell's real funeral, the funeral of free cross-cultural discussion, is now taking place: 'Had de Valera eaten Parnell's heart', 'Had Cosgrave eaten Parnell's heart...' Neither of the Civil War parties has absorbed the values which, for Yeats, link the eighteenth-century Protestant nation, Parnell and his own art. The poem's 'bitter wisdom' is contemporary.

This incomplete mutual digestion between Catholic and Protestant Ireland troubles *Purgatory* in the more extreme idiom of Yeats's last writings. His sexual and genetic metaphor implies that the Anglo-Irish have conspired in their own downfall. The 'bragging and drinking' groom evokes not only 'O'Connellite democracy' but the 'loose-lipped demagogues' of de Valera's Ireland, the figure unpleasantly characterised in the preceding rant of *On the Boiler* as 'some typical elected man, emotional as a youthful chimpanzee',[14] and perhaps that 'drunken, vainglorious lout' with whom Maud Gonne/Ireland had contracted a *mésalliance. On the Boiler* begins with 'Why Should Not Old Men be Mad?' which laments Maud's and Iseult's fall from Yeatsian grace. In *Purgatory* the old man who has killed his father in the burning house now kills his son to prevent further degeneration. But his ghostly parents must endlessly relive their mis-begetting – of a nation? Yeats's imagination seems to inhabit a purgatorial Ireland which so far mocks his hopes for cultural fusion: the many Anglo-Irish houses burned down in the 1920s are a quintessential symbol. Through the 'mad' licence of his old-man protagonist, he ironically torches the devalued 'great gazebo' and pursues Lear-like revenges. So the spirit that 'suffers because of its share...in the destruction of an honoured house'[15] derives more from the twentieth century than from the nineteenth as McCormack, or the eighteenth as Donald Torchiana suggests.[16]

In this reading *Purgatory* represses worse than sectarianism. Yet we should surely focus on Yeats's disaffection from ruling Nationalism in the 1930s, rather than on the historical or literal validity of his Ascendancy myths. (*Mutatis mutandis*, the same might be said

of Seamus Heaney, ruling Unionism, and Nationalist myths.) His
houses, dynasties and marriages do not only 'attend to the decline
of Ireland's landed gentry'.[17] As a form of cultural defence, they
are metaphors for a wider Protestant predicament. We evade its
nature, its cry of distress, if we exclusively follow Seamus Deane
following McCormack:

> Yeats's account of the Anglo-Irish tradition blurs an important distinction
> between the terms 'aristocracy' and 'Ascendancy'. Had he known a little
> more about the eighteenth-century, he would have recognised that the
> Protestant Ascendancy was, then and since, a predominantly bourgeois
> social formation. The Anglo-Irish were held in contempt by the Irish-
> speaking masses as people of no blood, without lineage and with nothing
> to recommend them other than the success of their Hanoverian cause
> over that of the Jacobites.[18]

Deane's counter-assumption of Gaelic aristocracy indicates that
the Yeatsian rhetoric has some bearing on the reality of sectarian
antagonisms both in the 1930s and the 1980s. In neither case does
the point seem to be getting eighteenth-century history right. Deane,
too, goes back to the Boyne. Elsewhere he doubts the indigenous
claims of the Irish Literary Revival (as Yeats's 'Irish Ireland' opponents had done): 'The whole Irish revival is...a movement towards
the colony and away from the mother-country, a replacement of
"Englishness" by "Irishness".'[19] And he avoids mentioning the
occasion (divorce) of Yeats's most famous Protestant protest: 'When
he told the Irish Senate that the Anglo-Irish were "no petty people"
...[he] was translating into a proud assertion an almost comically
absurd historical fiction.'[20] MacNeice, closer to the event, and 'Like
Yeats...brought up in an Irish middle-class Protestant family',[21] can
translate Yeats's translation: 'Living in the Irish Free State Yeats
had come to realise more vividly the drawbacks of Catholic Ireland
...and his opinion of the old Protestant Ascendancy rose accordingly.'[22]
Detailed studies of Yeats's politics in the 1920s and 1930s, particularly those by Bernard Krimm and Paul Scott Stanfield,[23] seem
more relevant than reading 'Ascendancy' back over Yeats's entire
career and its pre-history. Deane unhistorically contrasts 'Pearse's
line of heroes (Tone, Emmet, Davis, Lalor, Mitchel) and Yeats's
line (Berkeley, Swift, Burke, Goldsmith)',[24] thus rewriting Yeats's
Nationalist record. Was it for this he wrote 'September 1913'? And
when McCormack says 'I take Protestant Ascendancy to be the
central cultural assumption of Yeats's meditation on his own inheritance. By it he measured the politics of the Irish Free State...'[25] he
underplays the extent to which the measuring-instrument was shaped

by what it measured. Yeats's fictions of Anglo-Irish history were a latent strand in his imaginative weave which might not have stood out so prominently if his early hopes for the new state had been realised.

Deane, from his contemporary standpoint, may be picking up Unionist overtones in Yeats's later writings, as does Tom Paulin when he says that 'his mature verse combines muscle-flexing Protestant triumphalism with an élitist dedication'.[26] Yet to prove Yeats a colonialist or loyalist – complete with union-jack tattoos? – is again not to hear the distressed and squeezed Protestant Nationalist for whom 'crossing the Border'[27] was never really an option. MacNeice may phrase the matter more accurately when he refers to the 'complex peculiarities of that Protestant minority to which Yeats, like many another ardent nationalist, belonged'.[28] After quoting Shaw's preface to *John Bull's Other Island* ('I am violently and arrogantly Protestant by family tradition; but let no English government therefore count on my allegiance'), MacNeice comments:

> Yeats too was born and bred Protestant (which in Ireland does imply both violence and arrogance) and, whatever his flirtations with the Cabbala, the Upanishads, and so on, and however great and understandable his envy of Maud Gonne's conversion to Rome, his motto to the end was 'No Surrender'.[29]

Yeats's poetic strategies for avoiding surrender became more extreme as he felt more besieged. The mutations of ancestral houses and eighteenth-century Protestant names are a graph of marginalisation, which reaches its nadir in *Purgatory*. Besides the state-ideology's lack of attention to Protestant liberties, there was also continuing Protestant emigration and the gradual disappearance of Yeats's cultural world. Paul Scott Stanfield concludes:

> In the 1930s his solitude increased. The ascendancy of de Valera made the Anglo-Irish tradition of independent nationalism a virtually untenable faith. Most of those with whom Yeats had at one time or another made common cause – John O'Leary, John Synge, Lady Gregory, Kevin O'Higgins, George Russell – were dead.[30]

Marginalised groups assert their presence in territorial and genealogical terms:

> I declare this tower is my symbol; I declare
> This winding, gyring, spiring treadmill of a stair is my ancestral stair;
> That Goldsmith and the Dean, Berkeley and Burke have travelled there.
>
> ('Blood and the Moon')

The higher the rhetoric and the appeal to ancestry, the lower the influence and the population-level. Thus in claiming Augustan literary kin, Yeats stresses the enduring power of their (and his) 'mind', 'head', 'intellectual fire'. 'Blood and the Moon' is Yeats's response to the murder of that honorary Protestant, Kevin O'Higgins (in 1927). The illness and death of Lady Gregory also inspired a form of defiant elegy. However, 'Coole Park, 1929' concentrates on Coole as the symbolic locus of the Irish Literary Revival ('A dance-like glory that those walls begot'); whereas in 'Coole Park and Ballylee, 1931' Yeats leads up to the Revival's epitaph – 'We were the last romantics' – with two stanzas affirming a dynastic 'great glory' which underpins the artistic achievements. Presumably Yeats is using Coole to eulogise and elegise the totality of Anglo-Irish cultural effort culminating in the Revival:

> Beloved books that famous hands have bound,
> Old marble heads, old pictures everywhere...

But boasted antiquity and fame, the metamorphoses of family into house into art, cannot withstand the sense of cultural crisis. Whereas the 'meditative' movement of 'Coole Park, 1929' is centripetal, reflecting the Revival's group-dynamics ('That seemed to whirl upon a compass-point'), the 'rant' of 'Coole Park and Ballylee, 1931' is centrifugal and headlong. In the former the swallows come and go, in the latter 'the waters race' through seven monosyllabic verbs in the first stanza and, together with the swan, represent an intensifying flux:

> But all is changed, that high horse riderless,
> Though mounted in that saddle Homer rode
> Where the swan drifts upon a darkening flood.

The new context for the refrain of 'Easter 1916' must be deliberate.

However we judge Yeats's interest in fascism or General O'Duffy,[31] it was crucially conditioned by his darkening situation as a marginalised Southern Protestant, anxious to be influential on an élitist rather than a democratic basis. When O'Duffy's school, too, proved 'a crowd' (not to mention a potential Catholic Front), like Communism and Nationalist demagoguery, Yeats opted for 'Anglo-Irish solitude', thus making a virtue of necessity. In *On the Boiler* his obsession with eugenics – 'stocks' – clearly originates in the dwindling of a community and its power: 'As the nominated [i.e. Protestant] element began to die out – almost all were old men – the Senate declined in ability and prestige.'[32] The strident tone in Yeats's last poems, which approximates to that of *On the Boiler*, also issues from Protestant marginalisation:

> Or else I thought her supernatural;
> As though a sterner eye looked through her eye

On this foul world in its decline and fall;
On gangling stocks grown great, great stocks run dry,
Ancestral pearls all pitched into a sty,
Heroic reverie mocked by clown and knave,
And wondered what was left for massacre to save.

('A Bronze Head')

Whereas in the 1920s, and in the Coole Park poems, Yeats kept aristocracy at a metaphorical distance from art, or separated his tower from Coole, in the 1930s there can be a crude convergence of aesthetic and social superiority: 'Ancestral pearls', 'Sing whatever is well-made', 'We Irish...Climb to our proper dark, that we may trace/ The lineaments of a plummet-measured face'. The strained oxymoron 'Heroic reverie' betrays an imagination under siege. Yeats's rhetoric, like his imagery, climbs on top of all his precariously balanced assets, just as the mad McCoy – evidently a Northern evangelical Protestant – ascends the boiler 'to read the Scriptures and denounce his neighbours'.[33]

Tom Paulin considers that Yeats resorted to 'a formless mystic rage' instead of 'attacking specific targets and injustices'.[34] Rather, perhaps, his weariness with the latter activity – his senatorial efforts were geared to how the state might attract Northern Protestants – led him not to AE's (George Russell's) resigned exile, but to rhetorics of 'No Surrender' in which a mysterious élite driven to the margins broods on its restoration: 'In cavern, crevice, or hole,/Defending Ireland's soul' ('Three Marching Songs'). Obviously, 'that unfashionable gyre' also has to do with Yeats's traditionalist concept of art and his hatred of modern mechanical philosophies. But one might, for instance, contrast the demeanour of Henry Middleton in 'Three Songs to the One Burden' with 'the men of the old black tower'. Middleton is evidently a marginalised Protestant reduced to ineffectual moralising, and even doing his own housework in a 'small forgotten house'. Unlike Mannion, tinker and practical eugenicist, in the previous song, Middleton's lifestyle is ironically at odds with the refrain – or is 'burden' a pun? –

From mountain to mountain ride the fierce horsemen.

The men in the tower are certainly fierce, and would have been useful at the Siege of Derry ('they but feed as the goatherd feeds'), unlike Middleton's tame domesticity. *Inter alia* the black tower may be the last redoubt of the Anglo-Irish Protestant nation, of Yeatsian Nationalism, of the dead king, Parnell:

Those banners come to bribe or threaten,
Or whisper that a man's a fool

> Who, when his own right king's forgotten,
> Cares what king sets up his rule.
> If he died long ago,
> Why do you dread us so?

Perhaps this is the Williamite spirit transposed into a Jacobite mode.

Seamus Deane and Denis Donoghue have commented on Yeats's use of the term 'We Irish' at the end of 'The Statues':

> We Irish, born into that ancient sect
> But thrown upon this filthy modern tide
> And by its formless spawning fury wrecked,
> Climb to our proper dark, that we may trace
> The lineaments of a plummet-measured face.

Both, I think, take 'We Irish' to embrace Catholic Nationalist Ireland. Deane subjects what he sees as 'an abstract idea of essence' or 'mystique of Irishness' to a critique that seems more appropriate to Pearse than to Yeats.[35] Donoghue is kinder to 'an acceptable degree of self-consciousness',[36] but also misses the point that 'We Irish' secretes a mainly Protestant essence of Irishness (years earlier Yeats had noted in his journal that 'the sense of form...has always been Protestant in Ireland').[37] It marginalises Catholic Ireland, perhaps 'spawning' as much as 'this filthy modern tide', in a rhetorical turning of the tables. Like the 'indomitable Irishry' of 'Under Ben Bulben' – 'No Surrender' with an Anglo-Irish flourish – the last stanza of 'The Statues' parallels a notorious passage in *On the Boiler*:

> although the Irish masses are vague and excitable because they have not yet been moulded and cast, we have as good blood as there is in Europe. Berkeley, Swift, Burke, Grattan, Parnell, Augusta Gregory, Synge, Kevin O'Higgins, are the true Irish people, and there is nothing too hard for such as these. If the Catholic names are few, history will soon fill the gap.[38]

'The Statues' implies that Pearse could not have 'summoned Cuchulain to his side' if the Anglo-Irish or Yeatsian plummet had not first measured the nation. Hence Yeats's entitlement to reclaim the national soul even when his voices speak from their final dark margin: *old bones upon the mountain shake.*

II

It is a tribute to Yeats's powers of rhetorical reclamation, to his territorial presence in Irish poetry, that he attracts critiques like that of Seamus Deane. The social and cultural actualities were far different. To quote from K. Theodore Hoppen's *Ireland since 1880*:

> Amidst such attacks [like those of D. P. Moran in *The Leader*] the brief moment of Anglo-Irish cultural activism soon flickered into darkness, snuffed out as effectively as were the concurrent efforts of 'constructive' unionists like Horace Plunkett to create a new rural climate in which efficiency might draw strength from a common appreciation of the importance of agrarian improvement and change.[39]

> The tragedy of southern Protestantism lies in the fact that, by the time it had developed enough confidence to accept changed circumstances, it had virtually ceased to exist. In 1911 more than a tenth of the people in the twenty-six counties were Protestant. By 1926 this had fallen to 8 per cent, by 1961 to five per cent...What [despite its comparative wealth] the Protestant community so long fatally lacked was a sense of confidence ...Many of its spokesmen oscillated between private alienation and public expressions of gratitude for not having been driven out of the country entirely.[40]

After Yeats (and AE) Irish Protestant writers no longer proclaimed their right to define the national being and defend Ireland's soul. Nevertheless, a comparison between MacNeice and Hubert Butler shows them fighting back in various ways from the heroic impasse of Yeats's last stand. Whereas MacNeice's affiliations to Britain gave him a fresh vantage-point from which to criticise both Nationalism and Unionism, Butler tried to transform the impasse by inhabiting it positively and constructively. Yet, while their writings on national questions drastically modify the Yeatsian tones and tactics, certain continuities are apparent.

Hubert Butler's remarks, quoted earlier, about the 'amiable inertia' of Southern Protestants match Hoppen's analysis. And although he was himself far from inert, it must be significant that the formidable body of his prose has been properly recognised only in the last five years with the publication of *Escape from the Anthill* (1985), *The Children of Drancy* (1988) and *Grandmother and Wolfe Tone* (1990). These volumes of essays represent a lifetime of intellectual, moral and practical effort to comprehend Ireland from an inherited minor country house near Kilkenny. Butler also draws on relevant experience in Eastern Europe and what he sees as neglected parallels between Ireland and other small nations. Like Yeats, Hubert Butler engages in a form of genealogical and territorial insistence. The difference is that he builds up a set of local instances, a network of affiliations, rather than declaring a symbolic totality. Butler's mentors from the Revival period were 'practical visionaries':[41] the Co-operative pioneers, AE and Horace Plunkett. He wrote in 1984:

> AE had believed that, as the co-operative movement developed in Ireland, a real village community would grow round every creamery and that the principle of sharing would extend into every branch of life, spiritual, economic, cultural. The communal marketing of eggs and butter would lead to more intimate and domestic forms of sharing. AE saw the hedges planted with apple trees and gooseberry bushes, as in Germany, and gymnasiums and libraries, picture galleries and village halls...so that each village became a focus of activity and debate. Sixty years ago, an ingenuous young person could really believe this would happen.[42]

Although AE died disillusioned in England and Plunkett's house Kilteragh was burned down by Republicans, Butler had learned to be a utopian. His involvement with the Irish county libraries, and with cultural and economic projects specific to Kilkenny, made him value, too, the enterprise of earlier Protestant gentry. He never qualifies his scorn for those Unionist Anglo-Irish who 'rotted from the land', in Standish O'Grady's phrase, because they did not take enough interest in it: 'they were stupid and defenceless simply because since the Union they had exported all their brightest and their bravest to England...Waterloo may or may not have been won on the playing-fields of Eton, but Ireland was certainly lost there.'[43] (Butler several times warns Ulster Unionists against a similar fate.) Yet his essays enthusiastically set straight the historical record with regard to Anglo-Irish men and women who improved their neighbourhoods, who were custodians 'of historical continuity and of identity',[44] who 'decided to study the country which they could not rule',[45] and who by their scholarly activities 'managed to prove that [they were] Irish by being indispensable to Ireland'.[46] Lady Gregory might be an example, but Butler's family histories have an empirical persuasiveness which contrasts with Yeats's romantic versions of Coole. Yet his data make the same point as Yeats's loading of the adjectives 'ancestral' and 'old'.

Hubert Butler's Nationalism is essentially a heightened, unaggressive, religious sense of nationality. He believes in putting Ireland first, and also that the national can only be realised through the local: 'I have always believed that local history is more important than national history.'[47] Again and again – in the context of the Holocaust too – he returns to the warning that our aliveness to human obligations becomes diluted by distance, by science and technology, by metropolitan and megalopolitan thinking. His essays themselves are a proof that 'Close-cropped grass comes up again fresh and sweet'.[48] Their very structure filters large ideas through the precise instance. Butler implicitly perceives this localised national and moral responsibility as Protestant in spirit: derived not merely from land-lordly duty or the leisure for scholarship, but from a metaphysic at odds with Catholic universalism. Thus, despite his own international perspectives, he defended Anglo-Irish localism against Patrick Kavanagh's breezy dismissal of the Revival's 'pygmy literature':

> The Anglo-Irish writers who surrounded Yeats deliberately left the big world for the small one. They were more afraid of being culturally sub-merged in a big empire than of being stranded in sterile isolation in a small island. Time has justified them. Work of European significance was done under the stimulus of what might be considered parochial enthusiasms...[49]

He also notes that Kavanagh 'would sooner repudiate Irish National-ism than acknowledge any cultural indebtedness to Anglo-Ireland'.[50] (A variant of the same syndrome may be present in Seamus Deane's determination to reject a 'mystique of Irishness' that has anything to do with Yeats.)

Butler's willingness to engage with Kavanagh is only one instance of his dedication to debate, to an ethic of healthy critical exchange. This was the remedy he prescribed for more than one kind of border when he wrote the manifesto for a projected journal, *The Bridge*:

> The only way of holding [borders] at bay is to have an intelligent and vigorous public opinion. At present [1954] there is, south and north of the border, an almost unbelievable spiritual stagnation. A dumb, stupid antagonism breaks into an occasional muffled snarl or jeer. Where there is disagreement, there should, at least, be the stimulus of conflict. It is from challenge and response that civilisations have arisen in the past. Why are our differences so unfruitful?
>
> Here is one reason. Too many people would sooner be silent or untruthful than disloyal to their side.[51]

In 'Portrait of a Minority' he sums up Southern Protestant reluctance to criticise the political power of the Catholic Church, or to articulate 'an abiding Protestant resentment against much that is enshrined in our laws',[52] in the caricature-figure 'Mrs A'. Mrs A (Butler's equivalent of Henry Middleton) has adapted to the new status quo but privately retains Unionist prejudices:

> Her intellect, like a barrage-balloon that has lost its moorings, hovers uncertainly between Fishguard and Rosslare. She is really more con-cerned that England should get the ports than that the Anglo-Irish should be able to raise their voices again in Ireland...For thirty years and more she has grown used to the Cassandra-like mournings of her

hybrid race; gradually they have become less shrill and have the familiar monotony of a lullaby. They save thinking.[53]

In various essays and on several celebrated public occasions Hubert Butler violated his community's code of 'appeasement' and 'discreet silence', and suffered for it.[54]

At the same time, Butler does not accept that every critic has the credentials to attack the national ethos. It is instructive to compare his response to two critiques – Honor Tracy's *Mind You, I've Said Nothing!* (1953) and Brian Inglis's *West Briton* (1962) – with reviews by Louis MacNeice. For Butler, residential qualifications are crucial. Of Miss Tracy he asks: 'is it right for anyone to be so detached? Is she not like a doctor, who knocks at our door when we are ill, checks up on our heart-beats and pulse-beats, takes samples of our blood and urine, and then without a word or a pill makes off to win a gold medal for a thesis on our disease?'.[55] He also sees her as a typical English sceptic and humanist who fails to appreciate the 'passionate [religious] beliefs' in which Ireland is more representative of Europe than is secularised England.[56]

MacNeice as an expatriate, and one philosophically divided between sceptical humanism and an Irish concern with belief, takes more pleasure in 'this brilliant and unjust book': 'Miss Tracy says a great many things which few Irishmen would have the guts and few Englishmen the wits to put down in black and white.'[57] MacNeice maintains that while Honor Tracy's 'remarks [about the Catholic Church] will pain many truly religious people...it should be remembered that many good Catholics from Catholic countries on the Continent have been shocked and depressed by the narrowness and arrogance which their own Church shows in this "most Catholic of countries".' He adds: 'I only regret that Miss Tracy has not attended in equal detail to the Orangemen.'[58] And whereas Butler feels that she has given hostages to English patronage of Irish dottiness, Mac-Neice, living in England, sees her as correcting the English disposition to sentimentalise Ireland.

West Briton is an autobiography by a Southern Protestant who broke out of a constricting and shrinking circle of old Unionists, but eventually 'as an Anglo-Irishman found it difficult to carry out his wish to contribute to the new Ireland'.[59] MacNeice himself had written in the 1940s to E.R. Dodds (an expatriate Ulsterman and former Nationalist whom Butler saw as having taken the contrary path to his own): 'I wish one could either *live* in Ireland or *feel oneself* in England.' Thus he accepts Inglis's 'sense of political impotence', and endorses his conclusion that 'If the future relationship of Church and State was sooner or later going to become the most serious political issue in Ireland, this was something that no Protestant or Anglo-Irishman could do much about.'[60] To Butler, on the other hand, Inglis appears a 'defeatist', a 'sophisticated, guilt-ridden exile' and an 'intellectual absentee', even if 'For an Irish Protestant national loyalty is a difficult and fragile growth.'[61] He sees no reason why Protestants should not argue for the separation of Church and State, North and South ('the way of Jefferson and Tone'), and is provoked into neo-Yeatsian assertion:

> Ireland still offers opportunities to the countrymen of Tone. On the way to them there is a rich crop of slights and misunderstandings to be harvested, but it is better to be arrogant like Yeats and to stay than to be deprecating like Inglis and to go. As Yeats knew, Irish independence, like American, was primarily the notion of a small Protestant minority. It is in stark opposition to the imperialist universalism of the English and to the Catholic universalism of the Irish and derives from a handful of unpopular Trinity students and a few Belfast radicals.[62]

MacNeice steers between arrogance and deprecation. His *Poetry of W.B. Yeats* (1941) reads the vulnerable subtexts of Yeats's rhetoric which have eluded many subsequent commentators. His amused or ironic tone with regard to various Yeatsian postures also extends to Yeatsian Nationalism: 'In fact the nationalists dispensed almost entirely with these writers [Lady Gregory, Synge, etc.]. It was men like the Gaelic enthusiast, Pearse, and the dockhand balladist, Connolly, who made the rising.'[63] Exclusion of Protestants from shaping the state ideology, and from Catholic Ireland in general, seems to be a premise of MacNeice's reflections on his country during the 1930s: 'Banned for ever from the candles of the Irish poor' ('Carrickfergus'); 'she will not/Have me alive or dead' ('Dublin'). Thus valediction – which might be as retrospectively self-justifying as Butler's celebrations of staying on – is the form taken by MacNeicean invective. The mode itself oscillates between detachment and attachment. On the one hand, MacNeice's comments on 'Valediction' and section XVI of *Autumn Journal* objectify them as satirical eclogue or 'overstatement'. On the other, a tone of direct political anger breaks through: 'Your drums and your dolled-up Virgins and your ignorant dead'. But in so far as the persona lays claim to any authority, it is purely autobiographical as opposed to speaking for 'We Irish':

> And I remember, when I was little, the fear
> Bandied among the servants
> That Casement would land at the pier
> With a sword and a horde of rebels...

Terence Brown feels (as Hubert Butler feels about Honor Tracy) that MacNeice does assume undue authority in the matter of criticising a new state, 'attempting a painful self-sufficiency' and at economic war with Britain.[64] Yet distance lent him a useful licence to attack more openly than Yeats, to break out of the doubly cryptic black tower. And the nature of his perceptions in *Autumn Journal* XVI, his Northern and Protestant angles, may be more significant than the degree of contemporary accuracy. Thus MacNeice's special stress on Southern self-deception, repeated in other contexts, has partly to do with Nationalist unreality regarding Unionist objections to 'rebels', partly with Irish indifference to the forces threatening Europe in the 1930s:

> Let the round tower stand aloof
> In a world of bursting mortar!
> Let the school-children fumble their sums
> In a half-dead language;
> Let the censor be busy on the books; pull down the Georgian slums;
> Let the games be played in Gaelic.

A syntax of antithesis, earlier applied to incompatible ideologies and slogans in the North, diagnoses the same perceptual and moral distortion in the Southern packaging of civil-war history: 'Let them pigeon-hole the souls of the killed/Into sheep and goats, patriots and traitors.'

MacNeice's hostility to the state's Gaelicisation policy, as not only self-deceiving but anti-progressive ('fumble their sums'), certainly parallels Unionist derision. Dennis Kennedy in *The Widening Gulf* reports that 'In terms of newspaper coverage of the South [the Irish language] occupied much more space than, for instance, the original Unionist concern over Catholic domination of an Irish parliament. The insistence by Sinn Féin that language was an essential badge of nationhood could be turned around and used to disprove the existence of a distinct Irish nation.'[65] Yet Northern Protestant paranoia on this subject also manifests fears both of cultural coercion and of exclusion from Ireland on ethnic grounds. Yeats, when a senator, had opposed compulsory Irish, as off-putting to Unionists, culturally narrow, and 'a form of insincerity that is injurious to the general intellect and thought of this country and [which] creates an irritation against the Gaelic language'.[66] (Revisiting Dublin, John Hewitt's father 'was forever naming the streets like a litany, but the new names in Irish characters he ignored').[67] Nor was the economic war a clear-cut issue of 'painful self-sufficiency'. It was contested in the Free State itself (not only by Protestant farmers) as cutting off Ireland's nose to spite Britain's face. Hoppen concludes:

While the whole affair had proved economically foolish, that had never been the main consideration...Protection would of course have been on any sensible government's menu in the 1930s. But the gay abandon with which tariffs were imposed on crucial raw materials like coal and cement, the additional complications caused by the land annuities and the unrealistic hankerings for autarky, all made things far more complicated than they need have been. At the same time, however, Fianna Fail undoubtedly delivered some real gains in social welfare, while its encouragement of local industries was by no means without positive advantages.[68]

Joseph Lee's well-received *Ireland 1912-1985: Politics and Society* (1989) incorporates a scathing attack on the Free State's economic short-sightedness.

The critique of Nationalist Ireland in *Autumn Journal* is by a poet who always cherished long-term hopes for unity. It links Yeats's sense of Anglo-Irish exclusion with the state's failure to make room for British cultural dimensions intrinsic to MacNeice's Northern and English affiliations. In 'Dublin' he reminds the city which will not have him that her own pedigree is impure: 'She is not an Irish town/And she is not English'. For MacNeice, 'Anglo-Irishness' became not a matter of race but a practical state of affairs. While not feeling 'at home' in England[69] and criticising its culture from an outsider's perspective, he lacks (on the whole) the traditional Anglo-Irish contempt for the English. Further, he regarded the Irish hankering for autarky or self-sufficiency as a denial of complex ties ('Let the round tower stand aloof'). His earlier indulgence towards Irish neutrality changed sharply when his English friend Graham Shepard was drowned in the North Atlantic. His controversial accusation in 'Neutrality', that 'the mackerel/Are fat – on the flesh of your kin', raises unresolved issues about the 'kinship' of Ireland to Britain, about the intermediate position of Anglo-Irishmen and Ulster Protestants, about archipelagic interpenetrations. But many Catholic Irishmen fought in the Second World War. Hubert Butler found himself in unusual difficulties when he tried to square this fact with the state-policy, and to reconcile his Nationalism and his anti-Fascism.[70]

MacNeice's wartime situation as a 'nomad who has lost his tent',[71] and his pervasive imagery of transient homes, broadly belongs to the Anglo-Irish diaspora symbolised by the burnt house in *Purgatory*:

> I admit that for myself I cannot straiten
>   My broken rambling track
> Which reaches so irregularly back
>   To burning cities and rifled rose bushes
> And cairns and lonely farms
>   Where no one lives, makes love or begets children...
>   (*Autumn Journal*, XXIII)

And after the war, in 'Western Landscape', a poem of fleeting
return to Ireland, he characterised himself as 'neither Brandan/Free
of all roots nor yet a rooted peasant'. MacNeice's thirties' utopias
had tried, indeed, to conceive the best of British and Irish worlds:
to combine the assets of a traditional, rooted, 'island' society with a
modern fluidity. Thus he updates Yeats by pitting 'peasant' individuality more directly against the Marxist 'mass-production of neat
thoughts' ('Turf-stacks'); or by recasting unity of being and unity
of culture in democratic Socialist terms:

> a possible land...
> Where life is a choice of instruments and none
>   Is debarred his natural music,
> Where the waters of life are free of the ice-blockade of hunger
>   And thought is free as the sun...
> (*Autumn Journal*, XXIV)

Perhaps MacNeice's communal vision and his dialectic between
roots and mobility strike more chords in the contemporary Republic
than they once did. At the same time, his Protestant sense of 'dis-
franchisement' has a legacy in the reduced or tentative territorial
claims evident in the western landscapes of some Northern Irish
Protestant poets (Derek Mahon, Michael Longley), just as hesitant
when it comes to putting 'a stone on the cairn' or 'a word on the
wind'.

John Hewitt's claims are not tentative, though insecurities may
underlie them. But, confined to Northern Ireland, they lack the
residual Anglo-Irish possession in MacNeice's all-Ireland panoramas.
Yet Ulster gave Hewitt space to ponder his relation to Ireland and
to Nationalism: 'This is my home and country. Later on/perhaps
I'll find this nation is my own' ('Conacre', 1943). Hewitt's messianic
prospectus for regionalism in the 1940s and early 1950s may not,
as he later admitted, have sufficiently taken into account Catholic
or western Ulster. Nevertheless, it perhaps provided a more robust
social model than Hubert Butler's expanding parish based on the
receding big house, or MacNeice's hybrid utopias and western epiph-
anies. Hewitt took as a lifelong text Samuel Ferguson's 'Mesgedra':
'No rootless colonist of an alien earth'. His version of roots and
earth is less archetypal than Yeats's 'deep-rooted things' or 'contact
with the soil'. Founded on an agricultural proto-bourgeoisie, rather
than an ancient 'peasantry', it invokes planter-work and 'all the
buried men/in Ulster clay'. Also Hewitt's self-plantation as 'a
rooted man', his deliberate Ulster literary regionalism, may preclude
the grand inclusive parochialism of the Revival. Further back,

Hewitt found a touchstone in the 'rooted activity' of the Ulster-Scots rhyming weavers, rather than the 'English colonial' verses of Church of Ireland clergymen, doctors and schoolteachers.[72] For a combination of idealistic, artistic, socialist, and no doubt obliquely territorial motives, Hewitt embarked on an extensive recuperation of Ulster cultural history: for instance, researching all the writers and painters of the North-east to underpin the contemporary movement. His regionalist projects were undertaken *in opposition* to the 'English colonial' panic which led Unionism to cling culturally to 'the mainland' and forget its own history in Ireland. In the manifesto for *The Bridge* Hubert Butler says: 'the province has the artificial vitality of the garrison town and no organic life'. Meanwhile, Hewitt was acting on Butler's concern that 'Ulster would be of no value to Ireland if she were robbed of her rich history, her varied traditions'.[73] (Butler, MacNeice and Hewitt agree on their dislike of Unionist efforts to become 'more English than the English'.) Hewitt was always conscious of Ulster in Ireland, however regional his focus. Nevertheless, he relished his affiliations to certain English traditions, without hatred torturing him with love in Yeatsian or Anglo-Irish style:

> My mother tongue is English, instrument and tool of my thought and expression; John Ball, the Diggers, the Levellers, the Chartists, Paine, Cobbett, Morris, a strong thread in the fabric of my philosophy, I learned about in English history...I also draw upon an English literary tradition which includes Marvell, Crabbe, Wordsworth, Clare...[74]

Hewitt's writings betray an Ulster awareness of sectarian difference which contrasts with Butler's focus on mentalities and Yeats's refusal to admit directly (in his poetry at least) that he does not speak for the whole of Ireland. Thus when Hewitt is 'In the Rosses' he perceives 'the hospitable Irish' as other; when in the glens of Antrim, although an atheist, he distinguishes his Methodist family tradition from people 'of a vainer faith'; and among Catholic emigrants to Coventry he sits 'in enclave of my nation, but apart'. However, for all his wariness of the Anglo-Irish (which extends to a suspicion of high style) Hewitt must have modelled his Ulster regionalism on the Revival as well as on Scottish or Welsh literary Nationalism (themselves indebted to the Irish example). His cultural entrepreneurship resembles the hyper-activity of the early Yeats[75]. Also, 'Freehold', his rhapsodic celebration of the region (1946), might be retitled 'The Regional Being' by analogy with AE's *The National Being*. Thus Hewitt in the North complements Hubert Butler as a practical visionary, a pragmatic defender of

Ireland's soul. And his mystique of Ulsterness also owes something to Protestant Nationalist ideology, even if he left his utopian options open between 'a federated British Isles, or a federal Ireland':[76]

> I know my corner in the universe;
> my corner, this small region limited
> in space by sea, in time by my own dead...
>   ('Freehold')

A final word on Wolfe Tone, still the object of mixed literary idealism as well as of competition between Republican parties. Protestant and Catholic Nationalism also converge on Tone, but there the misunderstandings begin. The idea that an embryonic non-sectarian Eden or 'sweet/equal Republic' (Tom Paulin) was aborted in 1798 has been upset by research such as Marianne Elliott's: 'to assume that radicalism and anti-catholicism cannot exist within Presbyterianism is to misconceive its true nature. Anti-catholicism is part of that radicalism, and the United Irishmen were less tolerant in religious matters than later nationalist tradition cared to admit.'[77] Or, alternatively, as Hoppen puts it: 'The secular Republicanism of Tone, though not entirely destroyed, was to survive largely through the muffled and garbled filter produced by the sectarian concerns of the [Catholic] Defender tradition.'[78] I have suggested in 'Progressive Bookmen' that the interest of modern Northern Protestant (and indeed Catholic) writers in 1798 itself reflects diverse sectarian and political dispositions. Thus I feel that Paulin's *Liberty Tree* simplifies history and literary history when he mythologises too sharp a contrast between radical Presbyterianism and contemporary 'Desertmartin', ignoring all intermediate Protestant complexities: 'I see a culture of twigs and bird-shit/Waving a gaudy flag it loves and curses'. Hewitt, for instance, is much less interested in the Anglo-Irish Tone or the 'united' aspect of the United Irishmen, than in 'the stocky figure of James Hope': his 'fine, sinewy, balanced prose', his 'stubborn attitude'[79] ('stubborn' is Hewitt's stocky version of Yeats's 'indomitable') and his status as 'the only one of them all to grasp firmly the class complications in the struggle which they had waged'.[80] Hubert Butler, constant in his loyalty to Tone, interprets Tone's Nationalism as 'neighbourliness and shared experiences and a common devotion to the land in which you live'.[81]

As we have seen, such devotion need not term itself 'Nationalist'. The Protestant authors I have considered all in some sense unravel the dark encodings of Yeats's last writings. Their imaginative possession of Ireland is hedged, to varying degrees, by awareness that it might be disputed. Yet they have not quite surrendered the idea

that their works do as much to 'defend Ireland's soul' as does orthodox Nationalist faith. Whether fighting a brave rearguard action
(Butler), making occasional raids from across the water (MacNeice),
or securing a Northern 'corner' (Hewitt), they have not utterly
lost touch with the belief of William Drennan, Belfast Presbyterian
United Irishman, that: 'The Catholics may save themselves, but it
is the Protestants must save the nation.'

[1990]

'When Did You Last See Your Father?'

Perceptions of the Past in Northern Irish Writing 1965-1985

I

In Irish literature the past as a continuum looms larger than the past as mortality. Edward Thomas said that Villon 'inaugurated modern literature with the cry – *Mais où sont les neiges d'antan?*'[1] That cry pervades Hardy's poetry, for instance, which Seamus Heaney partly misreads in this Irish-angled comment on 'The Garden Seat':

> The poem is about the ghost-life that hovers over the furniture of our lives, about the way objects can become temples of the spirit. To an imaginative person, an inherited possession like a garden seat is not just an *objet*, an antique...rather it becomes a point of entry into a common emotional ground of memory and belonging. It can transmit the climate of a lost world and keep alive in us a domestic intimacy with realities that might otherwise have vanished.[2]

But the point about all Hardy's ghosts, unlike Heaney's, is that they are dead:

> Here was the former door
> Where the dead feet walked in.
> ('The Self-Unseeing')

Whereas Hardy is obsessed, to use Samuel Hynes's phrase, with 'the irreversible pastness of the past',[3] Irish writers are more likely to be obsessed with its irreversible presentness. David Martin punctuates his novel *The Ceremony of Innocence* (1977) with symbolic appearances by Shellshock Sam, still fighting the battle of the Somme in his head:

> Lieutenant Sam Ogilby, of the 36th (Ulster) Division, made up primarily of the Ulster Volunteer Force.
> Has he found his ghosts?
> His ghosts are real.[4]

Notoriously, the two communities in Northern Ireland cannot arrive at an agreed version of the past, let alone the present or future. (Prehistoric Navan Fort has been proposed as the mystic point where parallel lines might meet.) The increasingly subtle findings of historians have inspired no revisionist Orange banners or west Belfast murals. A soldier in Frank McGuinness's play *Observe the Sons of Ulster Marching Towards the Somme* (1985) – another gathering of ghosts in a character's head – speaks for many. As his comrades in the trenches pass the time by re-enacting the Battle of the Boyne (a play-battle within a play-battle) he calls anxiously 'Don't change

the result'. This scene registers historical cause and effect, and
the sacrosanct tribal tableau which secures the latter. The Somme
itself, of course, figures on Orange banners; while the play, as a
less immobilised account of history, indicates yet again how 1969
re-activated the past in the imagination of writers. The artistic
consequences need not only be painful or on the grand scale. An
unprecedented flood of personal and local reminiscence[5] signals
some effort at more total communal recall: to set down or set straight
small bits of the record. A recent addition to this literature is *The
Last Romantic Out of Belfast* (1984), a first novel by Sam Keery
(born 1930), who evokes his Second World War childhood. When
the hero Joe McCabe finally emigrates, he compares Belfast viewed
from a distance with Carlyle's history of *The French Revolution*,
and contrasts both with the intimate close-ups in his own memory
and by implication in the novel: 'The thought occurred to him
that history, like mountains, can be seen whole only from afar.'[6]

But if memoirs in the form of fiction, poetry and drama, as
well as 'straight' autobiography are complicating the map of the
past, for most Ulster people the changed present has rendered the
past more unchanging, confirmed the simplest stories the tribes
have formerly told themselves. Graham Reid's play *Remembrance*
(1984) centres on the intensified habit of mutually exclusive commemoration. A stylised cemetery dominates the stage, and the mother
of a dead IRA man and the father of a dead RUC man tend hostile
graves. Paul Muldoon's poem 'Come into My Parlour' also uses a
cemetery to represent history as not only fixed, but fixed in advance.
The poem hits at 'the vanity of ruling beyond the grave' by making
the graveyard rule, and pre-empt the individual's life history. Coulter
the gravedigger, predeterminantly named after a ploughshare, itself
an Ulster cultural determinant, 'knows' where everyone belongs:

> What Coulter took as his text
> Was this bumpy half-acre of common.
> Few graves were named or numbered
> For most were family plots.
> He knew exactly which was which
> And what was what...

'This bumpy half-acre of common' allegorises Ulster, Ulster history,
and history in Ulster: the past as the future. Muldoon obviously
supplies a 'text' and a reading (or moral) that query Coulter's posi-
tivism. This essay will conclude with a discussion of Muldoon's
poetry as historical and literary-historical revisionism. For instance,
'Come into My Parlour' might be read as an inversion and sub-

version of Seamus Heaney's 'Digging'. More generally, it suspects all invitations issued by ancestral voices.

II

'Come into My Parlour' exemplifies a tension between creative dynamic and historical stasis which contributes to the strengths of Northern Irish poetry in particular, and which has various issues in the work of Brian Friel, John Montague, Seamus Heaney, Michael Longley, Derek Mahon, Tom Paulin, Brian Moore, Maurice Leitch, David Martin and Bernard Mac Laverty. My quotation, 'When did you last see your father?', suggests one means of getting at the various configurations the past assumes in their imaginations. It implies, first, the amazing popularity of this motif; secondly, that father-figures may bear a changing relation to actuality even in Ulster. It's through parents that the individual locates himself or herself in history, and Irish history remains in many respects a family affair. (The Unionist parties sometimes call themselves 'the Unionist family', presumably aping the Mafia. Ditto the Republicans.) Ulster society, too, still revolves around family and kin. In 'Come into my Parlour' the speaker sees history's web as 'family plots' – punning on graves, conspiracies, and tales of the predictable: 'the grave of my mother,/My father's grave, and his father's...'

Introducing his anthology *Irish Poets 1924-1974* David Marcus notes 'the profusion of poems about the poets' fathers or mothers or other near-relations', and surmises 'that such ancestral homage could be a substitute for the fervorous patriotic themes beloved of earlier poets and denied by the changed times to their successors'.[7] It could indeed or, since times change so slowly in the North, might mark a staging-post. Marcus also underestimates the genealogical obsessions that pervade Irish culture. Of course the relationship between father and son (as increasingly between mother and daughter) has often focused new definitions of social and artistic identity – for example, in British literature of the 1950s. However, Ulster conservatism complicates filial rebellion, whether in fact or fiction. In Dan Magee's play *Horseman, Pass By* (1984) a father and son violently quarrel about the latter's involvement with the IRA.[8] In Bernard Mac Laverty's story 'Father and Son'[9] silent parallel monologues voice the same issue. Both works end in violence without essentially resolving the question of how the generations divide up reaction and revolution between them. Twenty years ago Brian Moore's novel *The Emperor of Ice-Cream*, set during the Second

World War, affirmed the values of freedom from the sectarian past. Gavin Burke's father, given to 'pious prate about Catholicism' and pro-Hitler 'fascist leanings in politics'[10] finally admits error, while Gavin thinks: 'His father was the child now; his father's world was dead.'[11] Maurice Leitch's *The Liberty Lad* published in the same year (1965), and also a *Bildungsroman*, follows Frank Glass's growing distance, as an upwardly mobile schoolteacher (courtesy of the 11-plus), from a Protestant working-class background. The novel ends with his mill-worker father's funeral, and these sentences:

> He thought that I was at last weeping for the loss of my father, but I wasn't. I was crying for the loss of someone else, me, as I had been once, three, four years...a year ago.[12]

The Liberty Lad features a Unionist MP, yet hardly touches on political matters. The MP resembles power-figures in British fifties and sixties fiction (such as *Lucky Jim* or *Room at the Top*) to whose class-patterns, and pattern-breaking, the novel adheres.

The social findings of *The Liberty Lad* are not necessarily contradicted by Leitch's later novel *Stamping Ground* (1975); but progress, mobility and growing pains are replaced by heavily emphasised circularity, the 'smug circling continuum' deplored by local historian Barbour Brown.[13] The novel's setting steps back in time to 1950, and in place from the small-town Ulster of *The Liberty Lad* (between country and city) to a Protestant rural heartland. And instead of Frank Glass's exploited father, sick and working in a dying trade, we meet a clutch of powerful and unpleasant patriarchs: notably, Henry Gault whose

> existence was as undeviating as a furrow he would set himself to plough... He moved through each day along a similarly straight course from dawn to an early bed-time and he judged everything and everyone he came in contact with – wife, son, servant, beast, implement – by the same standards he set himself.[14]

All the patriarchs in the novel blight the social, personal and sexual development of their offspring. Any prospect of 'liberty' seems minimal.

Outside my period, Sam Hanna Bell in *December Bride* (1951) created a more likeable Presbyterian farmer-patriarch; as does Seamus Heaney in 'The Other Side', which relishes 'each patriarchal dictum'. However, Presbyterianism and Protestantism have no monopoly of patriarchy. The allegory of Ireland as female and England as conquering, rapist male (re-cycled in Heaney's poem 'Act of Union') masks the masculine and authoritarian character of Catholic as well as

Protestant Irish culture.[15] In *Church and State in Modern Ireland*
John Whyte observes: 'deference to authority has been a feature
not just of Irish ecclesiastical life, but of Irish life in general'.[16] De
Valera as 'the chief', national founding-father and custodian of the
past, managed to fuse the auras of father as paterfamilias and
father as priest. Muldoon's poem 'Cuba' makes this link, together
with an Irish-American political connection. A father telling off his
daughter for 'Running out to dances in next to nothing' goes on:

> 'Those Yankees were touch and go as it was –
> If you'd heard Patton in Armagh –
> But this Kennedy's nearly an Irishman
> So he's not much better than ourselves.
> And him with only to say the word.
> If you've got anything on your mind
> Maybe you should make your peace with God.' [17]

In the last stanza the girl confesses 'Bless me, Father, for I have
sinned'. But the poem in fact exposes the sins of fathers, men laying
down the law, controlling women and taking up arms.

Fathers in Northern Irish literature calibrate tradition and transition, small shifts in the land of 'Not an Inch'. Muldoon calls it
'writing about what is immediately in front of me, or immediately
over my shoulder'.[18] If I now concentrate chiefly upon poetic
fathers, it is because poetry more radically transmutes the autobiographical into the symbolic, looks further round the corner of the
status quo. The actual fathers of poets include the following mixed
bag: a Belfast shipyard worker, a South Derry cattle-dealer and small
farmer, a Brooklyn exile, a market-gardener in Armagh orchard-
country, a headmaster, and an English furniture salesman who
fought in both world wars. The generation gaps span movements
from country to city, from country to country, and in all but one
case to a university education never achieved by the father.

Brian Friel's drama has close associations with poetry, and the
fathers in his plays since 1969 represent one pole of perception. In
Aristocrats and *Translations* they personify the inadequacy of what
the past has transmitted. The 'aristocratic' O'Donnells of Ballybeg
Hall are described, with Friel's evident sanction, as:

> four generations of a great Irish Catholic legal dynasty...a family with-
> out passion, without loyalty, without commitments; administering the
> law for anyone who happened to be in power; above all wars and famines
> and civil strife and political upheaval; ignored by its Protestant counter-
> parts, isolated from the mere Irish...[19]

Symbolically maimed by a stroke, the current head of the house
focuses the play's attack on collaborationist, Redmondite, West British

traditions in Irish politics. (Oddly, *Aristocrats* is usually interpreted as an exercise in Chekhovian melancholia.) Hugh, the hedge-school-master father in *Translations*, is more positively conceived. From the historical moment preceding the O'Donnells' amoral deracination, he hands on authentic qualities and traditions of 'the mere Irish'. Nevertheless, the play criticises his pandering to colonialist expectations about the drunken, verbalising Irishman, who speaks a 'language ...full of the mythologies of fantasy and hope and self-deception'.[20] Hugh's son Owen, once a literal and metaphorical 'collaborator' in the Ordnance Survey of Ireland (begun in the 1820s), finally rejects his own compromises and his father's 'confusion',[21] when the British soldiers threaten the community. In both these plays the sense of weak fathers having let down their children makes a political comment on the history of Northern Catholics since 1921. This may be why Friel misrepresents the Ordnance Survey as an imposed Anglicisation, rather than as an effort – supervised by the best Gaelic scholars – to standardise the orthography of Gaelic place-names. (J.H. Andrews, historian of the Ordnance Survey, has recently castigated 'the credulity shown by serious scholars in swallowing *Translations* as a record of historical truth or at any rate historical probability'.[22])

The work of three poets from Protestant backgrounds situates the father with reference to rejection, reinvention, dislocation. Derek Mahon's poetry takes as its premise, even its *sine qua non*, alienation from familial and tribal origins. In 'Ecclesiastes', which satirises the Protestant religious and political will to domination, the speaker resists blood-calls to 'nourish a fierce zeal' and

> love the January rains when they
> darken the dark doors and sink hard
> into the Antrim hills, the bog meadows, the heaped
> graves of your fathers.[23]

'Fathers', with its biblical ring, is a common Protestant word for ancestry and history. John Hewitt's best-known poem, 'Once Alien Here', begins 'Once alien here my fathers built their house', and Mahon's 'Canadian Pacific' evokes Ulster-Scots and Scots noncon-formist emigrants to the new world as 'Those gaunt forefathers'. Mahon has written no poem based on his actual father; but his early poems about anarchic male relatives – 'Grandfather' and 'Wicked Uncle' – imply a son's revolt by subverting 'adult' bourgeois Prot-estant respectability.His patriarchal poles seem to be the wrathful father and the renegade.

Tom Paulin's *Liberty Tree* (1983) attacks Protestant culture in more narrowly political terms: Protestantism as Unionism. In 'Father of History' he seems to invent an ideal forebear, a schoolmaster who builds

> Lisburn like a warm
> plain-spoken sermon on the rights of man.
> A sunned Antrim face, he maybe prays
> to the New Light in a relished dialect... [24]

Certainly a sunnier Antrim than Mahon's. This prelapsarian vision of the Protestant United Irishmen who *should* have begotten history, names the specific Republican fathers of its attitudes: 'Munro, Hope, Porter and McCracken.'

In Michael Longley's poetry the father focuses questions of belonging rather than longing: an Englishman who fought twice for his country. The poem 'Second Sight'[25] imagines a disorienting visit to London during which the speaker asks: 'Where is my father's house, where my father?', what of an English dimension in Ireland, an Irish dimension in England? There is a contrast between two poems about the father's war-service written before and after 1969. The earlier, 'In Memoriam',[26] sets out to 'read' the father's personal 'history' as a means of comprehending the 'death and nightmare' of the Great War. The later poem, 'Wounds',[27] uses the father's witness of the war – 'the Ulster Division at the Somme/Going over the top with "Fuck the Pope!"/"No surrender!" ' – as a perspective on civil war in Ulster, on the still more quintessential futility of deaths such as a bus-conductor

> shot through the head
> By a shivering boy who wandered in
> Before they could turn the television down
> Or tidy away the supper dishes.
> To the children, to a bewildered wife,
> I think 'Sorry Missus' was what he said.

Paul Fussell comments: 'the irony always associated with the Somme attack remains to shade that conclusion. But at least the Somme attack had some swank and style: one could almost admire, if afterward one had to deplore.'[28]

To digress briefly from fathers: the Somme occupies the imaginations of Longley, Martin, Leitch (Barbour Brown reflects: 'So many of his friends' names in the Deaths column of *The Ballymena Observer*'),[29] McGuinness. The latter, who comes from Donegal, is unique in approaching the theme from a background supposedly alien. More commonly, the world wars divide imaginations, if more subtly than the way Remembrance Day every November divides Dublin. Denial of any Catholic Irish participation in the wars resembles the cultural suppression that obliges Paulin's Protestant United Irishmen to 'endure posterity without a monument'. By a nice paradox, Stewart Parker's play about McCracken, *Northern Star* (1984), attracted Belfast audiences as much as *Observe the Sons of Ulster* drew Dublin. This may help to change something, if not any results. However, Seamus Heaney's poem 'In Memoriam Francis Ledwidge'[30] finds this Irish Catholic's involvement in the war imaginatively unresolvable, although the theme clearly compels him. Whereas for Longley the English 'soldier-poets' such as Isaac Rosenberg and Edward Thomas are declared literary-historical touchstones, Heaney's 'In Memoriam' regrets: 'In you, our dead enigma, all the strains/Criss-cross in useless equilibrium' ('strains' puns on another genetic definition of history). Nevertheless, the poem's own bloodline includes one trope of First World War poetry, the haunting rural flashback, in the beautiful image: 'Ghosting the trenches with a bloom of hawthorn'. Other elegies by Heaney recall Wilfred Owen.

In telling Ledwidge, 'You were not keyed or pitched like these true-blue ones', which may impute undue patriotism to the British dead ('True Blue' figures on Orange banners), manifests a deep Northern assumption about tribal inheritance. John Montague's *The Rough Field* is grounded on such assumptions. 'The Cage'[31] introduces the poet's father as 'My father, the least happy man I have known' and also refers to 'the lost years in Brooklyn'. 'Molly Bawn', in *The Dead Kingdom* (1984) still more explicitly places the father in the context of 'the embittered diaspora of/dispossessed Northern Republicans'. The next poem, 'A Muddy Cup', explores the poet's separation as a child, not only from his father, but from his mother who gave him to be fostered. This family 'diaspora', echoing in the repeated adjective 'lost', both underlies and underlines the historical losses mourned by *The Rough Field*: 'shards of a lost tradition'; a dead Gaelic civilisation; the vanished, vanquished O'Neills; the Flight of the Earls; the 'Loss' column of the New Omagh Road balance sheet; 'Our finally lost dream of man at home/ in a rural setting.'

Montague's Tyrone terrain shows how local as well as family history influences the shape of the past in a poet's imagination. Local historical societies are much thicker on the ground in the North than in the South, perhaps for obvious territorial reasons: every Northerner is an amateur local historian. Barbour Brown's obsessive researches into his 'Valley' parallel Leitch's own curiosity. Brown progresses from church records to 'lists of rocks and plants and buildings' to a voyeuristic interest in 'the forked animal again', thus becoming 'this spy creeping about the hedgerows'.[32] Similarly, Paul Muldoon's poetry can be read as alternative, transgressive parish-history. Seamus Heaney presents South Derry as a lusher field than Montague's Tyrone, and as the product of more complex geographical and historical co-ordinates. 'Terminus', from the pamphlet *Hailstones* (1984), ends on a vista of less than total loss:

> Baronies, parishes met where I was born.
> When I stood on the central stepping stone
>
> I was the last earl on horseback in midstream
> Still parleying, in earshot of his kernes.[33]

Heaney's midpoint 'parleying' gives rise to more than one version of the past in his poetry, even different fathers. At the outset (mid-sixties) the figure based on his actual father sums up a positive inheritance of skills and values which the poet transmutes within his own medium. Several poems dwell on the responsibility of 'following', and being followed by, earlier generations. In 'Follower' qualities of the father define qualities of the poetry: technical 'expertise', weight: 'His shoulders globed like a full sail.' The sense of ancestral solidity, rich rural continuity, in *Death of a Naturalist* (1966) is disturbed by those literal 'skeletons' from the past who appear in two Famine poems. Later, *Wintering Out* (1972) leads Heaney 'into [the] trail' of more insubstantial forebears than his farming fathers. Flitting wraiths symbolise discontinuities rather than continuity: the deprivations and repressions both of Irish history in the long term, and Ulster history in the short term. Heaney's gloss on 'The Tollund Man' initiates him into this tragic family: '[he] seemed to me like an ancestor almost, one of my old uncles, one of those moustached archaic faces you used to meet all over the Irish countryside.'[34] ('Moustached archaic faces' is, curiously, a quotation from Philip Larkin's poem 'MCMXIV'.) In contrast with the Tollund Man's attenuated condition, the early poem 'Ancestral Photograph' begins: 'Jaws puff round and solid as a turnip.' Heaney's most celebrated poem about his father, 'The Harvest Bow' in *Field Work* (1979), reinstates him as Jung's Wise Old Man archetype. A renewed vision of poetry as calling on the father's 'gift' and 'mellowed silence', rather than breaking silences of dispossession, poetry as peace-maker despite the changed 'spirit' of the times, attaches to

> a drawn snare
> Slipped lately by the spirit of the corn
> Yet burnished by its passage, and still warm.

III

Northern Irish poetry sometimes echoes, more often revises, philosophies of history articulated by historians and politicians. What might be termed 'the aspirational approach' tends to receive least modification – Nationalist history still proving its literary seductiveness. Exemplified by Paulin's *Liberty Tree* this approach derives from the corporate Field Day position, including more complex manifestations in Friel's drama. Seamus Deane's introduction to Friel's *Selected Plays* stresses how sundered Donegal haunts his imagination as 'a powerful image of possibility'.[35] This image crystallises Friel's protest against what Deane calls 'the sense of a whole history of failure concentrated into a crisis over a doomed community or group'.[36] Pointing to the sources of Friel's themes in a community robbed by history, robbed of history, Deane repeats such words and phrases as 'depressed and depressing atmosphere', 'apathy', 'desolation', 'failure', 'crisis', 'socially depressed and politically dislocated'. This language partly derives from psychology: the terminology for depressive psychosis. Friel in *Translations* applies a kind of therapy to this psychosis by offering Northern Catholics an alternative history, cultural self-respect, however 'doomed' that Gaelic culture itself is shown to be. *Translations* can be read as an 'image of possibility' to redeem the more recent past in the North: an aisling. It fits Oliver MacDonagh's phrase for the goal of Gaelic revivalists in the twenties: a 'land...repeopled, in imagination, by a pre-colonial society, free of the stains and shames of anglicisation'.[37] The aisling is the cultural figure that exemplifies the paralysing contradiction between epochalism and essentialism in Irish Nationalism.

Liberty Tree, too, sets out to 'father history', to sire the future on 'images of the past'. Paulin's 'image of possibility' for Ireland, for the Protestant people of the North, is a date – 1798. Another date, 1912, represents the contrasting nadir, and completes his vision of Ulster history as decline and fall from an ideal. 'Desertmartin' '[sees] a plain/Presbyterian grace sour, then harden,/As a free strenuous spirit changes/To a servile defiance'. Decline and fall, like failure and possibility, rules out merely developmental and evolutionary understandings of history. Even Paulin's 'critical position ...is founded on an idea of identity which has as yet no formal or institutional existence. It assumes the existence of a non-sectarian, republican state which comprises the whole island of Ireland.'[38] The aisling as literary theory? Similarly, Paulin's Field Day pamphlet, *A New Look at the Language Question*, proposes a more 'institutional existence' for

the English language in Ireland, a dictionary to codify what he
regards as linguistic and literary 'anarchy'.[39] This aspiration towards
an ideal language sometimes distracts the actual language of Paulin's
poetry. Words, on the whole, take an evolutionary view of themselves,
'Worn new' in Edward Thomas's paradox. Paulin's impatience to
establish a new vocabulary, to reconstitute 'a relished [Ulster] dialect',
gives words like the following little time to settle: 'glooby', 'scuffy',
'claggy', 'choggy'. As well as adjectives which aspire to exist, Paulin
also repeats adjectives of aspiration 'green', 'sweet', 'equal'. And
his poetry's general dependence on adjectives seems to me over-
insistent, willed, willing – an effort to institutionalise the future.

   Paulin aspires to redeem history, to start again from 1798 with
'a pure narrative before him' ('L'Envie de Commencement'). Derek
Mahon's greater pessimism about the sin of being born into history
begets a recurrent imaginative hankering to abolish 'daylong/twilights
of misery', to cut short its universally disastrous course. If Paulin
often approaches history with Calvinist denunciation, Mahon more
radically transposes the evangelist *alter ego* he satirises in 'Ecclesiastes'.
'Another Sunday Morning' in *The Hunt by Night* (1982) calls poetry
'A sort of winged sandwich board/El-Grecoed to receive the Lord'.
This disposition to say 'The End is Nigh' makes him in one sense
a son of his fathers. Mahon's fundamentalist view of Ulster Protestants as 'a lost tribe', rather than the elect, extends to the whole
human race, and its lack of truly human or spiritual qualities. His
poetry's grand prophetic sweep embraces 'civilisations', the beginning
and the end, 'the biblical span'; contracts history into a Beckettian
'instant'. 'Another Sunday Morning' casts the poet as 'A chiliastic
prig', i.e. a millenarian. John Wilson Foster, discussing millenarian
aspects of W.R. Rodgers's vision, cites millenarianism as a tradition
which looks for 'sudden divine intervention to destroy the existing
order'.[40] Mahon's less 'enthusiastic' version dispenses with divine
agency and ecstatic revelation, but projects spiritual renewal through
destruction (compare *Women in Love*). However, man may not be
among the worthy permitted to survive. In 'The Antigone Riddle'[41]

   Shy minerals contract at the sound of his voice,
   Cod point in silence when his bombers pass,
   And the windfall waits
   In silence for his departure
   Before it drops in
   Silence to the long grass.

'Matthew V. 29-30'[42] preaches an absurdist but logical sermon on
the text 'Lord, mine eye offended, so I plucked it out'. Here the

poet intervenes to destroy the 'offending' world himself, including 'evaporation of all seas,/the extinction of heavenly bodies'. Although the first line of 'A Disused Shed in Co. Wexford' gives history a last chance –

> Even now there are places where a thought might grow –

Mahon's historical consciousness, as guilty and punitive as Beckett's, not only turns biblical Protestantism inside out, but contradicts Whig history and deplores Belfast's industrial history. His poetry denies progress, views the rise of the bourgeoisie as a descent into 'barbarism', and cries woe to a houseproud 'civilisation':

> on
> stormy nights our strong
> double glazing groans with
> foreknowledge of death,
> the fridge with a great wound...
> ('Gipsies')[43]

Michael Longley's perception of history, lacking Paulin's and Mahon's religious and prophetic colouring, concentrates on the empirical issue of whether different histories can be accommodated, either imaginatively or communally, in a context symbolised by the last line of 'Letter to Seamus Heaney'[44] as 'A wind-encircled burial mound' – another cemetery. 'On Slieve Gullion'[45] specifically musters such histories:

> On Slieve Gullion 'men and mountain meet',
> O'Hanlon's territory, the rapparee,
> Home of gods, backdrop for a cattle raid,
> The Lake of Cailleach Beara at the top
> That slaked the severed head of Conor Mor...

One figure in the landscape is 'A paratrooper on reconnaissance' who 'sweats up the slopes of Slieve Gullion/With forty pounds of history on his back' – a sign of intertextual dialogue with Seamus Heaney's 'The Toome Road',[46] in which a speaker who encounters camouflaged armoured cars opposes to their intrusive presence 'The invisible, untoppled omphalos'. In 'On Slieve Gullion' Longley registers his own English connections in the phrase 'Both strangers here', and leaves the poem's mythic and historical ingredients in a state of suspension on the mountain. This implies the contemporary scarcity of such balm as 'slaked the severed head of Conor Mor'. As in 'Wounds', Longley's version of decline and fall differs from Paulin's.

But if 'On Slieve Gullion' finds no answers to the weight of the past, to 'forty pounds of history', it does not embrace the deter-

minism which characterises John Montague's vision and which
derives from the 'integrity of [the] quarrel' between the Ulster communities, 'two crazed peoples'[47] – an emphasis that contrasts with
Friel's concentration on the Catholic communal psyche. Montague
favours the word 'again': 'Again that note!', 'Once again, it happens';
'Again, the unwinding road'.[48] A hazard of perceiving events as
cyclical, is that style, too, can develop habits of repetition. 'Pattern'
and 'ritual', also favourite words, sometimes apply to Montague's
own technique, stiffening poems into a species of heraldry which
excludes or precludes the active verb, rhythmical dynamic. The main
process attributed to history concerns what is 'lost' or 'gone' (another
favourite word), with loss itself a pattern – familial in the poem
called 'Process':[50] 'time's gullet devouring/parents whose children/
are swallowed in turn'. After 1969 history repeats itself in Montague's
imagination, presents itself as pre-processed, or perhaps as an
impasse between the perspectives of 'mortality' and 'continuum'.

However, Ulster novelists also find it difficult to evade deterministic structures. Martin's *The Ceremony of Innocence* and *The Road to
Ballyshannon*, Mac Laverty's *Lamb* and *Cal*, all centre on characters
whose options narrow to a single historical necessity. The conclusion
of *Stamping Ground* falls into a similar mould, despite Leitch's
gesture towards the positive: a girl raped by three young men
implausibly feels 'sorry for them now more than anything'.[51] Hetty
essentially shares in the socio-sexual fatality, emanating from 'closed
places of the spirit',[52] which has already engulfed the Valley's older
generation. Her post-coital *joie de vivre* does not outweigh the past,
any more than does a wistful and wishful vision near the end of
The Road to Ballyshannon:

> 'I see it,' the sergeant said. 'I see it.' Through the mist and the broken
> cloud a dolphin swam among the stars. 'I see it. It's a dolphin, isn't it?
> And it's free.' It was then the sergeant realised that the boy's right hand
> was held up by a tree root and the eyes that glistened to the night sky
> were dead.[53]

Relentlessly deterministic, Martin's fictional techniques shoot home,
with loud clangs, the bolts which circumscribe existence. His epi-
graphs pre-condition the reader as well: from Marx in *The Ceremony
of Innocence*:

> Men make their own history, but they do not make it just as they please;
> they do not make it under circumstances chosen by themselves, but
> under circumstances directly encountered, given and transmitted from
> the past. The tradition of all the dead generations weighs like a night-
> mare on the brain of the living.

And from Nietzsche in *The Road to Ballyshannon*: '[Man] wonders
...about himself – that he cannot learn to forget, but hangs on the
past: however far or fast he runs, that chain runs with him.' *The
Ceremony of Innocence* incorporates quite a rich historical and social
panorama of Belfast since the Second World War; but all this gives
birth to a boy's destiny as 'a small black cross among the thousand
and more crosses that line the lawns of the City Hall when the peace-
marchers keep their silent, lonely vigil...'[54] A leaner, less rhetorical
work, set in 1922, *The Road to Ballyshannon* follows two Republican
fugitives and their RIC sergeant hostage to an inevitable rendezvous.
Although only the latter escapes with his life, his son has earlier
been killed by the Republicans. The sergeant is additionally doomed
to remain 'a hostage of the dead',[55] because during the enforced
journey he has become a surrogate father to the younger of his
captors – perhaps another touch of wistful transcendence.

Mac Laverty's *Lamb* also turns on surrogate fatherhood, but within
one community. To make altruistic amends for the authoritarianism
of a boys' borstal run by the Christian Brothers, Brother Sebastian
(Michael Lamb) takes rebellious Owen on an escape-journey. Its
time, money, and spirit 'inevitably' run out:

> He had started with a pure loving simple ideal but it had gone foul on
> him, turned inevitably into something evil. It had been like this all his
> life, with the Brothers, with the very country he came from. The beautiful
> fly with the hook embedded...Owen was dead. He had killed him to
> save him, although he loved him more than anyone else in his life.[56]

The sentimental tinge here, a counterpart to the melodrama informing
Martin's doomed odysseys, also weakens the impact of Cal's fate.
And if sex is dodged in *Lamb*, it seems unlikely in *Cal*. Cal's guilt-
ridden love affair with the widow of an RUC reservist, to whose
murder by the IRA he has been accessory, ends thus: 'he stood in
a dead man's Y-fronts listening to the charge, grateful that at last
someone was going to beat him to within an inch of his life'.[57] What
in the case of poetry causes predictable cadences, in the case of
fiction causes predictable plots, predictable emotional conformations:
ideal glimpses belying a masochism under history's iron crushers
which the novelist's sensibility shares with a passive victim-hero.

But the (would-be realist) novelist must work with society as it
is. Poetry has perhaps less excuse if it fails to maintain the tension
between creative dynamic and historical stasis, to detect hairfine
tremors or locate chinks in determinism's defences. Perhaps Paulin's
idealism weighs too hard on the dynamic scale-pan, Montague's
determinism too hard on the static. Both also, unlike Mahon, write

very explicitly about Irish history, which given half a chance will write the poems itself, turn idealism or aspiration back into determinism again, book the text in advance like Coulter's graves.

Seamus Heaney's 'Bogland'[58] famously does its own digging, conceives the past as a dimension to be explored dynamically rather than received statically: 'Our pioneers keep striking/Inwards and downwards', and so do the poem's rhythms. This conflates historical enquiry with psychic investigation, and Heaney's subsequent soundings resemble Jungian therapy, rather than Friel's implied prescription of electro-convulsion. Heaney's methods affirm the presence of depths and layers whereby the past imprints individual and community, a 'script indelibly written into the nervous system'.[59] Hence '*Broagh*,/its low tattoo/among the windy boortrees.'[60] Yet this begins to edge towards the mythic inevitabilities that take hold in *North* (1975) and give his forms, too, a more deterministic cast. Perhaps the concept of the 'Bog People', subsuming history in a single 'icon', 'an archetypal pattern', was bound to have such an effect.[61] Again, the two fathers of Heaney's poetry merge into generalised ancestor-worship: 'pinioned by ghosts/and affections' ('Viking Dublin'); 'god of the waggon,/the hearth-feeder' ('Kinship').

The iconography and rituals of *North* (which I have discussed elsewhere)[62] also freeze the fluid religious element which has always permeated Heaney's imaginative relation to the past. This – very different from Mahon's and Paulin's theologising – began with the animistic natural magic of Heaney's childhood landscape (captured in *Death of a Naturalist*) when the 'pump marked an original descent into earth...centred and staked the imagination, made its foundation the foundation of the *omphalos* itself'.[63] In his lecture 'The *Sense* of the Past' (my italics), Heaney traces a progression from the child's 'intimate, almost animal response' to 'the mystery and claims of time past...the sense of belonging to a family and a place', to 'those images which widen this domestic past into a community or a national past' and offer 'a dream of the past'.[64] In the latter connection he describes the enduring mystique within his imagination of a mass-rock picture with its 'emotional drama'.[65] Yet, these two ways of apprehending the past, as the second accrues political meanings, cease to be progressive or concentric. Do the ripples widen evenly from the pump in the yard to the historical nation? Are the two fathers *really* one? How far does the 'common emotional ground of memory and belonging' extend? Is history reducible to – whose? – collective unconscious? (In 'Bogland' this analogy is a matter of subtler metaphorical suggestion.) Similar problems arise from

Heaney's landscaped Magna Mater representing 'mother ground', origins: the eternal mythic presence of the past, as opposed to the father who at least participates in generational cycles.

Heaney's omphalos or Mother Ireland in his own backyard attempts a winning throw in the poetic, as well as political, game of naturalising religio-historical origins. Others, like Montague, have gambled on the dolmen as symbolic touchstone. Louis MacNeice reached back to the early Christian era when his aspiration to belong reached a qualified climax in 'The Once-in-Passing':[66]

> As though the window opened
> And the ancient cross on the hillside meant myself.

But beyond all monuments, the land remains 'the stable element' in poetry too, whether inscribed with Delphic essences or with revisionist desires. In 'Rocks' (after Guillevic)[67] Mahon uses geology, the durability of rocks ('Their dream of holding fast/In the elemental flux'), to dwarf the human episode 'Lying in their shadows/In the last traces of time'. More broadly, the (non-human) animal, vegetable and mineral harbour 'The Banished Gods',[68] who

> sit out the centuries
> In stone, water
> And the hearts of trees,
> Lost in a reverie of their own natures...

Longley partly integrates natural and human history; partly sees Nature as improving on man's record of environmental accommodation, 'rinsing' the burial-mound as does poetry itself:

> The spring tide circles and excavates
> A shrunken ramshackle pyramid
> Rinsing cleaner scapulae, tibias,
> Loose teeth, cowrie and nautilus shells
> Before seeping after sun and moon
> To pour cupfuls into the larks' nests,
> To break a mirror on the grazing
> And lift minnows over the low bridge.[69]
> ('Spring Tide')

The Southern Irish poet Paul Durcan, in 'Before the Celtic Yoke'[71], gets rid of the past by conceiving a platonic landscape, innocent of history's invasion. Pre-human, not post-human like Mahon's millenarian dream, at once Genesis and Revelation, re-visionary rather than revisionist, this variant on the aisling once again suggests that Irish poetic imaginations are caught between trying to transfix history, to finish it, and to begin it. Durcan imagines the aisling's object defying history-ridden poets and speaking for 'herself':

My vocabularies are boulders cast up on time's beaches;
Masses of sea-rolled stones reared up in mile-high ricks
Along the shores and curving coasts of all my island...

IV

Paul Muldoon's poetry does not assail the tyranny of the past by
any such bold strokes as 'Before the Celtic Yoke'. Instead, it suffers
death by a thousand cuts. Most fundamentally, Muldoon enquires
into the whole business of the writer, or anyone, looking to history
at all.

To begin with a digression: Muldoon's points of departure are
thrown into relief by the contrary methods of Heaney's long poem
'Station Island', and Brian Moore's fiction. The scenario of 'Station
Island' not only builds in religio-historical *pietas*, but an appeal to
(or for) higher authority. Heaney's theme of following or 'trailing'
returns on a larger scale as his pilgrim seeks spiritual and artistic
guidance by conversing with ghosts: various male voices from and
of the past, surrogate fathers or 'fosterers' – all from the Catholic
tradition – in the guise of priests, schoolmasters, mentors, master-
writers. A 'hard' macho Joyce is hailed as 'Old father, mother's son'.[71]
Although that last voice urges 'swim/out on your own' the poem
itself enacts an entrapment, not least in its thraldom to literary
history. 'Exemplary' is a favourite critical term of Heaney's, and
Seamus Deane salutes what seems more like dependency than
freedom, when he says: 'Heaney has begun to consider his literary
heritage more carefully, to interrogate it in relation to his Northern
and violent experience, to elicit from it a style of survival as a
poet.'[72] Thus 'Station Island' may stage an artificial liberation-
struggle. Indeed, its Joycean dénoument recycles, rather than revises,
the patriarchal/artistic will to power: the *schema* is that of initiation
into manhood, acceptance by elders of the tribe. Moore's *Fergus*
(1971), perhaps also seeking a style of literary survival, revisits the
past within a secular scenario very like that of 'Station Island'. Fergus
Fadden, serious novelist hoping to strike gold as a Hollywood script-
writer, is literally haunted in his Californian beach-house by ghosts
from his Irish family past. He too holds 'conversations with the
dead'[73] (and younger versions of the living). His dead father, a
socially and religiously conservative authority-figure, who resembles
Gavin's father in *The Emperor of Ice-Cream*, heads the haunters or
hunters of a less securely liberated psyche than Gavin's becomes.
Moore's resurrection of a 'father's world' bears very explicitly on

the theme John Wilson Foster sees as first surfacing in *An Answer from Limbo* (1962): 'primitivism and provincialism become virtues, bulwarks against the erosive hypocrisies of modern cosmopolitan life'.[74] Fergus articulates a crisis close to the novelist's own sensibility:

> He stood...hardly able to believe that a few moments ago, far from fleeing his ghosts, he had pursued them with questions...Until now, he had thought that, like everyone else, he exorcised his past by living it. But he was not like everyone else. His past had risen up this morning, vivid and uncontrollable, shouldering into his present.[75]

However, Moore's externalisation of interior or unconscious dialogue involves fairly stock characters and responses. The father's anticlimactic last words are: 'If you have not found a meaning, then your life is meaningless.'[76] Moore's fiction after *Fergus* oscillates within the terms of this over-neat antithesis. His protagonists find or lose some kind of faith, with the supernatural underlining the issue in *Catholics* (1972), *The Great Victorian Collection* (1975), *Cold Heaven* (1983) and *Black Robe* (1985). *The Mangan Inheritance* (1979) pursues, antithetically to *Fergus*, the question of faith in the past itself. Keeping the faith, whether religiously or historically, draws on the same font of Irish feeling. James Mangan, a Canadian not an expatriate Irishman, becomes obsessed with proving his kinship to the nineteenth-century poet James Clarence Mangan. His quest for genealogical ratification of his character and talents ends in tears, in 'hated self-images',[77] in the shattering of a talismanic ancestral daguerrotype, in a return home to healthier emotion about his father's death. Moore's dialectic between Irish total recall and Californian amnesia derives – like excessive determinism or idealism – from Ulster experience, but may be too much of a swinging pendulum to extend it artistically. Foster calls *Fergus* 'more of a re-hash than an advance'.[78] Despite his variations on a theme, Moore's historical imagination seems arrested between a futureless Ireland (doubly so since it belongs to his past) and a pastless North America.

Thirty years younger than Moore, Muldoon so far shows no signs of augmenting Foster's 'wry irony in the sight of yesterday's apostates becoming today's nostalgics'.[79] His poetry questions its own authority along with origins, foundations, heritage, precedent, preceptor and pedigree. For instance, in *Quoof* (1983) the trans-atlantic dimension of 'The More a Man Has the More a Man Wants'[80] is partly a way of suggesting the remoteness, the archaic distance, of Irish-American bloodlines:

> On the Staten Island Ferry
> two men are dickering

> over the price
> of a shipment of Armalites,
> as Henry Thoreau was wont to quibble
> with Ralph Waldo Emerson.

The scene then moves to the Algonquin where, in a parody of
Young Ireland's heroic genealogies, the protagonist encounters 'a
flurry/of sprites,/the assorted shades/of Wolfe Tone, Napper Tandy
...Then, Thomas Meagher/darts up from the Missouri/on a ray/of
the morning star/to fiercely ask/what has become of Irish hurling?'
(This poem is no respecter of ghosts.) 'The Frog'[81] attacks from a
different angle the notion that 'images of the past' hold lessons, can
be made 'exemplary'. The speaker to whom the frog-image occurs
seems poised between alternative politics of the poem: 'I set aside
hammer and chisel/and take him on the trowel'. 'Hammer and chisel'
implies the egotistical (and patriarchal) sublime: coercion of the
image to fit an agenda. 'Take him on the trowel', like the poem's
self-image as 'another small upheaval/amongst the rubble' ('Troubles'),
implies negative capability. 'The Frog' tries out the first approach,
but stops short:

> The entire population of Ireland
> springs from a pair left to stand
> overnight in a pond
> in the gardens of Trinity College,
> two bottles of wine left there to chill
> after the Act of Union.
>
> There is, surely, in this story
> a moral. A moral for our times...

This anti-Aesop, anti-Davisite fable plays down 1800 as much as
Paulin plays up 1798. It also criticises Heaney's 'Act of Union' as
not only portentously futile, but radical chic, a form of dilettante
dabbling in violent waters: 'What if I put him to my head/and
squeezed it out of him,/like the juice of freshly squeezed limes,/or
a lemon sorbet?' A related Muldoonian moral queries the status of
historical stories themselves. 'History'[82] embarks on research: 'Where
and when exactly did we first have sex?' and obliquely concludes
that only *imaginative* truth can be trusted since a possible location
is 'the room where MacNeice wrote "Snow",/Or the room where
they say he wrote "Snow".' MacNeice's poem emerges as the only
sure thing in a world of shaky facts. ('Exactly' belongs to aesthetics
in 'The Frog' too.) Similarly, the poet in 'Lunch with Pancho Villa'[83]
undermines a whole industry of publication on Northern Ireland
when he states: 'there's no such book, so far as I know,/As *How it
Happened Here*,/Though there may be. There may.'

Muldoon's poetry, then, attempts to loosen the grip of the past on both life and literature, perhaps as epitomised by a habituated pump attendant: 'grown so used/to hold-ups he calls after them,/ *Beannacht Dé ar an obair*'.[84] He 'interrogates history' in a more genuine sense than do many who make such a claim. His techniques sabotage all kinds of certainty about how 'far' we 'know' into the past or future. Hence the subjunctives, conditionals, syntactical ambiguities, refusals of historic tenses. The locus of the poetry is an uneasy present-continuous, at once an ironic echo of Ulster's 'eternal interim' ('Lull'), and 'exactly' where language tries to break into the future:

> How often have I carried our family word
> for the hot water bottle
> to a strange bed...[85]

> ('Quoof')

To defamiliarise is also to defamilialise. Throughout Muldoon's poetry the father is a persistent metaphysical shadow. Behind, rather than both behind and in front like Heaney's father-figure, he represents 'what is...immediately over my shoulder'. Some of Muldoon's early poems dramatise the son's psycho-sexual maturation – presented in Freudian, rather than Jungian, terms. 'The Waking Father'[86] (from *New Weather*, 1973) includes a disturbing infantile Oedipal fantasy:

> When my father stood out in the shallows
> It occurred to me
> The spricklies might have been pirhanas,
> The river a red carpet
> rolling out from where he had just stood...

In 'Duffy's Circus'[87] (from *Mules*, 1977) the speaker-son's drive towards individuation reaches adolescence. He ignores his father's Polonius-like 'nuts of wisdom', 'loses' him, and ends up absorbing rawer facts of life, sex and violence: 'From under a freighter/I watched a man sawing a woman in half'. This Freudian drama shades into the father's function as history-bearer. Sometimes (as part of Muldoon's running demurral with Heaney) he becomes an amalgam of archetypes/stereotypes. 'The Mixed Marriage'[88], with its 'school-mistress' mother and rurally atavistic father, parodies Lawrentian oppositions between super-ego and id. The father

> further dimmed the light
> To get back to hunting with ferrets
> Or the factions of the faction-fights –
> The Ribbon Boys, the Caravats.

Two poems in *Why Brownlee Left*, 'October 1950' and 'Immrama'[89], more directly challenge blood-conscious imperatives. The former presents conception not as determined or (wholly) determining but as 'chance' which might lead to 'Anything wild or wonderful'. The speaker of the latter at first seems eager to join the poetic paternity suite: 'I, too, have trailed my father's spirit', but orthodox Irish biography or literary cliché ('mud-walled cabin', 'farm where he was first hired out', 'building-site') has an unorthodox South American finale: 'That's him on the verandah, drinking rum/With a man who might be a Nazi...' This impugns not only any mythologised purity of family stock, but doctrines of such purity. Earlier the father's authority and factuality were revoked by the very dedication of Muldoon's *New Weather*: 'For my Fathers and Mothers.' His débutant historical pluralism prepared for other pluralities and mixtures in the poetry, subtler versions of those surrogacies or difficult mixed parentages in fiction: mongrels, mutations, doubles, androgyny and sexual ambivalence ('The Bearded Woman, by Ribera'[90] with her 'Willowy, and clean-shaven' consort), alter egos, alternative lives, promiscuity of cultural reference. Muldoon's puns and rhymes endow words themselves with multiple identities, strange bedfellows, surprisingly extended families, and his poems unfold through associations that unsettle the reader.

The title-poem of *Mules* presents a son witnessing a father witnessing an awkward birth:

> We had loosed them into one field.
> I watched Sam Parsons and my quick father
> Tense for the punch below their belts,
> For what was neither one thing or the other.[91]

Among other things, this problematic hybrid symbolises offspring of the so-called 'two traditions' in Ulster, including Muldoon's poetry itself. But fathers' breeding too, as 'Immrama' suggests, can be suspect. The longer poem 'Immram'[92] takes shape as a search for the father, for an explanation of some dirty business in the past which forces the son to re-think autonomy and free association:

> I was fairly and squarely behind the eight
> That morning in Foster's pool-hall
> When it came to me out of the blue
> In the shape of a sixteen-ounce billiard cue
> That lent what he said some little weight.
> 'Your old man was an ass-hole.
> That makes an ass-hole out of you.'
> My grandfather hailed from New York State.
> My grandmother was part Cree.
> This must be some new strain in my pedigree...

> I suppose that I should have called the cops
> Or called it a day and gone home
> And done myself, and you, a favour.
> But I wanted to know more about my father.

But, shifty and shifting, the father eludes pursuit: 'He would flee, to La Paz, then to Buenos Aires,/From alias to alias.' The son does not set out to avenge an entirely innocent father, as he does in *Immram Mael Duin*, the medieval voyage tale on which Muldoon's 'Immram' is loosely, if not licentiously, based. However, at the end of the poem he is released like Mael Duin from thraldom to the past, and 'happily' returns to 'Foster's pool-room' (a genetic pun on the fostering of Mael Duin). As he moves to rejoin the 'flow' of the living, the poem seems to resolve the father-son conflict on both its Freudian and its historical levels. In 'Gathering Mushrooms'[93] we glimpse the father once again as a familiarly solid rural figure: 'He'll glance back from under his peaked cap/without breaking rhythm'. Muldoon may partly allude to Heaney's father-figure, and, as elsewhere, to Heaney as a literary father-figure ('rhythm' in Heaney's poems fuses poetry and rural work). Such fathers are now perceived as sadly obsolescent: 'one of those ancient warriors/before the rising tide' – a helpless Canute or Cuchulain. Set 'fifteen years on', and thus straddling recent history, 'Gathering Mushrooms' presents the 'tide' of violence as psychedelic transformation. The substitution of magic mushrooms for the ordinary variety symbolises a grotesque mutation or regression of tradition. A reversed aisling, the poem is also a slow-motion reprise of 'Easter 1916' ('changed utterly') in which nothing – or a changeling – gets born. The speaker, his head 'grown into the head of a horse', finds in his mouth the words of a Republican dirty-protester instructing: '*If sing you must, let your song/tell of treading your own dung.*' The irony implicitly resists imperatives delivered by the past ('dung') in the name of the future ('*the day we leap/into our true domain*'), history's Davisite attempt to dictate to the poet.

If Mahon demolishes Whig history, you might say that Muldoon deconstructs its opposite. He exorcises the hovering 'ghost-life' of mythic history, what Oliver MacDonagh rather euphemistically terms 'an absence of a developmental or sequential view of past events'.[94] But his poetry does not simply or simplistically walk away from atavism into agnostic daylight. Nor does it weigh too heavily on either side of any antithesis, but resembles Brownlee's abandoned horses

> Shifting their weight from foot to
> Foot, and gazing into the future.[95]

Muldoon negotiates that small space, that inch, between necessity and possibility, with an integrity faithful above all to the present. 'Cherish the Ladies',[96] like other Muldoon poems, takes place in the present tense and is aware of itself as a tiny piece of historical process if not progress:

> In this, my last poem about my father,
> there may be time enough
> for him to fill their drinking-trough
> and run his eye over
>
> his three mooley heifers.
> Such a well-worn path,
> I know, from here to the galvanized bath.

The phrase 'my last poem' could mean either final or most recent, thus suggesting work-in-progress. 'Cherish the Ladies' (like 'Immram') braves the reader's imagined boredom with father-poems: 'Such a well-worn path/I know.' And it restores for the space of the poem the rural archetype of the father by insisting on the actuality of his opening 'the stand-pipe' – an image for begetting. Like 'Gathering Mushrooms', 'Cherish the Ladies' incorporates an italicised alternative poem, alternative history, alternative future controlled by the past:

> I know, too, you would rather
>
> *I saw behind the hedge to where the pride*
> *of the herd, though not an Irish*
> *bull, would cherish*
> *the ladies with his electric cattle-prod.*
>
> As it is, in my last poem about my father
> he opens the stand-pipe
> and the water scurries along the hose
> till it's curled
>
> in the bath – One heifer
> may look up
> and make a mental note, then put her nose
> back to the salt-lick of the world.

What might be going on, or written up, behind the hedge smacks of an abusive heritage (there are parodic references to folk-song). As ever, Muldoon discriminates between dead and living tradition, between apparent and real breaks with the past, between the oppressively, tribally progenitive 'pride of the herd' and the more admirable father who really 'cherishes' the future – even a female future – who makes available 'the salt-lick of the world'.

[1985]

From Cathleen to Anorexia

The Breakdown of Irelands

Northern Ireland has been called a 'failed political entity'. I think it's time to admit that both parts of Ireland are failed *conceptual* entities. That is, the ideas which created them and the ideologies which sustained them have withered at the root. If 'Northern Ireland' has visibly broken down, the 'Republic' as once conceived has invisibly broken down. And since 1969 each has helped to expose the inner contradictions of the other.

In his poem 'Aisling', written near the time of the hunger strikes, Paul Muldoon asks whether Ireland should be symbolised, not by a radiant and abundant goddess, but by the disease anorexia:

> Was she Aurora, or the goddess Flora,
> Artemidora, or Venus bright,
> or Anorexia, who left
> a lemon stain on my flannel sheet?

In blaming the hunger-strikers' emaciation on their idealised cause, the poem equates that cause with a form of physical and psychic breakdown. 'Anorexia' is thus Cathleen Ni Houlihan in a terminal condition. Anorexic patients pursue an unreal self-image – in practice, a death-wish. Similiarly, the Irish Nationalist dream may have declined into a destructive neurosis.

Feminists question any exploitation of the female body for symbolic or abstract purposes. So perhaps Anorexia should, rather, personify Irish women themselves: starved and repressed by patriarchies like Unionism, Catholicism, Protestantism, Nationalism. But here we come up against a difficulty. Not all Irish women resist these patriarchies. And for some, mainly from the North, Cathleen flourishes abundantly still. The Northern women's movement has been divided and retarded; while the Southern movement, preoccupied with church-and-state, has largely avoided 'nation'. Eavan Boland's feminist poem 'Mise Eire' (I am Ireland) destabilises Mise but not Eire – 'my nation displaced/into old dactyls'. There is some reluctance, partly for fear of further division, to re-open the ever-problematic, ever-central issue of 'Nationalism and feminism'. Later I will ask whether they are compatible. For the moment, I offer the reluctance as symptomatic.

This essay will mainly focus on the ideological breakdown of Nationalism because its breakdown is more complex and less obvious. Nationalism and Unionism are not in fact the same kind of ideology, nor do they function in the same manner. So they differ in their

modes of collapse as in their modes of construction. Unionism
since the first Home Rule bill has always been reactive: a coalition
of sects, interests, loyalties and incoherent hatreds in the face of a
perceived common emergency. No totalising philosophy covers the
whole coalition, even if religious and secular alarm fuse on its
fundamentalist wing. Orangeism and Paisleyism maintain a select
tribal memory-bank of historical persecutions, in which emblematic
events (1641, 1690) are reinforced by biblical parallels. But this has
never developed into a comprehensive symbolic system. You can't
personify Unionism. 'Orange Lil' is not the whole story.

As a separatist movement, Nationalism had to put together a more
elaborate ideological package and make more absolute claims. Also,
like Polish Nationalism, it is informed by Catholic theological habits.
When the SDLP and Sinn Féin deny any sectarian component in
their politics, these very habits blind them to the seamless join
betweeen Catholicism and Nationalism, a join which is a matter of
form as much as content. Nationalism thinks of Unionism as heresy
– hence past failures to analyse or understand it. And to come up
against the Church on integrated education is to be as chillingly
excluded as when one meets the guardians of the Republican grail.

Lapsed Nationalists are, therefore, more liable than lapsed Unionists to suffer from metaphysical *angst*. One example is Richard
Kearney's compulsion to redefine the platonic Republic. Other
Southern writers and intellectuals strangely complain that 'Ireland
does not exist'. This seems less an empirical judgement than a
state of unconscious mourning for a god, a goddess, a symbolic
future that failed. (It also evades the implications of the North.) Two
other post-Nationalist reactions are revisionism and cynicism. But
there has to be *some* reaction. Nationalism was internalised as God,
Nature and Family. So deeply absorbed as to become unnoticeable,
it can leave painful withdrawal symptoms as it recedes.

Unionism does not linger like bog-mist in unsuspected crannies.
For better or worse, you generally know it's there. Unionism exposes
its contradictions in public: in the gap between its interior monologues and what it can get the rest of the world to believe. All
ideologies work through unconscious assumptions as well as conscious
creeds. But the Unionist unconscious, in both its secular and religious
versions, has never been open to outsiders, whereas the reflexes of
the Nationalist unconscious have been widely accepted as norms.
The situation in the North is not helped by the tendency of Nationalist Ireland to swallow or re-import its own dated propaganda. Patrick
Kavanagh once said (with regard to the popularity of *The Quiet*

Man in Dublin): 'about the only place now where phoney Ould Oireland is tolerated is in Ireland itself'.[1] Unfortunately, he underestimated an export-market which continues to boom. When flattered by Irish-American sentiment or left-wing 'Brit guilt' (i.e. English over-compensation for historical sins), Nationalism becomes less disposed to self-criticism and forgets its inner malaise.

Literature plays a part in all this too. (We import some starry-eyed lit crit from the USA.) Now and then I will use contemporary writing as an index of the double ideological breakdown in Ireland. There are good historical reasons why Irish Nationalism so often reads like bad poetry and Ulster Unionism like bad prose. Cathleen, of course, has been Muse as well as goddess. Eoin MacNeill tried to lower the political temperature before the Rising by sending round a circular which plainly stated: 'What we call our country is not a poetical abstraction...There is no such person as Cathleen Ni Houlihan...who is calling upon us to serve her'. Ulster Protestantism, which prides itself on plain statement, has tried to discourage a self-critical prose tradition, let alone qualifying clauses. Literature remains the primary place where language changes, where anorexic categories are exposed. Thus from the 1920s most writers had no option but to constitute themselves an *opposition* to the ideological clamps holding both Irish entities together. In my lifetime, these clamps have distorted ethics, politics, social and personal relations, the lives of women, education, what passes here for religion, and our whole understanding of Irish culture.

Irish, Irisher, Irishest

'Irishness' is the most inclusive category for Irish Nationalist ideology – and also the most insidious. In the last paragraph of *Modern Ireland* Roy Foster criticises the recurring theme of 'being "more" or "less" Irish than one's neighbours; Irishness as a scale or spectrum rather than a simple national or residential qualification; at worst, Irishness as a matter of aggressively displayed credentials'.[2] During Easter 1989 the late Cardinal O'Fiaich proved how this theme persists in some collective unconscious. 'Many Protestants,' he said, 'love Ireland as devoutly as *any* Catholic does' (my italics). He then recited the litany of Patriot Prods (Tone, Emmet etc) usually produced in support of such statements. It sometimes seems as if Protestants have to die for Ireland before being allowed to live here.

The Cardinal meant his remarks kindly. But in so deliberately including Protestants, he excluded them. He fed the belief that Protestants have to work their passage to Irishness. Catholics, on the other hand, are born loving the country, knowing by instinct its entire history and literature, and generally 'kinned by hieroglyphic peat' to 'origins' (Seamus Heaney). This nonsense, out of date in the Republic is widely swallowed by both sides in the North. But Ulster Irishness, like Ulster Britishness, is a state neither of nature nor of grace. It is enforced and reinforced by socialisation, often by simplifications and stereotypes. In *Ripley Bogle* Robert McLiam Wilson satirises the conditioning processes of the North:

> I learnt of a great many things on my first day at school...I discovered that I lived in Belfast and that Belfast lived in Ireland and that this combination meant that I was Irish. The grim young bint we were loaded with was very fervent on this point. She stressed with some vigour that no matter what anyone else were to call us, our names would be always Irish...[she] told us that the occasional Misguided Soul would try to call us British but that of all things to call us this was the wrongest. No matter how the Misguided Souls cajoled, insisted or pleaded, our names would remain Irish to the core, whatever that meant...in the spirit of compromise (ever with me even then), I dubbed myself 'Ripley Irish British Bogle'.[3]

Roy Foster would replace the competing indoctrinations with 'a more relaxed and inclusive definition of Irishness, and a less constricted view of history'.[4] Who would not agree? Yet when he developed this idea in his lecture 'Varieties of Irishness', the Unionist David Trimble felt political pressures in the very term 'Irishness', however far its elastic might stretch.[5] Of course Unionists can be equally paranoid about being called Irish and not being called Irish (as Jews in pre-war Poland resented the alternatives of assimilation and expulsion). But this seeming paradox is in fact an accurate response to the rhetorical tactics famously admitted by Senator Michael Hayes in 1939: 'We have had a habit, when it suited a particular case, of saying they were Irish, and when it did not suit a particular case, of saying they were British or planters...'[6]

One way of circumventing an elaborate quadrille, in which the dancers contrive never to meet on the same ground, might be to accelerate the separation between political 'Irishness' and culture in Ireland. Culture in Ireland is a range of practices, expressions, traditions, by no means homogeneously spread nor purely confined to the island. Political Irishness, on the other hand, is the ideology of identity ('Irish to the core') mainly packaged by the Gaelic League, which, twined with Catholicism, served to bind the new state. In the Republic the strings of this package have got looser and looser, and much of its substance has leaked out. In the North, Sinn Féin still tries to deliver a fossilised and belated version. There, whether embraced or resisted, Irishness endures as an absolute abstract noun. When threatened by that absolute, Unionists reach for the security blanket of Britain or Ulster. Meanwhile, they are happy enough with relative or adjectival usages, Northern Irish, Irish Protestant, even Irish Unionist. In these usages Ireland stands for the country, not the nation, and 'Erin's Orange lily' feels at home. Protestant Northern Ireland retains institutions, self-images and insignia – harp, shamrock – associated with nineteenth-century Ireland under the crown. It is only since 1969 that it has predominantly identified itself as 'British' rather than as 'Irish in the UK'. The often-put question 'Are you British or Irish?' is strictly meaningless, since 'Irish' does double duty as an allegiance and as an ethnocultural description. 'British' is only an allegiance, an umbrella for English, Scots, Welsh and some Northern Irish. Allegiance has cultural effects, and culture influences allegiance. Yet 'Britishness' is not opposite to 'Irishness': it is the affiliation whereby Ulster Protestants seek to maintain those aspects of their identity which appear threatened or excluded by political Irishness.

Perhaps their reactions might seem less paranoid after we have visited the political unconscious of Alban Maginness, an SDLP councillor in Belfast. Here he is replying to an article by John Wilson Foster in which Foster contends that 'Northern Protestants have been excluded by the Nationalist majority in Ireland from being Irish'.[7] Maginness says:

> Curiously, in some non-political situations, the Northern Protestant, which Foster unapologetically claims to be, concedes, accepts or even claims Irishness...The train loads of rugby supporters from Belfast to Lansdowne Road...bear witness to this. A tired and over-worked example some might say, but it does raise the question, why can't this 'sporting' patriotism be translated into political patriotism? My understanding of modern Irish history is that the majority culture was and still is inclusive, not exclusive, and has an almost missionary zeal to persuade if not cajole Northern Protestants into realising or owning up to their innate Irishness...Why the absurd denial of Irishness? [8]

The above manifests a deep confusion between cultural and political Irishness. Nor does it recognise that Irishness depends on the definer. Maginness's rugby example should indeed be laid to rest since the only group *not* heading for Lansdowne Road are Ulster Catholics. The culture of sport is heavily politicised in the North, keeping talent from the great games of rugby and hurling. (Rugby is also a mainly middle-class pursuit.) And surely Maginness answers his own questions when he finds Irish Protestants, Irish Unionists relaxed about their affiliations to this country – a different matter from patriotic acceptance of the Republic – when the political heat is turned off. (People constantly generalise about 'Ireland' when they mean the Republic, although the English Left get it wrong the other way round by referring to Northern Ireland as 'Ireland'.) Maginness might also compare his own feelings whenever Unionism proposes to 'include' him, or professes 'missionary zeal' about persuading him to own up to his innate Britishness. And what exactly should Foster be *apologising* for?

As Unionists shy away from cultural areas that seem appropriated by Nationalists, so Nationalists assume that cultural 'Irishness', very narrowly defined, functions as a prelude to the political variety. A *cúpla focal* on the lips, a twiddle on the fiddle, and 'from their full and genial hearts/An Irish feeling [will] burst.' Labhrás O Murchú, head of the organisation that promotes traditional music, actually told the New Ireland Forum that 'any Unionist who is exposed to the *Tobar an Duchais* will come up with a much more legitimate status for himself than the status that was contrived'. (This is the same man who decided that traditional Irish music opposed abortion.) The celebrated dulcimer-player John Rea was an Orangeman who, although always friendly toward Catholic fellow-musicians, called them 'Them' to the end of his days. False hopes and fears are invested in 'the convert syndrome'. This encompasses the Protestant gaeilgeoir as well as the Protestant patriot. Unfortunately, all converts impress the congregation they join a lot more than the one they have left. (They may also be subtly patronised as heretics who have seen the light.) A type of Aran-knit Ulster Protestant is particularly misleading in this respect, and has no battalions at his (or her) back. But even if East Belfast were teeming with potential Douglas Hydes, it doesn't follow that the language leads to the nation. Rather, the nation has driven Ulster Protestants, often prominent in nineteenth-century efforts to preserve Gaelic, away from the language. Indeed, the poet and antiquarian, Samuel Ferguson set out to show that Gaelic literature is not the exclusive property of Catholics and Nationalists. Today mutterings to this effect have even been heard from the vicinity of the UDA.

What about literature in English written by Irish people? Does it belong to the nation, the country, the island, these islands, the world? Patrick Kavanagh knew he was on dangerous ground when he claimed that 'the writers of Ireland [are] no longer Corkery and O'Connor and the others, but Auden and George Barker':

> Saying this is liable to make one the worst in the world, for a national literature, being based on a convention, not born of the unpredictable

individual and his problems, is a vulnerable racket and is protected by fierce wild men. [9]

John Banville has been able to say more coolly that 'there is no such thing as an Irish national literature, only Irish writers engaged in the practice of writing'. Yet when progressive cultural thinkers in the Republic dwell on the Europeanism or Atlanticism of Irish writing, they sometimes forget that its Irishness has been shelved rather than interrogated. For naive readers some Irish writers and texts are still more Irish than others. And, thanks to the Irish Literary Revival, the canon retains a vaguely Nationalist aura, abroad if not always at home.

This is ironical, given that some literary critics have problems with Yeats's English literary connections, and with his latter-day cult of the Anglo-Irish tradition. But if Yeats's Protestant and English affiliations were more sympathetically regarded, it might illuminate the role of the North in Ireland's literary culture. Still quoted is AE's dictum: 'Unionism in Ireland has produced no literature.' This, like Irishness and Britishness, involves a false alternative, an asymmetry, whereby anything written by Irish people can be turned to the glory of Nationalism. Meanwhile, Protestant cultural expression is caricatured as drums and banners (not that the interest of these should be overlooked). Such perceptions reproduce an image foisted by political Irishness on to political Protestantism and sometimes internalised by it. This image excludes the dual Irish-British context, and what Protestants actually write, paint and perform, whatever their political allegiances.

In 1985 Gerald Dawe and I edited a collection of critical essays entitled *Across a Roaring Hill: The Protestant Imagination in Modern Ireland*. To some, the category appeared sectarian (whereas 'Irish' would have been taken for granted). One reviewer (Declan Kiberd) assumed that we had a hidden Unionist agenda; another (Enoch Powell) that we belonged to the Nationalist conspiracy. Brendan Kennelly quoted an acquaintance who reacted to the book's title by declaring that 'Protestants have no imagination at all'. This stereotype partly results from the inhibition of artistic expression within Scottish and Ulster Calvinism. But instead of putting down that culture with reference to 'the wonderfully rich Irish literary tradition etc' it should be understood in its own terms. Again, the relation of all Irish writing to Protestantism and Catholicism, an issue masked by homogenising 'Irishness', should be opened up – as should relations between Irish and English literature after 1921.

So I think that 'Irishness', with its totalitarian tinge, ought to be abandoned rather than made more inclusive. To include/exclude the Ulster Prods is a false and sterile alternative, the one exposed by Hayes, with underlying Nationalist assumptions. 1798 is no more practical use than 1916. Charles Haughey may have pragmatically modified his views since he made his opening speech to the Forum. Yet, in his psychic alarm, he identified the real agenda: 'The belief has been canvassed that we would have to jettison almost the entire ethos on which the independence movement was built and that Irish identity has to be sacrificed to facilitate the achievement of Irish unity.' In fact, some such sacrifice may be necessary for the sake of peace let alone unity as once dreamed. But cultural change and changing awareness of culture, in the Republic and even in the North, have already exposed political Irishness ('the ethos on which the independence movement was built') as now more than a prison than a liberation.

Northern Nationalists and Southern Revisionists

When Nationalism achieves its object it 'dies as a force'.[10] So said Sean O'Faolain in 1951. This means that the relation between Southern and Northern Nationalism is one of uneven development. The Southern state was gradually born into evolution, while Northern Nationalism (like Unionism) froze in an archaic posture. It stayed bent on realising what revisionism now seems wantonly to discard. But perhaps Northern Nationalists, nearly as anachronistic in Dublin as the Unionists in London, will have to accept that the Southern clock cannot be stopped or wound back.

As Clare O'Halloran shows in *Partition and the Limits of Irish Nationalism*, between Northern and Southern Nationalists there lies a distance not only of time but experience, a distance usually disguised by rhetorical togetherness. She quotes John A. Costello on the adversarial imperative that gives Northern Nationalism its distinctive shape: 'they have to fight their fight up there...as a minority and...every piece of Protestant bitterness in the North finds its counterpart, both politically and in a religious sense, in the hearts and in the actions of a Northern Catholic. We in the South have got to recognise that we cannot understand that problem or appreciate it to its full.'[11] That applies whether you are shocked by the atavisms of the North, or whether you don't want the North to rock the (relatively) secure Southern boat.

The largely unexamined relation between Northern and Southern Nationalist consciousness rarely reaches the political surface, because there is assumed to be not relation but identity: identity of perception, interest, objective, context, historical moment. For instance, there are taboos on criticising – or even analysing – John Hume, because psychic alarm-bells ring whenever Northern Nationalism and Southern revisionism touch.

In fact to deny any split or breakdown within the Irish Nationalist psyche is to deny well-attested trauma. The South's long neglect of Northern Nationalists (documented by O'Halloran) breeds guilty over-compensation – which does not necessarily heal underlying resentments. Austin Currie, formerly of the SDLP, now a TD, was told to 'go back' (North) during heated debate in the Dáil. Meanwhile slagging the South goes down well in west Belfast, and opinion in the Republic swings between indifference and feverish identification. The latter, however, is mostly roused by events which concern 'British justice' (the Gibraltar killings) and thus recall shared experience before 1922. In my view such philosophical and political incoherence serves neither side in the North, and retards the Republic's maturation into being part of the solution rather than central to the problem. It might advance the Hillsborough Accord if psychic separation were promoted not only between Britain and the Unionists, but also between the Irish Government and Northern Nationalists.

Even *Irish Times* editorials can regress towards political infancy when championing the SDLP: 'The SDLP and Provisionals may share, in part, a mistily defined political objective – the unification of Ireland. That is not an illegitimate objective: indeed it is a noble and attractive ideal' (22 April 1989). The last twenty years have seen the nemesis of misty definitions and attractive ideals. As for 'noble' (an adjective generally reserved for the male sex), in fits of crazed ecumenism Cardinal Cahal Daly has maintained that Unionism and Nationalism are *both* 'noble aspirations'. It would be preferable to downgrade Nationalism to the ignoble status traditionally enjoyed by Unionism, rather than cling to the notion that a 'good' or 'real' Nationalism exists in some zone uncontaminated by the Provos. We might also give 'aspirations' a rest. Fintan O'Toole has argued (*Irish Times*, 20 April 1989) that Section 31 permits physical-force Republicanism to function as the *id* of the body politic. It subsists at an unconscious level where it cannot be interrogated. And if Sinn Féin remains below interrogation, the SDLP (a political party after all) remains above it. Thus Southern Nationalism cedes control over its own redefinition. The very structure of the New Ireland Forum, in asserting the unity of the Nationalist family, excluded agonising reappraisal of other unitary principles. Nevertheless, *de facto* reappraisal takes place all the time: at the level of economic necessity, historical revisionism, cultural change, the cycles of shock and weariness over the Northern war.

Literature makes a good barometer of asymmetric consciousness in Ireland. As a literary critic who sometimes notices distinctive elements in Northern writing, I have been suspected equally of partisanship and partitionism. This looks like another over-anxious unitary reflex. It is absurd to contend that Northern Ireland and the Republic have had identical socio-political experiences since 1921, or since 1969. And if we believe that literature is (up to a point) conditioned by society, and criticises society, we should not sacrifice any insights it can offer. For instance, I have certainly learned about the culture of the North from Paul Muldoon's or Medbh McGuckian's or Seamus Heaney's poetry (even after his move to Dublin), and about that of the Republic from Paul Durcan's or Thomas McCarthy's.

Durcan's visionary radicalism, for instance, criticises a particular status quo. Unlike the majority of Southern poets, he broaches the North. But he does so from outside the territory, without inhabiting its tensions as do the imaginations of Muldoon or Heaney. And Durcan's special focus is to open up the Republic's implication in the war. Thus long before Enniskillen he wrote the satirical 'National Day of Mourning for Twelve Protestants'. Life slowly catches up with art. Durcan's poetry neither renounces its own cultural roots nor overlooks loyalist terror. But he concentrates on the spiritual failings of the society he knows and for which he feels responsible. So, generally, do other writers North and South. An exception that proves the rule may be recent fiction and drama from the Southern border counties, a channel of two-way perspectives from a neglected limbo and source of light. But the Republic's writers are distinctively obsessed with secularism, sexuality, socialism, versions of feminism, and other libertarian themes. Literature and theatre seem to be mounting a communal psycho-drama that releases what the official political culture won't admit.

Field Day is often perceived as speaking for Ireland. The company has indeed sometimes sponsored pluralism: in staging Stewart Parker's *Pentecost*, in publishing a pamphlet by Unionist Robert McCartney. But the pamphlet-topics so far chosen give a Northern Nationalist priority to cultural and political 'decolonisation'. The latest trio was written by foreign literary critics better acquainted with general theories of colonialism than with Ireland after 1921. For Edward Said and Terry Eagleton, all 'the Irish people' are still engaged in a single national struggle. Reviewing the pamphlets

(*Fortnight* no. 271), Colm Tóibín found a time-warp in Field Day's own perceptions: 'the social and cultural revolution of the 1960s has left the artists in the Field Day group singularly unmoved...They write as though nothing had ever changed: their Ireland is distinctly pre-decimal. Thus England is the problem and the enemy (and the dramatic *other*).' Field Day's production *Saint Oscar* looked odd and out of date in Dublin because it was an instance of the reimported Nationalist propaganda I mentioned earlier. Its author, Eagleton again, used Wilde to present a timeless thesis about imperialist oppression. Field Day's eagerness to collude with the hoary stereotypes of the English hard Left seems significant.

Common to Friel's drama and the critical writings of Seamus Deane is a powerful sense of Palestinian dispossession. The alienation of Friel's Ballybeg is utterly different from the post-Nationalist alienation of Tom Murphy's *Bailegangaire*. When speaking of Ireland's literary and political traditions, Deane repeatedly uses the terms 'crisis' and 'discontinuity'. These conditions he generalises to cover the total past and this total island now. But his perceptions cannot be divorced from the recent history of Derry with its lost hinterland. (The other side of this coinage is the now-displaced Derry Protestant.) The same affiliation may show itself in Deane's intellectual resistance to the 'mystique of Irishness' concocted by Yeats on the one hand, Corkery on the other. Perhaps his otherwise rather extreme (and contradictory) desire for 'new writing, new politics, unblemished by Irishness, but securely Irish' (*Heroic Styles*) reflects, and aspires to redress, the exclusion of Northern Nationalists from the self-images and cultural definitions that became operational in the new state. Certainly, critics associated with Field Day approach the Irish Literary Revival both as a colonial manifestation and as a present hegemony, not a receding phase in literary history. They question the Revival's cultural power as revisionists question the political power of 1916. As for Corkery, Tom Garvin argues that Munster, 'in many ways the most self-sufficient, insulated, and self-assured part of nationalist Ireland', and remote from *both* Ulster communities, played a disproportionate part in fuelling and theorising the revolution.[12] Today, the Cork historian and senator John A. Murphy has a knack of annoying Northern Nationalists.

Whatever its other purposes and qualities, the Field Day project for 'a comprehensive anthology' of Irish literature ('what writing in this country has been') shows a desire to influence definitions. Within the literary sphere it seeks to piece together a broken past, to go back behind all deforming colonisation, to return to origins (550 AD), and thus to clarify 'Irish reality' so that we can start again. In contrast, revisionism seeks to break down a monolithic idea of the past, to go back behind the revolution's ideology, to return to origins in 1922 and understand them more empirically. In my view the former project risks the dangerous fantasy that loss and breakdown can be retrieved. Rather than start a new literary and political clock, I think we should try to tell the time accurately.

John Hume and 'An Island Once Again'

Political language goes out of date when its objective basis shrinks. It's easy to see that Sinn Féin inhabits a rhetorical dead-end, although their terminology should be directly challenged in the Republic: *the only place where it can be.* But what about the political language of John Hume? Does he breathe new life into Nationalist ideology? Or (like Field Day at times) does he simply translate traditional concepts into an updated idiom?

Hume keeps his political unconscious under better control than do Haughey, Maginness and O'Fiaich. He thus seems a model of eloquent flexibility as compared with the monotonous negatives of Unionism. But Unionism may be a better critic than author – or at least a close reader of the subtexts that concern it. And on closer inspection Hume's language has much in common with George Orwell's metaphor for Marxist jargon: 'prefabricated phrases bolted together like the pieces of a child's Meccano set'.[13]

Hume likes to stress that he has moved beyond the old definitions. So let us test him on the questions of 'Irishness' and 'revisionism'. On the former topic he has criticised 'those who are so unsure of their Irishness that they need to remind us of it constantly' (thus acknowledging competition between the SDLP and Sinn Féin over degrees of Irishness). And he has rejected the Republican category of 'the Irish people', favouring instead: 'Protestant fellow Irishmen', 'the people of this island', 'the Unionist people and the rest of the people of this island' (*London Review of Books*, 2 February 1989). But is this quite as innocent and open as it looks? Or is it the 'particular case' which it suits to say that they are Irish? Hume's article does not call the Unionist people 'British', thus minimising the recent significance of this self-protective definition in their own consciousness. Again, while Ireland as island is an improvement on Ireland as nation, it omits 'the totality of relations in the archipelago'. Although Hume's vision is larger than that of most Northern politicians, he too selects the 'whole' on which he desires attention to concentrate. Nobody catches all the snooker-balls in the triangle.

Hume's *cultural* perception of his 'Protestant fellow Irishmen' is remarkably narrow. It excludes most of their affiliations to the other island – and indeed to this one. He characterises their 'long and strong tradition in Ireland' as religious, military, industrial: 'pride in their service to the crown... in their work ethic and in their faith'. Obviously there is truth here, but limited, stereotypical and dated. Meanwhile 'Irishness', so 'sure' as to be given no definition whatsoever, seems another matter entirely. (It also seems, unlike Unionism, to have no religious affiliation.) Hume's incomplete, and imperviously polarised, cultural awareness may reflect the binary geography of Derry. More recently (November 1993) he has said: 'Many Unionists feel some affinity for aspects of Irish life and culture.' This implies an already given, unified and timeless Irishness on which 'Unionists' intrude from outside.

As for revisionism: Hume contributed an article on 'Europe of the Regions' to Richard Kearney's compilation *Across the Frontiers: Ireland in the 1990s.* The contrast between it and the editor's own contribution illustrates once again the uneven development of Nationalist consciousness. This is the post-Nationalist Kearney:

> An Ireland without frontiers is obviously an Ireland without borders. This does not, however, entail a 'united Ireland' in the traditional sense of the term. For the Nation-States of Britain and Ireland, which constitute the very basis for the opposing claims of nationalist and unionist ideologies, would be superseded by a European constellation of regions.[14]

Hume's Europe, in contrast, becomes less and less regional the closer it gets to home. He does not advocate Ulster regionalism, or any other form of Irish Balkanisation, but emphasises what 1992 will do for the Gaeltacht. And, identifying region with nation, he falls into Nationalist idiom: 'the real "new republicanism"...rather than being any reversal of the national destiny...will allow us better to fulfil our potential as a people...and to enjoy properly the inchoate European outlook and vision which was lost in our oppressive and obsessive relationship with Britain'.[15] Wearing his SDLP hat, Hume remains interested in a relationship that his Euro-regionalist hat occludes.

When interviewed in the *Irish Times* by Frank Millar (13 January 1989), Hume endlessly repeated the unitary Meccano-phrase 'this island', *not* 'these islands': 'the central relationship being that of the Unionists and the rest of this island and *then* the relationship between Ireland and Britain' (my italics); 'Going to the heart of the problem is the relationship between the Unionist people and the rest of the people of this island'; 'do they want [to] work out

with the rest of the people of this island how we share the island?'
'What I want to see is the representatives of the divided people of
this island reaching an agreement on how they share the island...'

In a kind of linguistic tug-of-war, Hume first tries to yank the
Unionists off their UK base, then to pull them across the border,
while urging: 'stand on your own feet'. 'Island-sharing' (I wonder
how keen they are in Kerry?) is a very different matter from 'power-
sharing' within the existing framework. Hume is in fact skilfully
playing a political word and map game with specific origins in
Northern Irish politics. There, trying to control bounds and definitions has always been part of the territorial battle. (Another SDLP
MP, Seamus Mallon, never refers to 'Northern Ireland', always to
'the North of Ireland'.) But Unionists are unlikely to swallow his
island-Nationalism unless Nationalism equally swallows their
archipelagic-Britishness. The UK and the Republic find themselves
guarantors of communities more Unionist and more Nationalist
than themselves, for whose neurotic pathologies their own incoherence
is much to blame. Even apart from Northern Ireland, it is high
time that the massive traffic across the Irish Sea entered 'inter-
governmental' awareness. Only by rethinking their own relationship,
outside existing Nationalist and Unionist categories, will these two
European jurisdictions generate new political language for their
frontier-region. Borders can melt in two directions.

Women and Nationalism

I have compared Irish Nationalism to bad poetry. In bad poems
the relations between word, image and life break down. Political
images, like political language (from which they are never quite
distinct), eventually exhaust themselves or prove incapable of renewal.
I think this happens at the juncture where the image Women-Ireland-
Muse meets contemporary Irish women. There, I believe, the breakdown of Nationalist ideology becomes particularly clear.

In the film *Mother Ireland* (Derry Film and Video) Nell McCafferty
regrets that the Committee for the Liberation of Irish Women, to
avert a potential split, decided not to talk about the North. She
would now welcome general debate on topics like 'Feminism and
Physical Force'. While I might hope for a different outcome than
she does, I agree that the issue of women and Nationalism cannot
be dodged for ever. Southern women too are implicated in this
issue, although they may neither know it nor wish it. Even on her
death-bed Cathleen-Anorexia exerts a residual power over the image
and self-images of *all* Irish women. Both at home and abroad, she

still confers status on selected kinds of Irish femaleness (not, for instance, the Rhonda Paisley kind). An absurd 'Irish' edition of *Spare Rib* (August 1989), of which more anon, is a case in point.

Of course the Ulster Protestant community, though dragged forward faster by Westminster legislation, is as traditionally patriarchal as Catholic Nationalism. This tribe too has its cult of male chieftains: Carson, Moses, Paisley the 'Big Man' (compare Dev the 'Long Fellow', the Pope, the Boss). And the whole country abounds in Ancient Orders of Hibernian Male-Bonding: lodges, brotherhoods, priesthoods, hierarchies, sodalities, knights, Fitzwilliam Tennis Club, Field Day Theatre Company. But at least Unionism does not appropriate the image of woman or hide its aggressions behind our skirts. Nor does it – as a reactive ideology – seek ideological mergers. A Unionist feminist could be these things separately, though genuine feminism might erode her Unionism. A Nationalist/ Republican feminist, less readily regarded as a contradiction in terms, claims that her ideologies coincide. And in so doing she tries to hijack Irish feminism.

Terry Eagleton (in *Nationalism: Irony and Commitment*) develops an analogy between Nationalism and feminism as responses to 'oppression'. He argues that Nationalism must not prematurely sell its soul to revisionism and pluralism, just as feminism – until women have been truly liberated – must not sell its soul to 'a troubling and subverting of all...sexual strait-jacketing'.[16] As I will indicate later, with respect to the history of women and Nationalism, straitjackets tend to remain in place after the revolution unless their removal has been intrinsic to the revolution. Eagleton does not recognise that Catholic Nationalism has often been as great an oppressor of Irish people, Irish women, as British imperialism or Ulster Unionism. Perhaps the equivalent of advanced feminist 'troubling and subverting' is precisely what our Nationalist and Unionist patriarchal strait-jackets need.

Subversions occur wherever Protestants and Catholics in Ulster evade the binary ideological trap. But we need help from the Republic. I was surprised that Eavan Boland's LIP pamphlet, *A Kind of Scar: The Woman Poet in a National Tradition* ignored the extent to which the North has destabilised the 'nation'. Boland holds to unitary assumptions about 'a society, a nation, a literary heritage'. Troubled about 'the woman poet', she takes the 'national tradition' for granted – and perhaps thereby misses a source of her trouble. Because *A Kind of Scar* activates only one pole of its dialectic, it does not evolve the radical aesthetic it promises. By not asking why 'as a

poet I could not easily do without the idea of a nation', Boland
fails to challenge an idea of Irish poetry which is narrow as well as
patriarchal. She refers to 'marginality *within* a tradition' (my italics)
and regrets that 'the Irish nation as an existing construct in Irish
poetry was not available to me', without considering how that construct itself, both inside and outside poetry, has marginalised and
scarred many Irish women and men.[17]

Earlier I suggested that to over-stress the independence of Irish
literature from English literature (and *vice versa*) distorts literary
history and does not help contemporary politics. Boland, it seems
to me, feels unnecessarily guilty for (as an apprentice poet) having
read 'English court poetry' on Achill, and having imitated the English
'Movement' mode of the early sixties. To whom, to what avatar,
to what icon, is she apologising?[18]

In fact, it is to Mother Ireland herself. Although Boland criticises
male poets for having made woman a silent object in their visionary
odes (to 'Dark Rosaleen. Cathleen Ni Houlihan. The nation as
woman: the woman as national muse'), she insists: 'in all this I did
not blame nationalism'. Because she does not blame Nationalism,
her alternative Muse turns out to be the twin sister of Dark Rosaleen
etc: 'the truths of womanhood and the defeats of a nation. An
improbable intersection?' No, as Conor Cruise O'Brien said in a
similar context, 'a dangerous intersection'. Boland's new Muse,
supposedly based on the varied historical experience of Irish women,
looks remarkably like the Sean Bhean Bhocht. Her pamphlet begins
by invoking an old Achill woman who speaks of the Famine. The
'real women of an actual past' are subsumed into a single emblematic
victim-figure: 'the women of a long struggle and a terrible survival',
'the wrath and grief of Irish history'.[19] By not questioning the
nation, Boland recycles the literary cliché from which she desires
to escape.

Boland notes that 'the later Yeats' is a rare exception among
poets who 'have feminised the national and nationalised the feminine'.[20] There are good reasons why this should be so. Yeats's early
play *Cathleen Ni Houlihan* helped to propagate the feminine mystique
of Irish Nationalism. During the three years after 1916, in such
poems as 'On a Political Prisoner' and the much-misunderstood
'A Prayer for my Daughter', he broke the icon his poetry had gilded.
That is, he questioned Cathleen as then incarnated by Constance
Markievicz and Maud Gonne MacBride.

In 'A Prayer for my Daughter' Yeats criticises Ireland/Gonne
for her 'opinionated mind'. By 'opinion' he always means mechanical

dogma, particularly dogmatic Nationalism. So he is revising his
image of Woman-Ireland-Muse, and divining Anorexia in Gonne
'choked with hate':

> Have I not seen the loveliest woman born
> Out of the mouth of Plenty's horn,
> Because of her opinionated mind
> Barter that horn and every good
> By quiet natures understood
> For an old bellows full of angry wind?

That 'old bellows' is already full of destructive clichés. Yeats may
be patriarchal in the 'female' qualities he values above ideological
rigidity: 'natural kindness', 'heart-revealing intimacy', 'courtesy',
'rootedness'. But it might be argued that he replaces the aisling of
Nationalist male fantasy with a model for the Irish future that draws
on some qualities approved by feminists, or one that at least suggests
how to conceive the 'womanly times' for which Ian McEwan has
called.

However, Gonne, Markievicz and Maeve the warrior-queen have
enjoyed a new lease of life in Northern Republican ideology. Perhaps
we too readily assume that it's *always* a good thing when passive
versions of women are transformed into active ones (the militant
sliding into the military). Both have political uses.

Two passive images are the vulnerable virgin and the mourning
mother: images that link Cathleen with Mary. They project the self-
image of Catholic Nationalism as innocent victim, equally oppressed
at all historical periods. (Is there a subconscious admission that
Irish men victimise women?) This assigns to England the perpetual
role of male bully and rapist. In Seamus Heaney's 'Ocean's Love
to Ireland': 'The ruined maid complains in Irish'. In the mid-1970s
Heaney could still symbolise the Northern conflict as 'a struggle
between the cults and devotees of a god and a goddess'; between
'an indigenous territorial numen, a tutelar of the whole island, call
her Mother Ireland, Kathleen Ni Houlihan…the Shan Van Vocht,
whatever' and 'a new male cult whose founding fathers were Cromwell, William of Orange and Edward Carson'.[21] To characterise Irish
Nationalism (only constructed in the nineteenth century) as archetypally female both gives it a mythic pedigree and exonerates it
from aggressive and oppressive intent. Its patriarchal elements also
disappear. Here we glimpse the *poetic* (and Marian) unconscious
of Northern Nationalism. At the same time, Heaney's mouldering
'Bog Queen' in *North* may indirectly represent the cult of Cathleen
as a death-cult. The book contains an unresolved tension between

two Muses: a symbolic mummified or mummifying woman (not yet Anorexia) and the warmly creative, if domestic, aunt who bakes scones in the poem 'Sunlight'.

While Virgin-Ireland gets raped and pitied, Mother Ireland translates pity into a call to arms and vengeance. She resembles the white-feather-bestowing 'Little Mother' in First-World-War recruiting. Traditionally, it is her *sons* whom Mother Ireland recruits and whose *manhood* she tests. More recently, some of her daughters have also become 'freedom-fighters'. In *Mother Ireland* Bernadette (Devlin) McAliskey and Mairead Farrell differed in their attitudes to the personification. Devlin felt that Mother Ireland had empowered her as a strong woman; Farrell said: 'Mother Ireland, get off our backs'. But did she? Is there not collusion between all Nationalist images of women, between Queen Maeve and Mother Ireland, between the feminine-pathetic and the feminine-heroic? The latter disguises or softens aggression: the looks and deliberate dress of Gonne and Markievicz were propaganda-assets. On the cover of the biased *Only The Rivers Run Free: Northern Ireland: The Women's War* a glamorous young paramilitary woman fronts a desperate-looking Sean Bhean.

Such images of Irish women are among those selectively approved by Anorexia. The cover of *Spare Rib* (August 1989) features another: a west Belfast Mother Courage with child in pram, smoke and flames behind her, and insets of a British soldier and 'Stop Strip Searches'. Of course there are many courageous working-class mothers on the Falls – and on the Shankill too. But does it help them if this magazine distorts the profile of Irish women to include no police or UDR widows; no non-aligned social-workers, doctors or teachers; no members of the DUP; no Belfast or Dublin or London yuppies; no Southern feminists; no TDs? There are also articles with titles like 'Britain's War on Ireland' and 'Irish in Britain – Living in the Belly of the Beast' (an interesting variation on rape-images: cannibalism? John Bulimia? Siobhán and the whale?). And a literary section, among other poetic sentimentalities, reprints Susan Langstaff Mitchell's 'To the Daughters of Erin': 'Rise from your knees, O daughters rise!/Our mother still is young and fair... Heroes shall leap from every hill...The red blood burns in Ireland still'. Feminism, where are you? Hero-worship of the male Gael is part of the Nationalist pitch to women. *Spare Rib* has certainly provided the most ludicrous instance yet of the English Left's anach-ronistic and self-righteous pieties on the Irish question. But it's up to Irish women themselves to expose the loaded terms in a statement like: 'In the *Six Counties Irish* women experience *oppression* both as women and as members of a *colonised people*' (my italics). I attended a 'Time To Go' conference in London which offered a seminar on 'Ireland in Feminism'. I think feminism in Ireland should have something to say about that.

During the Irish revolution Nationalist women discovered, though not all acknowledged or cared, that their oppression as women did not end with the Dawning of the Day. The briefly eulogised '"Dáil Girl"…wielding a cudgel in one hand and a revolver in the other'[22] soon gave way to Dev's ideal of 'life within the home'. Nor had the Dáil girl necessarily taken up her cudgel for feminism. As a general rule: the more Republican, the less feminist. The ultra-Nationalism of the six women deputies who opposed the Treaty was, in Margaret Ward's words, governed by the 'ghosts of dead sons, husbands and brothers'.[23] Theirs were 'opinionated minds' with no – female? - capacity for compromise, and they set a pattern for the limited participation of women in the Free State/Republic's political life: almost invariably licensed by male relatives, by dynastic privilege. Rosemary Cullen Owens in *Smashing Times* (less romantic than Ward's *Unmanageable Revolutionaries*) brings out the tension between Nationalism and Suffragism: 'From 1914, with Home Rule on the statute book, it was the growing separatist movement which posed the greatest threat to a united women's movement.'[24]

Sinn Féin women (the only women quoted in *Spare Rib*) have recently adopted some feminist ideas. But they cling, like their elder sisters, to the prospective goodwill of Republican men, and to the fallacy that: 'there can't be women's liberation until there's national liberation'. Devlin in *Spare Rib* seems significantly wary of 'the gospel according to the Holy Writ of Feminism'. What a woman 'needs to know is that we, her sisters, will catch her if she stumbles, help her find the questions – the answers she must find herself'. Who are 'we, her sisters'? And what kind of élitism lurks in Devlin's assertion (in *Mother Ireland*) that 'the best young feminist women today are those who have come through the experience of the Republican movement'?

While admiring the bonding that tough circumstances beget, and perceiving these circumstances as tragic, I do not accept that either the supportiveness of the ghetto or the essential survival strategy in Armagh Gaol affords a model for Irish women in general. The basis of such bonding is tribal rather than sisterly. It remains true that the vast majority of Republican women come from traditionally Republican families – recruited by and for a patriarchal unit. The

Irish Women's Movement, instead of walking away or vaguely empathising, might examine the role of Nationalist conditioning in all this: the ideological forces which played a part in sending out Mairead Farrell to be shot.

Contrary to Nell McCafferty, I think that 'Feminism and Physical Force' is self-evidently a contradiction in terms. Years ago a member of the Irish Women's Franchise League said: 'It is our conviction feminism and militarism are natural born enemies and cannot flourish on the same soil.'[25] Militarism, that touch of Madame Defarge, gives the Sinn Féin sisterhood its faintly chilling aura. In *The Demon Lover: On the Sexuality of Terrorism* Robin Morgan argues that revolutionary terrorism, as much as 'official terrorism', inevitably involves a death-cult. It enacts the quest of the male hero who 'already lives as a dead man'. She asks: 'Why is manhood always perceived as the too-high price of peace?' and notes that when men take over any movement: 'What once aimed for a humanistic triumph now aims for a purist defeat. Martyrdom.'[26] The same syndrome can be detected in Protestant anticipations of Armageddon, apocalypse, their last stand (the ghosts of religious wars walk on both sides). Morgan's conclusion mirrors the Irish Nationalist historical pattern: 'The rebel woman in a male-defined State-that-would-be is merely acting out another version of the party woman running for office in the State-that-is.'[27] Unionist party-women have been equally acquiescent in militarism.

Cathleen-Anorexia encourages women to join a male death-cult given to a particularly masochistic martyrology. This cult's rituals deny the 'connectivity' that Morgan sees as the 'genius' of feminist thought: 'In its rejection of the static, this capacity is witty and protean, like the dance of nature itself...It is therefore a volatile capacity – and dangerous to every imaginable status quo, because of its insistence on *noticing*. Such a noticing involves both attentiveness and recognition, and is in fact a philosophical and activist technique for being in the world, as well as for changing the world.'[28] In 'Easter 1916' Yeats understands that 'Too long a sacrifice/Can make a stone of the heart', and contrasts that stone with 'the living stream'. Surely the chill, the stone, the self-destructiveness at the heart of Irish Nationalism shows up in its abuse of women and their gifts of life?

Conclusion: After Anorexia

I have argued that Nationalism and Unionism in Ireland are dying ideologies, death-cult ideologies. Yet these ideologies are also masks for an intensely local territorial struggle. Ulster's territorial imperative has produced a politics which pivots on male refusal to give an inch. John Hewitt characterises the Protestant people as 'stubborn'; Seamus Heaney characterises the Catholic people as 'obstinate'. The adjectives are inflected with an admiration that I cannot share.

But this polarised *macho* politics travesties the North's cultural complexity. In the 1989 report on *Cultural Traditions in Northern Ireland* Brian Turner emphasises how the thriving local studies movement has 'challenged the use of the "two traditions" terminology'.[29] And Anthony Buckley, in 'Collecting Ulster's Culture: are there really Two Traditions?', illustrates ways in which culture has been caricatured for the purpose of 'asserting group identities'.[30] A more negative term for this is 'cultural defence'. In fact insecurities underlie the self-assertive rhetorics of both Unionism and Nationalism. Cultural defence is the reflex of frontier-regions where communities fear extinction or absorption. It explains, for instance, the Catholic Church's not-an-inch attitude to integrated education. And it explains Unionism's perennial paranoia about the Irish language (only now to be properly supported and thus, perhaps, depoliticised).

That the Free State's Gaelicisation policy attracted more Unionist jeers than did Rome Rule indicates fears of ethnic exclusion (and also the counter-productiveness of Nationalist ideology). Yet Gaelicisation, which attempted an *impossible* separation of Irishness from Britishness, was itself a form of cultural defence against a powerful neighbour. Its errors are reproduced today by Sinn Féin's cultural self-ghettoisation. There can be a sad element of barren triumphalism in the west Belfast Festival.

Locked into dying ideologies, a territorial imperative and cultural defence, Northern Irish people do not immediately hold all the keys to their own salvation. One key is held by the Republic and the UK; another by a slow process of education.

Firstly, only the Republic and the UK together can defuse the mutual fear of their client communities. This should involve the Republic honestly re-examining its own Nationalism; making its constitutional claim as insignificant in theory as it is in practice; and adopting the same hands-off stance as the UK government. (John Hume's argument that the British have thereby 'neutrally' left matters up to the people of Ireland should be resisted, in so far as it promotes 'one more heave'.) Advance depends on an intricately engineered four-wheel drive which engages all parties to the dispute, and which encourages momentum within the North.

Secondly, without education in the broadest sense we cannot loosen the grip of Anorexia, of ideological *rigor mortis*. Progress will not only stem from official or institutional sources – changes in law, Fair Employment agencies, the Community Relations Council, re-conceiving school curricula, Education for Mutual Understanding, Cultural Diversity programmes etc – it occurs wherever people work together practically and constructively. The report of the Opsahl Commission (1993) testifies to many such efforts. Yet, as with the Irish language, we also need more formal means to dismantle the frameworks of cultural defence.

One pilot-model is the local studies movement. This, at the micro-level, breaks down monolithic versions of Nationalist and Unionist history. It also maximises the strength rather than the weakness of Ulster's territorial imperative: attachment to place. Local studies promote the 'noticing' that Robin Morgan values. Many Unionists (the OUP wing) refuse to notice the ground under their own feet, the very territory they claim. Since 1921 they have often imported an anxious, ersatz and self-mutilating Englishness to stand in for Britishness and fend off Irishness. The Campaign for Equal Citizenship (for getting British parties to organise in Northern Ireland) is a recent instance of Unionists staring across the water and trying to walk on it. Really, they are motivated by political sulks and cultural defence in the wake of the Anglo-Irish Agreement. This is not to say that British Toryism or socialism is 'alien' to Northern Ireland, as the Labour spokesman Kevin McNamara has claimed. But Unionist attempts to base themselves in London, like the SDLP inclination to identify with Dublin (or create a Derry-Dublin-Brussels-Boston axis that by-passes Belfast), show the vital importance of the regionalist concept. Some local councils now lead the way in power-sharing, as local studies do in culture-sharing.

Another model – which gives the lie to equations of the regional with the provincial – is Northern writing, especially since the early 1960s. At the start of this essay I called literature the primary place where language changes and anorexic categories are exposed (not always a conscious process). Writers born into an over-determined, over-defined environment, into a tension between political sim-plicities and cultural complexity, have felt impelled to redefine: to explore and criticise language, images, categories, stereotypes, myths. Northern writing does not fit the binary shapes cut out by National-ism and Unionism. It trellises the harsh girders with myriad details. It overspills borders and manifests a web of affiliation that stretches beyond any heartland – to the rest of Ireland, Britain, Europe. But the range of styles, histories, myths and influences perhaps could only enter the imagination in this unique zone of 'problems and cleavages' (John Hewitt's phrase). All the 'cultural traditions' count somewhere; nor are the political divisions discounted.

There is a third model in women's groups whose generally pragmatic priorities have theoretical implications. These groups exemplify how we learn and teach by doing. Recently, when the sectarianism of that male-dominated mayhem, Belfast City Council, blocked a grant to the Falls Road Women's Centre, their indignation was shared by the Women's Centre on the Shankill.

The image of the web is female, feminist, connective – as contrasted with male polarisation. So is the ability to inhabit a range of relations rather than a single allegiance. The great advantage of living in Northern Ireland is that you can be in three places at once. However, the term 'identity' has been coarsened in Ulster politics to signify two ideological package-deals immemorially on offer. To admit to more varied, mixed, fluid and relational kinds of identity would advance nobody's territorial claim. It would undermine cultural defences. It would subvert the male pride that keeps up the double frontier-siege. It would dismantle the dangerous ratchet that locks Catholic advance into Protestant demoralisation and emigration. All this would be on the side of life – like noticing, redefining and again redefining, doing.

Bernard Crick argues:

> while nationalisms are real and authentic in these islands, yet none are as self-sufficient as most of their adepts claim. In Northern Ireland most people are, in fact, torn in two directions: 'torn', that is, while their political leaders will not recognise that people can, with dignity, face in two directions culturally at once, and refuse to invent political institutions to match. In the world before nation-states such dualities and pluralities were common enough, as in some other border-areas today. [31]

Both Irish Nationalism and Ulster Unionism must accept the reality of the North as a frontier-region, a cultural corridor, a zone where Ireland and Britain permeate one another. The Republic should cease to talk so glibly about 'accommodating diversity' and face up to difference and division. This would actually help the North to relax into a genuinely diverse sense of its own identity: to function, under whatever administrative format, as a shared region of these islands. At which point there will definitely be no such person as Cathleen Ni Houlihan.

[1990]

Poetic Forms and Social Malformations

As they say in exam-questions, compare the following sonnets:

Someone on their way to early Mass
will find her hog-tied
to the chapel gates –
O Child of Prague –
big-eyed, anorexic.
The lesson for today
is pinned to her bomber jacket.
It seems to read *Keep off the Grass*.
Her lovely head has been chopped
and changed.
For Beatrice, whose fathers
knew Louis Quinze,
to have come to this, her perruque
of tar and feathers.

A BAD TIME

Having butchered everyone in the church
The soldiers explore the vaults underneath
Where the choicest ladies are hidden
Hoping to cheat the general death.
One of these, a most handsome virgin,
Kneels down to Thomas à Wood, with prayers
And tears, that he may spare her life.
Sudden pity; he takes her in his arms
Out of the church, intending her escape.
A soldier sees this and pikes her through.
à Wood, seeing her gasping, takes her money
And jewels, flings her down over the works.
Massacre flows for five days in succession.
A bad time for virgins, local people say.

The first sonnet is in fact a stanza: one of forty-nine making up 'The More a Man Has the More a Man Wants' in Paul Muldoon's *Quoof* (1983). This long poem is as much a sonnet-sequence as it is any other kind of sequence, since non-sequiturs constantly twist round its narrative signposts. *Quoof* as a whole stretches the elastic of sonnet-sequence even further; although once again 'sequence' seems too serial a term for a set of relations more akin to a Rubik cube. 'A Bad Time' comes from Brendan Kennelly's much longer sequence, the 146-page *Cromwell*, also published in 1983. A theme of this essay will be differences between Muldoon's poetry on the one hand, and *Cromwell* and the poetry of Paul Durcan on the other. It will discuss the pre-history of differing formal procedures and ask whether they reflect – up to a point – different cultural and social conditions in Northern and Southern Ireland. As Louis MacNeice says: 'A poem may be a bridge to the Unknown but it is a bridge essentially constructed in terms of the known.'[1] In another sense, poetry deals in what societies don't want to know.

Both sonnets quoted above concern violence against women in time of war. The first image derives from the tarring and feathering of Northern Catholic girls, punished (in the 1970s) for going with British soldiers. 'A Bad Time' condenses incidents from the sack of Drogheda by Cromwell's soldiers in 1649. But if the poems share fourteen lines and the matter of Ireland, do they also share lens and focus? Muldoon's allusive close-up does not waste words. Any physical impressions are inseparable from a tautly ironic linguistic fabric. 'Hog-tied', 'anorexic' and 'bomber jacket' tug against and intertwine with 'early Mass', 'chapel gate' and 'The lesson for today'. 'O Child of Prague' aligns a religious icon with totalitarian regimes. As always in Muldoon's poetry, puns bring to light incongruities or collusions – here, between authoritarian religion, misogyny, and violent politics. 'The lesson for today' finds in church-language a terrible contemporary imperative. *'Keep off the Grass'* puns on the poem's running motif of drugs, besides conveying more ominous prohibitions. 'Chopped/and changed' not only darkens the light slanginess of an everyday cliché, but visualises what it might mean. That 'head' not 'hair' is in question prepares for the French Revolutionary references to come. 'Beatrice' – one name for the poem's changing Muse, 'heroine' or female scapegoat – and 'Louis Quinze' exotically enlarge the literary and historical context. Yet this only highlights a tawdry smallness. 'Perruque' implies that victims of Republican terror, that terror itself, and its informing ideology have come down in the world since the 1790s. (At another level, the stanza deconstructs Seamus Heaney's 'Punishment', in which 'the exact/and tribal, intimate revenge' retains some mythic prestige: Muldoon exposes contradictions between Heaney's adjectives.) Muldoon's handling of sonnet-form is equally intricate. Lines 2-5 split pentameters where caesuras would not be emphatic enough. Again, the line-break 'chopped/and changed' goes beyond a local metrical pun to suggest that sonnet-form is mutating under brutal pressures; that its architecture is being determined by fault-lines.

'A Bad Time' faces its subject and the reader more directly. *Cromwell* comes at us from many angles, but Kennelly's prolific invention is less continuously linguistic than Muldoon's. Muldoon's poetry is a profound form of psycho-social linguistics which, by investigating structures of language, reveals 'the mechanism of the trap' (a favourite phrase of Auden's in the early 1930s). Kennelly's words are means to an end: the instruments of fact, fiction and fantasy, of a theatre which 'tries to present the nature and implications of various forms of dream and nightmare, including the nightmare of Irish history'. Some of this could apply to 'The More a Man Has', but in an inferred, introverted, implosive sense. *Cromwell* extroverts, explodes. It abounds in catalogues, accumulations, bad taste, bad jokes, bad language, melodrama, shock tactics, grotesque disproportions, hyperboles, going over the top. (Muldoon goes under it.) Thus the contradiction between Cromwellian 'butchery' and its church setting is not latent in idiom but made relentlessly explicit ('pikes her through') . The final absurd choric comment completes the picture and the sonnet-structure with heavier under-lining than the dispersed nuance of 'For Beatrice...to have come to this.' 'The More a Man Has' reserves explicit horror for climactic images:

> He slumps
> in the spume of his own arterial blood
> like an overturned paraffin lamp.

Cromwell sups full, piles on the narrative agony while hysteria rises under plain diction. 'A Bad Time' keeps tightening the screw until à Wood 'flings her down over the works'. Sonnet-form in *Cromwell* is also largely a means: a container for self-contained effects rather than an entertainer of its own possibilities. Kennelly takes sonnets as they come, regular or irregular, whereas Muldoon takes anarchic liberties that seem precisely calculated. Kennelly's incidental rhymes (underneath/death) do not raise the ghost of Petrarch as do Muldoon's delicate echoes (anorexic/perruque).

However, *Cromwell* is conscious of its medium in a broader and political sense. Half-masochistically the poem relishes the irony of an Irish poet following in the sonneteering footsteps of Spenser, Sidney and Shakespeare. 'Ed Spenser' actually becomes a character in a historical phantasmagoria which features not only Oliver Cromwell in various guises, but William of Orange, the giant, the Belly, Big Island, Little Island, and the put-upon protagonist M.P.G.M. Buffún. One of Buffún's burdens is the English literary tradition, which sometimes oppresses Irish writers if they feel dispossessed of their own language. Kennelly says in his introductory note:

> Because of history, an Irish poet, to realise himself, must turn the full attention of his imagination to the English tradition. An English poet committed to the same task need hardly give the smallest thought to things Irish.

This strand in the poem relates to Patrick Kavanagh's 'Memory of Brother Michael':

> It would never be morning, always evening,
> Golden sunset, golden age –
> When Shakespeare, Marlowe and Jonson were writing
> The future of England page by page
> A nettle-wild grave was Ireland's stage...

and Heaney's 'Bog Oak':

> Edmund Spenser,
> dreaming sunlight,
> encroached upon by
>
> geniuses who creep
> 'out of every corner
> of the woodes and glennes'
> towards watercress and carrion.

But Kennelly is neither as unpolitical as Kavanagh, angry about Irish dependence on the past for literary and other alibis ('Shall we be thus for ever?'); nor as political as Heaney, conscious of still-suppressed Northern genius. 'Master' both brings sunlit English myths of chivalry down to earth and admits a curious kinship between the artistic trials of Spenser and Kennelly:

> 'I am master of the chivalric idiom' Spenser said
> As he sipped a jug of buttermilk
> And ate a quaite of griddle-bread.
> 'I'm worried, though, about the actual bulk
> Of The Faerie Queene. She's growing out
> Of all proportions, in different directions.
> Am I losing control? Am I buggering it
> All up? Ruining my best intentions?
> As relief from my Queene, I write sonnets
> But even these little things get out of hand
> Now and then, giving me a nightmare head.
> Trouble is, sonnets are genetic epics.
> Something in them wants to grow out of bounds.
> I'm up to my bollox in sonnets' Spenser said.

A genetic epic, *Cromwell* conflates Spenser's two modes into one adapted to the 'tragic mess' of Irish history. Though no *Faerie Queene* (perhaps 'Demon King'), it might be termed 'primary epic' in the context of the Irish state since 1922; and in practice Kennelly's iconoclastic methods get 'the English tradition' off his back, as he bounces off it to pursue parallel purposes. If the tradition burdens Muldoon, he juggles rather than wrestles with it; remains technically within what he turns inside out. Heaney's complaint

> Ulster was British, but with no rights on
> The English lyric

suggests that Northern poets, from Catholic and Protestant backgrounds alike, have been motivated (as Yeats was) by a desire to show
English poets that they can make better use of that lyric inheritance.
Mixed literary motives – appropriation and separatism – persist.
Kennelly, on the other hand, questions the relevance of lyrical
concentration to his own artistic needs, and the needs of his society,
when the giant 'exhorts':

> This world bulges with chirping pissers like yourself,
> Melodious dwarfs fluting a dwarfing tune
> To other dwarfs who turn their backs
> On all songs hacked from nightmare.
>
> Shape up, my little bard! Rattle your rocks!
> Give us a twist to ring the ruined moon!

II

If the convergent subjects of the two sonnets with which I began
suggest Ireland's political disunity, their divergent techniques may
suggest its cultural hinterland. What inhibits a united Ireland and
a uniform Irish poetry – if the latter phenomenon were either possible or desirable – is refusal to acknowledge disunity or diversity,
to predicate unity on the recognition of differences. One can be
accused of 'Partitionism' for drawing any distinctions at all between
Northern and Southern, Protestant and Catholic literary expression,
as if no religious or regional factors applied. To describe is not to
prescribe. Words and forms usefully insist on cultural and social
realities, if at the expense of ideologies, ideals, and the author's
intention. Poetic units rarely coincide with political units. They
defeat or sabotage them by being simultaneously smaller and larger.
To say 'It's all Irish poetry' (as opposed to the incontrovertible 'It's
all poetry') is a pseudo-inclusive reflex, a premature homogenisation,
that actually devalues what poetry can tell us about Ireland. Indeed,
the politics of Irish poetry can be more revealing than the poetry
of Irish politics. Witness the contrasting premises and priorities of
Thomas Kinsella's *New Oxford Book of Irish Verse* and Paul Muldoon's
Faber Book of Contemporary Irish Poetry, both published in 1986.
    Kinsella's model of 'the Irish tradition' is singular, platonically
unified: 'a notable and venerable...tradition [surviving] a change of
vernacular'.[2] His first section makes primordial claims: 'From the
Beginning to the Fourteenth Century'. Given such awesomely long
vistas, it is not surprising that Kinsella fails to get the last mere

sixty years into focus. His small contemporary section fudges crucial issues of how Irish poetry has developed since Yeats and since the Treaty. He picks out Seamus Heaney and Derek Mahon, but mainly for ancestral *pietas*: 'it is in the context of a dual responsibility, toward the medium and toward the past, that Seamus Heaney's and Derek Mahon's poetry registers so firmly, rather than in any "Northern Ireland Renaissance"...[which] is largely a journalistic entity'.[3] It is difficult not to read these remarks politically (or, at very least, as literary politics). The appropriation of 'the past', once again singular, is itself a form of Irish political rhetoric, Nationalist and Unionist. Conor Cruise O'Brien queries Kinsella's concept of 'one single thing called "Irish poetry" which has "two bodies". "Irish poetry" turns out to be a cultural Siamese twin'.[4] Kinsella may be uncertain about the dynamics of Irish poetry today because his platonic ethnicity discounts historical process: the shaping role of poetry's linguistic body and plural social contexts.

The Faber Book, with its counter-bias towards the North (six of the eight living poets included), at least takes a bet on the music of what happened after Yeats. It also differs from the *New Oxford Book* in writing off the past as dominant Muse. Muldoon's prolonged epigraph, in lieu of an introduction, is an extract from a radio-discussion between F.R. Higgins and Louis MacNeice broadcast in 1939. Higgins speaks up for 'our blood-music that brings the racial character to mind'; MacNeice for 'impure' poetry, and the poet as 'a sensitive instrument designed to record anything which interests his mind or affects his emotions'. In part of the discussion not included by Muldoon, MacNeice refers to the poetry that can be got from 'a changing society, or a jumble of clans'. He also says: 'if you are inside a changing society the only kind of poetry you will write must recognise the changes going on'. Muldoon implicitly backs MacNeice's creative eclecticism rather than the essentialism that links Higgins to Corkery, Kinsella, and perhaps Heaney. Higgins praises in Irish poetry 'a belief emanating from life, from nature, from revealed religion, and from the nation'. (Heaney, detecting a Muldoon subtext, was inclined to defend Higgins at the International Writers' conference, Dublin 1989). As for the anthology's contents, although excluded Southern poets might not agree, Muldoon's politics again seem more intrinsically aesthetic than Kinsella's in that he favours a concentration akin to his own, and his criteria bar John Hewitt as well as Brendan Kennelly.

My Introduction discussed some of the cultural factors, now unique to Ulster, which made Anglo-Irish and English forms a *living* challenge – not just a kink in the 'post-colonial' psyche or a dazzle on the Spenserian page – to all poets whatever their background. More homogeneous literary as well as social conditions then obtained in Dublin, even if Trinity had already cradled some 'Northern' poetry. Muldoon, twelve years younger than the first wave of poets, has this perspective on his own cradle:

> for [older poets] and for a lot of the younger poets there was a sense of an audience not only in Ireland but in England – and that seemed to give, in a provincial way, some kind of credibility to what was happening. Now people may dispute this, but the fact is our sense of the London scene was very important, because then – perhaps less so now [1985] – London was seen as the cultural centre of those islands. Dublin had already declined, and Kavanagh had just died [1967], so that particular Irish literary scene had to some extent disappeared.[5]

Although Dublin's literary traditions are so much older and richer than Belfast's, in another sense they are younger. A seismic transition has taken place in this as in so many areas. During the 1930s and 1940s certain poets in the Free State declared aesthetic independence too. It seemed important to break or weaken Anglo-Irish and English literary links infinitely complicated by a shared language. One route to separateness was Austin Clarke's absorption in and of Gaelic poetry. Another was Modernism. It is relevant that Kinsella should have subsequently tried to fuse Gaelicism with Modernism – and that MacNeice should have asked: 'When will well-known Irish writers who publish nothing but English stop preaching nothing but Gaelic?'[6] Joyce (understandably) seemed to provide a more liberating artistic role-model than Yeats, and Modernism also opened up continental and transatlantic horizons. Not only Beckett, but writers such as Denis Devlin and Brian Coffey lived abroad. Michael Smith compiled his anthology *Irish Poetry: The Thirties Generation* (first published in 1971) in order 'to demonstrate that, since Yeats, Irish poetry written in English was not all rural in content and simplistically popular in technique, but also possessed a body of truly modern work, reflecting urban consciousness, experimenting with new techniques and concerned with non-nationalist experience'.[7] Some of these polarities are much too cut and dried. Thomas MacGreevy fought at the Somme and wrote a book on T.S. Eliot, but retained a 'fierce patriotic Irish Catholicism, which was really an anti-Protestant, anti-Englishism'.[8] Reasons for rejecting 'the Yeatsian big-top' (Smith) may be complex, and turn on the acceptability of Anglo-Irish versions of Nationalism.

Thus MacNeice's background made it easier for him to become the Irish poet of his generation who most thoroughly, if dialectically, absorbed Yeats into his creative and critical systems. Similarly, Derek Mahon has been able to say: 'I was never oppressed by Yeats'.[9] Hubert Butler, in reply to Kavanagh's sniping at the Revival (see p.141), diagnosed unadmitted literary trauma together with canonical uncertainties:

> The Anglo-Irish contribution to letters is today [1954]...a chief focus of psychological disturbance...Mr Kavanagh...will not see that the Abbey Theatre Group not only nursed Irish talent at home but also created abroad a favourable atmosphere for its reception. Every Irish writer who travels to London is in their debt...In an essay on F.R. Higgins he accuses Irish Protestants of trying to 'by-pass Rome on the way to the heart of Ireland', and several times he argues with different degrees of candour that you cannot be Irish if you are not Catholic...What Mr Kavanagh is trying to do is to bypass Anglo-Ireland on the way to the heart of London. And it is sure that while Anglo-Ireland, north and south, may ultimately be assimilated (a very slow process of reciprocal adjustment), it cannot conceivably be by-passed. The Anglo-Irish were not only the cruel stepmothers of Gaelic civilisation, they were also the indulgent nurses and governesses of Irish literature in the English language.[10]

Although Butler discerns total hostility to literary Nationalism, because constructed by Anglo-Irish Protestants, there are Catholic-Nationalist undercurrents in this 'disturbance'. (Kavanagh, as I hope to show, is a special case.) Subject to changing fashions of theoretical idiom, these undercurrents recur in critiques of the Revival from the 1930s to the 1980s – from Leslie Daiken in *Goodbye, Twilight* (see page 116) to Michael Smith to Field Day. The sub-text of 'urban internationalist' consciousness, even of urban internationalist socialist consciousness, can be unexamined Nationalism. Declan Kiberd's categories still simplify literary and political issues when he prefers the Ireland 'pioneered by men like Connolly and James Joyce' to 'the one led by Yeats and de Valera'.[11] Yeats would be surprised to learn that de Valera had eaten his heart.

Whether because it had not put its ideological house in order, or for other reasons, Irish poetic Modernism never matched up to the prose with its Joycean head's start. Beckett is the Modernist of the 1930s generation who has most deeply influenced later poetry, especially Derek Mahon's images and ironies. Mahon fits the bill if urban consciousness and internationalism are required, though not as regards free verse. And verse is the key-factor (as ever with poetry) on which other structural elements depend. Irish poetry needed indigenous new rhythms such as those D.H. Lawrence had created in England. Poetic Modernism could not be imported at a stroke by exchanging F.R. Higgins's pastiche Yeats for pastiche Eliot:

> I am tired, tired, tired. I will go home now,
> The train clattering between the tenements,
> The train clanking through the greasy fog...
> Eyes stare me, black sunken holes,
> Faces of dead men, pearl sweat on the forehead...
>   (Brian Coffey, 'Dead Season')

Kinsella's methods in 'Nightwalker' (1968) are surely not much of an advance:

> I only know things seem and are not good.

> A brain in the dark, and bones, out exercising
> Shadowy flesh; fitness for the soft belly,
> Fresh air for lungs that take no pleasure any longer.
> The smell of gardens under suburban lamplight...

The revolutionary Irish free-verse achievement of the early forties, the poem which liberated the ears of Brendan Kennelly and Paul Durcan, does not sing to Eliot's tune. Kavanagh's *The Great Hunger* (1942) begins:

> Clay is the word and clay is the flesh
> Where the potato-gatherers like mechanised scarecrows move
> Along the side-fall of the hill – Maguire and his men...

This combines parodic yet powerful incantation with colloquial ease, and initiates symbolic depth-charges. Michael Smith is misled by the recurrent red herring of rural subject-matter when he describes Kavanagh as 'wanting not so much to make it new as to replace the fraudulent with the genuine'.[12] To deny Kavanagh's innovatory shock is to imply that all natural or country images, whatever their purposes, belong to a single reactionary aesthetic. Indeed, an embryonic tension in Kavanagh's imagination is that between 'country poet' and 'nature poet'. But in so far as *The Great Hunger* attacks discrepancies between official ideology and social practice, it targets the functional hypocrisies of Dublin as much as Inniskeen, de Valera's developing myth of 'frugal comfort' and 'cosy homesteads'[13] as much as Yeats's singing of the peasantry. This remarkable poem can be read not only as anti-pastoral but as national counter-epic:

> The hungry fiend
> Screams the apocalypse of clay
> In every corner of this land.

It was *because* Kavanagh had something passionate to say that he could 'make it new' technically. He read *The Waste Land* (just before writing *The Great Hunger*) but transmuted its method to fit his own necessities. What Kavanagh says about literary-political poses (in 'Violence and Literature') applies to the faking of *Waste Land angst* in Irish poetry: 'Putting on the agony, any kind of agony, is silly and a form of weakness. It must come to you and you must be helpless.'[14] That also applies to putting on the (Modernist) style.

The Faber Book of Contemporary Irish Poetry makes it clear that Paul Muldoon considers Kavanagh and MacNeice to be the presiding geniuses after Yeats. The relative prominence accorded to MacNeice in anthologies might be used as one graph of perceptions. His poem 'Dublin' (1939) anticipates that the city 'will not/Have me alive or dead': an accurate prophecy of his absence from Smith's 'Thirties Generation' (France seems a more acceptable place of exile than England), and from Maurice Harmon's *Irish Poetry After Yeats* (1979). Kinsella includes MacNeice, but the 'two poetic careers that demand special attention'[15] are those of Clarke and Kavanagh. He also queries the legitimacy of MacNeice's possible Northern paternities: 'the search for special antecedents usually [fastens] on Louis MacNeice'.[16] Harmon's bias is less deliberate than Kinsella's, but he offers few aesthetic criteria and assumes too readily that the dust has settled regarding Ireland's poetic let alone political traditions:

> the poetic tradition has been strengthened. Its separate elements are visible, the poets are conscious of being part of it and work confidently within it. We see this sense of tradition in broad terms in the lines that connect Kavanagh, Montague and Heaney, or in the links between Joyce, Clarke and Kinsella.[17]

Besides disregarding MacNeice's posterity, Harmon's summary limits Kavanagh's. Just as MacNeice and Kavanagh took Irish poetry to ideologically incorrect but creatively enriching places (urban England, rural Ireland), so their one-man 'revivals' are not bounded by these contexts. It is – or should be – the measure of genuine poets that they excite a wide range of responses in their successors. But history and geography also placed Kavanagh at a strangely nodal point – 'Inniskeen Road: July Evening', perhaps.

> Half-past eight and there is not a spot
> Upon a mile of road, no shadow thrown
> That might turn out a man or woman, not
> A footfall tapping secrecies of stone.

This is an ironic portrait of the poet contemplating his creative locus whose 'code of mysteries' the sonnet has already tapped. The coding of Kavanagh's Inniskeen contributes to his position at a literary crossroads. Neil Corcoran, while rightly stressing his influence on Northern poets, wrongly terms him 'a kind of honorary Ulsterman'.[18] There is nothing honorific about the title. Inniskeen is in Co. Monaghan, one of the three Ulster counties (the others are Donegal and Cavan) assigned to the Free State at the time of Partition. Even though Kavanagh comes from a homogenously Catholic area, and though some Monaghan Protestants crossed the border in the 1920s, the county retains a Northern grasp of sectarian differences. Kavanagh's own reflex sectarianism, discussed by Antoinette Quinn in her fine study *Patrick Kavanagh: Born-Again Romantic* (1991), underlies the literary prejudices with which Hubert Butler takes issue. For example, in *The Great Hunger* Patrick Maguire's mother, castrator of the male psyche, personification of the repressive collusion between small-farm economics and Catholic morality, is called 'tall hard as a Protestant spire' – an interesting transference. Quinn persuasively argues that Kavanagh fulfils, albeit in a critical spirit, Daniel Corkery's agenda for the 'native' writer, especially as regards two imperatives: 'The Religious Consciousness of the People' and 'The Land'.[19]

On the other hand, Kavanagh's South Ulster origins may partly explain his wary attitude towards the third pillar of Corkery's trinity – i.e. Nationalism. The cultural ideology which Kavanagh assailed in Dublin was strongly influenced by Corkery's Munster preoccupations. Kavanagh's black hills 'look north towards Armagh' ('Shancoduff'). Co. Louth to the East once belonged to Gaelic Ulster. Inniskeen, in fact, sits within a more authentic 'borderlands' than the actual Northern Irish border. Due to geography and Gaelic lordships, 'there are few examples where boundaries so finely reflect a borderland as the Monaghan-Armagh-Louth county boundaries coinciding with the southern edge of the most extensive drumlin belt in western Europe'.[20] 'Living among small farmers in the north of Ireland', as Kavanagh terms it in 'Living in the County', was not necessarily an identical experience for Kavanagh, for the young Heaney in south Derry, and for the young Muldoon in Co. Armagh. Nevertheless, Kevin Whelan has pointed to the distinctiveness of Ulster's historical development as a densely populated proto-industrial area 'festooned with myriad small farmer-weaver holdings, especially within the linen triangle of Belfast, Dungannon and Newry'.[21] The agricultural map of Ulster, with its network of small farms, has contributed to other forms of territorial intensity.

From his move to Dublin in 1939 until his death in 1967 Kavanagh obsessively tried to comprehend a dislocation, a split:

> In many ways it is a good thing to be cast into exile
> Among strangers

> Who have no inkling
> Of The Other Man concealed
> Monstrously musing in a field.
> ('Living in the County')

It was a good thing in that The Other Man, Kavanagh's Monaghan self, re-created his local co-ordinates as a poetic microcosm: 'I cannot die/Unless I walk outside these whitethorn hedges' ('Innocence'). It was a bad thing in that it cast him into cultural limbo and a posture of perpetual opposition – the hedges also mark a defensive perimeter. His language of internal exile can be linked to regional factors as well as to the broader tensions between culchie (countryman) and Jackeen (Dubliner), or between 'peasant poet' and literary metropolis. For instance, Kavanagh's objections to the cults of Gaelic poetry and western landscape stem not only from rivalry with Austin Clarke and F.R. Higgins, but from his belief in the literary potential of a cultural terrain different to that fetishised by 'Paddy of the Celtic mist' or 'Paddy Connemara West' ('The Paddiad'). He says in *The Green Fool*:

> I stayed a week in Connemara and was disappointed with the scenery and the people. When you have seen one bit of Connemara you have seen it all, and it is all stones. The folk there were inclined to laugh at me. They spoke Gaelic and yet I felt that the English-speaking peasants of my own country were nearer to the old tradition. There was no culture in Connemara, nothing like County Monaghan where the spirit of the old poets haunted the poplars.[22]

In fact, Kavanagh (who grew up inside the border of Scottish influence on both languages in Ireland) wrote a poem dedicated to the south Armagh Gaelic poet Art McCooey, a poem of shared territorial precisions:

> I recover now the time I drove
> Cart-loads of dung to an outlying farm –
> My foreign possessions in Shancoduff –
> With the enthusiasm of a man who sees life simply.
>
> The steam rising from the load is still
> Warm enough to thaw my frosty fingers.
> In Donnybrook in Dublin ten years later
> I see that empire now and the empire builder.

Despite Kavanagh's guerrilla-campaigns against the Yeatsian aftermath, Yeats's representations of Sligo and Galway helped to release other Irish local (and regional) muses. While still a farmer, Kavanagh used to arrange Yeats poems along the hedge of a field where he was ploughing. When he eventually formulated his own aesthetic of 'parochial enthusiasm' (Hubert Butler's phrase), it opposed the totalising propensities of Nationalism. Hence Heaney's failure to remake the parish poem in a national image. For Kavanagh,

> nationalism is seldom based on those sincerities which give any truly spiritual force its power. Good work cannot survive in an angry atmosphere ...English literature...seems to me largely divorced from England the nation, the often scoundrelly nation...the protective atmosphere which fed the English poetic world had little to do with politics or patriotism. Love of the land and landscape is of course a different kettle of potatoes altogether. Constable, Wordsworth, Clare...were great patriots in that sense.[23]

As both Seamus Heaney and Antoinette Quinn have demonstrated, Kavanagh 'found his voice' amidst the conflict between literary idioms that already existed and the speech he heard around him:

> The sun sinks low and large behind the hills of Cavan,
> A stormy-looking sunset. 'Brave and cool.'
>
> ('Art McCooey')

Within the zone of 'Northern poetry', it may be that Ulster-Catholic localisms shadow the larger, unstable Ulster regionalism conceived by John Hewitt. Kavanagh's persona, cultivated for purposes of defence and offence in Dublin, included his self-image as the honest plain-speaker from out-of-town: 'Paddy Conscience' agonised by a 'nondescript land' where 'Everything is secondhand', by a 'sneering', 'insincere' city. His rarely-quoted poem 'The Twelfth of July' links sincerity and authenticity with 'the voice of Ulster speaking,/Tart as week-old buttermilk from a churn/Surprising the tired palates of the south'. Kavanagh's 'Ulster imagined' includes 'All that was sharp, precise and pungent-flavoured', and he recruits 'young men out of Ulster' as his imagined allies against the metropolitan sneers of 'Dublin's lounge-bar panzers'.

Terence Brown was right to conclude *Northern Voices* (1975) 'With Kavanagh in Mind'. He praises Kavanagh's sonnet 'The Hospital' for combining 'that European and English form' with 'the conditions of his own bitter, difficult Irish experience' in a way that 'transcends' the latter.[24] However, Brown may be premature and inaccurate in proclaiming Kavanagh the same thing to all Irish poets: a model of 'the free, exhilarated imagination', which he contrasts with the degree to which Ulster poets' 'imaginative life... has been limited by the horizons defined by the colonial predicament'.[25] The polarity 'freedom versus constraint' is no more straightforward a yardstick as applied to societies than to metres, or to the relation between political and poetic structures. Kavanagh's sonnets and problematic horizons face two ways: towards *Cromwell* and *Quoof*.

III

MacNeice's reasons for finding free verse uncongenial were that: 'In the arts bars can be cross-bars and limitations an asset.'[26] This dictum holds culturally as well as formally, even if it took the 'narrow ground' of the North as long to flower as the 'stony grey soil of Monaghan'. It is indeed the 'territorial' Kavanagh who most appeals North of the border. 'That original townland' (to transfer a phrase from Heaney's 'The Harvest Bow') strikes home where the language, metaphors and mentality of territory go so deep as to render poetry a form of multi-dimensional map-making. This reproduces, in A.T.Q. Stewart's words, the 'unavoidable fact of coexistence [which] dictates the most important aspect of the enduring conflict, which is that it must always be conducted in terms of topography'.[27]

Heaney's significantly named essays ('From Monaghan to the Grand Canal' and 'The Sense of Place') relish Kavanagh's poetry for being 'earthed in the actual' and weighted rather than weightless, for possessing a keen 'appetite for the living realities of Patrick Maguire's world'. He finely terms Kavanagh 'a parish priest'.[28] Kavanagh's doctrine that the 'parochial mentality...is never in any doubt about the social and artistic validity of his parish',[29] however compensatory, is often cited by Northern poets who follow him in translating local specificities on to symbolic planes. Whatever else may be in doubt, the stanza from 'The More a Man Has' intimately knows where it is. Even if Muldoon's parodic 'Moy' incorporates a bleak critique of parishes and priests, it upholds the spaciousness of specificity: 'I'm very interested in the way in which a small place, a parish, can come to stand for the world.'[30] Yet both Heaney and Muldoon pull Kavanagh further North. Heaney reads into Kavanagh's poetry some of his own 'weightedness' ('weight', laden with aesthetic and cultural value, is a term he borrows from Ted Hughes), obsession with 'growing down and in', and political interest in 'raising the inhibited energies of a subculture to the power of a cultural resource'.[31] Kavanagh perceived his culture as self-inhibited, not externally oppressed, and his imaginative trajectory as to do with growing up and out.

For Kavanagh, 'a peasant is all that mass of mankind which lives below a certain level of consciousness. They live in the dark cave of the unconscious and they scream when they see the light.'[32] Heaney, removed from farmwork by education, revisits the rural unconscious in a Romantic quest for archetypes, endowing it with prehistory as well as mystery. He finds 'opulent', rather than oppressive,

'the mill-race heavy with the Lammas floods' and perceives as lack
or absence the fact that at 'the bottom of Kavanagh's imagination
there is no pagan queen, no mystique of the national, the mythic or
the tribal'.[33] Heaney can't or won't see the social and personal history,
the communal crisis, written into *The Great Hunger*. Kavanagh's
mystique or healing myth centres on 'light of imagination' – 'winking
glitter' – not dark. The recalcitrant clay that symbolises the defor-
mations of Patrick Maguire's world (where a 'monster hand lifted
up children and put down apes') never takes on the amniotic aura
of Heaney's bog – 'nesting ground,/outback of my mind'. Kavanagh's
'In Memory of My Mother' repeatedly detaches her from 'the wet
clay'. There are evidently psychological as well as cultural or political
differences here. Whereas, in Jungian terms, Heaney's 'mother
ground' (rather unusually) reunites the male anima with maternal
origins; Maguire's purgatorial entrapment, from which the narrative voice cannot or does not wholly extricate itself, resembles the
hero's failure to 'deliver himself from the mother archetype (and
from the infantile unconsciousness that the hero's bondage to her
authority represents for the conscious personality)'.[34] Poetry delivered
Kavanagh into consciousness, but not into full personal articulation.
His blockage in Dublin suggests that a rite of passage was never
completed on a psychic as well as a cultural level. Hence those only
partially healing poems that re-constitute Inniskeen as a pre-ado-
lescent Eden. To recover innocence or his mother means accepting
loss. In 'Innocence' 'I know nothing of women,/Nothing of cities'
is a cry both of defiance and despair.

Besides earthing their foundations, territorial cultures develop
orienteering skills above ground, which poets' strategies and structures
may imitate or interrogate. Parleying 'on the central stepping stone'
('Terminus') is only one among Heaney's many self-images as

> picking a nice way through
> the long toils of blood
>
> and feuding.
>   ('The Last Mummer')

The wary walker along networks of boundaries, who has 'an eye
for weather-eyes//at cross-roads and lane-ends', emerges from a more
pressing objective reality than do the spy-ridden landscapes of early
Auden. On this internalised map divisions run within, as well as
between, groups. Thus Muldoon's poetry features a comically elusive
figure 'Golightly' as alias of the poet. However, he also becomes the
tragically fugitive protagonist of 'The More a Man Has', pursued

by furies and 'Keeping down-wind of everything'. Muldoon's techniques, too, of course involve artful dodging, disguises, shape-changes, riddles, undercover puns, cunningly subjunctive syntax. His poetry manoeuvres in a one-dimensional charmed space between irresistible forces – a fictive *reductio* of the Ulster constraints:

> They came bearing down on me out of nowhere.
> A Buick and a Chevrolet.
> They were heading towards a grand slam.
> Salami on rye. I was the salami.
> So much for my faith in human nature.
> The age of chivalry how are you?
> But I side-stepped them, neatly as Salome...
>
> ('Immram')

A dance of veils, an ingenious rhyme, may be a lifesaver. Similarly, 'The Boundary Commission' challenges the binary terms of Heaney's 'Other Side' by reducing territorial maps to absurdity:

> *You remember that village where the border ran*
> *Down the middle of the street,*
> *With the butcher and baker in different states?*
> Today he remarked how a shower of rain
>
> Had stopped so cleanly across Golightly's lane
> It might have been a wall of glass
> That had toppled over. He stood there, for ages,
> To wonder which side, if any, he should be on.

The typical protagonist of Ciaran Carson's first-person poems, in *The Irish for No* (1987) and *Belfast Confetti* (1989), seems to have the fewest strategic options amid boundary-wars. Bemused by the 'labyrinth' of the city, he cannot read (or write) a shifting battle-ground where survival and syntax have become arbitrary:

> Suddenly as the riot squad moved in, it was raining exclamation marks,
> Nuts, bolts, nails, car-keys. A fount of broken type. And the explosion
> Itself – an asterisk on the map. This hyphenated line, a burst of rapid fire...
> I was trying to complete a sentence in my head, but it kept stuttering...
>
> ('Belfast Confetti')

Free from the perplexities of 'Golightly's lane', 'man-killing parishes', the 'hyphenated line', Paul Durcan and Brendan Kennelly recreate the visionary rather than 'earthed' dimension of Kavanagh's poetry. The priest means more than the parish, spirit than technique; although here a contrast with Heaney's version of 'vision' is relevant. Heaney's more recent work, in *The Haw Lantern* (1987) and *Seeing Things* (1991), has links with the changed emphasis of his later essay on Kavanagh, 'The Placeless Heaven':

> Where Kavanagh had once painted Monaghan like a Millet, with a
> thick and faithful pigment in which men rose from the puddled ground,
> all wattled in potato-mould, he now paints like a Chagall, afloat above
> his native domain, airborne in the midst of his own dream place rather
> than earthbound in a literal field.[35]

Yet this may be too clearcut an opposition, or too determined by
Heaney's own artistic agenda. Now he exaggerates Kavanagh's
airiness, as formerly his weightiness. Kavanagh's transcendental
assertions are most poetically persuasive when hard-won from contingency. He 'recovers' Inniskeen not at will, but in the context of
Dublin pressures. Experience – and the incapacity for experience
– shadows the 'whitethorn hedges' of 'Innocence': 'They laughed
at one I loved...' When Heaney discusses 'Innocence' in terms of
'luminous spaces within [Kavanagh's] mind', 'sites where the mind
projects its own force','the white light of meditation',[36] he may miss
the emotional point. Certainly, it is not the same point as Heaney's
trope of the felled chestnut tree transfigured into 'a bright nowhere',
which symbolises the perpetual presence of his own past or (in
'Clearances') of his dead mother. Perhaps Heaney comes closest to
one of Kavanagh's later parochial blends in 'The Harvest Bow', a
poem which revisits 'that original townland', and its parish priest,
for therapy in time of war: '*The end of art is peace*/Could be the
motto of this frail device'. Nonetheless, all Heaney's re-writings or
significant misreadings of Kavanagh depend on place – placeless-
ness being merely a variant. Durcan, on the other hand, sees his
relation to Kavanagh as a religious allegiance:

> I have not 'met' God, I have not 'read'
> David Gascoyne, James Joyce, or Patrick Kavanagh:
> I believe in them.
> Of the song of him with the world in his care
> I am content to know the air.

This exudes Kavanagh's own belief in the poet as spiritual legis-
lator: a concept that blends Romantic theory with a Catholic absoluteness. Northern poets, in their statements about poetry, more pragmatically emphasise the poem, the word, the artifact. (This is true
of Heaney's remarks about Millet and Chagall.) Durcan edited
Kavanagh's long-buried poem *Lough Derg* (1978), and his Foreword
expounds the text as a book of revelation:

> much of his work – *Lough Derg* being a classic example – demands of the
> reader spiritual courage as well as highly sensitive powers of perception...
>   Besides being a great poem *Lough Derg* is also a spiritual document:
> for not only was Kavanagh himself a mystical (in the strict sense of
> the word) man but he had a tremendous understanding of the fact...that

ordinary people undergo mystical experiences. In a wider spiritual sense, Lough Derg is also a religious document: e.g. he pinpoints the inextricable relation in Ireland between Religion and Emigration...

Lough Derg is about the terrible need to love which Kavanagh sees as even more terrible than the need to be loved: and he sees the need to love, first in terms of the personal isolation of the individual, and secondly, in terms of the communal isolation of Ireland in 1942 because of de Valera's neutrality policy. At each of these levels... he pinpoints tragic flaws which are redeemed through the purgatorial fires of real, spiritual love.[37]

Kennelly added Lough Derg to the second edition of his Penguin Book of Irish Verse (1981). The language and tone in which he glosses this inclusion also take a religious view of Kavanagh, poetry, and the poem. Further, the passage suggests that Kennelly shares with Durcan a social context and a social mission – although Durcan's historical and political awareness is sharper than this rather scatter-gun indictment:

The claustrophobia and congestion that marked Irish life and literature in the forties, fifties and early sixties are gradually being dispelled and are being replaced by a much more *open* attitude to experience and expression; though the country, North and South, can still be horrifying for its attitudes of barbarism and stupidity, for intolerance both savage and subtle. Poetry is a vital part of our struggle to be free from, and critical of, all such attitudes, and of futile gloom, bumptious self-conscious modernism, the diligent pursuit of ugliness (Dublin is fast becoming an offensively *ugly* city), the dominance of philistinism in public life, pomposity, religiosity, iron respectability, sad suspicion, the cherished profession of cynicism, humourless self-importance and the grotesque, manic materialism of Holy Ireland. More than any other poet of recent times, Patrick Kavanagh is responsible for this liberation...The far-reaching consequences of Kavanagh's confrontation of the full spiritual range of Irish life, from grovelling squalor to unconscious magnanimity, have yet to be realised.[38]

Durcan and Kennelly revere Kavanagh for divining today's malformations in the womb of the earlier 'Ireland that froze for want of Europe'. If Lough Derg lacks the intensity of The Great Hunger (to an extent that makes their excess of praise significant), it broadens the social panorama: 'Solicitors praying for cushy jobs/To be County Registrar or Coroner', 'A Leitrim man/With a face as sad as a flooded hayfield', Aggie Meegan with a tale of 'Birth, bastardy, and murder' which might anticipate the Kerry Babies. Perhaps Lough Derg unfolds the earlier poem's symbolism, attempts to translate a concentrated parochial microcosm into a society and literally locate 'the apocalypse of clay/In every corner of this land'. It should be said, however, that Lough Derg (in Co. Donegal), site of 'that most penitential and most protracted of all Irish pilgrimages' [39], is peculiarly associated with the culture of Ulster Catholicism.

If *Lough Derg* spells out the meaning of *The Great Hunger*, Durcan spells out the meaning of Lough Derg, the detailed ramifications of Kavanagh's primary insight into 'The grey and grief and unlove,/The bones in the backs of their hands,/And the chapel pressing its low ceiling over them'. Yet *Lough Derg* already pulls back from the apocalyptic insights of *The Great Hunger*. On this occasion Kavanagh fails to bring the Church, 'ordinary people', sexual and economic misery, the special position of the poet, within a broadly consistent range of perspective or tone. His inability to revise, resolve, or publish the poem once again suggests blockage. He may have feared the genies that he had earlier let out of the bottle: 'There are some queer and terrible things in *The Great Hunger*, but it lacks the nobility and repose of poetry.'[40] Although several critics have accepted this at face value, it reeks of sublimation rather than the sublime. Perhaps Kavanagh felt that he had violated codes of silence, bans on criticism in front of outsiders, communal taboos – and, most crucially, his own taboos. Did St Patrick re-inhibit his poet-namesake at Lough Derg? It is therefore Durcan who resumes the full range of his predecessor's social anger (which declined into a narrower, paranoid focus on literary Dublin), and re-connects it with 'queer and terrible things' in the unconscious. Derek Mahon has said: 'Paul Durcan takes the madness of public life personally.'[41] In a sense Durcan rewrites *Kavanagh's Weekly* (a shortlived polemical journal edited by Kavanagh and his brother Peter in 1952) more powerfully by using parody newspaper-items to satirise hypocrisies: 'Minister Opens New Home for Battered Husbands', 'National Day of Mourning for 12 Protestants', 'Margaret Thatcher Joins IRA', 'The Perfect Nazi Family is Alive and Well and Prospering in Modern Ireland', 'Archbishop of Kerry to have Abortion'. Durcan's furious fantasies assail verbal pieties which mask materialism, sexism, the commodification of relationships and of art, authoritarianism in the Church, and the violent subtext of Nationalism. Although he also writes elegies for victims of loyalist violence, these are not on the conscience of his poetry like the deeds and attitudes represented by the following dialogue:

> Don't suppose Derrylin will ever be as prestigious as Auschwitz:
> *So what?...*
>
> A thirty-nine year old father-of-two in Derrylin:
> *So what?...*

Waiting to drive busload of Derrylin schoolkids to swimming pool:
So what?

Shot at the wheel, staggered up aisle of the bus, shot dead:
So what?

Killers cheered as they climbed out of the bus into getaway car:
Maybe so.

Drove off across the Border into the Republic of Ireland:
Maybe so.

Children had to wait for three hours before removal of corpse:
So what?...

The hypocrisy, cruelty, indifference and evasion diagnosed by Durcan's socially explicit poems, condition the schizophrenia in his strange dark visions:

And I take a look out from my bunk bed
As if all the world were a black silhouette

Or an infinite series of black silhouettes
Brokenly riding the white skyline:
'Rider Haggard, Rider Haggard:
Storm Jameson, Storm Jameson':
And just as my father thought God was a woman
I think God is a man: are both of us wrong?
Oh if only a horse could write a song:

Oh if only a horse could write a song.

('The Daughter Finds her Father Dead')

Here neither the self, nor self and society, can be put back together again. Durcan follows up Kavanagh's tragic intuition by brooding on a deranged family, the vicious circle of whose neurosis extends into the body politic:

Ireland 1972
Next to the fresh grave of my beloved grandmother
The grave of my firstlove murdered by my brother.

Images of men murdering women, or murdering what Durcan sees as the female principle, are central to his social psychology. (Once again, 'Beatrice' has come to grief.) He subverts oppressive patriarchy by playing around with gender-roles and with male expectations of women's status and behaviour. Thus nuns – of an unorthodox, relaxed order – outrank priests in the hierarchy of his imagination. 'The Nun's Bath' celebrates 'A buxom nun who scrubbed herself as if/The early morning air was itself the water'; 'Sister Agnes Writes to her Beloved Mother' announces: 'The big news is that

Rev Mother is pregnant;/The whole convent is simply delighted'. Durcan's stress on the familial titles *Sister* and *Mother* underlines his appropriation of the matriarchal residues in Catholicism for a utopian ideology – or perhaps liberation theology – that unites the spiritual and the secular. Not mother ground, but active, anarchic reverend mothers. However, Durcan's idealisation of women has not always found favour with feminists. In poems such as 'Theresa's Bar' or 'Fat Molly' a sensual, generous, permissive mother/lover may simply invert more austere representations of Cathleen Ni Houlihan. And the sequence for his estranged wife, in *The Berlin Wall Café* (1985), might be seen as exploitative, despite the male protagonist's self-abnegation. Nonetheless, Durcan recognises and unlocks the repressed feminine of *The Great Hunger*. There Maguire's mother is called 'venomous' and his spinster-sister 'spits poison'. They receive less sympathy and insight as victims of the same forces that oppress Maguire. Thus male power-systems are displaced on to 'the wind-toughened navel-cord' while, with unconscious irony, Maguire's sexual inhibition is personified as 'the enclosed nun of his thought'.The very title of 'The Haulier's Wife Meets Jesus on the Road Near Moone' addresses social class, the subjugation of women, and spiritual salvation. Many of Durcan's concerns meet in this monologue (perhaps modelled on letters to agony aunts) by one of the distressed gentle women who at least personify his poetry's recoil from patriarchal violence:

> I live in the town of Cahir,
> In the Glen of Aherlow,
> Not far from Peekaun
> In the townland of Toureen,
> At the foot of Galtee Mór
> In the County of Tipperary.
> I am thirty-three years old,
> In the prime of my womanhood:
> The mountain stream of my sex
> In spate and darkly foaming;
> The white hills of my breasts
> Brimful and breathing;
> The tall trees of my eyes
> Screening blue skies;
> Yet in each palm of my hand
> A sheaf of fallen headstones.
> When I stand in profile
> Before my bedroom mirror
> With my hands on my hips in my slip,
> Proud of my body,
> Unashamed of my pride,

> I appear to myself a naked stranger,
> A woman whom I do not know
> Except fictionally in the looking-glass,
> Quite dramatically beautiful.
> Yet in my soul I yearn for affection,
> My soul is empty for the want of affection.

Durcan's use of place-names here contrasts with Muldoon's 'Golightly's lane' or Heaney's 'Anahorish', even if they all go back to Kavanagh's 'Cassidy's hanging hill' or 'the God of imagination waking/In a Mucker fog'. (However, Muldoon's deployment of names owes a little to the 'Jonsonian, emblematic' tradition',[42] Heaney's to Edward Thomas.) Durcan's place-names, like Blake's, signpost the gulf between ideal and actual: between a New Jerusalem heralded by 'magic passwords into eternity', and the grim *de facto* resonance of Derrylin or 'I've got the Drimoleague Blues'. The lingering litany which starts off 'The Haulier's Wife' sets the scene for the potential and frustration that the woman personifies. Even 'the townland of Toureen' does not really qualify for Heaney's 'sense of place', but provides the site for a representative sociology:

> I am married to a haulier,
> A popular and a wealthy man,
> An alcoholic and a county councillor,
> Father by me of four sons,
> By repute a sensitive man and he is
> Except when he makes love to me:
> He takes leave of his senses,
> Handling me as if I were a sack of gravel...
>
> We live in a Georgian, Tudor, Classical Greek,
> Moorish, Spanish Hacienda, Regency period,
> Ranch-House, Three-Storey Bungalow
> On the edge of the edge of town...

Indeed, what the second passage pinpoints is the absence of the sense of place, dislocation, human constructs at odds with the landscape. If Heaney's names sometimes warn off outsiders, they profoundly know the disputed place, so known because disputed: 'that last/*gh* the strangers found/difficult to manage' ('Broagh'). The haulier's wife, not knowing where she is, doubting the validity of her parish and her sexuality, dresses up to the nines and takes the restless provincial's road to Dublin to watch 'My favourite actor, Tom Hickey'. However, she is diverted on the way to Damascus by meeting 'a travelling actor' called 'Jesus' who kisses her. The last stages of the poem develop another litany which maintains the extraordinary fusion of sexual and spiritual, real place and promised land:

As I drove on into Dublin to the Shelbourne Hotel
I kept hearing his Midlands voice
Saying to me over and over, across the Garden of Gethsemane –
Our night will come.

By admitting the world and the flesh, renounced by pilgrims at Lough Derg, into his vision of redemption, Durcan symbolises a solution to the problems of 'strangled impulse' tragically posed in Kavanagh's poetry.

There is, of course, a lot of spilt Catholicism in all this. However, Durcan and Kennelly wear differently the priestly vestments inherited from Kavanagh. Durcan prays to God in the sight of the congregation. His incantatory voice sounds from the altar like some of Kavanagh's revelatory parochial communions. Kennelly, within whose sensibility the spirit, world, flesh and devil still conduct their quarrels, speaks in a secular voice from the pulpit:

The Catholic bombed the Protestant's home
The Protestant bombed the Catholic's home
The Protestant castrated the Catholic
The Catholic castrated the Protestant...

Besides making no bones about the lesson for today, this contrasts tactically with Durcan's dialogue about Derrylin. Yet, even if Durcan's persona is more that of the withdrawn visionary, Kennelly's more that of the worker-priest, they share certain assumptions about their flock or audience. The Catholic Church in the Republic, its lay social and political manifestations, and even its critical poetic counter-selves take it for granted that a homogeneous body is there and willing to be addressed. (This spills over into unitary generalisations about Ireland.) Not so as regards the discretions and reticences between, and often within, the religious cultures of the North. As well as mirroring such codes, Northern poetry respects the ethic that words must be weighed in complex, menacing and poet-humbling circumstances. The Republic's movement towards 'a much more open attitude to experience and expression' (though the 1986 Divorce Referendum rebuffed this for a time) partly takes place in the media, and might be epitomised by the RTE *Late Late Show*, on which Kennelly has often appeared. Similarly, his poetry and Durcan's have the air of participating in some public forum. The popularity of their poetry-readings is bound up with qualities in the writing. Thus their methods not only draw on the ritual formulae of the Church, but imitate press-reports, television commentary, anecdote, advertising, ballads (not only Irish), blues, pop-songs,

documentary programmes, revue-monologues, pub-talk. Perhaps
the urban-demotic revolution in poetic diction, achieved in England
with the help of MacNeice during the 1930s, only reached Southern
Ireland during the 1970s. (Derek Mahon, writing about 'Subsidy
Bungalows', shocked Trinity poetry circles in 1960.) Durcan, who
has recorded with Van Morrison, absorbed the sixties – the music,
the protest, the pacifism, although Kennelly's populist sources are
more traditional. Nevertheless, both contribute to an urban idiom
which seems partly specific to Dublin of the last twenty years. This
is perhaps another proof of uneven development, and that the pace
of literary change cannot always be forced. It would be ironical if
the arrival of a new 'urban consciousness' derived from Kavanagh,
not from the 1930s Modernists, and not just from Kavanagh's
'Dublin' poems, which began in Monaghan. The public-address
systems of Kennelly and Durcan once again go back to *Lough Derg*,
in its explicitness and expansiveness:

> A woman said her Litany:
>
> That my husband may get his health
>   We beseech Thee to hear us
> That my son Joseph may pass the Intermediate
>   We beseech Thee to hear us
> That my daughter Eileen may do well at her music
>   We beseech Thee to hear us
> That her aunt may remember us in her will
>   We beseech Thee to hear us
> That there may be good weather for the hay
>   We beseech Thee to hear us...

Here, as elsewhere, Kavanagh also shows his successors how to free
their verse by listening to how people speak. Forms – even free
verse – cannot be prescribed if the poet's ear has not caught the
Frostian 'sentence-sounds' around him. And it is not just a cliché
that Dublin's rhetorical and social styles are generally more extro-
verted than Belfast's. 'Lettering' throws light on Kennelly's poetic
mission, an urgency to get through which can never assume such
hopeful energy in Northern poetry:

> I belong to that silent minority
> Who do not write letters to *The Irish Times*
> But I swear to Christ I felt like writing
> This morning when, on getting the 16A
> And lurching through the city
> Of Parnell, O'Connell, Emmet, Grattan,
> I saw, scrawled on a wall in red lettering,
> BOOM WENT MOUNTBATTEN!

Durcan's 'Ireland 1977' condenses a similar motivation:

> 'I've become so lonely, I could die' – he writes,
> The native who is an exile in his native land:
> 'Do you hear me whispering to you across the Golden Vale?
> Do you hear me bawling to you across the hearthrug?'

Whereas 'The Boundary Commission' presents the poet as infinitely pondering the parameters of territorial obsession, 'Ireland 1977' presents him as passionately broadcasting to a deaf country.

Durcan's and Kennelly's readiness to 'speak for Ireland' in expansive and accessible terms may not be the only thematic or technical focus in contemporary Southern Irish poetry, but it is a distinctive phenomenon. Today, their writings illuminate the condition of Ireland in the 1980s – a period of preparation for Mary Robinson. At the same time, Kennelly's diffuseness finally dissolves the boundary between poetry and prose in a way that highlights the necessity for the haiku or the Greek epigram (Craig Raine has dubbed some Northern poetry the o' haiku). The 364 pages of *The Book of Judas* (1991) are in danger of succumbing to what they attack, and to an imitative fallacy that dissolves the literary medium too: 'In this poem I wanted to capture the relentless, pitiless anecdotalism of Irish life, the air swarming with nutty little sexual parables, the platitudinous bonhomie sustained by venomous undercurrents, the casual ferocious gossip...' Another caveat is that autobiographical and regional factors produce different forms of *couvade* with the gestating Irish future. Durcan seems to base his poetic authority, which has a metropolitan cast, on a dissident, post-sixties mutation of his family's involvement with the institutions of the state (see Introduction, p.65). The dialectics in Kennelly's work – between Buffún and Cromwell, Ireland and England, Judas and Christ – pivot on an older insecurity about the seat or voice of authority. This insecurity, although projected across the water, again implicates a patriarchal church, and partly arises from cultural distances between Dublin and his native Kerry. In that sense Kennelly's quarrel with himself and Ireland parallels Kavanagh's dislocations. A subtext in *Cromwell* and *Judas* is the unease of traditional rural small-town Ireland (not only west of the Shannon) with the culture of an increasingly dominant east coast 'Pale'.

IV

Of course there is ultimately no iron border between poetry written by Northerners and Southerners. Not least of the overlaps is the poets' fruitful awareness of one another, the cross-border influences now at work. But poetry, feeling its way through form, with its utopian pull against the biases of society, is in one sense an art of the possible that qualifies theoretical buzz-words, e.g.: 'crisis', 'colonialism', 'identity'. Republicans and Marxists insist on their undifferentiated application to the whole of Ireland, but the poetry discussed in this essay supports plural usages. Contrasting vocabularies define 'crisis' as chiefly territorial in the North; chiefly one of faith and identity in the South: 'Holy Ireland' and fundamentalist Nationalism battling it out with forces of pluralism, secularisation and liberalisation. *Cromwell* intertwines this growing-pain with post-Independence, post-civil-war trauma to create a communal psychodrama which exorcises some over-familiar ghosts. A therapeutic primal scream, the poem internalises – as *The Great Hunger* did – neuroses which cannot perpetually be laid at the door of Big Island. Kennelly understands that you don't exorcise the curse of Cromwell merely by cursing Cromwell.

That Buffún's consciousness of England (rather than Britain) should bulk so large, reflects a distinctively Southern version of Irish historical experience. For me, a good image of the Northern version is the sight (denoting an already established Ulster territoriality) that horrified O'Connell's emissary, John Lawless, in 1828:

> Soon, thousands of armed Orangemen faced more thousands of armed Catholics from opposite hills overshadowing the town [Ballybay, Co. Monaghan]. At the eleventh hour, Lawless took fright, mounted a grey horse, rode through the ranks behind him – and fled.[43]

Thus, regarded as anti-colonial exercises, Brian Friel's *Translations* seems largely a play about power and territory, about ground that strangers find difficult to manage; Thomas Kilroy's *Double Cross*, largely a play about residual inferiority complexes. (Though Kilroy's scenario, in which Brendan Bracken and William Joyce strive to become 'English', might be complemented by another drama in which figures such as Mícheál MacLiammóir or Terry Eagleton would re-invent themselves as 'Irish'.) Again, there are overlaps. But Anglicised Irishmen, the Anglo-Irish Ascendancy, hardly haunt Northern Catholics as compared to the actual presence of Ulster Protestants and UK rule. *Cromwell*, like *Double Cross*, asks who am I?

> I am that prince of liars, Xavier O'Grady,
> I am Tom Gorman, dead in the bog...
> Men astound me, I am outside women,
> I have fed myself on the bread of hate...
> I am a safe-hearted puritan

> Blaming it all on the Jansenists
> Who, like myself, were creatures on the run.
> I am a home-made bomb, a smuggled gun.
> I like to whine about identity...

The protagonist of Muldoon's 'The More a Man Has', certainly a creature on the run, might seem to have similar problems:

> Gallogly, or Gollogly,
> Otherwise known as Golightly,
> Otherwise known as Ingoldsby,
> Otherwise known as English,
> Gives forth one low cry of anguish
> And agrees to come quietly.

But these aliases reflect territorial street-wisdom, the names Ulster people try to impose on each other, and the pointlessness of it all. The metamorphic plurality of 'the sign' is at ironic odds with actual fixity and fate. Gallogly, at once guilty and persecuted, is too caught up to have an identity-problem in Buffún's sense. Identity for him is defined by the pursuing alter ego: no existential *angst*, but the 'anguish' of survival, a security-problem. Ulster Catholics and Protestants perhaps suffer from an excess of identity (always underscored by the pack on the other hill), from what is really an identification-problem (who will guarantee these identities?) Of course 'The More a Man Has' profoundly questions such voracious categories, the necessities obliterating Gallogly. Some of the history that is a hang-up for Buffún, remains an operational force for him and other victims like the 'hog-tied' girl. Muldoon, who has said 'I'm very sceptical about how much we direct anything that happens to us',[44] has written a bleaker sonnet-sequence than Kennelly. Its historical narrative closes in disintegration, a tragic chaos (see below), rather than potential integration ('I hear the makers calling'). Certainly these conclusions converge and complement one another.

'Malformation' implies birth-defect. *The Great Hunger*, indeed, is conceived as a parody of Genesis in which the Word, human consciousness, fails to be born from clay. Clearly, Maguire's notional utopia 'back of the hills [where] love was free/And ditches straight' requires more than an unpartitioned Ireland. The 'colonial predicament' (Brown) may be read, or written, into other neurosis. Again, malformation of one kind or another is the condition of most societies, even if violence announces special distortions. Thus 'malformation' in this essay also implies the pathological elements in culture which transfer to institutions and power-systems. Equally, hegemonies induce or aggravate pathologies. Hence the special position of the

Catholic Church in Irish literary imaginations. The work of these three generations of male poets from various Irish Catholic backgrounds confirms its historically repressive role within the body politic and the individual psyche. This hegemonic reach has helped twentieth-century Irish poetry to fulfil Auden's desire that poetry should roam between the zones of Marx and Freud – which of all the Sweeneys is most astray? At the same time, the rituals of the Church have positively influenced sensibility and aesthetics. Patrick Maguire at mass cannot reconcile 'the prayer phlegm' with 'the pregnant Tabernacle lifted a moment to Prophecy/Out of the clayey hours'.

Kavanagh's 'pregnant Tabernacle' is relevant to Seamus Heaney, whose relation to Catholicism (though not as a believer) seems almost entirely positive. Heaney's poetry has developed the animistic 'natural magic' captured in Kavanagh's

> The Holy spirit is the rising sap,
> And Christ will be the green leaves that will come
> At Easter from the sealed and guarded tomb.

Heaney goes beyond Kavanagh in paganising Catholic feeling. Perhaps he has also responded to the vestiges of an older church, 'a vernacular religion', still accessible in parts of rural Ulster. Kevin Whelan argues that Ulster-Connaught escaped some of the centralising reforms of nineteenth-century 'ultramontane' Irish Catholicism.[45] Hence the ties of the christian calendar, or of pilgrimages such as Lough Derg, to local custom, to the landscape, and to more ancient superstition. Perhaps Heaney's animism – in conjunction with the anima – at once bandages and bypasses the psychic trauma apparent elsewhere. 'Station Island', for all its Joycean denouement, stages no Dedalian rebellion. At another level, in that his myth draws on anti-Partitionist assumptions, Heaney may occlude the religious question in Northern contexts. However, 'First Kingdom', one of the 'Sweeney Redivivus' poems in *Station Island*, begins by parodying Kavanagh's 'A Christmas Childhood' ('The queen mother hunkered on a stool/and played the harpstrings of milk'); then covertly criticises rural Ulster Catholic culture, though with a Nationalist subtext:

> They were two-faced and accommodating.
> And seed, breed and generation still
> they are holding on, every bit
> as pious and exacting and demeaned.

But if this (and the whole sequence) corresponds to the parthian shots of a MacNeice or Mahon, Heaney's poetry has not – so far

– directly or indirectly engaged with any other society. His 'placeless heaven' can be interpreted as socio-political limbo, a portable
parish, a place of waiting like Brian Friel's Ballybeg, within which
malformations are to be transcended by a slightly threatening 'jurisdiction of achieved form'.[46]

Kennelly's epics do not quite transcend malformation. His extraordinary confessional method mediates between oppressor and victim,
sinner and confessor, patient and analyst. But, having recited the
trauma, laid out the dossier, he stops short of jurisdiction, of diag-
nostic or formal closure. *The Book of Judas* ends – though there is
no reason why therapy should not go on for ever –

> If the song comes right, the true thing may find a name
> Singing to me of who, and why, I am.

Durcan and Muldoon, to make a final comparison, more precisely
distinguish, and more precisely connect, the psychological and
political analysis of neurotic societies. This is partly because they
are interested in personal and sexual relations for their own sake –
a sphere in which Kennelly's continuously extraverted voice has
been less successful. Thus Durcan is able to build in more specific
therapy than Kennelly, models of loving-kindness, prospects of
sexual-spiritual redemption. The refrain 'Our night will come' is
in pointed opposition to Sinn Féin's 'Our day will come'. Muldoon's
opposition to violence (in 'Ireland') comes across more wistfully:

> The Volkswagen parked in the gap,
> But gently ticking over.
> You wonder if it's lovers
> And not men hurrying back
> Across two fields and a river.

However, if Durcan's utopia is predicated on a likely reform of
relations between the sexes, Muldoon generally represents these
either as metaphors for the social problematic or as vitiated by the
same power-games that govern the political jungle. Sex, often discussed as a theoretical function of his texts, does 'refer'. In 'When
Did You Last See Your Father?' I argued that Muldoon's poetry
negotiates its way through and beyond an authoritarian paternal
blockage. But, the (fainter) maternal presence in his work also
seems inhibiting: 'My mother slams the door/on her star-cluster of
dregs' ('Trance'), and may be identified with the Lawrentian 'law'.
As with Heaney, the locus of the 'father' is closer to poetic origins. William A. Wilson notices a reservation, too, about 'female'
promiscuity: 'the essential pattern of Muldoon's sexual poetics is

that 'the principle of male unity *comes down to, falls into* female division'.[47] Thus his textual pluralities may be more positively nuanced on a political than on a psycho-sexual level, his gender-bending more darkly ambiguous than Durcan's. So all difficulties do not end with the advent of *différance*. The scenarios of Muldoon's 'love poems' are generally provisional or precarious. A characteristic motif is a couple mutually incommunicado in a restaurant, as if they have emptied or eaten one another. There are several desolate one-night stanzas. Many of Muldoon's sexual images allude to sadism, voyeurism, fetishism, pornography, prostitution, exploitation. His 'Beatrice' figures as both victim of abuse and *femme fatale*. Yet, whatever Freudian 'family romance' may be inscribed here, like those of Kavanagh, Durcan and Heaney it intersects with a communal romance. Thus Muldoon poses a particularly stark question about human societies. Some of his early poems reproduce Philip Larkin's fear that to compromise selfhood (and artistic single-mindedness) is to enter the destructive element – but as one of the destroyers: 'It is no real fire./They are breaking each other' ('Wind and Tree'). 'Merman' is a parable of the solitary *versus* the social, and of different artistic trajectories. The speaking 'I' who farms bounded land and asks 'What of friendship, love? Such qualities?' has been obliterated by the end of the poem, while the merman still effectively pursues his 'single furrow' despite its promise of only the 'wind-scythe, the rain-harrow'. This may portend much that Muldoon's poetry has chillingly harvested.

Perhaps Muldoon refuses all utopian indulgence for the sake of clarifying the status quo. In his poetry no punk-nuns usurp the Hierarchy. So, despite deconstructing fixed identities and edging into the future by dint of comic ridicule and linguistic mutations, he implies that social therapy can go no further or faster. The vengeful 'apache' doppelganger pursuing Gallogly ends up in bits with a 'pump attendant...mouth[ing] an Act of Contrition/in the frazzled ear'. An image of poetry's failure at the impasse of the split self and the split community. The last image is a severed hand gripping Robert Frost's truth or pebble of quartz – 'a lunimous stone' in the local dialect. The protagonist of 'Bran' suffers another kind of split, one that severs sexuality from emotion. He experiences woman as both manipulative ('let') and as object, and seeks to reinstate the narcissism of childhood:

> While he looks into the eyes of women
> Who have let themselves go,
> While they sigh and they moan
> for pure joy,

> He weeps for the boy on that small farm
> Who takes an oatmeal Labrador
> In his arms,
> Who knows all there is of rapture.

'Bran' rewrites Kavanagh's 'Innocence', but is not an innocent poem.

The core of ice in Muldoon's imagination, possibly where religion has frozen, as contrasted with Durcan's explicitly curative and utopian tendency, might have various origins. But there is no doubt about poetic outcomes. The one inclines to Gramsci's 'pessimism of the intellect', the other to his 'optimism of the will'. Thus Durcan's 'Beyond the Celtic Yoke' involves the reader in a primal dream rather than primal scream, and proposes a visionary natural model for the integrated Irish psyche:

> In Ireland before the Celtic yoke I was the voice of Seeing
> And my island people's Speaking was their Being;
> So go now brother – cast off all cultural shrouds
> And speak like me – like the mighty sun through the clouds.

But while cultural shrouds remain in place, poets must often labour under differently repressive yokes.

[1988/1993]

No More Poems About Paintings?

In 1955 Kingsley Amis famously declared that, among other taboo topics, 'nobody wants any more poems about paintings...or art galleries'.[1] That Amis was whistling in the wind is suggested by John Dixon Hunt's statement in 1980 at the start of a lecture 'On Poems on Paintings': 'The incidence of poems on paintings, especially in the twentieth century, is quite astonishing. And they form only one part of a group which, besides poems on actual historical artworks, includes poems on imaginary paintings, poems on actual artists and on imaginary ones; poems on visual arts generally, and poems that employ the trope of "painting"...as a metaphor for the poetic act'.[2] In his lecture Hunt gives some bad poems over-respectful attention. And I think Amis has a point: possibly more poems about paintings than about almost anything else are likely to end up in a *Pseuds' Corner* column. Also, addiction to the practice (e.g. Wallace Stevens) can be a form of imaginative auto-eroticism. Certainly, quality is unevenly spread. In this essay I will be suggesting that Ireland comes off well. I will also be asking whether there is any broader significance for Irish poetry in the fact that Derek Mahon and Paul Durcan, for instance, have so notably defied the Amis fiat. Two of Mahon's collections take their names from paintings: *Courtyards in Delft* and *The Hunt by Night*; two others have Munch and Botticelli images on their covers. Two Durcan covers reproduce pictures by Edward McGuire; one reproduces *Ortachala Belle with a Fan* by the Russian Niko Pirosmani. *Going Home to Russia* backs up its cover by containing five poems intriguingly said to be *after* various painters. *Crazy about Women*, Durcan's variations on selected paintings in the National Gallery of Ireland, appeared in 1991; *Give Me Your Hand*, his response to paintings in the National Gallery of London, followed in 1994. Again, in Paul Muldoon's recent collections references to painting and painters have multiplied.

Whenever the issue of 'poetry and painting' comes up, so do the Pre-Raphaelites. Does the fact that Yeats 'learned to think in the midst of the last phase of Pre-Raphaelitism'[3] still influence the practice of his successors? Poetry's consciousness of painting inevitably highlights and measures its *aesthetic* self-consciousness, tilts the see-saw away from history. As Bram Dijkstra says, in an essay on Wallace Stevens and William Carlos Williams: 'The study of the influence of painting on literature is primarily a study of motive and method...A poet's response to painting can tell us why he is a poet and why his poetry has taken its specific form.'[4] (Stevens notoriously bought new paintings when he ran out of inspiration.)

But such response can also tell us about aesthetic history and the history of poetry. Ernst Gombrich worries about the way in which both historians of ideas and philosophers of aesthetics downgrade 'mechanisms of tradition' i.e. the conventions of particular art forms.[5]

In my view, some of the best contemporary Irish poetry still has an illuminating context in English post-Romanticism and in mechanisms which Yeats made central to that tradition. (There are more neutral and positive ways to track the 'aestheticism' that Yeats transplanted to Ireland than to construe it simply as the mark of the coloniser.) Ian Fletcher, writing about 'Leda and the Swan' as a Rossettian iconic sonnet, records as 'One of the curiosities of Yeats criticism...that the source-materials most accessible to the master, most likely to become a permanent part of his mental history, poems and paintings of the middle and late nineteenth century, have been generally ignored for more modish zones'.[6] Likewise, more modish critical approaches may have neglected some of the specific aesthetic courses pursued by poets for whom Yeats is inescapably part of their mental history.

The rest of this essay will first touch on the well-worn business of *ut pictura*. Then I will revert to Yeats and the shading of Pre-Raphaelitism into Symbolism. After that, I will refer briefly to Louis MacNeice and John Hewitt in the post-Yeatsian phase. My ultimate objective is to examine a few poems by Seamus Heaney, Paul Muldoon, Derek Mahon, Medbh McGuckian and Paul Durcan in the light of previous theorising.

The late American poet and art critic Frank O'Hara wrote a delightful poem called 'Why I am Not a Painter'.[7] In this poem the painter Mike Goldberg puts the word SARDINES into a painting. Some time later the poet-speaker starts off a poem by thinking about the colour 'orange'. But Goldberg's finished work contains 'just/letters' and O'Hara's poem ends:

> My poem
> is finished and I haven't mentioned
> orange yet. It's twelve poems. I call
> it ORANGES. And one day in a gallery
> I see Mike's painting, called SARDINES.

Sardines and Oranges. Chalk and Cheese. The image begins where the word vanishes. The word begins where the image vanishes. I agree with O'Hara's implied separation of artistic powers after the mysterious point of imaginative origin. Since Lessing's demolition of *ut pictura poesis* many commentators have pressed further the distinction between spatial and sequential art-forms. These tend to be specialist art and literary critics, for example, Rudolph Arnheim's *Visual Thinking* on the one side, P.N. Furbank's *Reflections on the Word 'Image'* on the other. It is the philosophers, who, in the words of W.J.T. Mitchell, 'crave unity, analogy, harmony and universality'.[8] Hence the 'linguistic determinism' which Arnheim criticises,[9] Derrida cutting off the ear to universalise the text, and the tendency of new semiotics to sophisticate old *ut pictura*. Perhaps theorists might explore relationship-in-difference – sardines and oranges – rather than try to homogenise. Mitchell, despite his critique of the search for a master-theory, attaches a homogenising title to his study: *Iconology: Image, Text, Ideology*. And by underprivileging the aesthetic in his argument, he is able to contend that the politics of different critics and periods, rather than *essential* distinctions, govern discussion of 'the text-image difference'.[10] I shall suggest that the literary politics of Modernism itself have obscured a primarily aesthetic issue. And, even if politics condition (rather than govern) discussion of 'the text-image difference', including Mitchell's and my own, it does not follow that no distinctions can be made. Nor can 'essentialism' mean the same thing as in, say, discussion of the Irish-English difference. Religion, too, is implicated in these issues.

Not only theorists but practitioners can be seduced by analogy and harmony. Two contemporary English poets who, in my view, lose their balance are Charles Tomlinson and Craig Raine. Some of their poems make a useful contrast with those by the Irish poets. Even when not writing about paintings, Tomlinson tends to produce art theory rather than poems, art-criticism rather than criticism of life. His poem 'Paring the Apple'[11] relates to Pieter de Hooch's 'Woman Peeling Apples' (a genre painting also relevant to Seamus Heaney's sonnet about peeling potatoes in the sequence 'Clearances'):

> There are portraits and still-lifes.
>
> And there is paring the apple.
>
> And then? Paring it slowly,
> From under cool yellow
> Cold-white emerging...

Tomlinson's poem glosses the painting rather than discovers fresh artistic possibilities in its mode, colours and shapes. The punning punchline merely *announces* a fusion of form with emotion, of looking at the painting with reading the poem:

> The cool blade
> Severs between coolness, apple-rind
> Compelling a recognition.

In contrast with Tomlinson's effort to reproduce 'stillness' by re-
peating single words – cool, blade – Heaney's sonnet creates its
own formal and moral relation between objects and people. And he
exploits the resources of his sequential medium to 'break the silence'
and thus emphasise it:

> When all the others were away at Mass
> I was all hers as we peeled potatoes.
> They broke the silence, let fall one by one
> Like solder weeping off the soldering iron:
> Cold comforts set between us, things to share
> Gleaming in a bucket of clean water.
> And again let fall. Little pleasant splashes
> From each other's work would bring us to our senses.

The pulse beating between 'solder...soldering' and 'let fall...And
again let fall' amounts to more than repetition. It underscores a
momentum which introduces life into the still shot of the iconically
posed memory.

Where Tomlinson abstracts, Craig Raine over-visualises, tries
to beat visual representation at its own game. His sequence of poems,
'Pre-Raphaelite Paintings',[12] gilds the Pre-Raphaelite lily:

> Suddenly there are little green vultures
> hatched from varnished petits fours.
>
> They perch like envious angels, plotting
> in groups of two and three, with cloak wings.
>
> I was expecting a more expansive gesture,
> a coup d'état, not these little stings of green
>
> that will go through a pineapple stage...
> Things seem, well, frivolous –
>
> the wych elm buds and wafts its drying
> fingernails, careful to keep them apart.
>
> In the autumn martyrdoms,
> tonsured heads will fall.

('Chestnut Trees')

'Chestnut Trees' invites us to visualise vultures, petits fours, angels,
pineapples, fingernails and monks. (The phrase 'little stings of
green' works better, because it evokes the visual as sensation instead
of sensationalising the visual.) Neither as image-cluster nor as
rhythm does the poem fully cohere: 'Things seem, well, frivolous...'
seems a fairly frivolous *primum mobile*. Gilbert Adair, in his brilliant
Myths & Memories, argues that 'the characteristic trait of Raine's
metaphors (similes, rather) is, paradoxically, their pedantic, funda-

mentally tautological literalness. "This looks like that" is what they say, over and over again; and, so in most instances, it does; and that, it would seem, is that.'[13] Adair finds that words themselves fail to 'reverberate' in Raine's poetry because that 'would fatally compromise the analogy which is often [a word's] sole *raison d'être*'.[14] The poems by Tomlinson and Raine, I would suggest, are parasitic upon another medium in proportion as they are deficient in their own. This indicates an impaired relation to the tradition which they implicitly and explicitly invoke.

That tradition is the late nineteenth and early twentieth century interaction between English Pre-Raphaelitism and elements in French Symbolism. Scholars and critics increasingly stress the indigenous contribution, especially to Yeats's consummation of the movement. Frank Kermode's insistence on 'native Romantic roots'[15] has been developed, for instance, by John Dixon Hunt in *The Pre-Raphaelite Imagination 1848-1900* and Alan Robinson in *Poetry, Painting and Ideas 1885-1914*. Hunt argues that 'the symbolism which [their] discussions of Blake document and support is perhaps the central mode of the Pre-Raphaelite imagination'.[16] He describes Yeats as 'the first to appreciate how much the actual practice of the Pre-Raphaelite arts endorsed the more vocal and formulated programme of French symbolism'.[17] In 'Art and Ideas' (1913) Yeats conceived 'our reintegration of the mind, our more profound Pre-Raphaelitism'[18] specifically to counter the Modernist view of verbal/visual relations put forward by Pound, Wyndham Lewis and the Vorticists. This project for 'reintegration', together with the Pre-Raphaelite doctrine of mutual support between the arts, culminates in what one critic has termed 'Yeats's masterpiece in the Rossettian mode'[19] i.e. 'Lapis Lazuli'. The poem's last section is an iconic sonnet.

In *New Poems* and *Last Poems* the solidarity of the arts functions as a metaphor and rhetoric for the solidity of Yeats's 'old man's eagle' vision. The opening line of 'The Municipal Gallery Revisited' – 'Around me the images of thirty years' – invokes image as perception, image as painting, image as poetry. Painting constitutes the intermediary stage, as the visual arts often did in Yeats's creative process ('Leda and the Swan' is only a particularly rich instance). In 'Lapis Lazuli', as in 'The Municipal Gallery Revisited', Yeats lets us watch him transpose a visual art-object into a verbal one. Animating the stone, giving it movement, historical sequence and finally sound suggests how Yeats activated mechanisms of poetic tradition which eluded his Pre-Raphaelite predecessors. More profound Pre-Raphaelitism betokened more profound symbolism: a symbolism which did not drain vitality from syntax and rhythm; a symbolism which reintegrated, not only intellect and history, but speech and drama into Yeats's nineties sister-arts aesthetic of sounds, colours and forms (see the twin essays 'Symbolism in Painting'/ 'The Symbolism of Poetry'). Perhaps, as a result, poets who follow Yeats negotiate more adroitly with the visual arts than do those who follow Pound.

Indeed, it's possible to see Symbolism as splitting into two, or as parting company with Modernism, over a different conception of such relations. The paths diverge at Imagism. It seems significant that two important poet-adversaries of Pound and Imagism, Robert Frost and Edward Thomas, based their critique on this poetry's aspiration to the condition of the visual arts, its demotion of speech and rhythm. 'Kiln-dried tabule poetry'[20] Frost called it, and he scorned 'eye readers' and eye writers: 'the ear is the only true writer and the only true reader'.[21] Of course, Modernist verse-layout often tries to exploit spatiality instead of providing a verbal structure which alerts the reader's ear and cues the voice (and perhaps alerts the intelligence: W.J.T. Mitchell plays down some links, traced by Kermode and others, between the spatial aesthetics of Modernism and the rise of Fascism). A recent off-shoot of this is the post-modernist concept of 'radial reading' which collapses language, meaningful sequence, and history into collage. Jerome McGann has said: 'every verse form is a spatialised form once it is committed to a written mode'[22] (would he say the same of a musical score?). Interestingly, Gombrich interprets Lessing's *Laoköon* primarily as *resistance* to the encroachment on literature of principles derived from the visual arts.

Alan Robinson – the title of whose book revealingly contrasts with Mitchell's – reminds us how deeply discussions of art and literature interpenetrated at the turn of the century. His map, like Frost's, marks a crossroads at Imagism. He argues that Imagism repudiated the transcendental impulses, the Hegelian idealism, which had hitherto unified different branches of avant-garde aesthetics. Robinson terms Imagism 'a truncated Symbolist aesthetic'[23] (contrast Yeats's 'great rooted blossomer'). And the theory of T.E. Hulme, as well as the practice of Pound and others, underlines the direct challenge presented by *visual* Imagism to Yeats's *rhythmic* Symbolism (even in the nineties rhythm, if 'wavering' rather than 'energetic', was intrinsic to the Yeatsian aesthetic). Hulme says: 'Regular metre to this impressionist poetry is cramping, jangling, meaningless, and out of place. Into the delicate pattern of images and colour it introduces the heavy, crude pattern of rhetorical verse'.[24]

I would argue that the methods of Heaney, Muldoon, Mahon, McGuckian and Durcan – not only in poems about paintings – belong to the tradition of more profound Pre-Raphaelitism rather than of Modernist spatial aesthetics; and that the varied uses to which they put the visual arts illustrate the diversity of that tradition as well as differences between their own aesthetics.

* * *

Obviously since Yeats the small change of the sister-arts has continued in Ireland– Irish painters supplying designs and images for pamphlets, poets eulogising painters in exhibition-catalogues, Louis le Brocquy emblems all over the literary shop. Much of this collaboration descends, like the Cuala Press (run by Yeats's sisters) and the Dolmen Press, from William Morris and the decorative-craft aspect of Pre-Raphaelitism. An outstanding instance of cross-inspiration from the visual arts side is the portraiture of the late Edward McGuire – though inspired by *poetry* rather than *poems*: a reaction against his commissioned paintings of the likes of Charles Haughey. McGuire painted twenty-five portraits of poets and other writers: the best-known appears on the back-cover of Heaney's *North*. Three aspects of these portraits tie in with Pre-Raphaelite visual literariness: firstly, what Dorothy Walker terms their 'applied rather than inherent' colour [25]; secondly, their combination of meticulous detail with an aura of mystery; thirdly, their culturally revealing substitution of the male poet (eyes and hair to the fore) for the iconic female Muse.

On the other side of the post-Yeatsian fence it is remarkable that two poets who mediate in contrasting ways between Yeats and the contemporary, namely Louis MacNeice and John Hewitt, should have had formative connections with the visual arts. These connections also exemplify two kinds of affiliation which need not be mutually exclusive: consciousness of the international avant-garde and closeness to local artists. It is not widely appreciated that Mac-Neice's first intellectual mentor was Anthony Blunt, once chiefly celebrated as an art critic, and already such at Marlborough where he and MacNeice were contemporaries in the early 1920s. Blunt played truant to attend art exhibitions in Paris. MacNeice's accounts of his own early attitudes to poetry are permeated by allusions to painting. He read Eliot *after* becoming habituated to reproductions of Picasso and Matisse. Blunt's artistic credo at this time was Pure Form, an aesthetic of severe geometric outlines advocated by the young Le Corbusier among others. MacNeice's retrospects on Pure

Form are invariably ironical. Thus his 'Eclogue for Christmas' (1933) attacks Pure Form and abstraction for selling humanity short:

> abstracting and dissecting me
> They have made of me pure form, a symbol or a pastiche,
> Stylised profile, anything but soul and flesh.

However, MacNeice distinguished between the degrees to which painting and literature could afford to ditch 'soul and flesh'. The following statement (1936) repudiates Modernist homogenisation, and is relevant to the issues of semiotics and radial reading: 'It is no doubt possible to use words merely for decoration, as the Moors used tags of the Koran to decorate their walls at heights where no one could read them [SARDINES again]. To do this in literature seems a perversion.'[26]

Yet MacNeice did not emulate Blunt's conversion from Pure Form to Marxism (indeed, he saw it as *plus ça change*). In 1936 they visited Spain together, less to sniff civil war than to frequent the Prado. In MacNeice's autobiography *The Strings are False* painting focuses his aesthetic-political disagreements with Blunt. MacNeice enthuses over Goya's creative vitality and ideological self-contradiction as against Blunt's dream of 'in every parish a Diego Rivera'.[27] In *Autumn Journal VI* MacNeice uses Goya-images to imply the intractable condition of contemporary Spain: 'in the Prado half- / wit princes looked from the canvas they had paid for /(Goya had the laugh – / But can what is corrupt be cured by laughter?)'

Further, a *conflict* between poetry and painting contributes to MacNeice's most fundamental formal preoccupation: how to reconcile the claims of flux and pattern. In fact, his painterly obsession with colours and with shifting prismatic light – initially, a response to Ireland's 'water-shafted air / Of amethyst and moonstone' ('Valediction') – meant that he wished his poetry to follow 'the living curve' not turn it into a static geometry. (This has implications for MacNeice's imaginative relation to politics as contrasted with Pound's.) So it's another case of resisting *ut pictura*; indeed, *moving* pictures, cinema, helped to resolve the problem. MacNeice's early sonnet 'Poussin' (Blunt was to write definitive works on Poussin) turns a classical painting into a post-Impressionist painting by seeing it in a light, and seeing in it an image, not literally present, and by stressing the flow of perception over its surfaces. The poem also indicates the influence of Virginia Woolf on MacNeice:

> In that Poussin the clouds are like golden tea,
> And underneath the limbs flow rhythmically,
> The cupids' blue feathers beat musically,

And we dally and dip our spoon in the golden tea.
The tea flows down the steps and up again,
An old-world fountain, pouring from sculptured lips,
And the chilly marble drop like sugar slips
And is lost in the dark gold depths, and the refrain
Of tea-leaves floats about and in and out,
And the motion is still as when one walks and the moon
Walks parallel but relations remain the same.
And thus we never reach the dregs of the cup,
Though we drink it up and drink it up and drink it up,
And thus we dally and dip our spoon.

'Poussin' is another Rossettian sonnet: one which explicitly substitutes perpetual motion for the sculptural model of such a poem. And it does so by means of a rhythmic rhetoric which would have pained T.E. Hulme: refrain, internal rhyme, dynamic assonance. The poem, indeed, uses self-referential words like 'rhythmically', 'musically', 'refrain' in opposition to images within the picture of 'sculptured lips' and 'chilly marble'. So MacNeice animates 'cold pastoral', solves the problem of stillness and motion in a verbal medium – partly by suggesting that the poem will never quite end: 'And thus we drink it up and drink it up and drink it up'. This both makes the sequential run on the spot, and imitates the potential infinity of looking and of the painting's effect. Perhaps the difference between this and the Tomlinson poem is that 'Paring the Apple' looks at a picture; 'Poussin' dramatises looking.

John Hewitt's poetry received no particular *formal* impulse from painting, and his taste in the visual arts always stopped short of Pure Form. Instead, his role as 'art gallery man' at the Ulster Museum in Belfast, from the 1930s to 1950s, consorted with his whole effort to generate cultural self-awareness in the North. This agenda owed something to Yeats and the utopian (William Morris) wing of Pre-Raphaelitism, as well as to contemporary Scottish and Welsh movements. Thus in his book *Art in Ulster* Hewitt defines the credentials of the Ulster visual artist as 'not primarily a question of birth, of blood or accent; [but] the condition of being involved in Ulster life and Irish landscape, and finding therein the material for…art'.[28] In his purchases for the museum, then civically controlled, Hewitt did his best with limited money and city councillors who objected to nudes. Colin Middleton and John Luke were the local painters he particularly favoured. Hewitt's long poem 'Freehold' (1946) names the artists first in its fervent regional cultural 'Roll Call'.[29] The revised version forty years later (in the collection *Freehold*) retains a central episode in which Hewitt and Luke, poet and painter, walk near Armagh sharing a landscape and its expression: 'The long five miles of road to Killylea / Held only half the things we had to say.' However, Middleton and Luke are far from being realist painters, either as regards landscape or anything else, and Hewitt always insisted on Ulster painters acquainting themselves with international activity in the visual arts.

Hewitt's curatorship at the Ulster Museum undoubtedly helped to give young writers and others 'loftier thought,/Sweeter emotion'. Seamus Heaney, who most directly follows up the links that Hewitt forged between landscape poetry and painting, says as much in his introduction to an exhibition he selected from the museum's holdings: 'I began to visit the Ulster Museum when I was an under-graduate at Queen's University in the late fifties...John Hewitt's career as a curator probably established that vital connection between *pictura* and *poesis*.' [30]

* * *

In fact it was Middleton rather than Hewitt who represented the older literary-artistic generation to young writers in the Belfast of the early 1960s (Middleton and his wife Kate both wrote poetry). Hewitt was then running the Herbert Art Gallery in Coventry. The first collections of Heaney, Mahon and Longley all contain a poem dedicated to Colin Middleton. Heaney's 'In Small Townlands' sees Middleton as subsuming and surpassing those physically engaged rural craftsmen whom his early poetry envies and mimics:

> In small townlands his hogshair wedge
> Will split the granite from the clay
> Till crystal in the rock is bared:
> Loaded brushes hone an edge
> On mountain blue and heather grey.
> Outcrops of stone contract, outstared.
>
> The spectrum bursts, a bright grenade,
> When he unlocks the safety catch
> On morning dew, on cloud, on rain.
> The splintered lights slice like a spade
> That strips the land of fuzz and blotch,
> Pares clean as bone, cruel as the pain
>
> That strikes in a wild heart attack.
> His eyes, thick, greedy lenses, fire
> This bare bald earth with white and red,
> Incinerate it till it's black
> And brilliant as a funeral pyre:
> A new world cools out of his head.

Heaney compares the painter's brush to a spade and it might be acting on the land itself as much as on the canvas. It 'splits' and 'hones'. Further, Middleton's creation of a 'new world' from the shapes and textures of County Down resembles an act of aggression. (Compare Heaney's rendering of Goya in 'Summer 1969': 'painting with his fists and elbows...as history charged' – a different version from MacNeice's Goya as artist-survivor who 'has the laugh' on history.) This is again a rhetoric of the visual arts – like Yeats's – which boosts poetry's own solidity, male mastery, and self-confidence. Heaney's poem 'Bogland' leans on the painter T.P. Flanagan in a contrasting way. 'Bogland' is not only dedicated to Flanagan. It resulted from Heaney watching Flanagan at work in Donegal on his series 'Boglands'. Heaney has said of Flanagan's images: 'what invites the eye back again and again is the fetch of water and air, their mutual flirtation, their eternal triangle with a moody light'.[31] This version of the interchange between artist, landscape and viewer is more feminine, less aggressive: Middleton's 'greedy lenses' recall the animal-eye in Ted Hughes's poetry. 'Bogland' begins by looking through the painter's eye as direction-finder for the poet's imagination: 'Everywhere the eye concedes to / Encroaching horizon'. And the eye of the land, 'the cyclops' eye/Of a tarn', looks back at the perceiver. (Incidentally, the 'Great Irish Elk' in the third quatrain is another debt to the Ulster Museum.) But as the poem moves into history and meditates upon it, the visual recedes.

The aesthetic bias of Heaney's preferences in the Museum somewhat contradicts Richard Kearney's view of his poetry (in *Transitions*) as struggling towards post-modernism to be born.[32] Heaney chose 'paintings, photographs and objects that housed some charge of primal energy or embodied some remembered feeling'.[33] As well as landscapes, he included basalt axeheads (mentioned in *Station Island*), a quilt evocative of slower 'customs and rhythms', and R.J. Welch photographs of 'Flax Harvest' and 'Fishing Nets' which 'conjure up that older, less disinfected world of seasonal work'.[34] (Welch was a remarkable Ulster photographer and field-naturalist at the turn of the century.) This is not the aesthetic of a poet who, in Kearney's words, rejects 'parochial *pietas*' and 'antiquated mythologies of "tradition" and "nature"'.[35] Heaney has said in a symposium on Irish Expressionist Painting: 'Things are not yet at the post-modernist, self-cancelling, ironical stage for most people in [Ireland]'.[36] His relief is obvious. Again, the numinous glow of calligraphy in the sequence 'Sweeney Redivivus' and in 'Alphabets' would seem to rebut the arbitrariness of the sign:

> Yet shape-note language, absolute on air
> As Constantine's sky-lettered IN HOC SIGNO
> Can still command him...

With this in mind, I want to compare two further iconic sonnets by Heaney: 'Strange Fruit' and 'The Seed Cutters'. Heaney's poems about the Bog People substitute a generally sculptural model for the painterly model that can be detected in his first two collections. Religious sculpture too: as when 'The Grauballe Man' seeks to create/'perfect'/exhibit the figure it venerates. This creation requires a set of visual or tactile similes: 'basalt egg', 'swan's foot'. As with the Raine-simile, analogical 'this looks like that' tends to promote iconography over verbal and historical complication. In 'Punishment' the speaker terms himself an 'artful voyeur'. I am not sure that *North* always follows through the self-critical logic of this: the possible suppression of dialectic, the ethics of 'spectatorial' attitudes [37] (for which Edward Thomas criticised Walter Pater). The ambiguous status of the Bog People makes it tempting to contemplate or reify life as art, death as still life. 'Strange Fruit' seems to me among the most successful poems, all the more powerfully iconic because it admits dialectic and subverts its own iconicity:

> Here is the girl's head like an exhumed gourd.
> Oval-faced, prune-skinned, prune-stones for teeth.
> They unswaddled the wet fern of her hair
> And made an exhibition of its coil,
> Let the air at her leathery beauty.
> Pash of tallow, perishable treasure:
> Her broken nose is dark as a turf clod,
> Her eyeholes blank as pools in the old workings.
> Diodorus Siculus confessed
> His gradual ease among the likes of this:
> Murdered, forgotten, nameless, terrible
> Beheaded girl, outstaring axe
> And beatification, outstaring
> What had begun to feel like reverence.

Perhaps that fits one of Rossetti's categories for the iconic sonnet – a 'dire portent'. Heaney has described how he altered the ending of 'Strange Fruit' because his emotion had become too literary and 'reverent'.[38] In fact the sonnet's belated 'turn' in the eleventh line wakes up to the implications of 'made an exhibition' and 'gradual ease' for the poem itself. At this point too the verbal medium asserts its priority. The girl 'outstares' the voyeuristic artist and reader (contrast Heaney's celebration of Middleton as 'outstaring' his natural subject-matter). Un-aesthetic language of moral and historical rather than visual definition shatters religious sculpture, 'beatification', 'reverence': 'Murdered, forgotten, nameless, terrible...'

'The Seed Cutters' contrasts with 'Strange Fruit' in being painterly and secular. It again employs the visual-arts 'trope' (Dixon Hunt) but belongs to a different Rossettian iconic category: the 'moment's monument' which is also 'a lustral rite'. Presumably the sonnet invokes Pieter Brueghel, though Heaney does praise a picture from the Ulster Museum, 'Landscape with Windmills', attributed to Jan Brueghel the Elder, for its 'eagerness to preserve and celebrate a well-known world'.[39] Incidentally, in a recent reading Heaney called the companion poem 'Sunlight' 'a Dutch interior set in Ulster'. In 'The Seed Cutters' Heaney's technique again proves equal to suggesting momentum as well as moment and monument:

> They seem hundreds of years away. Brueghel,
> You'll know them if I can get them true.
> They kneel under the hedge in a half-circle
> Behind a windbreak wind is breaking through.
> They are the seed cutters. The tuck and frill
> Of leaf-sprout is on the seed potatoes
> Buried under that straw. With time to kill
> They are taking their time. Each sharp knife goes
> Lazily halving each root that falls apart
> In the palm of the hand: a milky gleam,
> And, at the centre, a dark watermark.
> O calendar customs! Under the broom
> Yellowing over them, compose the frieze
> With all of us there, our anonymities.

The mid-line sentence-breaks at once poise the poem and give it impetus. This is epitomised by the watermark at the sonnet's own centre. It turns on a lovely chiasmus of word, syntax and stress: 'with time to kill / They are taking their time'. This warm pastoral shows a Flemish respect for calendar customs, for getting detail 'true', and for numinous precisions to be central in Heaney's aesthetic. The speaker's receptive, absorbed demeanour, and its likeness to the seed-cutters' strategy, also poise Heaney's variable aesthetic politics of subject and object. Here the poet-painter is subdued to what he works in. Thus, half-aspiration, half-elegy, the last three lines appeal to traditional collectivities, to 'custom' in art and community. The speaker becomes absorbed in a different sense as 'I' and 'them' turn into the 'all of us' of folk-art.

Paul Muldoon's poetry generally fits Kearney's account of postmodernist collage much better than anything by Heaney. Thus his long poem 'The More a Man Has the More a Man Wants' alludes to works of art and literature from different periods and countries. However, the poem does not carry collage so far as to collapse history, argument and linguistic sequence. Muldoon's cultural relativism is not there for its own sake but serves specific purposes. For example, two Belfast assassins ride into 'a picture by Edward Hopper / of a gas station'. By evoking the American painter's image of 'such a desolate oval' Muldoon gives local violence the further context of a bleak modern nowhere. Again, his wounded scapegoat Gallogly is said to 'get right under the skin, / the spluttering heart / and collapsed lung, / of the horse in *Guernica*'. Then we are told: 'He flees the Museum of Modern Art / with its bit between his teeth'. This gives full weight to the incongruity of Museum and Modern, Museum and Art. It confronts art with its suffering object trapped in history, modern art with its impotence, even post-modernism with its irrelevance. Muldoon's poem 'Christo's' also trangresses the boundary between life and art, as does this artist who covers stretches of landscape. But Muldoon imagines 'the whole of Ireland ...under wraps' in order to convey claustrophobia and menace during the period of the hunger-strikes.

Two Muldoon poems more exclusively about paintings are: 'Edward Kienholz *The State Hospital*' and 'Paul Klee: *They're Biting*'. Since Muldoon writes so many sonnets it seems perverse of him not to do so when iconic sonnets are called for. But certainly these poems are iconic portents. The two pictures may have attracted him because they already incorporate rudimentary shapes or signs associated with writing: Kienholz's comic-strip 'dream-bubble', Klee's 'exclamation-mark//at the painting's heart'. Muldoon's methods contrast with Heaney's, not only in calling attention to fictionality and artifice (Heaney in 'The Seed Cutters' seeks to reconcile beauty and truth in a Keatsian 'frieze'), but in weaving narratives rather than dwelling on images. With regard to *The State Hospital*, the poem 'assumes' details the picture cannot supply:

> Where a naked man, asleep, is strapped
> to the lower bunk of a bed.
> The bed-pan is so tantalisingly out of reach
> we may assume he has trouble
> with his bowels.
> He will have been beaten by an orderly,
> a bar of soap wrapped
> in a towel.

Another procedure is to superimpose a different picture (as MacNeice does with the 'golden tea' in 'Poussin'):

> His head, when we come to examine the head
> we would never allow ourselves to touch,
> is a fish bowl
> in which two black fish, or mauve,
> take it in turns to make eyes and mouths
> or grapple with one bright idea.
> Yet the neon-lit, plastic dream-bubble
> he borrowed from a comic strip –
> and which you and I might stretch
> to include Hope, Idaho –
> here takes in only the upper bunk of the bed
> where a naked man, asleep, is strapped.

The head-shape becoming a fish-bowl yields a further narrative of the man's interior state. Here Muldoon translates ambiguous shapes into the verbal shape-changing his poetry relishes: 'take it in turns to make eyes and mouths'. The fish-bowl metaphor also comments on the visual correlation between head and 'dream-bubble' as the same enclosed space. The framing chiasmus – chiasmus recurs in poem/painting crossovers – both seals the poem's iconic fixity and finds a verbal formal equivalent for an alarming, 'hopeless' fixity whereby the man can dream only his own predicament.

'Paul Klee: *They're Biting*' is divided between an account of the painting and a doubtfully 'connected' personal narrative. The chiasmic repetition 'caricature anglers – fish caricatures' again tracks a visual relation: one which asks 'who is being caught?'

> The lake supports some kind of bathysphere,
> an Arab dhow
>
> and a fishing-boat
> complete with languorous net.
>
> Two caricature anglers,
> have fallen hook, line and sinker
>
> for the goitred,
> spiny fish-caricatures
>
> with which the lake is stocked.
> At any moment all this should connect.

Muldoon translates Klee's joke into the idiom 'fall hook line and sinker', which secretes the further punning ambiguity of 'falling for' in the senses of loving, being deceived, naively looking or reading. The painting then prompts another visual-verbal 'connection' within the speaker's consciousness:

> When you sent me a postcard of *They're Biting*
> there was a plane sky-writing

> I LOVE YOU over Hyde Park.
> Then I noticed the exclamation-mark
>
> at the painting's heart.
> it was as if I'd already been given the word
>
> by a waist-thick conger
> mouthing NO from the fishmonger's
>
> otherwise drab window
> into which I might glance to check my hair.

I LOVE YOU, sky-writing, NO, conger eel and the speaker's reflected self-image are not quite surreally disconnected even if they disorient his and our reading. Here we have a bleak love-story, an omen of narcissism and mutual deception. In 'giving the word' these poems read pictures rather than look at them. And Muldoon chooses pictures that potentially tell a story or whose morally emblematic quality he can translate into verbal parables. Text usurps image.

Derek Mahon, as if correcting a contrary bias, comes nearest to developing the Yeatsian intensification of Pre-Raphaelitism into Symbolism. Like Yeats and the Pre-Raphaelites, too, he opposes art to materialism and progress. Thus the visual arts as such constitute a source of value in Mahon's poetry. For example, in 'North Wind: Portrush' French Impressionism represents high civilisation as opposed to what Antrim and Ulster have to offer:

> Elsewhere the olive grove,
> *Le déjeuner sur l'herbe,*
> Poppies and parasols,
> Blue skies and mythic love.
> Here only the stricken souls
> No spring can unperturb.

Again, towards the end of Mahon's verse-epistle 'The Sea in Winter' the 'luminous geometry' of Botticelli's Dante-drawings prefigures utopia: 'Diagrams of that paradise / Each has his vision of'.

In his poetry Mahon has adopted the personae of three painters: Van Gogh, the forger van Meegeren and Edvard Munch. He seems attracted to puritanical zeal translated into expressionist art. Thus he links Van Gogh's mission to the miners with the 'fierce fire' of his sunflowers. Even van Meegeren he credits with 'agony', 'fanaticism' and sheltering a 'light to transform the world'. 'Edvard Munch', later re-titled 'The Studio', concentrates on the instruments of expression as it comes into being. Based, I think, on the well-known photograph of Munch in his studio, the poem shows us round the structures in the artist's head. Pain, fury and despair are displaced on to 'furniture'. This workshop, despite its failure to produce a definitive, healing artefact whose elements will 'meet, sing and be one', strangely refuses to dissolve into the existential flux. Rather than 'roar into the floor' it continues its expressionist function:

> But it
> Never happens like that. Instead
> There is this quivering silence
> In which, day by day, the play
> Of light and shadow (shadow mostly)
> Repeats itself, though never exactly.
>
> This is the all-purpose bed-, work- and bedroom.
> Its mourning faces are cracked porcelain only quicker,
> Its knuckles door-knobs only lighter,
> Its occasional cries of despair
> A function of the furniture.

The poem has allowed us to glimpse the pressures behind Munch's paintings, Mahon's poems.

'The Studio' might be an inversion, the shadow or unconscious, of a Dutch interior, implying all that numinous rooms brush out of sight. 'Courtyards in Delft' and Mahon's response to Munch's 'Girls on a Bridge' tell us more about the art with which he can and cannot identify. 'Courtyards in Delft', based on de Hooch's series of that name, takes less pleasure in the Flemish school than Heaney does: 'Oblique light on the trite'. The poem criticises a production, not only a reproduction, of the Protestant work ethic ('chaste / Precision of the thing and the thing made'). It dwells on the paintings' sins of omission and omission of sins:

> No spinet-playing emblematic of
> The harmonies and disharmonies of love;
> No lewd fish, no fruit, no wide-eyed bird
> About to fly its cage while a virgin
> Listens to her seducer, mars the chaste
> Precision of the thing and the thing made.
> Nothing is random, nothing goes to waste:
> We miss the dirty dog, the fiery gin.

An excluded lust, chaos and ruin threaten the 'vividly mnemonic' and iconic:

> That girl with her back to us who waits
> For her man to come home for his tea
> Will wait till the paint disintegrates
> And ruined dykes admit the esurient sea;

Yet – the poem has a 'Yet' – the ironic does not completely rule out the iconic:

Yet this is life too, and the cracked
Out-house door a verifiable fact
As vividly mnemonic as the sunlit
Railings that front the houses opposite.

I lived there as a boy and know the coal
Glittering in its shed, late-afternoon
Lambency informing the deal table,
The ceiling cradled in a radiant spoon.
I must be lying low in a room there,
A strange child with a taste for verse,
While my hard-nosed companions dream of war
On parched veldt and fields of rainswept gorse.

On the one hand, Mahon's language half-relishes the immanent 'lambency' and 'radiance' with which de Hooch's secularised Protestant art-form invests the ordinary; on the other, Dutch/Ulster Protestant war-mongering haunts the house-work ethic and its aesthetic. Thus the last stanza's proto-poet suggests how this way of life, this way of art, incubates its anti-self: a Munch, a Mahon.

I think that Mahon gets closer to Munch in 'The Studio' than in 'Girls on the Bridge'. But the contrast between the poems brings out two elements in his approach to paintings: firstly, a concern with the aesthetic and its psychological roots (this also applies to his 'writer' poems such as 'Homage to Malcolm Lowry'); secondly, a concern with moral explication. Thus the girls on the bridge are located on the road of life between a Flemish version of home ('Beds, / Lamplight and crisp linen') and Munch's 'Scream'. The human figure is prominent in the visual arts as processed by Mahon's poetry. But if he seems comparatively uninterested in abstraction, his symbolism develops the 'play/Of light and shadow' he (like MacNeice) notices in painting. His poetry of course draws on, and translates, French Symbolism directly, without Yeats's mediation. Nevertheless, the sequence 'Light Music' underscores affinities with the Pre-Raphaelite and the *fin-de-siècle*. Here the human figure largely disappears from poems that point towards a therapeutic, aesthetic realm where all the arts – as the punning title suggests – cohabit. 'Light Music' offers poetry as the best of visual and rhythmical worlds.

The sequence's sub-headings include: 'Architecture', 'Aesthetics', 'Byzantium', 'Joyce in Paris', 'Rembrandt', 'Mozart', Magritte'. The brevity of the poems might recall Imagism, but their symbolism (as in the case of symbolic light) is not truncated but transcendental. Thus Magritte's surrealist placing of a woman's torso over clouds adumbrates the birth of new categories: 'Now what pale thighs/ open the door in the cloud?' And in 'Revelation' – a title that links the Bible with poetic epiphany – the sounds, colours and forms of poetry outdo painting by imagining an unimaginable colour:

> A colour the fish know
> we do not know, so
> long have we been ashore.
>
> When that colour
> shines in the rainbow
> there will be no more sea.

Mahon's revelatory aesthetics might be used to define the genesis of Medbh McGuckian's poetry, which is suffused and obsessed with colour and light. The extent to which her poems dwell on the metaphysics of their own creation makes her Ireland's nearest equivalent to Wallace Stevens. And, as with Stevens (or Yeats in the 1890s), the fact that her images seem projections of imagination and language, rather than tokens of sensory presence, bring poetry and painting very close together: 'The sounds that shapes make in the air/The shapes that sounds make' ('Death of a Ceiling'). 'Lime Trees in Winter, Retouched', from *Venus and the Rain* (1984), illustrates McGuckian's ease with 'the trope of "painting"...as a metaphor for the poetic act':

> Black is my continuum, my black wheat ripens
> From peach black, vine black, to the resins
> Of darkness. That is how good a picture
> Should be, oil abetting, light disturbing,
> Hoisted between two windows like the soul
> Of modesty, constantly straightening against them.

Yet her resort to this metaphor once again differentiates the sister arts (very sisterly in McGuckian's case) by exploiting the greater physicality of painting as act and artifact. Some poems also evoke writing in terms of paper, ink, book, letter-shapes, 'my yellow/ Pencil, my green table'. However, this still encroaches on the visual arts domain, much as Virginia Woolf envied her painter-sister, Vanessa, and stood up at a desk to write. Some of McGuckian's poems recall Lily Briscoe's surrogacy for Woolf in *To the Lighthouse*: Lily's problems about perceiving/painting Mrs Ramsay and achieving her own 'vision'. 'Woman with Blue-Ringed Bowl', from *On Ballycastle Beach* (1988), responds to a woman's portrait with a Woolfian, Impressionist care for variations of light and perspective:

> If I was possessed of a pen that wrote in four colours,
> I could patrol how differently each tree contains the sun.
> Hold me in the light, she offers, turn me around,
> Not the light controlled by a window, but the cool gold
> Of turning leaves after their short career in the sky.

The aesthetic attributed to the portrait, and operative in the poem, accords with a feminist politics of representation. 'Mr McGregor's Garden', in McGuckian's first collection, *The Flower Master* (1980), wittily uses Beatrix Potter to sort out power-relations between female artist and male muse:

> Some women save their sanity with needles.
> I complicate my life with studies
> Of my favourite rabbit's head, his vulgar volatility,
> Or a little ladylike sketching
> Of my resident toad in his flannel box...

But the representation of her own sex also causes problems for the woman painter-poet. In 'The Sitting' (from *Venus and the Rain*) the sitter resists what she sees as imposition and distortion: 'she questions my brisk/Brushwork, the note of positive red/In the kissed mouth I have given her'. 'Bright', 'positive' colours may stand for self-assertion and sexuality, which the painter properly rescues from the repression suggested by her subject's 'making a tunnel with her/Hands over her dull-rose dress'. Or the sitter, seemingly the hidden, unarticulated side of the speaker's psyche ('My half-sister'), may properly criticise 'Wishfulness, the failure of the tampering rain/To go right into the mountain'. This implies the need for some new aesthetic, not one based on existing premises – political or sexual – if the inner woman is to be reached. Conversely, in an earlier poem, 'The Seed-Picture', the artist speaks as a traditional woman who represses a younger, freer woman by fixing her image: 'enclosing her/In the border of a grandmother's sampler'. Yet, as 'The seeds dictate their own vocabulary', that vocabulary turns angry, and sexually vengeful: 'the irises/Of Dutch blue maw, black rape/For the pupils, millet/ For the vicious beige circles underneath'. The creator of the seed-picture finds her handiwork, her alter ego, her ego and id, coming alive (like the woman in the yellow wallpaper) to 'make women/Feel their age, and sigh for liberation'.

McGuckian brings her own twists to the motif of the woman artist liberating herself, and thereby other women. Her poetry engages in an oblique, continuous dialectic with her Northern male precursors and contemporaries. For instance, 'Next Day Hill' (in *The Flower Master*) proposes to surprise male poets, inscribed by quotation into the poem, with an art-object: 'A book with primrose edges and a mirror/In the cover'. This, of course, *The Flower Master* already is: indeed, the title-poem (with some irony) completes a course of female pupillage in 'the principle/Of enfolding space'. Evidently, the mirror does not promise to flatter. 'The Flitting',

also in *The Flower Master*, dramatises a relevant tension between
motherhood and an 'immortality' postponed. As in 'Courtyards in
Delft', Flemish painting implies repression and false security, but
this time as it affects the housewife-artist forcibly identified with
the house:

> 'You wouldn't believe all this house has cost me –
> In body-language terms, it has turned me upside down.'...
>
> Now my own life hits me in the throat, the bumps
> And cuts of the walls as telling
> As the poreholes in strawberries, tomato seeds.
> I cover them for safety with these Dutch girls
> Making lace...

However, one Dutch painting prompts the ambiguous speculation:
'Her narrative secretes its own values, as mine might/If I painted
the half of me that welcomes death/In a faggotted dress, in a peacock chair'. This shadow-self adumbrates the counterpart of Mahon's
'studio': a creative locus for a narrative contrary to that of the
patriarchal 'house', a narrative spelling out the painful subtext of
'The Flitting'. The speaker has been passively transferred 'from
one structure to the other', i.e. from being a daughter to being wife
and mother, *via* 'a chair of human arms...that *fraternity* of clothes'
(my italics). The male portraits of women in her house/head belong
to what is, in fact, a single controlling 'structure', but also insinuate
'otherness', the possibility of 'a garden escape'.

McGuckian's most recent collection, *Marconi's Cottage* (1991),
includes a poem about Gwen John, implicitly in the shadow of her
brother Augustus as well as of a lover/artist who imposes his light,
his masculine aesthetic: 'a station of candles//In wine bottles' –
perhaps an allusion to Seamus Heaney. Thus 'Her fear of light
began/While his coat still hung over a chair'. The candlelight ob-
scures, leaving 'a film of woodsmoke' (a critical thrust on McGuckian's
part); whereas, during their relationship, the woman denies her
subtle colour-sense and her complex awareness of *natural* light
remains unexpressed. The poem's title, 'Road 32, Roof 13-23, Grass
23', comes from Gwen John's notebooks, and 'signifies the graduated
numbers of the spectrum of colours she used'. This note, supplied
by McGuckian, itself stakes an aesthetic claim.

The claim is at once metaphorical and highly specific. My quotations would suggest that McGuckian uses a graduated spectrum
of colour-coding, to provide psychological key-signatures and define
balances of artistic and sexual power. As with the emphasis on
colour in Woolf's prose, the effect is primarily metaphysical. Mc-

Guckian's spectrum runs from 'a sisterly length/Of flesh-coloured silk' to erotic 'flag-red,/Flag-gold, storming flowers', from whites of effacement or obliteration to crimsons of passion and a purple unconscious. Colour may be applied to flowers, clothes or décor: 'I kept insisting/On robin's egg blue tiles around the fireplace'; its emblematic shading may be a touch ('dull-rose') or a broader brush-stroke: 'Your eyes were ever brown, the colour/Of time's submissive-ness'. Some associations seem fairly constant: brown is recessive as compared with bronze, for instance; the relatively rare green and yellow may be colours of writing and renewal. But the way in which McGuckian rings changes on blue, at an interesting stage of the spectrum, indicates how she prevents this technique from becoming predictable: 'Bone-deep blue', 'designer-blue air', 'hard-blue dress', 'my youngest, speedwell blouse', 'stone-blue/Hours', 'a blue vigour', 'unpronounceable blue', 'the usefulness of blue', 'the perfect narra-tive nature of blue', 'a careful, sad, a Marie-Louise blue'. Two poems parody her obsession with blue. 'Catching Geese' is ironical about 'my soon-to-be-famous blue style', and 'A Small Piece of Wood' (in *Marconi's Cottage*) sends up this among other mannerisms:

> While my numberless blues
> Have neither end nor beginning,
> Arranged like a tribe of lovers
> In a circle...

For all McGuckian's artifice, her aesthetic theory paradoxically comes down on the side of nature, on the garden beckoning beyond the house: 'Not the light controlled by a window...' Her dialectic not only turns the historical tables by situating the male artist indoors, but transforms the stereotyping of 'woman-as-nature' into a source of artistic strength. Artwork with flowers or seeds is one of her favoured models for making poems. McGuckian aligns her-self with Woolf's and MacNeice's 'flux' in that she tends to portray the patriarchal sublime as lacking fluidity – less of a 'river's art' – the male artist-lover as unduly architectonic. 'Rowing', which involves a conflict between 'perfect', 'classical' light and 'artless' 'dark tobacco golds' 'from the room below', may allude to 'Sailing to Byzantium': 'Your body renovates me like an artisan,/A gold-smith, none too delicate'. In 'Head of a Woman' an insensitive male sculptural 'hand waits to give the movement/Completing my head'. 'Painter and Poet' (in *Venus and the Rain*) brings these strands together. The woman speaker is, significantly, the painter, taking her cues from the natural world. The male, the poet, confines himself to a hothouse room whose 'crimson flock/Wallpaper' she

chokes 'with sheets of mimosa'. Finally, his 'perfection' and 'exact-
ness' yield to her desire for ' his quenched eyes' to be opened.
Painter and poet, female and male principles, mysteriously blend
into some new imaginative order 'until even/The ghosts of paths
were out of sight'.

If Mahon's poetry evokes the *fin-de-siècle*, and McGuckian's an
even further aesthetic extreme, Paul Durcan seems to reconstitute
the starting-point of Romantic interaction between poetry and
painting. His approach recalls Blake, Yeats's 'chanticleer of the new
dawn'.[40] Durcan may not be a painter – though he attracts labels
like surrealist and expressionist – but he is certainly a poet who
responds to painting with the utmost intensity. Paintings 'inspire'
him in the full Romantic sense, and women in paintings become
Muses. Thus Durcan's poetry moves among paintings as it does
among other phenomena, sometimes insisting that the paintings
are more real than what passes for 'the real world'. This can be
gauged from his poems 'The National Gallery Restaurant' and
'Round the Corner from Francis Bacon'. The former is spoken by
a business-man who complains: 'One of the snags about the National
Gallery Restaurant / Is that in order to gain access to it / One has
to pass through the National Gallery': he objects to 'being looked
at by persons in pictures'. In contrast, the impecunious young
lovers in 'Around the Corner from Francis Bacon' consider their
'haven for peaceful revolutionaries' to be sanctified by the artist's
proximity.

As part of a holistic revolutionary vision, Durcan's poems *after*
paintings are without aesthetic self-consciousness. And they bear a
much looser relation to their inspiration than do the poems about
paintings I have been looking at. For example, Durcan says of his
poem 'EI Flight 106: New York – Dublin' that it derives both from
meeting a lively old woman on that plane, and from looking long
and hard at Turner's painting of a shipwrecked slave-ship. But all
that *apparently* survives of Turner's contribution is a brief fancy
whereby a plane-crash would plunge the passengers into the sea 'All
sunset and chains'. Similarly, 'The Jewish Bride' (*after Rembrandt*)
sparks off a meditation on husband and wife as fascist and victim,
and only the last line reproduces any feature of the painting itself
– its eloquent hands. 'The Rape of Europa' gives Titian more space,
but frames his picture with a dialogue between a father and daughter
about life and sex. Zeus becomes the 'man who works in Mr Con-
way's field'. The poem makes us visualise the metamorphosis of
man into bull, as the picture cannot. Durcan, in combination with

Titian's seductively soft-focus animal, produces a much less patriarchal, if more idealised, effect than Yeats's swan god – the awakening of sexuality without fear:

> He lowed as if the dusk was a towel on his brow
> And I put flowers on his head.

In a poem whose refrain is 'Life is a dream', the bull comes alive to look at us in the way the business-man dislikes.

Durcan's somewhat mixed bag of painterly inspirations either have a visionary intensity of their own, or lend themselves to *his*. And he finds the poet in paintings as well as the Muse – not only in the obvious Chagall ('Poète Allongé'), but in Kitaj's 'The Orientalist',[41] Veronica Bolay's 'Hay Carrier' or Michael Cullen's 'Running Clown'. Durcan's attention to two of the newer Irish painters, Cullen and Bolay, confirms his bias towards the non-representational in modern art, but towards the symbolist as opposed to the abstract. The human figure is as constant as in Mahon. However, Durcan's transcendental symbolism is as all-embracing as Blake's, not Mahon's site of residual aspiration. He greatly admires Stanley Spencer – a painter very much in the Blake tradition – and Spencer's transmogrified Cookham may cast light on Durcan's Ireland, on the fantasy landscape of 'Europa and the Bull'. Hostile to the term 'primitive', Durcan speaks as 'a sophisticated primitive' in his poem about Pirosmani's *Ortachala Belle*. This accords with Blakean innocence, as does Durcan's interest in Cullen's exploitation of forms from children's art. The naif child-art manner of Cullen's 'Clown Running', as well as its images, contributes to Durcan's figure of the 'Clown Witness': an innocent menaced by the machinery of war and aggression ('The Michael Cullen Show at the Fenderesky').

Besides making pictures tell unlikely, perception-cleansing stories, Durcan's most characteristic twist of style when inspired by paintings is to make a mantra of word or phrase-structure equivalent to the painter's focus on certain colours or shapes. Thus Michael Cullen's 'Strawberry Nude gets her full strawberry due, in a tone that (like the painting) blends voyeurism and vision:

> On either side of her, concertinas of strawberry men
> Queue up to give her a strawberry kiss;
> Isn't it strawberry, strawberry, that it's all so strawberry!
>
> There is a life after language! Bury me –
> O my strawberry girl – bury me.

Durcan's most powerfully iconic poem about/after a painting is 'The Hay-Carrier' *after Veronica Bolay*. His submission to Bolay's strong image shows in that he neither selects nor embroiders but enters fully into the picture's own intensity (as Blake's poetry into his visual images and *vice versa*):

> Have you ever saved hay in Mayo in the rain?
> Have you ever made hay in Mayo in the sun?
> Have you ever carried above your head a haycock on a pitchfork?
> Have you ever slept in a haybarn on the road from Mayo into Egypt?
> I am a hay-carrier.
> My father was a hay-carrier.
> My mother was a hay-carrier.
> My brothers were hay-carriers.
> My sisters were hay-carriers.
> My wife is a hay-carrier.
> My son is a hay-carrier.
> His sons are hay-carriers.
> His daughters are hay-carriers.
> We were always all hay-carriers.
> We will always be hay-carriers.
> For the great gate of night stands painted red –
> And all of heaven lies waiting to be fed.

Here the whole poem becomes a cosmic symbol where Mayo elides into Egypt as England into Jerusalem. The genealogy of hay-carrying suggests a perennial spiritual mission. Whereas 'Michael Cullen's Strawberry Nude' affirms 'There is a life after language' – a point where words stop and image takes over – in 'The Hay-Carrier', as in Mahon's 'Revelation', words take over from image. As Mahon imagines an unknown colour, so Durcan elaborates colour-detail in Bolay's picture to define the visionary and utopian common pursuit of painter and poet:

> For the great gate of night stands painted red –
> And all of heaven lies waiting to be fed.

[1988]

The Room Where MacNeice Wrote 'Snow'

Louis MacNeice has influenced redefinitions of Irish poetry and Irish identity. He has done so not only by virtue of what he says about Ireland, but because he is such a good poet. It may also be significant that his poetry mediated between traditionalism and Modernism at an important juncture in twentieth-century poetry. MacNeice's relation to Ireland and England, to Yeats and Eliot, and to his 1930s contemporaries makes his poetry a remarkably broad conduit for the materials and techniques of twentieth-century poetry. And a conduit, too, for its crises of faith: one theme of this essay will be the different ways in which MacNeice, Derek Mahon, Paul Muldoon, and Ciaran Carson have reinterpreted the tension between poetry and history. This tension they inherited more immediately from Yeats, further back from English Romanticism and the aesthetic tradition.

Yet not only MacNeice's 'Anglo' dimension but also Yeats's is sometimes marginalised or criticised in accounts of 'Irish poetry'. After Independence there was increasingly no obvious Yeatsian constituency in the Free State/Republic. And, as Yeats's indigenous cultural context became more remote, so did certain aspects of the Irish-British literary connection. In terms of poetic history, we must not forget that the Celtic Twilight fogged up the entire archipelago. Again, from the other side of the Irish Sea, the impact of Yeats on English poets – W.H. Auden, Philip Larkin – has not always been understood. Here the connection is often to do with form, with formal traditionalism, with the 'ancient salt' in which Yeats insisted poetry should be packed lest it decay. In *The Poetry of W.B. Yeats* (1941) MacNeice draws a firm formal circle around Yeats, Auden and himself:

> We admired [Yeats] too for his form. Eliot in 1921 had argued that, as the modern world is so complex, the poet must become 'more allusive, more indirect, in order to force, to dislocate if necessary, language into his meaning'. A chaotic world, that is, could only be dealt with by the methods of *The Waste Land*. Yeats went back to an earlier tradition and suggested by his example that, given a chaotic world, the poet is entitled, if he wishes, to eliminate some of the chaos, to select and systematise. Treatment of form and subject here went hand in hand. Yeats's formalising activity began when he *thought* about the world; as he thought it into a regular pattern, he naturally cast his verse in regular patterns also. A parallel process can be observed in W.H. Auden...[1]

At the same time, as we shall see, MacNeice also assimilated *The Waste Land*'s challenge to such 'formalising activity'. But my immediate point is that Yeats's posterity has been more dispersed than Eliot's. Indeed, the prominence of Modernism in academic theorising of twentieth-century poetry may owe something to the fragmentation of a Yeatsian opposition. Critics loosely refer to Yeats as a 'Modernist' – even though he called Pound his 'opposite'[2] – without regard to tradition and the individual country. But poets pick up what critics miss. And if certain contexts for Yeats went down the plughole of Irish separation from Britain, it's not surprising that Northern Irish poets, born into uneasy cultural dualities, should home not only towards MacNeice's 'treatment of form and subject', but towards Yeats's. In the case of MacNeice, as compared with the Modernists I discussed in 'Poetic Forms and Social Malformations', we have an Irish poet strategically placed to weigh Yeats against Eliot. On the one hand, his cultural affiliation to Yeats went much deeper than Auden's; on the other, a poet from Ireland encountered Eliot in a context – 1930s Britain – which enforced a re-examination of the formal means whereby poetry could cope with historical pressures. Recent esteem for the rarefied politics of Modernist texts might recall that thirties revision. Nevertheless, *The Poetry of W.B. Yeats*, written across the outbreak of war, does not propose any easy or obvious correlation between literary forms and the historical moment. Rather, Hitler's invasion of Poland has blasted open all the artistic options once again, making equally 'unreal' for MacNeice 'Yeats and his poetry...modern London, modernist art...Left Wing politics [and] the poetry that professes to be "realist"'.[3]

His successors attend to MacNeice because MacNeice attended to his predecessors. Such genealogical awareness is itself an Irish trait, with literary as well as political repercussions. Though a less devout ancestor-worshipper than Yeats, MacNeice warned in his essay 'Poetry Today' (1935) against the abolition of tradition:

> [poets and readers] must avoid the two extremes of psittacism and aphasia. There are cultured people in England today who write poems which are mere and sheer Shelley: these are psittacists; they are betraying themselves (and, incidentally, betraying Shelley). There are also the enthusiasts (mostly Americans in Paris) who set out to scrap tradition from A to Z; this should logically lead to aphasia; that they do not become quite aphasic is due to their powers of self-deception. How are we to do justice, not to the segregated Past or Present, but to their concrete antinomy?[4]

MacNeice goes on to frame this question in terms which we would now call post-modernist:

> The problem is especially difficult for us because, unlike our more parochial predecessors, we have so many Pasts and Presents to choose from. We have too much choice and not enough brute limitations. The eclectic is usually impotent.[5]

But MacNeice does not seek relief from creative 'impotence' in notions of the self-pleasing text. His solution is 'clique-literature', i.e. interaction between a group of contemporaries. MacNeice's Irishness sharpened his sense of both poetic community and poetic tradition. His book *Modern Poetry* (1938) is the critical work of the period which most obsessively addresses the point where the poet's own generation activates that 'concrete antinomy' of 'Past and Present'. And none of his *English* contemporaries discriminated so carefully between what they could use and what they could not in the practice and theory of Yeats and Eliot. Nor did any Irish poet subject Yeats to such detailed interrogation. They mostly dealt with anxiety of Yeatsian influence by psittacism (F.R. Higgins) or by would-be aphasia (Austin Clarke). Measured from the 1930s, MacNeice saw Yeats, Eliot and even Joyce as still unduly implicated in aestheticism, in 'Pater's closed circle of exalted moments'.[6] He considered that Auden and himself had more thoroughly broken the aesthetic circuit by virtue of their attention, not only to subject-matter and history, but also to language. MacNeice always stresses the social contexts of the language that reaches the poet: language as a community-product, conditioned by the 'vulgar' social and political world. He would not have accepted that this world was already textually inscribed or pre-empted. For instance, he endorsed Geoffrey Grigson's dislike of Ezra Pound's 'cultural reference rock-jumping style' and criticised the 'monotonous...cadences' of Poundian free verse.[7] For MacNeice, poetic rhythms must listen to the speech and sounds that invade the poet's ear. They must also (unlike Pound) know when to stop. He believed that the thirties poets, in their resumption of traditional forms, could now take in their stride techniques 'previously...exploited for their own sakes by experimenters'.[8] 'Poetry Today' ends with MacNeice's sense of the formal and metaphysical issues in the mid 1930s:

> We [poets] want to have the discoveries of other poets in our blood but not necessarily in our minds. We want just enough *a priori* to make us ruthless so that when we meet the inrush of *a posteriori* (commonly called 'life') we can sweep away the vastly greater part of it and let the rest body out our potential pattern; by the time this is done, it will be not only a new but the first pattern of its kind and not particularly ours...[9]

This anticipates Adorno's view that art-works 'are neither pure impulse nor pure form, but the congealment of the process obtaining between impulse and form. This process is a social one.'[10]

MacNeice's early poems worry at the problem of closure; or, to use his own terminology, flux and pattern. Both directly and subtextually they question the disposition of form and language to simplify or petrify the existential flow. However, in 'Nature Morte' the senses, too, are represented as fallible:

> So we whose senses give us things misfelt and misheard
> Turn also, for our adjustment, to the pretentious word
> Which stabilises the light on the sun-fondled trees
> And, by photographing our ghosts, claims to put us at our ease...

Then MacNeice inverts the premise that artistic 'reconstructions' are necessarily either stable or stabilising:

> no matter how solid and staid we contrive
> Our reconstructions, even a still life is alive
> And in your Chardin the appalling unrest of the soul
> Exudes from the dried fish and the brown jug and the bowl.

This undermines both the artist's and the viewer's control over meaning, but in terms of emotional turmoil as much as aesthetic theory. Just as a Chardin painting destabilises its own apparent poise, so with the long irregular couplets of 'Nature Morte' itself. 'Appalling unrest of the soul' hangs in the air between speaker and reader. In other poems of the 1930s MacNeice similarly uses the long couplet as a halfway house between traditional forms and freer techniques, testing sonnet or stanza against the weight of life that bulkier line-units and cheeky enjambement can introduce. For example, the couplets of 'Birmingham' are fraught with socio-political traffic up to the end:

> On shining lines the trams like vast sarcophagi move
> Into the sky, plum after sunset, merging to duck's egg, barred with
>   mauve
> Zeppelin clouds, and Pentecost-like the cars' headlights bud
> Out from sideroads and the traffic signals, crème-de-menthe or bull's
>   blood,
> Tell one to stop, the engine gently breathing, or to go on
> To where like black pipes of organs in the frayed and fading zone
> Of the West the factory chimneys on sullen sentry will all night wait
> To call, in the harsh morning, sleep-stupid faces through the daily
>   gate.

In so elasticating the eight-line stanza, MacNeice revises the favourite medium of Yeats who, in his view, 'avoided flux, the sphere of the realist proper'.[11]

MacNeice agreed with Yeats that the lyric poem was a dramatic structure, but he re-designed theatre, actors and set. This revision has implications both for 'who speaks' in a poem and for 'closure'. 'Nature Morte' and 'Birmingham' distribute and collectivise the lyric voice in a way that differs from the Yeatsian phantasmagoria with its centre-stage rhetorical 'I'. The artist-'we' of 'Nature Morte' shares in a pervasive and continuous maladjustment; the reporter-'we' of 'Birmingham' (not that the poem is 'realism proper') merges into the urban-capitalist neurosis, the 'fidgety machines', on which he reports. MacNeice distrusted T.S. Eliot's claims to multi-vocal impersonality, arguing that he merely dodged the first-person singular. MacNeice's own handling of pronouns combines the democratic and the dramatic. His later poetry extends this principle into the creation of a third-person Everyman, a locus for riddling questions about the human and modern condition. Such questions hardly stop at the point where the self is discovered to be a construct. MacNeice's poetry enquires into the constructing agencies (not represented as wholly social), and asks whether these can be perceived and which should be resisted. As 'The Habits' puts it: 'When they put him in rompers the habits/Fanned out to close in'. This echoes, more lightly and ironically, the wartime intensity of 'Prayer before Birth': 'Let me not make me a stone and let them not spill me'. Here the self, like poetry shuttles between flux and pattern, petrifaction and fluidity, in a context where ethical choice (a necessary 'closure') rather than 'autonomy', marks its coming into being. All of which renders 'vulgar Marxist' disapproval of lyrical transcendence mostly beside the point. However, the genres of 'Nature Morte' and 'Birmingham' (both written in 1933) can be distinguished, in that the former mainly addresses the soul or psyche, the latter situates itself in history, 'the daily gate'. Thus 'Nature Morte' ends with a defining if hardly consoling image, whereas the final impressions of 'Birmingham' emphasise a continuum. Yet the distinction is not absolute, since both poems cast us back upon flux.

Sometimes together, sometimes apart, the unrest of the soul and the traffic of history surge through MacNeice's poetry of the 1930s. Flux invades pattern with language, rhythms and data that derive from the assumed sphere of 'the realist proper'. Auden's poetry retains more stanzaic system (also more philosophical system) and can become rhythmically formulaic. MacNeice, responding to flux 'On the tongue on the eyes on the ears in the palms of one's hands', retextured form from the inside out. His adverse comments on free verse ('Some traditional verse forms are like ladders with rungs every few inches; you get stuck in them or stub your toes on them. But a ladder without any rungs...?') [12] do not rule out adjustments between the two kinds of ladder.

Autumn Journal (1939) metrically, structurally and metaphysically consummates MacNeice's early dialectic between flux and pattern.

It also re-opens channels between Modernist poetry and history. In 'Eclogue for Christmas' (1933), which both derives and deviates from *The Waste Land*, MacNeice had criticised the abstract direction of Modernist forms as no answer to the alienation that they reproduce:

> I who was Harlequin in the childhood of the century,
> Posed by Picasso beside an endless opaque sea,
> Have seen myself sifted and splintered in broken facets,
> Tentative pencillings, endless liabilities, no assets,
> Abstractions scalpelled with a palette-knife
> Without reference to this particular life...

Although MacNeice broadly accepted a relativistic universe, his politics, together with his reading of philosophy and the classics, led him to assert the social claims of 'this particular life' – not a defence of autonomy, but the cry of the 1930s against the 1920s. 'Impotent eclecticism' is no ground for society any more than for art. (Marxist critics who complain that post-modernism leaves no basis for critique should look into the thirties MacNeice.) Accordingly, *Autumn Journal* could be called 'Beyond *The Waste Land*'. It takes off from London (and Europe) in pre-war rather than post-war crisis, although 'the end-all mud' of 1914-18 remains in view. And it places the relation of splintered self to splintered culture within an explicitly historicised and politicised context. Thus, for example, Eliot's classical fragments become MacNeice's post-Munich version of the Ancient World as populated by

> the crooks, the adventurers, the opportunists,
> The careless athletes and the fancy boys,
> The hair-splitters, the pedants, the hard-boiled sceptics
> And the Agora and the noise
> Of the demagogues and the quacks; and the women pouring
> Libations over graves
> And the trimmers at Delphi and the dummies at Sparta...

He adds: 'and lastly/I think of the slaves'. Broadly speaking, English writers of the 1930s followed Eliot's ambiguous signpost either towards Marx (John Cornford) or towards God (Evelyn Waugh). *Autumn Journal* politicises the *Waste Land* scenario but does not eliminate questions of humanist and spiritual value – 'And Conscience still goes crying through the desert'. MacNeice's impulse is to re-integrate 'broken facets', or at least bring them into the proximity of a fine and flexible formal mesh. His capacious verse-medium itself puts back in what Eliot's imagist methods (or Pound's editing) took out – discursiveness, persona. Yet the poem's structural model is the Heraclitean stream. It defers closure in the precisely contingent

sense of accepting an ominous 'inrush' of history without succumbing
to necessity:

> The dead are dead as Nineteen-Thirty-Eight.
> Sleep to the noise of running water
>   Tomorrow to be crossed, however deep...
>   There will be time to audit
> The accounts later, there will be sunlight later
>   And the equation will come out at last.

In section XVI of *Autumn Journal* Ireland, South and North,
figures as a set of attempts to freeze history: 'Let the round tower
stand aloof/In a world of bursting mortar!' This image, with its
Yeatsian echo, suggests the extent to which MacNeice's aesthetic as
well as his politics (although they cannot finally be separated) was
shaped by a recoil from Irish absoluteness. Yet he stops short of
relativising the imagination into the closed circuit of infinitely decon-
structible texts. We can see the importance of this for his successors
by considering how poems by Derek Mahon, Paul Muldoon and
Ciaran Carson receive MacNeice's celebrated poem 'Snow'.

In the last section of *Autumn Journal* MacNeice himself rewrites
'Snow', placing the poem at a receding historical point:

> Sleep, my past and all my sins,
>   In distant snow or dried roses...

But the great shock of 'Snow' is its perennial immediacy:

> The room was suddenly rich and the great bay-window was
> Spawning snow and pink roses against it
> Soundlessly collateral and incompatible:
> World is suddener than we fancy it.
>
> World is crazier and more of it than we think,
> Incorrigibly plural. I peel and portion
> A tangerine and spit the pips and feel
> The drunkenness of things being various.
>
> And the fire flames with a bubbling sound for world
> Is more spiteful and gay than one supposes –
> On the tongue on the eyes on the ears in the palms of one's hands –
> There is more than glass between the snow and the huge roses.

'Suddenness' and 'fancy' are versions of flux and pattern. The
challenge of suddenness to fancy tests the conjunctive powers of
poetry as well as metaphysics. Can it follow and fathom what is
'between the snow and the huge roses'? 'Between' is famously
ambiguous in opening up distance, yet perhaps retaining closeness.
It suggests not only the richness but the risk of pluralities, of the

modern cognitive destabilisation: 'World is...more of it than we think'. Mahon and Muldoon, too, accept the challenge of life's disjunctions to poetic conjunction, of 'incorrigible' plurality to the aesthetic rage for order. The poems in which they refer to 'Snow' are Mahon's elegy for MacNeice, 'In Carrowdore Churchyard' (written in 1964), and Muldoon's 'History' (published in *Why Brownlee Left*, 1980). In the last stanza of the former, 'Snow' comes to epitomise MacNeice's whole poetic enterprise – its tonal and ethical spectrum – the whole enterprise of poetry:

> Locked in the winter's fist, these hills are hard
> As nails, yet soft and feminine in their turn
> When fingers open and the hedges burn.
> This, you implied, is how we ought to live –
>
> The ironical, loving crush of roses against snow,
> Each fragile, solving ambiguity. So
> From the pneumonia of the ditch, from the ague
> Of the blind poet and the bombed-out town you bring
> The all-clear to the empty holes of spring;
> Rinsing the choked mud, keeping the colours new.

Mahon's oxymoronic adjectives reproduce the paradoxical poise, the metaphysical conundrum of MacNeice's poem. But the stanza goes on to claim that poetry can in some sense 'solve' or at least sieve the 'inrush' of phenomena and history. Rhythmically and rhetorically it moves beyond 'ambiguity'.

Paul Muldoon's 'History', as it ostensibly tries to reconstruct a sexual encounter is partly a joke against rigid understandings of history in Ulster and Ireland. It sabotages the assumption that we can 'remember' 1690 or recover the spirit of 1916:

> Where and when exactly did we first have sex?
> Do you remember? Was it Fitzroy Avenue,
> Or Cromwell Road, or Notting Hill?
> Your place or mine? Marseilles or Aix?
> Or as long ago as that Thursday evening
> When you and I climbed through the bay window
> On the ground floor of Aquinas Hall
> And into the room where MacNeice wrote 'Snow',
> Or the room where they say he wrote 'Snow'.

The names teasingly evoke Ulster's British connection (Fitzroy, Notting Hill – both a district of London and a location in Belfast), foreign entanglements (the Marseillaise?), and religious oppositions (Cromwell/Aquinas). The cream of the joke is that Aquinas Hall, later a hostel for Catholic women students, was the palace of Anglican bishops of Down, Connor and Dromore when MacNeice's father held that office. Thus Muldoon smuggles in some factual and transgressive local history.

'History' and 'In Carrowdore Churchyard' articulate two Mac-Neicean premises and imply them as *a priori*: premises that evolved from his reaction against the 'choked mud' of Ireland and exposure to 1930s Britain. Firstly, poetry must lay itself open to a flux of consciousness and history. Secondly, by doing so it can arrive at unpredicted patterns. But Mahon and Muldoon process and develop these premises differently. Flux in 'History' belongs more exclusively to consciousness than do Mahon's existential 'rough winds' (partly akin to 'that wind / That shakes the shutter' in 'In Memory of Major Robert Gregory'). Again, where Mahon stresses image and formal clarification, Muldoon stresses language and the puzzles of cognition. Yet, Muldoon's irony points to the writing of 'Snow' as the only 'exactitude' amid the cognitive instability. Poetry, then, puts history (and literary history – 'they say') in its place and solves once again, if at a further remove from MacNeice's original inrush of snow and roses. However, the intensity of their afterglow does not diminish. Muldoon invokes 'Snow' less as written text than as creative act or touchstone or stay against confusion.

Their rewritings of 'Snow' show Mahon as more preoccupied with poetry's 'formalising activity', and Muldoon with its cognitive activity: with knowing and saying rather than with shape and image. This suggests that both preoccupations and their tension – intrinsic to the tension between Romantic aesthetics and Modernism – are manifested in MacNeice's poetry, not only in the quintessential 'Snow'. To put it another way: MacNeice embraces and counter-poses the double origins of poetry in song and riddle. Some of his poems declare themselves one or the other. 'Snow' might be both.

As anthologists of Irish poetry Mahon and Muldoon agree on MacNeice's importance, but weight it differently. Mahon's *Sphere Book of Modern Irish Poetry* (1972) mainly features the early MacNeice, Muldoon's *Faber Book of Contemporary Irish Poetry* (1986) mainly the later. These emphases are borne out by their statements else-where. For instance, in 1961, when he was producing his own *juvenilia*, Mahon reviewed *Solstices*, the collection in which Mac-Neice's new kind of parable-poem became central to his poetry. Putting pressure on word, phrase and syntax, parable developed the linguistic means and ends of MacNeice's metaphysic. But Mahon commented briskly: 'Many of the fifty [poems] are pretty sterile, and when a poet who was once capable of "Cradle Song" or the more haunting passages in *Autumn Journal* proffers a poem telling you how to play shove-halfpenny, you begin to suspect that he is only writing now out of force of habit'.[13] 'Shove Halfpenny', one of a riddling sequence called 'Indoor Sports', may not be an epic; but its angled syntax and puns set up a suggestive emblem of sexual relations:

> One disc can knock another one into place
> With skill and join her there. No, not like that;
> Like this.

The effect is certainly more proto-Muldoon than proto-Mahon.

Mahon, to employ MacNeice's own metaphors for his own style, warms to its 'bloom or frill or...floating image', rather than to its later 'syntax and bony feature'.[14] In Mahon's early poetry we can detect debts to MacNeice's 'bloom or frill', and to his 'falling twigs of song' ('Entirely'), as much as to his absorption of the 'industrialised, commercialised'[15] tracts that MacNeice saw Yeats (and even Eliot) as excluding. 'In Carrowdore Churchyard' encapsulates the MacNeicean tension between countryside and city, the natural and historical worlds. But it does so by further concentrating the procedure whereby urban data in early MacNeice become image rather than reportage. In late MacNeice such data – e.g. traffic – acquire a parabolic significance distributed through a poem. Mahon, rather, compresses statement into cadence and image into symbol. The 'bombed-out town' and bringing 'the all-clear to the empty holes of spring' not only represent poetry as a therapeutic process, and conflate MacNeice's imaginative worlds, but distil the processes of his poetry. This accords, too, with Mahon's revival of the Yeatsian and aesthetic theme of art, significantly muted in MacNeice's *corpus*. Like Muldoon, Mahon writes against his own religious grain. However, art, poetry as form, has been humbled by its exposure to historical inrush, and MacNeice's dramatisation of that exposure in the mid twentieth century. Distinctive psychological and sociological factors also condition Mahon's poetry. But he has learned from MacNeice that traditional forms must take the imprint of flux. This deeply assimilated knowledge stood Mahon in good stead, when, after 1969, he wrote poems such as 'Rage for Order' and 'The Snow Party', poems which involve an ironic collision between Romantic aesthetics ('Idea of Order at Key West', 'Lapis Lazuli') and the Ulster troubles – a new version of 'the bombed-out town':

> Somewhere beyond
> The scorched gable end
> And the burnt-out
> Buses there is a poet indulging his
> Wretched rage for order –

Or not as the
Case may be...

Additional literary influences reinforce Mahon's attraction to the symbolic mystery of 'the snow and the huge roses', Muldoon's attraction to the linguistic mystery of what might be between them. For instance, Robert Graves as well as Yeats steered Mahon towards stanzaic shape (nothing as baggy as 'Birmingham'), Robert Frost steered Muldoon towards the insight that 'all the fun's in how you say a thing'. It was, indeed, with reference to Frost that MacNeice compared syntax in poetry to squash rather than tennis, saluting Frost as 'a master of angles'.[16] Idioms and clichés can also rebound at unexpected angles in poetry ('No, not like that...'). Whereas Mahon developed MacNeice's earlier way with the revitalised cliché, which partly involves sheer punning delight in the act of revitalisation ('suits you down to the ground'), Muldoon's practice resembles MacNeice's later interrogation of cliché's deep structures ('Your place or mine?'). This may occur locally or govern a whole poem.

Ciaran Carson's poetry also inclines towards riddle or riddling narrative, rather than song. Its long lines (more reminiscent of MacNeice's bulking-out of lyric form in the 1930s than of the supposed model, C.K. Williams) place syntax and sentence-sounds in the foreground. Carson's 'Snow' begins:

> A white dot flicked back and forth across the bay window: not
> A table-tennis ball, but 'ping-pong', since this is happening in another era,
> The extended leaves of the dining-table – scratched mahogany veneer –
> Suggesting many such encounters, or time passing: the celluloid
>   diminuendo
> As it bounces off into a corner and ticks to an incorrigible stop.

This verbal game seems more extraverted than Muldoon's semantic squash, with its drop-shot puns and unexpected finesses ('Or the room where they say...'). Carson's generally cumulative methods can be referred to MacNeice's dialectic between conjunction and disjunction. I have already quoted (p.52) Neil Corcoran's comment on Carson's 'scepticism about how much can be made to cohere in any given narrative'. This scepticism has a precedent in MacNeice's obsession with flux and pattern. Some of Carson's poems recall, on the one hand, the precarious synthesis effected by the 'ands' of *Autumn Journal*; on the other, the black holes, the 'dissolving map', presented by the asyndeton of parables like 'Charon':

> We just jogged on, at each request
> Stop there was a crowd of aggressively vacant
> Faces, we just jogged on...

'Charon', which moves deathwards through an underworld London, is a miniature deconstruction of *Autumn Journal*. As such, its syntactical deviations may be even more disturbing than the gaps in the *Waste Land* collage. MacNeice was interested in the prose of Apuleius: 'an arithmetical or cumulative technique, a succession of fairly short phrases, roughly equal in length and often rhyming, often without conjunctions, just adding up and adding up' [17]. Carson's 'Snow' adds up in a way that makes words as well as things part of the catalogue: 'all the haberdashery of loss – cuff buttons,/Broken ball-point pens and fluff, old pennies, pins and needles'. MacNeice and Carson have catalogues in common. MacNeice's urge to 'mention things' and 'vulgarise' poetic language in the 1930s anticipates the dispersal of human beings into 'brand name, advertising slogan and list' that Corcoran notices in Carson's work. [18] The same might be said of 'Birmingham', in which the consumers seem to be consumed: '(Chromium dogs on the bonnet, faces behind the triplex screens)…Cubical scent-bottles artificial legs arctic foxes and electric mops'. MacNeice's 'Snow' is also about the incorrigible plurality of language itself, from 'spit the pips' to 'Soundlessly collateral and incompatible': language that creates, as well as re-creates, a perplexing world. Yet the plus side of post-modernist Babel is that you can say, not nothing, but anything. Like the classicist-populist MacNeice, Carson mocks linguistic hierarchies, savouring poetry as a promiscuous thesaurus.

At the same time, Carson's 'Snow' criticises its prototype. It plays on the historical distance, the 'glass', between the progressive 1930s and the Northern Irish war, quotes key-words from 'Snow' in ironic contexts ('incorrigible stop'), and translates roses and snow into blood and death. Disjunction, incompatibility, prevails:

> Someone
> Has put up two trestles. Handshakes all round, nods and whispers.
> Roses are brought in, and suddenly, white confetti seethes against the
> window.

But if the celebratory shine goes off 'Snow' – 'the pith was a wordless bubble', Carson's poem remains within the darker orbit of its ambiguity: 'world/Is more spiteful and gay than one supposes'.

Of the three poets, it is Muldoon who brings this politics of form to the ideological surface. He uses MacNeice in the same spirit as they both use the cliché: as a stalking-horse, as a mask for subversion, as a mask for himself. And it is through MacNeice that Muldoon obliquely comments on the current state of poetry, in Ireland and elsewhere. He does so, firstly, in his epigraph to the

Faber Book of Contemporary Irish Poetry – the found eclogue between
MacNeice and F.R. Higgins discussed earlier (p.201); secondly, in
the long poem '7, Middagh Street' (*Meeting the British*, 1987). The
poem, like the epigraph, suggests that Muldoon is interpreting the
present through the prism of English and Irish literary arguments
in the 1930s.

In '7, Middagh Street', with its literary subject, cultural reference
rock-jumping, and formal bungee-jumping, Muldoon leans nearer
to (post) Modernism. (Mahon's Modernist leanings are principally
channelled through Beckett.) At the same time, the poem's anti-
thetical gyre is rootedness – in place, tradition, the sonnet, communal
responsibilities, political commitment, art. As Muldoon imaginatively
leaves Ireland, following the Modernist path of exile, he gets a fix
on his own situation through the unstable literary-historical moment
when Auden, MacNeice, Carson McCullers, Benjamin Britten, Gypsy
Rose Lee, and other artists bizarrely passed through a New York
boarding-house. The year was 1940. '7, Middagh Street' consists of
inter-related monologues, the framing monologues being spoken by
'Wystan' and 'Louis'. In contrast with his role in the *Faber Book*,
MacNeice now personifies roots. Unlike Auden, he went back to
London, the Blitz ('bombed-out town') and the war. (He told his
father that he didn't want to 'miss history'.) 'Wystan' in '7, Middagh
Street' declares, contrastingly: 'The roots by which we were once
bound // are severed here'. In writing the poem, Muldoon probably
drew on Humphrey Carpenter's biography of Auden which quotes
him as 'trying deliberately to live without roots in America', and
also cites Edmund Wilson's opinion that America was enabling
Auden to become an international poet who took in 'the whole
modern world'.[19] Accordingly, 'Wystan' rejects Marx, the collective
thirties dream, and his own false position as a radical literary leader.
His artistic quest, now governed by *eros* and *thanatos*, has become
arcadian rather than utopian: a solitary, Freudian, American dream:
'each straining for the ghostly axe/of a huge, blond-haired lumber-
jack'. At the other end of '7, Middagh Street', however, 'Louis'
finds himself transported, via the 'dream logic' he and Muldoon
share, back to the sectarian 'daily gate' of Belfast:

> falling in with
> the thousands of shipyardmen who tramped
> towards the front gates of Harland and Wolff.
>
> The one-eyed foreman had strayed out of Homer;
> 'MacNeice? That's a Fenian name.'
> As if to say, 'None of your sort, none of you

> will as much as go for a rubber hammer
> never mind chalk a rivet, never mind caulk a seam
> on the quinquereme of Nineveh.'

In counterpointing Auden's emigration with MacNeice's return (and fusing contemporary Belfast with blitzed London), Muldoon keeps his own personal and artistic options open; the poles of home and abroad in a magnetic relation. His relativist aesthetic, like Mac-Neice's, does not forget its home-port of 'one-eyed' absolutes. Thus he might imply that a Modernist cosmopolitan freedom is not so easily achieved. Or that it is too easily achieved. Here Muldoon reproduces MacNeice's own weighing of Yeats against Eliot. As for the question of 'missing history', Auden having been more political than MacNeice had ceased to be political at all. MacNeice queried the abruptness of the switch, significantly with reference to Auden's views in 'The Public v. the Late Mr William Butler Yeats' (1939). This dialogue, in fact, represents another poet arguing with himself. It is the thirties Auden who speaks for the prosecution, arraigning Yeats as irredeemably anti-progressive: 'For the great struggle of our time to create a juster social order, he felt nothing but the hatred which is born of fear.'[20] The embryonic forties Auden speaks – with more conviction – for the defence:

> For art is a product of history, not a cause…The case for the prosecution rests on the fallacious belief that art ever makes anything happen, whereas the honest truth…is that, if not a poem had been written, not a picture painted, not a bar of music composed, the history of man would be materially unchanged.[21]

In '7, Middagh Street' Muldoon has 'Wystan' say:

> If Yeats had saved his pencil lead
> would certain men have stayed in bed?
>
> For history's a twisted root
> with art its small translucent fruit
>
> and never the other way round.

This has sometimes been cited as Muldoon's last word. But in fact he gives the last word to 'Louis' who quotes Yeats's 'In dreams begin responsibilities' and goes on to contradict Auden: 'For poetry *can* make things happen –/ not only can, but *must*.'

Yet it may not be quite accurate to say that '7, Middagh Street' *has* a last word. Its form is that of a corona – i.e. each monologue takes off from the concluding word or phrase of its predecessor. So the poem has its tail in its mouth. Masefield's 'Quinquereme of Nineveh', symbolising poetry, circumnavigates for ever in a

characteristic Muldoonian *immram* or mystery-voyage. Or the design
might be termed a deconstructed pair of gyres. But it is certainly
not a Paterian 'closed circle'. Nor does it vindicate the dualism of
'twisted' history and 'translucent' art. In *The Poetry of W.B. Yeats*
MacNeice answers Auden, with Yeats's influence on Ireland in mind:

> The case for the prosecution does rest on a fallacy but it is not this.
> The fallacy lies in thinking that it is the *function* of art to make things
> happen and that the effect of art upon actions is something either direct
> or calculable. It is a historical fact that art *can* make things happen and
> Auden in his reaction from a rigid Marxism seems in this article to be
> straying towards the Ivory Tower.[22]

In '7, Middagh Street' the fate of all expression depends on incalcu-
lable twists and turns. Surrealism does not save 'Salvador' from
André Breton's 'kangaroo-court'. And 'Gypsy' says:

> Shakespeare's Sonnets,
> *Das Kapital*, Boethius,
> Dainty June and her Newsboy Songsters –
> all would succumb to Prohibition...

Thus, where history boards art's quinquereme, and what cargo it
carries into history, can never be predicted. 'Ben' says: 'In this, as
in so many things,/it won't be over till the fat lady sings'.

As the arguments of '7, Middagh Street' rotate on the axis provided by 'Wystan' and 'Louis', its form imitates the ceaseless engage-
ment between flux and pattern. And (as for Mahon in a different
way) Yeats, especially the Delphic dialogue of 'The Man and the
Echo', remains in view behind MacNeice. Despite appearances, the
poem is neither ludicly post-modernist nor eclectically impotent.
This suggests how the devolution of Romanticism and traditionalism
through Yeats and Ireland still counts in contemporary poetry.

* * *

In Yeats's poetry the Romantic quest for transcendence – Muldoon's quinquereme – is repeatedly dashed against the rocks of
history. As MacNeice acknowledges, this obliged Yeats to exchange
(if less radically than his successors) the Paterian 'closed circle' for
'the Heraclitean doctrine of creative conflict'.[23] Contemporary
Northern Irish poetry finds itself on that same 'dolphin-torn [and]
gong-tormented sea', not only because of history's content but
because of its raised insistence. Hence the chastened demeanour
of art in Mahon's 'The Snow Party', whose imagery echoes Joyce's
'The Dead' as well as MacNeice:

> everyone
> Crowds to the window
> To watch the falling snow...
>
> Elsewhere they are burning
> Witches and heretics
> In the boiling squares...
>
> But there is silence
> In the houses of Nagoya
> And the hills of Ise.

Like other effects in Mahon's poetry, this self-effacing closure corresponds to Adorno's remark in *Aesthetic Theory* (1970) that: 'Aesthetic transcendence and disenchantment achieve unison in the speechlessness that characterises Beckett's work.'[24] (That Beckett should be his model modern artist again implicates Ireland in these issues.) Yet Mahon's 'Tractatus', a defence of the aesthetic principle, directly affirms 'Everything that is the case imaginatively'. So the volume of transcendence may be turned up or down according to occasion; the admixture of riddle and song; decisions taken deep within form. For Adorno, all artistic transcendence is necessarily (and desirably) 'fragmented', as a result of its divorce from 'the magical and cult functions of archaic art'.[25] But he allows this transcendental residue a significant space ('breath'), threatened both by reductionist ideologies and by magic:

> Works of art become works of art when they produce that surplus which is their transcendent quality. They are not however the arena where transcendence occurs, which is why they are also separated from transcendence. The true arena of transcendence in works of art is the integration of their moments. [26]

This applies to the ambiguous epiphany of 'Snow' and to Muldoon's circuitous *immrama* as well as to Mahon's 'fragile' solutions. In 'Snow' it is the pattern of the poem itself that links 'snow' and 'roses', and produces surplus along with ambiguity. For example, in the phrase 'Soundlessly collateral and incompatible' threads of sound pull against the surface meaning. Transcendence as an outcome of Mahon's poetry is less 'suddenly rich', and might be compared to the faint aura around an eclipse. It 'gasps for light and life' from various metaphorical twilight zones: dusk, the small hours, 'dawn rain', lonely rooms, wintry seashores, waste heaps, historical margins. 'Aesthetics', from his sequence 'Light Music', defines its subject and itself as 'the single bright/landing light/ghosting an iodine cloud'. To quote Adorno again:

> Art's Utopia, the counter-factual yet-to-come, is draped in black. It goes
> on being a recollection of the possible with a critical edge against the
> real; it is a kind of imaginary restitution of that catastrophe which is
> world history; it is freedom which did not come to pass under the spell
> of necessity and which may well not come to pass ever at all.[27]

The same quotation might also be applied to Muldoon's poetry, except that its 'radical spiritualisation' is more concealed by its simultaneous 'chaotic moment'.[28] Here frozen, rather than spilt, religion keeps overt transcendence permanently on hold and in perpetual quarantine. Yet early poems, such as 'Good Friday, 1971. Driving Westward', do not imply a wholly secular direction.

For Mahon, poetry is a 'religious impulse'.[29] Even in its inverse mode of introducing chaos into order, this seems broadly true of Northern Irish poetry – so lately post-religious. However, both generic and overt transcendence are as various as their theological origins. For example, Seamus Heaney's poetry has become more ardently 'counter-factual' and less inclined to trust a poem's integration of its moments. Among some fine poems in *Seeing Things* (1991) are others which 'seek transcendence as an effect',[30] thus piling surplus on surplus:

> Deserted harbour stillness. Every stone
> Clarified and dormant under water,
> The harbour wall a masonry of silence.
>
> Fullness. Shimmer...

The 'perfected vision' ends: 'Omnipresence, equilibrium, brim'. Certainly, such confident transubstantiation contrasts with Mahon's frail 'wands of sunlight'. The latter rarely irradiate personal vision or earthly epiphany, but point to the collective guilt of history as an urgent case for salvation. Objects in Mahon's poetry acquire a displaced glow that denotes what is absent from human epistemology – 'the banished gods' – not what is 'omnipresent'.

Heaney's theory at the end of the 1980s argued that contingency can be a constraint on 'song'. He set up an antithesis between 'Song and Suffering', between creative joy and external pressures:

> the essential thing about lyric poetry, Mandelstam maintained, was its
> unlooked-for joy in being itself, and the essential thing for the lyric poet
> was therefore a condition in which he was in thrall to no party or pro-
> gramme, but truly and freely and utterly himself...Mandelstam had no
> immediate social aim. Utterance itself was self-justifying and creative,
> like nature.[31]

Yet the content and context of Mandelstam's utterance placed him at odds with Stalin. Being in thrall to no party or programme makes poetry oppositional as well as independent. And to describe Mandelstam as 'singing in the Stalinist night'[32] is to identify him, sentimentally, with Paul McCartney's blackbird. Also, poem rather than poet mediates the inrush or unrest that constitutes the impulse. Subjective creative satisfaction should not be conflated with the objective variables of poetic pattern. Nevertheless, the 'idealistic hubris'[33] of *Seeing Things* functions as an intertextual foil to Muldoon's *Madoc* – that bumper book of riddles.

MacNeice's poetry kept – and keeps – all these dialectics in play. His poems 'Reflections' and 'Variation on Heraclitus' (from *Solstices*) complement each other as projections of the self/writer coping with an unstable and relativistic cosmos. They also represent poles of introversion and extroversion. In 'Reflections' a solipsistic hall of mirrors, cognitive nihilism, dissolves an identity whose defining terms are reading, writing, and 'warmth':

> a taxi perhaps will drive in through the bookcase
> Whose books are not for reading and past the fire
> Which gives no warmth and pull up by my desk
> At which I cannot write since I am not left-handed.

However, in 'Variation on Heraclitus' the stream of perceptions and consciousness positively liberates the 'I' who 'signed/On a line that rippled away with a pen that melted'. His dizzy text is always becoming and so can defy authoritarian systems including ways in which it might be read: 'none of your slide snide rules can catch what is sliding so fast'. The arguments between these poems, their rearrangements of the same 'room', their variations and reflections on lyric form, fully embrace the challenge of Modernism without abandoning 'formalising activity' in a more traditional sense. Similarly, the open ending of *Autumn Journal* leaves solution, transcendence, 'imaginary restitution' on the long finger, but does not quite rule it out. The grain of belief that MacNeice inherited from his clergyman father informs his pattern-making.

'The Truisms' (also from *Solstices*), which begins as a riddle and ends as a song, encapsulates the passage of transcendence from religion to poetry. The protagonist, who has abandoned his father's 'box of truisms/Shaped like a coffin', experiences a dispersed history which is not merely autobiographical:

> met love, met war,
> Sordor, disappointment, defeat, betrayal,
> Till, through disbeliefs he arrived at a house
> He could not remember seeing before,

> And he walked straight in; it was where he had come from
> And something told him the way to behave.
> He raised his hand and blessed his home;
> The truisms flew and perched on his shoulders
> And a tall tree sprouted from his father's grave.

At one level, this is a parable of revisionist processes between Irish generations. At another, the 'tall tree' represents MacNeice's poetry – and now its variegated offshoots. Mahon's 'In Carrowdore Churchyard' marks these transitions:

> Your ashes will not stir, even on this high ground,
> However the wind tugs, the headstones shake.
> This plot is consecrated, for your sake,
> To what lies in the future tense. You lie
> Past tension now, and spring is coming round
> Igniting flowers on the peninsula.

The high ground and consecrated plot are also the elegy itself, enlisting Nature to steal authority and transcendence from the churchbuilding ('reverend trees' occurs later). To return to Mahon's version of 'Snow' and its legacy: 'ironical, loving', 'fragile, solving'. Although within each pair of adjectives there is echo rather than elision, the pairs rhyme – 'loving' and 'solving' with peculiar intricacy. However, this was before the 'pneumonia', 'ague' and bombs of the 1930s and 1940s returned in new guises.

MacNeice said of his last collection *The Burning Perch*: 'I would venture the generalisation that most of these poems are two-way affairs or at least spiral ones: even in the most evil picture the good things, like the sea in one of these poems, are still there round the corner.'[34] This (continuing) spiral or gyre, as MacNeice recognises, goes back to 'poems I was writing thirty years ago' – such as 'Snow'. The room where MacNeice wrote 'Snow' signifies space or breath opened up by poetry. It is a room, to quote 'Variation on Heraclitus', whose 'walls are flowing'. Thomas Flanagan once suggested that much Irish poetry in English rests on the 'hard deal board' in Samuel Ferguson's 'Cashel of Munster'. The same might be said of 'There is more than glass between the snow and the huge roses'.

[1989/1993]

NOTES

Introduction: Revising 'Irish Literature' *(pp.9-68)*

1. T.W. Adorno, *Aesthetic Theory*, translated by C. Lenhardt (Frankfurt, 1970; London, 1984), p.328.

2. Louis MacNeice, *The Poetry of W.B. Yeats* (Oxford, 1941; London, 1967), p.46.

3. James Lydon, 'The Silent Sister: Trinity College and Catholic Ireland', in *Trinity College and the Idea of a University*, edited by C.H. Holland (Dublin, 1991), p.30.

4. 'The Silent Sister', p.35.

5. Quoted by Lydon, 'The Silent Sister', p.35.

6. 'The Silent Sister', p.37.

7. In his review of James Hardiman's *Irish Minstrelsy* over several issues of the *Dublin University Magazine*. The review is a landmark in the history of translating Irish poetry into English.

8. *The Bell* 8, 3 (June 1944), p.222.

9. *The Bell* 8, 3 (June 1944), p.220.

10. *The Bell* 8, 3 (June 1944), p.185.

11. *The Bell* 8, 3 (June 1944), pp.186-7.

12. *The Bell* 8, 3 (June 1944), p.192.

13. *The Bell* 8, 3 (June 1944), p.196.

14. See 'Boycott Village', *Escape from the Anthill* (Mullingar, 1985), pp.134-44.

15. His memorial tribute to Sheehy-Skeffington, who died in 1971, is included in *Escape from the Anthill*, pp.197-200.

16. In 'Crossing the Border' (1955), a manifesto for a projected journal *The Bridge*, Butler complains that 'the art of free controversy was never so neglected'. See Hubert Butler, *Grandmother and Wolfe Tone* (Dublin, 1990), p.65.

17. *Grandmother and Wolfe Tone*, p.65.

18. Hubert Butler, 'Portrait of a Minority', *Escape from the Anthill*, p.118.

19. Denis Donoghue, 'T.C.D.', in *We Irish: The Selected Essays of Denis Donoghue*, I (London, 1986), p.173.

20. Lydon, 'The Silent Sister', p.49.

21. Gordon L. Herries Davies, 'Hosce meos filios', in *Trinity College Dublin and the Idea of a University*, p.328.

22. 'Hosce meos filios', p.327.

23. Quoted by Lydon, 'The Silent Sister', p.40.

24. Seamus Deane, *Heroic Styles: the tradition of an idea* (Derry, 1984), p.10.

25. Letter to the *Daily Express* (Dublin), 7 February 1895. See *Collected Letters of W.B. Yeats*, 1, edited by John Kelly (Oxford, 1986), p.437.

26. *The Field Day Anthology of Irish Writing*, edited by Seamus Deane [henceforth *FDA*], 2, (Derry, 1991), pp.969-70.

27. *FDA* 2 p.971.

28. *FDA* 2, p.971.

29. *The Leader*, 5 January 1901; *FDA* 2, p.973.

30. Brian Fallon, 'Laureates, divines, Francophiles and poor MacFlecknoe', 'Trinity Weekend', *Irish Times*, 9 May 1992, p.8.

31. John Wilson Foster, Introduction, *Colonial Consequences: Essays in Irish Literature and Culture* (Dublin, 1991), p.1.

32. Derek Mahon, interviewed by William Scammell, *Poetry Review* 81, 2 (Summer 1991), p.4.

33. Seamus Heaney, interviewed by Seamus Deane, *Crane Bag* 1, 1 (Spring 1977), p.61.

34. Seamus Heaney, 'The Placeless Heaven: Another Look at Kavanagh', *The Government of the Tongue* (London, 1988), pp.6-7.

35. Neil Corcoran, 'One Step Forward, Two Steps Back', in *The Chosen Ground: Essays on the Contemporary Poetry of Northern Ireland*, edited by Neil Corcoran (Bridgend, 1992), p.213.

36. Louis MacNeice, review of *Poetry Now*, edited by G.S. Fraser, reprinted in *Selected Literary Criticism of Louis MacNeice*, edited by Alan Heuser (London, 1987), p.209.

37. Letter to Lady Gregory, 11 May 1916, *The Letters of W.B. Yeats*, edited by Allan Wade (London, 1954), p.613.

38. Edna Longley, 'Poetry and Politics in Northern Ireland', *Poetry in the Wars* (Newcastle upon Tyne, 1986), pp.185-210.

39. Kevin Barry, 'Anthology as History: *The Field Day Anthology of Irish Literature*', *Irish Review* 12 (Spring/Summer 1992), p.51.

40. The 'Dialogue', which appeared in the *Dublin University Magazine* 2 (November 1933), is reprinted in *FDA* 1, pp.1177-85.

41. John Wilson Foster, 'Culture and Colonisation', *Colonial Consequences*, p.276.

42. Deane, *Heroic Styles*, p.18.

43. John Wilson Foster, 'Culture and Colonisation', *Colonial Consequences*, p.271.

44. Compare Declan Kiberd, *Anglo-Irish Attitudes* (Derry, 1984), p.22; and F.S.L. Lyons, *Culture and Anarchy in Ireland 1890-1939* (Oxford, 1979), p.137.

45. See Deane, *Heroic Styles*, pp.17-18.

46. Seamus Deane, 'Canon Fodder: Literary Mythologies in Ireland', in *Styles of Belonging: The Cultural Identities of Ulster*, edited by Jean Lundy and Aodán MacPóilin (Belfast, 1992), p.31.

47. 'Canon Fodder', p.32, p.23.

48. Foster, 'A Complex Fate: The Irishness of Denis Donoghue', *Colonial Consequences*, p.212.

49. Colm Tóibín, in a debate on the *FDA* at the American Conference for Irish Studies conference, Galway, July 1992. A slightly altered version of his talk appears, together with other contributions to the debate (by Anthony Bradley, Siobhan Kilfeather, and myself), in the *Canadian Journal of Irish Studies* 18, 2 (December 1992). Tóibín reviewed the *FDA* in the *Sunday Independent*, 24 November 1991, p.8.

50. Seamus Deane, Introduction to *Nationalism, Colonialism and Literature*, a reprint of Field Day pamphlets by Terry Eagleton, Fredric Jameson and Edward Said, (Minneapolis, 1990), pp.6-7.

51. Deane, General Introduction, *FDA* 1, p.xxi.

52. E.P. Thompson, *The Poverty of Theory and Other Essays* (London, 1978), p.303.

53. Sabina Lovibond, 'Feminism and Pragmatism: A Reply to Richard Rorty', *New Left Review* 193 (May/ June 1992), p.61.

54. Tom Dunne, 'New Histories: Beyond "Revisionism"', *Irish Review* 12 (Spring/Summer 1992), p.6.

55. *FDA* 3, p.1316.

56. *FDA* 3, p.1398.

57. Deane, General Introduction, *FDA* 1, p.xx.

58. Deane, Introduction to *Nationalism, Colonialism and Literature*, p.6.

59. Joseph Lee, *Ireland 1912-1985: Politics and Society* (Cambridge, 1989), p.627.

60. Fredric Jameson, *Modernism and Imperialism* (Derry, 1988), pp.19-22.

61. Edward Said, *Yeats and Decolonisation* (Derry, 1988), p.19.

62. Terry Eagleton, *Nationalism, Irony and Commitment* (Derry, 1988), p.13.

63. Hubert Butler, 'The Sense of Evil and the Sense of Guilt', *Escape from the Anthill*, p.173.

64. Robin Glendinning, 'The Quality of Laughter', *Irish Review* 8 (Spring 1990), p.5.

65. See for instance, *Natives and Newcomers: The Making of Irish Colonial Society 1534-1641*, edited by Ciaran Brady and Raymond Gillespie; Hiram Morgan, 'Mid-Atlantic Blues', *Irish Review* 11 (Winter 1991/92), pp.50-5.

66. Liam Kennedy, 'Modern Ireland: Post-Colonial society or Post-Colonial Pretensions?', *Irish Review* 13 (Winter 1992/93), pp.118-19.

67. Robert Hughes, *Culture of Complaint: The Fraying of America* (New York, Oxford, 1993), p.101.

68. Edward Said, *Culture and Imperialism* (London, 1993), p.xi.

69. *Culture and Imperialism*, p.266.

70. David Lloyd, *Anomalous States: Irish Writing and the Post-Colonial Moment* (Dublin, 1993), pp.5-7.

71. Foster, *Colonial Consequences*, p.271.

72. *Colonial Consequences*, p.272.

73. John Whyte, *Interpreting Northern Ireland* (Oxford, 1990), p.203.

74. Jameson, *Modernism and Imperialism*, p.20.

75. Deane, General Introduction, *FDA* 1, p.xx.

76. Deane, *FDA* 3, p.3 ; *FDA* 1, p.xxiii.

77. Hubert Butler, *Grandmother and Wolfe Tone* (Dublin, 1990), p.143.

78. *FDA* 3, p.315.

79. *FDA* 3, p.685.

80. *Sunday Independent*, 24 November 1991, p.8.

81. Seamus Deane, *Celtic Revivals: Essays in Modern Irish Literature 1880-1980* (London, 1985), p.76.

82. Sabina Lovibond, 'Feminism and Pragmatism', *New Left Review* 193 (May/June 1992), p.67.

83. Frances Gardiner, 'Political Interest and Participation of Irish Women 1922-1992: The Unfinished Revolution', *Canadian Journal of Irish Studies* 18, 1 (July 1992), p.17 .

84. 'The Unfinished Revolution', p.18.

85. Deane, General Introduction, *FDA* 1, p.xxii.

86. Deane, General Introduction, *FDA* 1, p.xix.

87. Anne Rigney, *The Rhetoric of Historical Representation: Three Narrative Histories of the French Revolution* (Cambridge, 1990), p.47ff., p.xii.

88. Michael Laffan, 'Insular Attitudes: The Revisionists and their Critics', in *Revising the Rising*, edited by Theo Dorgan and Máirín Ní Dhonnchadha (Derry, 1991), p.114.

89. 'Insular Attitudes', p.118.

90. Tom Paulin, Introduction, *The Faber Book of Political Verse* (London, 1986), p.15.

91. Deane, General Introduction, *FDA* 1, p.xxi.

92. Deane, General Introduction, *FDA* 1, p.xix.

93. See, for instance, *The Collected Letters of W.B. Yeats*, 1, edited by John Kelly (Oxford, 1986), pp.433-50.

94. See note 24.

95. Jan Gorak, *The Making of the Modern Canon: Genesis and Crisis of a Literary Idea* (London, 1991), pp.245-6.

96. *The Making of the Modern Canon*, p.246.

97. Deane, *FDA* 1, p.xxi.

98. Deane, *FDA* 3, p.554, p.463.

99. Deane, *FDA* 3, p.383.

100. Deane, *FDA* 3, p.383.

101. Deane, *FDA* 3, p.383.

102. Debating the *FDA*, *Canadian Journal of Irish Studies* 18, 2 (December 1992), p.122.

103. Deane, *FDA* 3, p.383.

104. Damian Smyth, Review of *FDA*, *Fortnight* 309 (September, 1992), p.26.

105. *FDA* 3, p.1375, p.1380.

106. A comment on Sean O'Faolain's view of 'The Gaelic Cult', *FDA* 3, p.562.

107. *FDA* 3, p.574.

108. *FDA* 3, p.568.

109. *FDA* 3, p.566.

110. Declan Kiberd, 'The Elephant of Revolutionary Forgetfulness', *Revising the Rising*, p.18.

111. 'The Elephant of Revolutionary Forgetfulness', p.18.

112. Deane, 'Wherever Green is Read', *Revising the Rising*, p.97.

113. John Waters, *Jiving at the Crossroads* (Belfast, 1991), pp.24-6.

114. Damian Smyth, *Fortnight* 309, p.27.

115. *FDA* 3, p.1375.

116. Robert Garratt, *Modern Irish Poetry: Tradition and Continuity from Yeats to Heaney* (Berkeley and London, 1986), pp.5-102.

117. Deane, General Introduction, *FDA* 1, p.xix.

118. Garratt, *Modern Irish Poetry*, p.275.

119. *Contemporary Irish Poetry*, edited by Anthony Bradley, new and revised edition (Berkeley and Los Angeles, 1988), Introduction, p.1.

120. See Terence Brown, *Ireland's Literature: Selected Essays* (Mullingar and New Jersey, 1988), pp.77-90.

121. Seamus Heaney, *FDA* 2, p.789.

122. Heaney, *FDA* 2, p.786.

123. Heaney, *FDA* 2, p.787.

124. Michael Allen, review of *The Penguin Book of Contemporary Irish Poetry*, *Irish Review* 9 (Autumn 1990), p.101.

125. Introduction, *The Penguin Book of Contemporary Irish Poetry*, edited by Peter Fallon and Derek Mahon (Harmondsworth, 1990), pp.xix-xx.

126. *Penguin Book of Contemporary Irish Poetry*, pp.xvii-xxii.

127. Introduction, *The New Oxford Book of Irish Verse*, edited by Thomas Kinsella (Oxford and New York 1986), p.xxiii.

128. Introduction, *Penguin Book of Contemporary Irish Poetry*, pp.xix-xx.

129. *The Chosen Ground: Essays on the Contemporary Poetry of Northern Ireland*, edited by Neil Corcoran (Bridgend, 1992), p.7.

130. *The Inherited Boundaries: Younger Poets of the Republic of Ireland*, edited by Sebastian Barry (Portlaoise, 1986), pp.13-14.

131. Dermot Bolger, *Picador Book of Contemporary Irish Fiction* (London, 1993), p.ix, xxvi.

132. *Wildish Things: An Anthology of New Irish Women's Writing*, edited by Ailbhe Smyth (Dublin, 1989), Introduction, p.9.

133. Dillon Johnston, *Irish Poetry after Joyce* (Notre Dame and Portlaoise, 1985), p.45.

134. Introduction, *The Penguin Book of Contemporary British Poetry*, edited by Blake Morrison and Andrew Motion (Harmondsworth, 1982), p.20.

135. *The Penguin Book of Contemporary British Poetry*, p.16.

136. Hugh Kearney, *The British Isles: A History of Four Nations* (Cambridge, 1989), pp.7-8.

137. Robert Crawford, *Devolving English Literature* (Oxford, 1992), p.9.

138. John Hewitt, 'The Bitter Gourd: Some Problems of the Ulster Writer', *Ancestral Voices: The Selected Prose of John Hewitt* (Belfast, 1987), p.109.

139. *Ancestral Voices*, p.115.

140. Stan Smith, 'The Distance Between: Seamus Heaney', *The Chosen Ground*, p.35.

141. Thomas Docherty, 'Initiations, Tempers, Seductions: Postmodern McGuckian', *The Chosen Ground*, p.205.

142. Alan Robinson, *Instabilities in Contemporary British Poetry* (London, 1988), p.7.

143. Neil Corcoran, 'One Step Forward, Two Steps Back: Ciaran Carson's *The Irish for No*', *The Chosen Ground*, p.232.

144. *The Chosen Ground*, p.191.

145. Clair Wills, 'The Perfect Mother: Authority in the Poetry of Medbh McGuckian', *Text and Context* 3 (Autumn 1988), p.109 .

146. Interviewed by Kevin Smyth, *Rhinoceros* 4 (1990), p.90.

147. John Goodby, review of *Madoc*, *Irish Review* 10 (Spring 1991), p.134.

148. Louis MacNeice, *Modern Poetry: A Personal Essay* (London 1938, 1968), Preface.

149. In *Quoof* (London, 1983), p.40ff.

150. Clair Wills, *Improprieties: Politics and Sexuality in Northern Irish Poetry* (Oxford, 1993), p.235.

151. *Improprieties*, pp.236-7.

152. *Improprieties*, p.242.

153. *Improprieties*, p.224.

154. Vàclav Havel, 'Growing Up "Outside"', *Disturbing the Peace* (London, 1990), p.9.

155. Interviewed by Kevin Smyth, *Gown (Literary Supplement)*, May 1984.

156. John Whyte, *Interpreting Northern Ireland* (Oxford, 1990), pp.258-9.

157. Frank Wright, *Northern Ireland: A Comparative Analysis* (Dublin, 1987), p.xii.

158. Hubert Butler, *Escape from the Anthill* (Mullingar, 1985), p.259.

159. *Escape from the Anthill*, p.272.

160. Neal Ascherson, *Independent on Sunday*, 16 May 1993.

161. Anthony D. Smith, *National Identity* (London, 1991), p.176.

162. Patrick Kavanagh, 'Nationalism and Literature', *Collected Pruse* (London, 1967), p.269.

163. Mary Kaldor, 'Yugoslavia and the New Nationalism', *New Left Review* 197 (January/February 1993), p.108.

164. 'Yugoslavia and the New Nationalism', p.111.

165. Dzevad Karahasan, interviewed by Frederick Baker, *Guardian*, 8 July 1993.

166. W.B. Yeats, *Memoirs* (London, 1972), p.196.

167. Letter to Ernest Boyd, 20 January 1915, *The Letters of W.B. Yeats*, edited by Allan Wade (London, 1954), p.591.

168. John Banville, 'A Fiddler's Curse', *Irish Times*, 28 September 1991.

169. David Bromwich, *Politics by Other Means* (New Haven and London, 1992), p.119.

170. Peter Washington, *Fraud: Literary Theory and the End of English* (London, 1989), p.20.

171. Ernest Gellner, *Postmodernism, Reason and Religion* (London and New York, 1992), p.74.

172. E.P. Thompson, *The Poverty of Theory* (London, 1978), p.iv.

The Rising, the Somme and Irish Memory *(pp.69-85)*

1. Tom Dunne, *Theobald Wolfe Tone: Colonial Outsider* (Cork, 1982), p.12.

2. See his contribution to *16 on 16*, edited by Dermot Bolger (Dublin, 1988), pp.41-2.

3. Seamus Heaney, *Preoccupations: Selected Prose 1968-1978* (London, 1980), p.56.

4. See p.148 and note 77, p.285.

5. *The Bell* 9, 3 (December, 1944), p.190.

6. See William Irwin Thompson, *The Imagination of an Insurrection* (New York, 1967), pp.120-1.

7. *The Imagination of an Insurrection*, p.125.

8. *The Imagination of an Insurrection*, p.122.

9. Anthony D. Buckley, 'The Chosen Few: Biblical Texts in the Symbolism of an Ulster Secret Society', *Irish Review* 2 (1987), p.39.

10. 'The Chosen Few', p.32.

11. Seamus Heaney, 'The Sense of the Past', *Ulster Local Studies* 9, 20 (Summer 1985), p.112.

12. 'The Sense of the Past', pp.112-13.

13. 'The Sense of the Past', p.113.

14. Seamus Heaney, 'Feeling into Words', *Preoccupations*, p.57.

15. Belinda Loftus, *Mirrors: William III and Mother Ireland* (Dublin, 1990), p.44.

16. *Mirrors*, p.82

17. Gordon Lucy, *The Ulster Covenant: A Pictorial History* (Belfast, 1989), p.vii.

18. *The Ulster Covenant*, p.43.

19. *The Ulster Covenant*, p.43.

20. Paul Fussell, *The Great War and Modern Memory* (Oxford, 1975), p.21.

21. Philip Orr, *The Road to the Somme* (Belfast, 1987), p.54.

22. *The Road to the Somme*, p.54.

23. Keith Jeffery, 'The Great War in Modern Irish Memory', in *Men, Women and War*, edited by T.G. Fraser and Keith Jeffery (Dublin, 1993), p.150.

24. See *The Great War: A Tribute to Ulster's Heroes 1914-1918*, first published in

1919 by 'the Citizens Committee, City Hall, Belfast' (reprinted Belfast, 1991), p.127.

25. Orr, *The Road to the Somme*, p.217.

26. *The Road to the Somme*, p.218

27. Thompson, *The Imagination of an Insurrection*, p.130.

28. Quoted in *The Imagination of an Insurrection*, pp.94-95.

29. W.B. Yeats, *Tribute to Thomas Davis*, 20 November 1914 (Cork, 1947), p.15.

30. *Tribute to Thomas Davis*, p.19.

31. See *Free Thought in Ireland*, supplement to *Fortnight* 297 (July 1991), pp.17-18.

32. Bolger, *16 on 16*, p.16; p.10.

33. Robert Ballagh, '1916 – Goodbye to all that?', *Irish Reporter* 2 (1991), pp.6-8.

34. Sean O'Faolain, *The Bell* 3, 2 (November 1941), p.103. See epigraph to this book.

'A Barbarous Nook': The Writer and Belfast *(pp.86-108)*

1. This heroic-couplet, non-sectarian eulogy was printed in Belfast by Joseph Smyth. Patrick Curley directed my attention to the poem.

2. In *The Unpardonable Sin* (1907).

3. George Birmingham, *The Red Hand of Ulster* (London, 1912), p.21.

4. *The Red Hand of Ulster*, p.14.

5. E.M. Forster, *Two Cheers for Democracy*, Abinger edition, p.263.

6. *Icarus* 42 (March 1964), p.31.

7. *The Drennan Letters*, edited by D.A. Chart (Belfast, 1931), p.375.

8. *The Drennan Letters*, p.349.

9. *Lagan* 2 (1944), p.27.

10. *The Irish Sketch Book*, chapter 27.

11. Note to *Awake! and Other Poems* (London, 1941).

12. *Lagan* 3 (1945), p.98, reprinted in *Ancestral Voices: Selected Prose of John Hewitt*, edited by Tom Clyde (Belfast, 1987), p.114.

13. *Lagan* 3 (1945), p.98, *Ancestral Voices*, pp.113-4.

14. Milton, *Prose Works*, 3, p.334. See A.T.Q. Stewart, *The Narrow Ground* (London, 1977), pp.88-90.

15. John Montague, *The Rough Field* (Portlaoise, 1972), p.10.

16. M.F. Caulfield, *The Black City* (London, 1952), p.9.

17. James Patrick Madden 'saw the grimy half-tones of this ugly town, saw the inevitable rain obscure the window-pane...' *The Lonely Passion of Miss Judith Hearne* (London, 1955), Penguin edition, pp.42-3.

18. Reid, for instance, defiantly used this heading for an article on the Lane pictures. which W.B. Reynolds commissioned for *Uladh*. Reynolds had tried to make Reid subscribe to his own belief in 'The Ulster Genius'. See *Private Road* (London, 1940), pp.34-40.

19. *Zoo* (London, 1938), pp.78-84 (reprinted in *Selected Prose of Louis MacNeice*, Oxford, 1990). Compare Mahon's 'tide of sunlight between shower and shower' ('In Belfast'); MacNeice, *The Strings are False* (London, 1965), p.222.

20. '1957-1972', *The Collected Poems of John Hewitt*, edited by Frank Ormsby (Belfast, 1991), p.222.

21. Caulfield, *The Black City*, pp.9-10.

22. E.M. Forster, 'Forrest Reid', *Abinger Harvest* (1936), Penguin edition, p.90.

23. Mary Beckett, *A Belfast Woman* (Swords, Co. Dublin, 1980), p.98.

24. C.S. Lewis, *Surprised by Joy* (London, 1955), p.147.

25. John Boyd, Preface to *Belfast: The Origin and Growth of an Industrial City*, edited by J.C. Beckett and R.E. Glasscock (London, 1967), p.viii.

26. 'If the rest of our society mirrored the truly ecumenical spirit of the dole queue the likes of me would be forced to work for a living. Here citizens who had driven one another from factory and building site with bomb and bullet mingle in good fellowship, all venom uniting against the pleasant young men and pretty girls behind the counter.' John Morrow, *The Confessions of Proinsias O'Toole* (Belfast, 1977), p.25. See, for a factual account of fleeting solidarity during the Depression, Paddy Devlin, *Yes We Have No Bananas* (Blackstaff Press, 1981). The title derives from 'the only neutral tune' available to Orange and Green.

27. London, 1965.

28. Derek Mahon, *Night-Crossing* (Oxford, 1968), p.6.

29. John Wilson Foster, *Forces and Themes in Ulster Fiction* (Dublin, 1974), p.37 ff.

30. 'Webs of Artifice', *The New Review* 3, 32 (November 1976), p.44.

31. Michael McLaverty, *Call My Brother Back*, Poolbeg Press edition, p.59.

32. *Call My Brother Back*, p.62.

33. Michael McLaverty, *Lost Fields*, Poolbeg Press edition, p.1.

34. *Lost Fields*, p.79.

35. *Lost Fields*, p.12.

36. *Lost Fields*, p.19.

37. *Lost Fields*, p.101.

38. George Orwell, *The Road to Wigan Pier* (1937), Penguin edition, p.17.

39. McLaverty, *Lost Fields*, p.135.

40. *Lost Fields*, p.29.

41. Foster, *Forces and Themes in Ulster Fiction*, p.41.

42. McLaverty, *Lost Fields*, p.205.

43. *Lost Fields*, p.208.

44. McLaverty, *Call My Brother Back*, p.15.

45. *Call My Brother Back*, p.68.

46. *Call My Brother Back*, p.122.

47. *Call My Brother Back*, p.184.

48. 'The Best Books on Ulster', chosen by Twelve Writers, *The Bell* 4, 4 (July 1942), p.252.

49. McLaverty, *Lost Fields*, p.107.

50. See 'Fosterage', *North* (London, 1975), p.71.

51. Seamus Heaney, *Preoccupations* (London, 1980), p.30.

52. James Randall, 'An Interview with Seamus Heaney', *Ploughshares* 5, 3 (1979), p.17.

53. Published (1946) by the *Irish News*; reprinted (1982) by Blackstaff Press.

54. Kenneth McNally (Belfast, 1972). Jonathan Bardon's *Belfast: An Illustrated History* (Belfast, 1982) was a landmark.

55. Raymond Williams, *The Country and the City* (London, 1973), p.297.

56. *The Collected Poems of John Hewitt*, p.303.

57. John Campbell, *Saturday Night in York Street* (Belfast, 1982), p.13.

58. London, 1953.

59. Herbert Moore Pim, *Unknown Immortals* (Dublin; London, 1917), p.36.

60. London, 1960.

61. Belfast, 1978; Dublin, 1981. See also *The Sinking of the Kenbane Head* (Belfast, 1977).

62. 'Funerals Have Lost Their Style', *Sam McAughtry's Belfast*, p.36.

63. Belfast, 1979.

64. John Morrow, 'Moved to Tears', *Northern Myths*, p.5.

65. Belfast, 1977.

66. Belfast, 1982.

67. *Belfast: A Poem, Descriptive and Tributary*, p.21. Earlier Lyons has celebrated 'Those works of quick productive trade,/Where Chemistry's prolific art/The fruits of science can impart – /Where COATES'S Iron-works display/ Their owner's ingenuity...' *Belfast: A Poem, Descriptive and Tributary*, pp.19-20.

68. *Belfast: A Poem, Descriptive and Tributary*, 'To the Public'.

69. Peter Denman, *The Achievement of Samuel Ferguson* (Gerrards Cross, 1990), p.11.

70. Printed in *The Honest Ulsterman* 50 (Winter 1975), pp.4-64. For another perspective (pride in trade and tradition) see Sam Hanna Bell: 'I work down the Island', *Erin's Orange Lily* (London, 1956), pp.37-49.

71. *Selected Poems* (Dublin and London, 1991), p.61. See also Mahon's soliloquy for Bruce Ismay, 'As God is my Judge', re-titled 'After the Titanic' in *Selected Poems*.

72. George Birmingham, *Pleasant Places* (London, 1934), p.1.

73. Birmingham, *The Red Hand of Ulster*, p.72.

74. St John Ervine, *Some Impressions of My Elders* (New York, 1922), p.65.

75. London, 1914.

76. London, 1927.

77. Foster, *Forces and Themes in Ulster Fiction*, p.131.

78. Sam Hanna Bell, *December Bride* (London, 1951; Belfast, 1974), pp.128-9.

79. Sam Hanna Bell, *A Man Flourishing* (London, 1973; Belfast, 1986), p.35.

80. Bonar Law McFall's death 'for Ireland' is reported in the same newspaper as David Minnis's selection to play 'for Ireland'. *The Hollow Ball* (London, 1961; Belfast, 1990), pp.240-1.

81. Lord Dunseveric and his son Maurice help their Presbyterian neighbour and antagonist, Neal Ward, to escape execution, *The Northern Iron* (Dublin, 1909), pp.236 ff. Neal leaves Ireland for a utopian America, while subsequent realities of the North are glossed over.

82. *New Review* 3, 32 (November 1976), p.43.

83. *The Emperor of Ice-Cream* (London, 1965), Mayflower edition, p.107.

84. *The Emperor of Ice-Cream*, p.79.

85. *The Emperor of Ice-Cream*, p.152.

86. Moore, *Judith Hearne*, Penguin edition, p.155.

87. Heaney, *Preoccupations*, p.28.

88. See note 18 above.

89. David Kennedy, 'The Ulster Region and the Theatre,' *Lagan* 2, 1 (1946), p.51.

90. Introduction, *Lagan* 1, 1 (1943), p.7.

91. Editorial, *Rann* 5 (Summer 1949).

92. These include: Samuel Ferguson, William Allingham, William Alexander, James H. Cousins, ballads, translations from the Gaelic. A whole issue (*Rann*,

11) is devoted to poems by William Drennan, James Orr, Samuel Burdy, Hugh Porter, and others. McFadden refers humorously to Hewitt 'turning over... mossy stones to uncover creashy weavers and reverend gentlemen with poems in their pockets', *Rann* 10 (Autumn 1950).

93. Eiléan Ní Chuilleanáin, 'Drawing Lines', *Cyphers* 10 (Spring 1979), p.50.

94. See, for instance, *The Bell* 4, 4 (July 1942); 4, 5 (August 1942). The editorial of the former 'Ulster Issue' includes the following passage, in which O'Faolain's generosity verges on stereotype: 'the strength of the North is that she does live and act in the Now. Belfast has immediacy. Ulster has contemporaneity – our southern curse is that we have never cut the umbilicus. Of course it is also true that Belfast *is* a city of mixed grills and double whiskies, of stalking poverty and growling hate. But even if these things generate fierceness, by the challenge of hideous enmities and rivalries, what is the important thing? Cork is a far more pretty town, Dublin a finer city by far, but how we who come from them loathe and curse them for their soapy softness and their shrugging vacillations as of a smoke in a south wind! The important thing is that so long as the gantries go on producing writers like these in this and the next issue the victory is not with the brutality of nineteenth century industrialism, nonconformity, the kirk, the lodges, the bosses, but with the fine and intelligent humanity of the natural, wide-awake Ulsterman.'

95. 'The primary impulse of the artist springs, I fancy, from discontent, and his art is a kind of crying for Elysium.' The opening sentence of *Apostate* (London, 1926).

96. Moore, *The Emperor of Ice-Cream*, p.9.

97. *The Emperor of Ice-Cream*, p.10.

98. *The Emperor of Ice-Cream*, p.58.

99. *Time Was Away*, edited by Terence Brown and Alec Reid (Portlaoise, 1974), p.115.

100. Louis MacNeice, *Modern Poetry* (Oxford, 1938, 1968), p.74.

101. *Modern Poetry*, p.103.

102. Retitled 'The Death of Marilyn Monroe', *Poems 1962-1978* (Oxford, 1979), p.7.

103. We are supposed to feel sympathetic to Sheila Redden when she praises to her husband a man who '*has* been abroad, he's interesting to talk to, he can talk about something else besides Paisley and the Provos'. Brian Moore, *The Doctor's Wife* (London, 1976), Corgi edition, p.24.

104. 'Once more, as before, I remember not to forget'. The last line of the first stanza of 'In Belfast'.

105. See 'Rage for Order', *Lives* (Oxford, 1972), p.23.

106. What will be left/After the twilight of cities,/The flowers of fire,//Will be the soft/Vegetables where our/Politics were conceived'... ['Thammuz', *The Snow Party* (Oxford, 1975), p.11. ['Thammuz' was renamed 'The Golden Bough' when it was published in *Poems 1962-1978* (1979)]; 'Matthew V', *Poems 1962-1978*, p.13.

107. 'Already in a lost hub-cap is conceived/The ideal society which will replace our own'. 'After Nerval', *The Snow Party*, p.23, re-titled 'The Mute Phenomena' in *Selected Poems*. 'Recognising,/As in a sunken city/Sea-changed at last, the surfaces/Of once familiar places./With practice you might decipher the whole thing/Or enough to suffer the relief and the pity'. 'A Dark Country', *Lives*, p.18.

108. 'The Last of the Fire Kings', *The Snow Party*, p.10; *Selected Poems*, p.59.

109. *Selected Poems*, p.50.

Progressive Bookmen *(pp.109-129)*

1. Sam Hanna Bell, *The Hollow Ball* (London, 1961; Belfast, 1990), pp.143-4.
2. Published in the *Northman* 2, 6 (June 1930).
3. Note to *Awake! and Other Poems* (London, 1941); quoted by John Hewitt in 'The Bitter Gourd: Some Problems of the Ulster Writer' (1945), reprinted in *Ancestral Voices: The Selected Prose of John Hewitt*, edited by Tom Clyde (Belfast, 1987), p.119.
4. Louis MacNeice, *I Crossed the Minch* (London, 1938), p.125.
5. Valentine Cunningham, *British Writers of the Thirties* (Oxford, New York, 1988), p.33 .
6. *British Writers of the Thirties*, p.218; pp.358-9 .
7. John Hewitt, 'No Rootless Colonist' (1972), *Ancestral Voices*, p.149.
8. Henry Patterson, *Class Conflict and Sectarianism* (Belfast, 1980), p.149.
9. Letter to Patrick Maybin, 11 February 1942.
10. See Foreword to *Labour in Irish History* (Dublin, 1910), p.xxx.
11. *Labour in Irish History*, pp.xxx-xxxi.
12. Sean O'Faolain, *The Bell* 9, 3 (December 1944), p.190.
13. *The Bell* 4, 6 (September 1942), p.392 .
14. Patterson, *Class Conflict and Sectarianism*, p.148.
15. Hewitt, *Ancestral Voices*, p.150.
16. On a TV discussion, chaired by Tariq Ali, in which he defended the *Field Day Anthology* against Irish feminists, July 1992. Paulin's collection *Liberty Tree* (1983) celebrates the 'dissenting green' and 'rebel minds' of the Presbyterian United Irishmen.
17. In conversation with the author.
18. 'James Hope, Weaver, of Templepatrick', Hewitt, *Ancestral Voices*, p.137. Originally published in *Northern Star* 2, 2 (April 1941).
19. *The Bell* 4, 4 (July 1942), p.251.
20. Denis Ireland, *Six Counties in Search of a Nation: Essays and Letters on Partition* (Belfast, 1947), p.68. For a portrait of Denis Ireland see John Boyd, *The Middle of My Journey* (Belfast, 1990), pp.20-2.
21. The original text of a line from 'The Glens' (1942), which now reads 'the lifted hand against unfettered thought'. Hewitt changed the line after realising that it was 'arrogant' and 'gave offence to kindly and gentle Catholics'. See Frank Ormsby, *The Collected Poems of John Hewitt* (Belfast, 1992), p.626.
22. *Goodbye, Twilight*, edited by Leslie Daiken (London, 1936), Introduction, pp.xii-xiv.
23. *Forum*, supplement to *Irish Jewry* (January 1937).
24. Another review of *Goodbye, Twilight*, *Irish Democrat* (?1937).
25. *Forum*, supplement to *Irish Jewry* (January 1937).
26. *Forum*, supplement to *Irish Jewry* (January 1937).
27. Louis MacNeice: *The Poetry of W.B. Yeats* (London, 1941, 1967), p.186.
28. *The Poetry of W.B. Yeats*, p.184.
29. In conversation with the author.
30. John Boyd, *Out of My Class* (Belfast, 1985), p.147, p.177.
31. *North Light* MS; 'No Rootless Colonist', *Ancestral Voices*, p.151.
32. 'The Peace League', *Northman* 2, 3 (Autumn 1934), p.20.
33. 'No Rootless Colonist', *Ancestral Voices*, p.151.
34. Louis MacNeice, *The Strings are False* (London, 1965), p.134, p.154.

35. 'Adelphi Centre', *North Light* MS.

36. MacNeice, *The Strings are False*, p.146.

37. *The Strings are False*, p.157.

38. Margot Heinemann, 'Louis MacNeice, John Cornford and Clive Branson: Three Left-Wing Poets', in *Culture and Crisis in Britain*, edited by Jon Clark et al (London, 1979), p.110.

39. *Forum*, supplement to *Irish Jewry* (January 1937).

40. MacNeice, *The Strings are False*, p.161.

41. *Forum*, supplement to *Irish Jewry* (January 1937).

42. 'The War Years II', *North Light* MS.

43. 'London Letter 4', in *Selected Prose of Louis MacNeice* edited by Alan Heuser (Oxford, 1990), p.127; 'Notes on the Way', *Selected Prose*, p.180.

44. Christopher Caudwell, *Illusion and Reality: A Study of the Sources of Poetry* (London, 1937), p.155.

45. 'The War Years', *North Light* MS .

46. John Wilson Foster, 'The Dissidence of Dissent', in *Colonial Consequences* (Dublin, 1991), p.120.

47. *The Bell* 4, 6 (September 1942), p.392 .

48. Editorial: *The Bell* 4, 6 p.381.

49. Editorials: *Lagan* 3 (1945), p.11; *Lagan* 1 (1943), p.6.

50. Quoted in 'Regionalism: The Last Chance', *Ancestral Voices*, p.123; 'The Bitter Gourd', *Ancestral Voices*, p.120. Hewitt was profoundly influenced by E. Estyn Evans's *Irish Heritage* (Dundalk, 1942).

51. F.L. Green, *Odd Man Out* (London, 1945), pp.187-8.

52. 'The Bitter Gourd', *Ancestral Voices*, p.108.

53. 'Regionalism: The Last Chance', *Ancestral Voices*, p.125. For one update of Hewitt's ideas, see John Wilson Foster, 'Radical Regionalism', *Colonial Consequences*, pp.278-95.

54. In ' "The Dissidence of Dissent": John Hewitt and W.R. Rodgers', *Colonial Consequences*, pp.114-132.

55. See 'Alec of the Chimney Corner', *Honest Ulsterman* 4 (August 1968), pp.5-12 (p.7): an extract from *A North Light*.

56. *Honest Ulsterman* 4 (1968), p.7.

57. *Honest Ulsterman 4* (August 1968), p.9; and see *The Bell* 16, 1 (April 1948), pp.27-36.

58. *Belfast Telegraph*, 19 May 1966.

59. In a lecture 'Caliban and Ariel: Louis MacNeice and the BBC', John Hewitt International Summer School, July 1991.

60. Louis MacNeice, review of *Over the Bridge*, *Observer*, 31 January 1960, p.23.

61. Douglas Carson, lecture at John Hewitt International Summer School, July 1991.

62. 'Ulster's position in this island involves us in problems and cleavages for which we can find no counterpart elsewhere in the British archipelago', 'The Bitter Gourd', *Ancestral Voices*, p.109.

'Defending Ireland's Soul': Protestant Writers and Irish Nationalism after Independence *(pp.130-149)*

1. W.J. McCormack, *Ascendancy and Tradition in Anglo-Irish Literary History from 1789 to 1939* (Oxford, 1985), p.396.

2. 'Varieties of Irishness', printed in *Cultural Traditions in Northern Ireland: Varieties of Irishness*, edited by Maurna Crozier (Belfast, 1989).

3. Louis MacNeice, *The Strings are False* (London, 1965), pp.78-9.

4. *Selected Prose of Louis MacNeice*, edited by Alan Heuser (Oxford, 1990), p.189.

5. A.T.Q. Stewart, *The Narrow Ground* (London, 1977), p.99.

6. Tom Paulin, *Ireland and the English Crisis* (Newcastle upon Tyne, 1984), p.202.

7. MacNeice, 'A Personal Digression' (*Zoo*, 1938), *Selected Prose*, pp.61-2.

8. Hubert Butler, *Escape from the Anthill* (Mullingar, 1985), p.116.

9. In a lecture at the John Hewitt Summer School, August 1990.

10. *Variorum Edition of the Poems of W. B. Yeats*, edited by Peter Allt and Russell K. Alspach (New York, 1957), p.833.

11. McCormack, *Ascendancy and Tradition*, p.370.

12. 'Modern Ireland: An Address to American Audiences 1932-1933'; quoted by Paul Scott Stanfield, *Yeats and Politics in the 1930s* (London, 1988), p.18.

13. 'Commentary', *Variorum*, p.835.

14. W.B. Yeats, *On the Boiler* (Dublin, 1938), p.12.

15. Yeats's gloss on 'Purgatory', *Irish Independent*, 12 August 1938; quoted by Donald Torchiana: *W.B. Yeats and Georgian Ireland* (Evanston, Illinois, 1966), p.357.

16. *W.B. Yeats and Georgian Ireland*, p.340ff.

17. McCormack, *Ascendancy and Tradition*, p.393.

18. Seamus Deane: *Celtic Revivals* (London, 1985), p.30.

19. *Celtic Revivals*, p.48.

20. *Celtic Revivals*, p.30.

21. Louis MacNeice, *The Poetry of W.B. Yeats* (London, 1941; 1967), p.50.

22. *The Poetry of W.B. Yeats*, p.134.

23. Bernard Krimm, *W.B. Yeats and the Emergence of the Irish Free State 1918-1939: Living in the Explosion* (New York, 1981) and Paul Scott Stanfield *Yeats and Politics in the 1930s* (London, 1988).

24. Deane, *Celtic Revivals*, p.94.

25. McCormack, *Ascendancy and Tradition*, p.12.

26. Tom Paulin, Preface to *The Faber Book of Political Verse* (London, 1986), pp.41-2.

27. Yeats was accused of having said this, when he opposed somewhat Soviet proposals for Irish copyright legislation in the Senate.

28. *Selected Literary Criticism of Louis MacNeice*, edited by Alan Heuser (Oxford, 1987), p.191.

29. *Selected Literary Criticism of Louis MacNeice*, p.191.

30. Stanfield, *Yeats and Politics in the 1930s*, p.185.

31. See Stanfield's review of the issues, pp.40-77.

32. Yeats, *On the Boiler*, p.12.

33. *On the Boiler*, p.1.

34. Paulin, *Ireland and the English Crisis*, p.203.

35. Seamus Deane, *Heroic Styles: the tradition of an idea* (Derry, 1984), p.17.
36. Denis Donoghue, *We Irish* (Brighton, 1986), p.9.
37. W.B. Yeats, *Memoirs* (London, 1972), pp.212-13.
38. Yeats, *On the Boiler*, p.30.
39. K. Theodore Hoppen, *Ireland since 1800* (London and New York, 1989), p.133.
40. *Ireland since 1800*, pp.241-2.
41. Hubert Butler, *Grandmother and Wolfe Tone* (Dublin, 1990), p.29.
42. Butler, *Escape from the Anthill*, pp.96-7.
43. *Escape from the Anthill*, p.87.
44. *Escape from the Anthill*, p.102.
45. *Escape from the Anthill*, p.55.
46. *Escape from the Anthill*, p.55.
47. *Escape from the Anthill*, p.93.
48. *Escape from the Anthill*, p.2.
49. *Escape from the Anthill*, pp.156-7.
50. *Escape from the Anthill*, p.157.
51. Butler, *Grandmother and Wolfe Tone*, p.65.
52. Butler, *Escape from the Anthill*, p.118.
53. *Escape from the Anthill*, p.120.
54. *Escape from the Anthill*, p.139. See, for instance 'The Sub-Prefect Should Have Held His Tongue' (*Escape from the Anthill*, p.270 ff.) for Butler's account of the outrage he occasioned when he was alleged to have insulted the Papal Nuncio by disclosing facts about Croatian Catholic pogroms against Orthodox Serbs during the Second World War.
55. *Escape from the Anthill*, p.127.
56. *Escape from the Anthill*, p.129.
57. MacNeice, *Selected Prose*, p.189.
58. *Selected Prose*, p.191.
59. *Selected Prose*, p.255.
60. *Selected Prose*, p.256.
61. Butler, *Grandmother and Wolfe Tone*, p.138ff.
62. *Grandmother and Wolfe Tone*, p.144.
63. MacNeice, *Poetry of W.B. Yeats*, p.119.
64. See Terence Brown, 'MacNeice's Ireland, MacNeice's Islands', in *Literature and Nationalism*, edited by Vincent Newey and Ann Thompson (Liverpool, 1991), pp.225-38 (p.230).
65. Dennis Kennedy, *The Widening Gulf* (Belfast, 1988), p.182.
66. *The Senate Speeches of W.B. Yeats*, edited by Donald R. Pearse (London, 1961), p.79.
67. *Ancestral Voices: The Selected Prose of John Hewitt*, edited by Tom Clyde (Belfast, 1987), pp.24-5.
68. Hoppen, *Ireland since 1800*, p.213.
69. MacNeice, *Selected Prose*, p.88.
70. See 'The Two Languages', *Grandmother and Wolfe Tone*, p.37ff.
71. MacNeice, *The Strings are False*, p.17.
72. Hewitt, *Ancestral Voices*, p.66.
73. Butler, *Grandmother and Wolfe Tone*, pp.67-8.
74. Hewitt, *Ancestral Voices*, p.148.
75. See *Ancestral Voices*, pp.149-50 for Hewitt's response to the Revival.
76. *Ancestral Voices*, p.125.

77. Marianne Elliott, *Watchmen in Sion: The Protestant Idea of Liberty* (Derry, 1985), p.9.

78. Hoppen, *Ireland since 1800*, p.13.

79. Hewitt, *Ancestral Voices*, pp.133-5.

80. *Ancestral Voices*, p.130.

81. Hubert Butler: *Wolfe Tone and the Common Name of Irishman* (Mullingar, 1985), p.12.

'When Did You Last See Your Father?': Perceptions of the Past in Northern Irish Writing 1965-1985 *(pp.150-172)*

1. *The South Country* (London, 1909), p.109.

2. 'The Sense of the Past', *Ulster Local Studies* 9, 20 (Summer, 1985), p.109.

3. Samuel Hynes, *The Pattern of Hardy's Poetry* (Chapel Hill, NC, 1961), p.4.

4. David Martin, *The Ceremony of Innocence* (London, 1977), p.32.

5. For example, autobiographies, books about historical Belfast or rural communities, more specialised social and economic histories. The Blackstaff Press's list includes, for instance: *Out of My Class*, the autobiography of John Boyd (socialist, playwright, BBC producer), and *Voices and the Sound of Drums*, autobiography of Patrick Shea, a Catholic civil servant at Stormont; John Hewitt's autobiographical sonnet sequence *Kites in Spring*; Sam McAughtry's family memoir of the thirties and Second World War, *The Sinking of the Kenbane Head*; Jonathan Bardon's *Belfast*; Michael J. Murphy's *Tyrone Folk Quest*; Brian M. Walker's *Sentry Hill*; Alan McCutcheon's *Wheel and Spindle*; Paddy Devlin's *Yes We Have No Bananas: Outdoor Relief in Belfast, 1920-39*; and R.M. Arnold's seductively titled *The Golden Years of the Great Northern Railway* – in two volumes.

6. Sam Keery, *The Last Romantic Out of Belfast* (Belfast, 1984), p.174.

7. *Irish Poets, 1924-1974*, edited by David Marcus (London, 1984), p.16.

8. Printed in *Theatre Ireland* 6 (April/June 1984), pp.119-42.

9. In *A Time to Dance* (Belfast, 1982).

10. Brian Moore, *The Emperor of Ice-Cream* (London, 1965), Mayflower edition, p.29.

11. *The Emperor of Ice-Cream*, p.250.

12. Maurice Leitch, *The Liberty Lad* (London, 1965; Belfast, 1985), p.208.

13. Maurice Leitch, *Stamping Ground* (London, 1975), Abacus edition (1984), p.30.

14. *Stamping Ground*, pp.41-2.

15. See also 'From Cathleen to Anorexia', p.189 above.

16. See the section 'The authoritarian strain in Irish culture' in Chapter 1 ('Some Traditions of Irish Catholicism') of J.H. Whyte, *Church and State in Modern Ireland, 1923-1979* (Dublin, 1980), pp.21-3. This section includes a comment on rural father-son relations.

17. Paul Muldoon, *Why Brownlee Left* (London, 1980), p.13.

18. Interview with John Haffenden, *Viewpoints: Poets in Conversation with John Haffenden* (London, 1981), p.130.

19. *Selected Plays of Brian Friel* (London, 1984), p.294.

20. *Selected Plays of Brian Friel*, p.418. Hugh's description of the Irish language evidently applies to his own speech.

21. *Selected Plays of Brian Friel*, p.446.

22. J.H. Andrews, 'Notes for a Future Edition of Brian Friel's Translations', *Irish Review* 13 (Winter 1992/93), pp.93-106.

23. Derek Mahon, *Selected Poems* (Dublin and London, 1991), p.28.

24. Tom Paulin, *Liberty Tree* (London, 1983), p.32.

25. Michael Longley, *Poems 1963-1983* (Edinburgh/Dublin, 1985), p.151.

26. *Poems 1963-1983*, p.48.

27. *Poems 1963-1983*, p.86.

28. Paul Fussell, *The Great War and Modern Memory* (London, 1975), p.325.

29. Leitch, *Stamping Ground*, p.101.

30. Seamus Heaney, *Field Work* (London, 1979), p.59.

31. John Montague, *The Rough Field* (Dublin, 1972), p.41.

32. Leitch, *Stamping Ground*, pp.31-2.

33. Seamus Heaney, *Hailstones* (Dublin, 1984), p.14.

34. James Randall, 'An Interview with Seamus Heaney', *Ploughshares* 5, 3 (1979), p.18.

35. *Selected Plays of Brian Friel*, p.11.

36. *Selected Plays of Brian Friel*, p.17.

37. Oliver MacDonagh, *States of Mind* (London, 1983), p.119.

38. Tom Paulin, *Ireland and the English Crisis* (Newcastle upon Tyne, 1984), p.17.

39. Tom Paulin, *A New Look at the Language Question* (Derry, Field Day Pamphlet Number 1, 1983), p.13.

40. John Wilson Foster, 'The Dissidence of Dissent', *Colonial Consequences* (Dublin, 1991), p.124.

41. Mahon, *Poems 1962-1978* (Oxford, 1979), p.67.

42. *Poems 1962-1978*, p.69.

43. Mahon, *Selected Poems*, p.43.

44. Longley, *Poems 1963-1983*, p.84.

45. *Poems 1963-1983*, p.98.

46. Heaney, *Field Work*, p.15.

47. John Montague, 'Red Branch (A Blessing)', *The Dead Kingdom* (Belfast/Dublin, 1984), p.51.

48. Montague, *The Rough Field*, p.60; p.67.

49. Montague, *The Dead Kingdom*, p.25.

50. *The Dead Kingdom*, p.18.

51. Leitch, *Stamping Ground*, p.202.

52. *Stamping Ground*, p.47.

53. David Martin, *The Road to Ballyshannon* (London, 1981), Abacus edition (1983), p.155.

54. Martin, *The Ceremony of Innocence*, p.280.

55. Martin, *The Road to Ballyshannon*, p.156.

56. Bernard Mac Laverty, *Lamb* (Belfast/London, 1980), p.152 (Penguin edition).

57. Bernard Mac Laverty, *Cal* (Belfast/London, 1983), p.170.

58. Heaney, *Door into the Dark* (London, 1972), p.55.

59. Heaney, 'Mossbawn', *Preoccupations*, p.20.

60. Heaney, 'Broagh', *Wintering Out* (London, 1972), p.27.

61. Heaney, *Preoccupations*, p.57.

62. '*North*: "Inner Emigré" or "Artful Voyeur"?' in *Poetry in the Wars* (Newcastle upon Tyne, 1986), pp.140-69.

63. Heaney, 'Mossbawn', *Preoccupations*, p.20.

64. *Ulster Local Studies* 9, 20 (Summer, 1985), p.113-14.

65. *Ulster Local Studies* 9, 20 (Summer, 1985), p.112.
66. Louis MacNeice, *Collected Poems* (London, 1966), p.450.
67. Mahon, *Poems 1962-1978*, p.35.
68. *Poems 1962-1978*, p.78.
69. Longley, *Poems 1963-1983*, p.156.
70. *The Selected Paul Durcan* (Belfast, 1982), p.55.
71. Seamus Heaney, *Station Island* (London, 1984), p.93.
72. Seamus Deane, *Celtic Revivals* (London, 1985), p.186.
73. Brian Moore, *Fergus* (London, 1971), p.31.
74. John Wilson Foster, *Forces and Themes in Ulster Fiction* (Dublin, 1974), p.174.
75. Moore, *Fergus*, p.37.
76. *Fergus*, p.227.
77. Brian Moore, *The Mangan Inheritance* (London, 1979), p.308.
78. Foster, *Forces and Themes in Ulster Fiction*, p.179.
79. *Forces and Themes in Ulster Fiction*, p.84.
80. Paul Muldoon, *Quoof* (1983), p.40.
81. *Quoof*, p.29.
82. Muldoon, *Why Brownlee Left*, p.27.
83. Muldoon, *Mules* (London, 1977), p.11.
84. In 'The More a Man Has', *Quoof*, p.63.
85. *Quoof*, p.17.
86. Paul Muldoon, *New Weather* (London, 1973), p.19.
87. Muldoon, *Mules*, p.51.
88. *Mules*, p.42.
89. Muldoon, *Why Brownlee Left*, p.9; p.23.
90. Muldoon, *Mules*, p.38.
91. *Mules*, p.52.
92. Muldoon, *Why Brownlee Left*, p.38.
93. Muldoon, *Quoof*, p.7.
94. MacDonagh, *States of Mind*, p.6.
95. Muldoon, *Why Brownlee Left*, p.22.
96. Muldoon, *Quoof*, p.25.

From Cathleen to Anorexia: The Breakdown of Irelands
(pp.173-195)

1. Patrick Kavanagh, 'The Story of an Editor who was Corrupted by Love', *Collected Pruse* (London, 1967), p.155.
2. R.F. Foster, *Modern Ireland 1600-1972* (London, 1988), p.596.
3. Robert McLiam Wilson, *Ripley Bogle* (London, 1989), pp.13-14.
4. Foster, *Modern Ireland*, p.596.
5. See *Cultural Traditions in Northern Ireland: Varieties of Irishness*, edited by Maureen Crozier (Belfast, 1989), pp.5-23; p.48ff.
6. Quoted by Clare O'Halloran in *Partition and the Limits of Irish Nationalism: An Ideology Under Stress* (Dublin, 1987), p.31.
7. John Wilson Foster, 'Who Are The Irish?', *Studies* 77, 308 (Winter 1988), pp.403-16. Reprinted in *Colonial Consequences* (Dublin, 1991), pp.248-62.
8. Alban Maginness, 'Who Are The Irish?', *Studies* 77, 308 (Winter 1988), pp.417-20.

9. Patrick Kavanagh, 'Waiting for Godot', *Collected Pruse*, p.266.

10. Sean O'Faolain, 'The Death of Nationalism', *The Bell* 17, 2 (May 1951), p.44.

11. O'Halloran, *Partition and the Limits of Irish Nationalism*, p.59.

12. See Tom Garvin, *Nationalist Revolutionaries in Ireland 1858-1928* (Oxford, 1987), p.51; pp.7-8; pp.92-4.

13. George Orwell, 'The Prevention of Literature', *Collected Essays, Journalism and Letters of George Orwell*, 4 (1968), Penguin edition, p.89.

14. *Across the Frontiers: Ireland in the 1990s*, edited by Richard Kearney (Dublin, 1989), p.18.

15. *Across the Frontiers*, p.56.

16. Terry Eagleton, *Nationalism: Irony and Commitment* (Derry, 1988), p.5.

17. Eavan Boland, *A Kind of Scar* (Dublin, 1989), pp.7-8; p.20.

18. *A Kind of Scar*, p.5; p.10.

19. See *A Kind of Scar*, pp.12-13; p.20.

20. *A Kind of Scar*, p.18.

21. Seamus Heaney, 'Feeling into Words', *Preoccupations* (London, 1980), p.57.

22. Margaret Ward, *Unmanageable Revolutionaries* (Dingle and London, 1983), p.152.

23. *Unmanageable Revolutionaries*, p.165.

24. Rosemary Cullen Owens, *Smashing Times: A History of the Irish Women's Suffrage Movement 1889-1922* (Dublin, 1984), p.108.

25. Quoted in *Smashing Times*, p.99.

26. Robin Morgan, *The Demon Lover: On the Sexuality of Terrorism* (London, 1989), p.63; p.99; p.169.

27. *The Demon Lover*, p.214.

28. *The Demon Lover*, p.53.

29. Brian Turner, report on 'Local Studies', in *Cultural Traditions in Northern Ireland: Varieties of Irishness*, edited by Maurna Crozier (Belfast, 1989), p.110.

30. A.D. Buckley, 'Collecting Ulster's Culture: are there really Two Traditions?', *The Uses of Tradition*, edited by Alan Gailey (Cultra, 1988), p.49.

31. Bernard Crick, 'An Englishman Examines His Passport', *Irish Review* 5 (Autumn 1988), p.10.

Poetic Forms and Social Malformations *(pp.196-226)*

Quotations from the poetry of Paul Muldoon, Brendan Kennelly and Paul Durcan throughout this essay are taken from the following volumes: Paul Muldoon, *Why Brownlee Left* (London, 1980), *Quoof* (London, 1983); Brendan Kennelly, *Cromwell* (Dublin, 1983; Newcastle upon Tyne, 1987); Paul Durcan, *The Selected Paul Durcan* (Belfast, 1982), *The Berlin Wall Café* (Belfast, 1985).

1. Louis MacNeice, *The Poetry of W.B. Yeats* (London, 1967), p.25.

2. *The New Oxford Book of Irish Verse* (Oxford, 1986), Introduction, p.xxvii.

3. *New Oxford Book*, p.xxx.

4. Review of *New Oxford Book*, *Observer*, 8 June 1986.

5. Michael Donaghy, 'A Conversation with Paul Muldoon', *Chicago Review* 35, 1 (Autumn 1985), p.77.

6. Louis MacNeice, 'An Alphabet of Literary Prejudices', *Selected Literary Criticism of Louis MacNeice*, edited by Alan Heuser (Oxford, 1987), p.144.

7. *Irish Poetry: The Thirties Generation*, edited by Michael Smith (Dublin, 1983), Preface, p.2.

8. Interview with Mervyn Wall, *Irish Poetry: The Thirties Generation*, p.85.

9. 'An Interview with Derek Mahon', by Terence Brown, *Poetry Ireland Review* 14 (Autumn 1985), p.17.

10. Hubert Butler, '*Envoy* and Mr Kavanagh', *Escape from the Anthill* (Mullingar, 1985), pp.156-7.

11. Declan Kiberd, 'Inventing Irelands', RTE/UCD Lectures, *Ireland: Dependence and Independence*, *Crane Bag* 8, 1 (Spring 1984), p.13.

12. *Irish Poetry: The Thirties Generation*, p.3.

13. Quotations from a notorious St Patrick's Day broadcast by de Valera in 1943.

14. Patrick Kavanagh, 'Violence and Literature', *Collected Pruse* (London, 1967), p.273.

15. Kinsella, *New Oxford Book*, Introduction, p.xxviii.

16. *New Oxford Book*, p.xxx.

17. *Irish Poetry After Yeats*, edited by Maurice Harmon (Dublin, 1979), Introduction, p.28.

18. *The Chosen Ground: Essays on The Contemporary Poetry of Northern Ireland*, edited by Neil Corcoran (Bridgend, 1992), Introduction, p.7.

19. See Antoinette Quinn, *Patrick Kavanagh: Born-Again Romantic* (Dublin, 1991), Chapter 5, 'Writing Catholic Ireland'.

20. P.J. Duffy, 'A Geographical Perspective', *The Borderlands: Essays on the History of the Ulster-Leinster Border* (Belfast, 1989), p.11.

21. Kevin Whelan, 'Settlement and Society in Eighteenth Century Ireland', *The Poet's Place* (Belfast, 1991), edited by Gerald Dawe and John Wilson Foster, p.57.

22. Patrick Kavanagh, 'Tramping', *The Green Fool* (London, 1938, 1971), p.309.

23. Patrick Kavanagh, 'Nationalism and Literature', *Collected Pruse*, pp.268-9.

24. Terence Brown, *Northern Voices* (Dublin, 1975), p.220.

25. *Northern Voices*, p.215.

26. 'Free Verse', 'An Alphabet of Literary Prejudices', MacNeice, *Selected Literary Criticism*, p.143.

27. A.T.Q. Stewart, *The Narrow Ground* (London, 1977), p.180.

28. Seamus Heaney, *Preoccupations* (London, 1980), pp.119-24.

29. Patrick Kavanagh, 'The Parish and the Universe', *Collected Pruse*, p.282.

30. Interview with Paul Muldoon, *Viewpoints*, edited by John Haffenden (London, 1981), pp.130-1.

31. Heaney, *Preoccupations*, p.116.

32. Patrick Kavanagh, 'Self Portrait', *Collected Pruse*, p.19.

33. Heaney, *Preoccupations*, p.122, p.142.

34. C.G. Jung, *Aspects of the Masculine*, edited by John Beebe (London, 1989), p.xi.

35. Seamus Heaney, 'The Placeless Heaven: Another Look at Kavanagh', *The Government of the Tongue* (London, 1988), p.13.

36. Heaney, *Government of the Tongue*, p.5.

37. *Lough Derg* (London, 1978), Foreword, pp.vii-ix.

38. *The Penguin Book of Irish Verse* (Harmondsworth, 1981), Note to the Second Edition, pp.41-2.

39. Quinn, *Patrick Kavanagh: Born-Again Romantic*, p.173.

40. Kavanagh, 'Self Portrait', *Collected Pruse*, p.21.

41. Quoted by Eileen Battersby, Profile of Paul Durcan, *Irish Times*, 10 November 1990.

42. Interview with Paul Muldoon, *Viewpoints*, p.140.

43. Quoted by Oliver MacDonagh in *States of Mind* (London, 1983), p.19.

44. Interview with Paul Muldoon, *Viewpoints*, p.140.

45. See Kevin Whelan, 'The Regional Impact of Irish Catholicism 1700-1850', *Common Ground*, edited by William J. Smyth and Kevin Whelan (Cork, 1988), pp.253-74, especially pp.271-2.

46. Seamus Heaney, 'The Government of the Tongue', *Government of the Tongue*, p.92.

47. William A. Wilson, 'Paul Muldoon and the Poetics of Sexual Difference', *Contemporary Literature* 28, 3 (1987), p.324.

No More Poems About Paintings? *(pp.227-251)*

1. *Poets of the 1950s*, edited by D.J. Enright (Tokyo, 1955), p.17.

2. John Dixon Hunt, *Self-Portrait in a Convex Mirror: on Poems on Paintings*, Inaugural Lecture (Bedford College, 1980), p.1.

3. W.B. Yeats, 'Art and Ideas', *Essays and Introductions* (London, 1961), p.346.

4. Bram Dijkstra, 'Wallace Stevens and William Carlos Williams: poetry, painting and the function of reality', in *Encounters: Essays on Literature and the Visual Arts*, edited by John Dixon Hunt (London, 1971), p.156.

5. E.H. Gombrich, 'The Necessity of Tradition: An Interpretation of the Poetics of I.A. Richards', in *Tributes* (London, 1984), p.185.

6. Ian Fletcher, *W.B. Yeats and his Contemporaries* (Brighton, 1987), p.226.

7. Frank O'Hara, *Collected Poems* (New York, 1972), p.261.

8. W.J.T. Mitchell, *Iconology: Image, Text, Ideology* (Chicago, 1987), p.157.

9. Rudolph Arnheim, *Visual Thinking* (London, 1970), pp.236-8, 242-6.

10. Mitchell, *Iconology: Image, Text, Ideology*, p.49.

11. This appears facing 'Woman Peeling Apples' in *Voices in the Gallery*, edited by Dannie and Joan Abse (Tate Gallery, 1986). The anthology also includes Heaney/Goya, Longley/Lowry, and Mahon/Munch pairings.

12. In *The Onion, Memory* (Oxford, 1978), p.46ff.

13. Gilbert Adair, *Myths & Memories* (London, 1986), p.135.

14. *Myths & Memories*, p.136.

15. Frank Kermode, *Romantic Image* (London, 1957), p.5.

16. John Dixon Hunt, *The Pre-Raphaelite Imagination 1848-1900* (Nebraska, 1968), p.175.

17. *The Pre-Raphaelite Imagination*, p.128.

18. W.B. Yeats, 'Art and Ideas', *Essays and Introductions*, p.355.

19. Lynn Lundgaard, unpublished thesis: 'The Importance of the Visual Arts in the Aesthetic of W.B. Yeats' (University of Oklahoma).

20. *Selected Letters of Robert Frost*, edited by Lawrance Thompson (London, 1965), p.127.

21. *Selected Letters of Robert Frost*, p.113.

22. 'Theory of Texts', *London Review of Books* 10, 4 (18 February 1988), p.21.

23. Alan Robinson, *Poetry, Painting and Ideas 1885-1914* (London, 1985), p.75.

24. T.E. Hulme, *Further Speculations*, edited by Sam Hynes (Minneapolis, 1955), p.74.

25. Dorothy Walker, 'Sailing to Byzantium: The Portraits of Edward McGuire', *Irish Arts Review* 4, 4 (Winter 1987), p.21.

26. 'Subject in Modern Poetry', in *Selected Literary Criticism of Louis MacNeice*, edited by Alan Heuser (Oxford, 1987), p.59.

27. Louis MacNeice, *The Strings are False* (London, 1965), p.161.

28. John Hewitt, *Art in Ulster*, 1 (Belfast, 1977), p.146.

29. *Lagan* 2, 1 (1946), pp.23-4.

30. Seamus Heaney: *A Personal Selection*, exhibition catalogue introduction (Ulster Museum, 1982).

31. *The Irish Imagination*, exhibition catalogue, Rosc (Dublin, 1971).

32. Richard Kearney, 'Heaney and Homecoming', in *Transitions* (Dublin, 1988), pp.101-22.

33. *A Personal Selection* catalogue, introduction.

34. *A Personal Selection* catalogue.

35. Kearney, *Transitions*, p.102.

36. *Irish Review* 3 (1988), p.37.

37. Edward Thomas, *Walter Pater* (London, 1913), pp.94-6.

38. John Haffenden, *Viewpoints: Poets in Conversation* (London, 1981), p.61.

39. *A Personal Selection* catalogue.

40. W.B. Yeats, 'Symbolism in Painting', *Essays and Introductions*, p.150.

41. Kathleen McCracken discusses Durcan's response to Kitaj's portrait in 'Canvas and Camera Translated: Paul Durcan and the Visual Arts', *Irish Review* 7 (Autumn 1989), pp.18-29. With respect to paintings in general she argues that they 'are there not as "objective correlatives" but as "corroborators" in an instinctive appreciation of human concerns outside cultural and chronological boundaries' (p.28).

The Room Where MacNeice Wrote 'Snow' *(pp.252-270)*

1. Louis MacNeice, *The Poetry of W.B. Yeats* (Oxford, 1941; London, 1967), pp.156-7.

2. W.B. Yeats, *A Vision* (London, 1962), p.3.

3. MacNeice, *The Poetry of W.B. Yeats*, pp.17-18.

4. *Selected Literary Criticism of Louis MacNeice*, edited by Alan Heuser (Oxford, 1987), pp.13-14.

5. *Selected Literary Criticism of Louis MacNeice*, p.14.

6. MacNeice, *The Poetry of W.B. Yeats*, p.81, p.176.

7. *Selected Literary Criticism of Louis MacNeice*, p.17.

8. *Selected Literary Criticism of Louis MacNeice*, p.33.

9. *Selected Literary Criticism of Louis MacNeice*, p.43.

10. T.W. Adorno, *Aesthetic Theory* (London, 1984), p.190.

11. MacNeice, *The Poetry of W.B. Yeats*, p.175.

12. 'An Alphabet of Literary Prejudices', *Selected Literary Criticism of Louis MacNeice*, p.143.

13. *Icarus* (literary magazine of Trinity College Dublin) 34 (June, 1961), p.51.

14. MacNeice's gloss on *Visitations* (1957), *Selected Literary Criticism*, p.211.

15. MacNeice, *The Poetry of W.B. Yeats*, p.178.

16. *Selected Literary Criticism of Louis MacNeice*, p.245.

17. *Selected Literary Criticism of Louis MacNeice*, p.131.

18. Neil Corcoran, 'One Step Forward, Two Steps Back: Ciaran Carson's *The Irish for No*', in *The Chosen Ground: Contemporary Poetry of Northern Ireland* (Bridgend, 1992), edited by Neil Corcoran, p.223.

19. Humphrey Carpenter, *W.H. Auden: A Biography* (London, 1981), p.289.

20. *The English Auden* (London, 1977), edited by Edward Mendelson, p.390.

21. *The English Auden*, p.393.

22. MacNeice, *The Poetry of W.B. Yeats*, p.192.

23. MacNeice, *The Poetry of W.B. Yeats*, p.154.

24. Adorno, *Aesthetic Theory*, p.117.

25. *Aesthetic Theory*, pp.184-5.

26. *Aesthetic Theory*, p.116.

27. *Aesthetic Theory*, p.196.

28. 'The chaotic moment and radical spiritualisation coincide in their rejection of shiny comforting notions of what life is all about.' Adorno, *Aesthetic Theory*, p.138.

29. 'Derek Mahon Interviewed' (by William Scammell), *Poetry Review* 81, 2 (Summer 1991), p.6.

30. Adorno, *Aesthetic Theory*, p.116.

31. Seamus Heaney, 'The Interesting Case of Nero, Chekhov's Cognac and a Knocker', in *The Government of the Tongue* (London, 1988), p.xix.

32. Heaney, *Government of the Tongue*, p.xix.

33. Adorno, *Aesthetic Theory*, p.245.

34. *Selected Literary Criticism of Louis MacNeice*, p.248.

ACKNOWLEDGEMENTS

'The Rising, the Somme and Irish Memory' first appeared in *Revising the Rising*, edited by Theo Dorgan and Máirín Ni Dhonnchadha, (Field Day Publications, Derry, 1991); ' "A Barbarous Nook": The Writer and Belfast' first appeared in *The Irish Writer and the City*, edited by Maurice Harmon (Colin Smythe, Gerrards Cross, 1984); an early version of 'Progressive Bookmen' appeared in *Irish Review* 1 (1986); ' "Defending Ireland's Soul": Protestant Writers and Irish Nationalism after Independence' first appeared in *Literature and Nationalism* (a *Festschrift* for Philip Edwards), edited by Vincent Newey and Anne Thompson (Liverpool University Press, 1991); ' "When Did You Last See Your Father?" ' first appeared in *Cultural Contexts and Literary Idioms in Contemporary Irish Literature*, edited by Michael Kenneally (Colin Smythe, 1988); 'From Cathleen to Anorexia' was published by Attic Press, Dublin as a pamphlet in their *LIP* series (1990) and reprinted in *A Dozen LIPS* (Attic Press, 1994); the original version of 'Poetic Forms and Social Malformations' appeared in *Tradition and Influence in Anglo-Irish Poetry*, edited by Terence Brown and Nicholas Grene (Macmillan, 1989); 'No More Poems about Paintings?' first appeared in *Irish Literature and Culture*, edited by Michael Kenneally (Colin Smythe, 1992); the original version of 'The Room Where MacNeice Wrote "Snow" ' appeared in *The Crows Behind the Plough: History and Violence in Anglo-Irish Poetry and Drama*, edited by Geert Lernout (Rodopi, Amsterdam, 1991).

The author and publisher are grateful for permission to reprint the following copyright material:

Ciaran Carson: extracts from *The Irish for No* (1987), *Belfast Confetti* (1989) reprinted by permission of the Gallery Press and Wake Forest University Press.

Paul Durcan: extracts from *The Selected Paul Durcan* (1982), *The Berlin Wall Café* (1985), *Going Home to Russia* (1987), *Daddy, Daddy* (1990), reprinted by permission of Blackstaff Press.

Seamus Heaney: extracts from *Death of a Naturalist* (1966), *Door into the Dark* (1969), *Wintering Out* (1972), *North* (1975), *Field Work* (1979), *Preoccupations* (1980), *Station Island* (1984), *The Haw Lantern* (1987), *The Government of the Tongue* (1988), *Seeing Things* (1991), reprinted by permission of Faber and Faber Ltd and Farrar, Straus and Giroux Inc.

John Hewitt: extracts from *The Collected Poems of John Hewitt* (1991), reprinted by permission of Blackstaff Press; extracts from unpublished chapters of *A North Light*, reprinted by permission of the estate of John Hewitt.

Patrick Kavanagh: extracts from the poetry and prose, by permission of the estate of Patrick Kavanagh, c/o Peter Fallon, Loughcrew, Oldcastle, Co. Meath.

Brendan Kennelly: extracts from *Cromwell* (1983), *The Book of Judas* (1991), reprinted by permission of Bloodaxe Books Ltd.

Michael Longley: extracts from *Poems 1963-1983* (1985), reprinted by permission of Peters, Fraser & Dunlop Ltd.

Medbh McGuckian: extracts from *The Flower Master* (1982), *Venus and the Rain* (1984), *On Ballycastle Beach* (1988) and *Marconi's Cottage* (1991), reprinted by permission of the Gallery Press.

Louis MacNeice: extracts from *Collected Poems* (1966), reprinted by permission of Faber and Faber Ltd.

Derek Mahon: extracts from *Night-Crossing* (1968), *Lives* (1972), *The Snow Party* (1975), *Poems 1962-1978* (1979), *The Hunt by Night* (1982), published by Oxford University Press, later collected in *Selected Poems* (Gallery/Viking, 1991), reprinted by permission of the Gallery Press.

John Montague: extracts from *The Rough Field* (1972), *The Dead Kingdom* (1984), reprinted by permission of the Gallery Press and Wake Forest University Press.

Paul Muldoon: extracts from *New Weather* (1973), *Mules* (1977), *Why Brownlee Left* (1980), *Quoof* (1983), *Meeting the British* (1987), reprinted by permission of Faber and Faber Ltd and Wake Forest University Press; extracts from *Madoc: A Mystery* (1990), reprinted by permission of Faber and Faber Ltd.

Tom Paulin: extracts from *Liberty Tree* (1983), reprinted by permission of Faber and Faber Ltd.

INDEX

Word-by-word alphabetical arrangement is used here. The suffix *n* to a page reference indicates that the entry is a note on that page.

Index compiled by Stephanie J. Dagg